A BOOK THAT CAN CHANGE...

Did you know?

- As many as 30 percent of American children are underachieving in math, spelling, reading, and writing because they do not learn in the same way that their classmates learn.

- A struggling child's self-image can be indelibly damaged if timely, first-rate remedial assistance is not provided.

- Defe... ...spiration and then...

- Infor... ...e system and are fa... ...than passive parer...

- Marg... ...ceive little or no le...

- Most... ...delayed, or intell...

- Defici... ...dy skills are major...

- Paren... ...skills deficits and, i...

"Greene... ...mmonly af-flict so i... ...options for overcom... ...re skilled at maneuv...

...author of ...D/ADHD

"Finall... ...ls. Parents learn th... ...ning prob-lems... ...ey!"

...reenburg, ...California

"A pow... ...tion they need to... ...be must-reading

...Meanings

OTHER BOOKS BY LAWRENCE J. GREENE

Kids Who Hate School
Learning Disabilities and Your Child
Kids Who Underachieve
Getting Smarter
Study Smarter, Think Smarter
Smarter Kids
1001 Ways to Improve Your Child's Schoolwork
The Life-Smart Kid
Finding Help When Your Child Is Struggling in School

e-Matter
(at Barnes & Noble.com)

Helping Your Child Succeed in School
Building Your Child's Self-esteem and Self-confidence
Helping Your Child Make Wise Decisions
Shortchanging Kids Who Learn Differently
Helping Your Child Become More Independent

ROADBLOCKS TO LEARNING

Understanding the Obstacles That Can Sabotage Your Child's Academic Success

LAWRENCE J. GREENE

WARNER BOOKS

An AOL Time Warner Company

Copyright © 2002 by Lawrence J. Greene
All rights reserved.

Warner Books, Inc., 1271 Avenue of the Americas, New York, NY 10020

Visit our Web site at www.twbookmark.com.

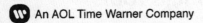 An AOL Time Warner Company

Printed in the United States of America

First Printing: July 2002

10 9 8 7 6 5 4 3 2

Library of Congress Cataloging-in-Publication Data

Greene, Lawrence J.
    Roadblocks to Learning: Understanding the Obstacles That Can Sabotage Your Child's Academic Success / Lawrence J. Greene
      p. cm.
    Includes bibliographical references and index.
    ISBN 0-446-67901-1
    1. Learning disabilities—Handbooks, manuals, etc. 2. Learning disabled children—Education—Parent participation—Handbooks, manuals, etc. I. Title.

LC4704.G72   2002
649'.15—dc21

                                            2001026258

Cover design by Brigid Pearson
Book design and text composition by Stanley S. Drate / Folio Graphics Company, Inc.

For my son, Joshua Ryan Greene

Six years and running . . . everywhere! Your spirit
and zest still enthrall me. I shall always be thankful
for the joy you have brought into my life.

Acknowledgments

Marisa Cammarata deserves special thanks for her encouragement during the writing of this book. She is a consummate educational therapist and an equally consummate school principal. I would also like to thank Mark Steinberg, Ph.D., for his professional input and friendship. My six-year-old son Joshua deserves a heartfelt acknowledgement for letting me use "his" computer. Those many mornings when he allowed me to work while he turned over all the furniture and built forts in the living room were a blessing and are much appreciated. He is clearly destined to become either an architect or a soldier. Dan and Evie Greene, as always, were there for me with their unconditional love. And so, too, were Evan and Lisa Greene. Thank you all.

Contents

▲

APPLIED INTELLIGENCE

▲

BEHAVIOR

▲

PERCEPTUAL PROCESSING

▲

PSYCHOLOGICAL FACTORS

▲

SPEECH AND LANGUAGE

▲

ROADBLOCKS TO LEARNING

Introduction

At any given time in American classrooms, 7 million children are struggling academically. This translates into approximately 15 percent of the school population. Yet in most school districts only 3–4 percent of these marginally performing students are actually being provided with formal learning assistance.

In the world's wealthiest and most technologically advanced country, vast numbers of students have abysmal academic skills. This sad state of affairs is documented by nationally administered achievement tests that indicate that underachievement has reached epidemic proportions. The scores testify to the fact that millions of American children with normal-to-superior intelligence are unable to read effectively, spell accurately, do basic math, and write comprehensible, grammatically correct essays. That the average eighth-grader in a city such as Los Angeles is reading at the fourth-grade level attests to the gravity of the problem.

Given the dismal level of student achievement in school districts throughout the United States, there can be little doubt that our educational system is failing to meet the legitimate scholastic needs of a large segment of the student population. Far too many potentially capable children with learning difficulties are receiving a sub-par education. These youngsters are struggling to learn effectively and are clearly working below their full potential. Despite compelling evidence that many American students are failing to acquire decent academic skills, the educational system is either oblivious to the plight of these underachieving children or unable or unwilling to address the fundamental problems. The repercussions from the instructional inadequacies threaten the very fabric of our society.

After having spent more than thirty years as an educational therapist, diagnostician, curriculum developer, university instructor, counselor, child advocate, and school consultant and after having diagnosed and treated more than 14,000 learning-disabled children, I have had innumerable opportunities to witness the repercussions of the failure to provide struggling learners with needed learning assistance. I have seen firsthand the disastrous academic and emotional consequences when students are allowed to founder in school; the frustration, demoralization, and psychological scarring; the damage that results when parents are oblivious of, or apathetic to, the perils and discover too late that their child is in crisis. I have also witnessed the self-concept and spirit of potentially capable youngsters disintegrate because they cannot learn in the same way as their classmates.

At the same time, my years on the educational front line and in the trenches have provided me with another more positive perspective. I have seen dramatic improvement in the skills and self-image of struggling children when their parents confront the issues head-on, become informed, and intervene effectively. I have also seen how the life of academically demoralized children can literally be transformed when they are provided with timely, first-rate remedial assistance and appropriate parental support.

My experiences have shaped my thinking and have led me to a firmly held philosophical position. I am unequivocally convinced that every child of normal intelligence is genetically programmed to learn, absorb information, and acquire the requisite skills to survive, compete, and prevail in a demanding, highly competitive world. The natural instinct to learn is voracious and is one of the unique characteristics hammered into the DNA of the human species. This inborn passion to acquire knowledge does not die easily. It must be extinguished through neglect, deprivation, degradation, insensitivity, lack of access to required remedial services, and/or abysmal teaching.

When the educational needs of poorly performing students are disregarded, emotional damage is inevitable. As struggling children become increasingly discouraged and demoralized, they are all but certain to conclude that they are hopelessly incompetent and that academic success is not a viable option. Once they acquiesce to their scholastic "limitations," they will begin closing doors that they may never again be able to reopen.

The most potent antidote to this waste of human ability is to provide parents with the information they need to understand their child's learning difficulties and make informed choices about their child's educational needs. Parents who conclude that their child requires specialized assistance and that their child's school is unwilling or unable to provide effective help must be prepared to function as proactive advocates of their child's legitimate educational rights. To do so effectively, they must understand the issues.

The basic premise of this book is that the American educational system has a compelling obligation to help *all* children who are struggling to learn, not just those who have incapacitating learning disorders. Ironically, students with less severe learning difficulties that might otherwise be easily and quickly remediated typically receive little or no formal assistance. In far too many instances, their deficits are overlooked, misdiagnosed, or dismissed as inconsequential. Once children conclude that they cannot succeed in school, they will respond by lowering their expectations and aspirations. The consequences can be life altering. Children will demand less from themselves and for themselves, and their talents may never be actualized. Rewarding careers may never be launched, and vital contributions to society may never be realized.

Make no mistake—something is profoundly amiss when children shut down and spend twelve years treading water in school. The academic and emotional disintegration parallels the effects of a life-threatening, metastasizing disease. If the illness is to be kept from spreading, it must be accurately diagnosed and effectively treated using the best resources available. Timely intervention is vital. To disregard the symptoms guarantees disaster.

Most parents of children with learning difficulties are painfully aware of the academic, emotional, and vocational risks their children face. Profoundly apprehensive about the long-range implications, these parents crave incisive information, guidance, and solutions. They realize that without knowledge they are powerless and can only watch passively as their child falls further and further behind and becomes increasingly demoralized. They also realize that once they become informed, they can galvanize the available resources and become highly effective and proactive champions of their child's legitimate educational rights and needs.

Three critically important questions must be asked:

- Why are millions of academically deficient children being denied formal learning assistance in school?
- What are the consequences of allowing academic deficiencies to go untreated?
- What can parents do to make certain their child receives effective help before often-irreversible psychological damage occurs?

Why are millions of academically deficient children being denied help?

The answer to this question is simple and disturbing. The bottom line is that there are too many underachieving students and too little money to fund programs that could get them on track academically. Economics and the laws of supply and demand determine how precious remedial services are allocated. By necessity, hard-pressed schools prioritize the needs of the most seriously learning disabled and send the "walking wounded"—those whose learning difficulties do not conform to rigid and often arbitrary diagnostic criteria— back to the front lines without meaningful treatment. That the ostensibly "minor" wounds of these neglected children often become incapacitating is a reality that our educational system conveniently chooses to disregard.

What are the consequences of allowing academic deficiencies to go untreated?

When schools fail to provide learning assistance for marginally per-forming students, the effects are predictable: deficient academic skills, frustration, demoralization, resistance to learning, and behav-ior problems. Left to their own devices, some of these neglected youngsters continue to work diligently and valiantly. Most, however, choose the path of least resistance and shut down in school.

As the self-concept of poorly performing students unravels, they will begin to accept the inevitability of diminished achieve-ment. Once they do, they are destined to arrive at the end of the school production line poorly educated, emotionally bruised, de-moralized, and learning-phobic. These children are also likely to end up at the bottom of the food chain, with few, if any, marketable skills or vocational options.

What can parents do to make certain their child receives learning assistance?

The importance of effective parental advocacy cannot be overstated. Involved, knowledgeable, and empowered parents can play a criti-cally important role in making certain that their child's legitimate educational needs are identified and addressed.

Having a child who is struggling with learning difficulties can be a nightmare. No sentient, responsible parent wants to stand on the sidelines and watch a child suffer. No parent wants to feel help-less as his or her child becomes increasingly discouraged and aca-demically incapacitated.

Many factors can interfere with a child's capacity to learn effi-ciently. The impediments may involve deficits in perceptual pro-cessing (e.g., dyslexia), focusing, memory, reading comprehension, following directions, planning, organization, time management, test preparation, and written or spoken expressive language. Emotional and behavioral issues can also obviously undermine the efficiency with which children learn. Test anxiety, reading or math phobias, learned helplessness, resistance, procrastination, sloppiness, and diminished self-confidence can erect formidable barriers to efficient learning.

Being unknowledgeable about the educational issues that are undermining a child's academic performance can have disastrous implications. Soluble problems that might have been accurately identified in first grade, effectively addressed, and resolved by the time a child enters third grade may go untreated. By fourth grade, these problems may have become intractable and may pose monumental barriers to scholastic achievement and self-concept development. For example, parents may be acutely aware that their second-grader is struggling when reading aloud, but they may have no idea about what is causing the problem. If they are unfamiliar with the basic information about the dynamics of reading, they are unlikely to link their child's chronic reading inaccuracies with possible causative factors that may include deficits in the areas of auditory discrimination, visual memory, phonics, word attack, blending, or near-point focusing.

In an era in which the parents of children with learning problems and school personnel often find themselves in adversarial roles because of limited funding for special-education services, *Roadblocks to Learning* levels the playing field. It provides parents with the vital information they need to represent their child's interests competently.

Roadblocks to Learning is designed to provide the insight you need to help your child. To evaluate your child's educational needs intelligently, you must have critical information. Once you become knowledgeable about the issues, you can assume an effective, proactive, and if necessary, aggressive role in making certain your child's educational problems are addressed. Armed with key information, you will be able to:

- understand the dynamics, symptoms, and implications of your child's learning difficulties
- identify the causative factors
- comprehend the terminology
- make intelligent decisions about testing and treatment options
- interface effectively with school personnel
- make certain that your child's educational needs are being met

How to Use This Book

———▲———

Roadblocks to Learning defines and explains virtually every type of learning disorder and counterproductive behavior that can block academic achievement. You can use the book to acquire immediate information about a particular problem, or you can use it as a road map for more comprehensive research. You can quickly familiarize yourself with jargon, testing methods, and treatment protocols. You can also refer to the guide for a quick review before an important school conference or when you are communicating with a teacher or resource specialist on the telephone. Within a few minutes, you'll understand what a *decoding dysfunction* is. You'll recognize the relationship between *logic* and *critical thinking*. You'll realize how *articulation difficulties* and an *auditory-discrimination deficit* may be linked. This information will enable you to communicate more productively and confidently with educational specialists and other professionals.

The book lists the common symptoms associated with each difficulty, clearly defines terminology and educational jargon, and when appropriate, describes testing procedures and suggests remediation strategies. Each term or condition is listed alphabetically under appropriate categories. For quick reference, you will find a concise definition of the specific deficiency. A more comprehensive description of the particular learning difficulty follows, which includes the etiology (origins), physiology (metabolic and physical causes), and academic and/or emotional implications. You will find a highlighted list of the red-flag academic and behavioral symptoms associated with the particular area of difficulty. If there are formal or informal tests designed to assess the difficulty, these protocols are listed and briefly described. A description of specific methods or programs that can be used to treat the problem has also been included. If these remedial programs are not likely to be available in a public-school special-education program, this is noted. At the end of each entry you will find a list of cross-references that will help you pinpoint symptoms and identify possible overlapping deficits that could be having a negative impact on your child's ability to function efficiently and effectively in school. Finally, at the back of the book, there is an extensive index.

The information on the following pages will allow you to assume a pivotal role in assuring that your child's educational needs are identified and addressed. Your proactive involvement could alter the course of your child's life.

ACADEMICS

A learning disability can undermine performance exclusively in one subject area, such as reading, or in multiple academic subjects. In most cases, the tendrils of a learning dysfunction will invade every content area. For example, dyslexic children are likely to have problems not only with deciphering words but also with spelling and language arts. Their decoding difficulties will probably affect their ability to solve word problems in math and their reading comprehension in history, science, and English.

Children with auditory-discrimination deficits (i.e., difficulty differentiating the sounds that individual letters and blends produce) invariably struggle to master phonics and spell accurately. Those with auditory- and visual-memory problems can be expected to have difficulty retaining the information they read in their textbooks and hear in class. Those who cannot follow instructions or pay attention are destined to be confused when their teachers give directions about how to do an assignment or when they explain such procedures as finding the common denominator when adding mixed fractions.

The marginal academic success experienced by children with learning disabilities produces predictable consequences that include frustration, discouragement, diminished effort, poorly developed skills, and reduced self-confidence. To avoid work they find painful and cope with feelings of inadequacy, many of these students compensate by resorting to counterproductive behavior and attitudes. They may procrastinate, submit sloppy, incomplete, and late assignments, blame others for their difficulties, and resist help. These misguided defense mechanisms provide no real protection and only exacerbate the educational challenges.

Having to do homework is a dreaded experience for children with deficient skills. Many of these academically defeated youngsters choose the path of least resistance and do anything possible to avoid studying. They then unconsciously rationalize and justify their behavior by deluding themselves into thinking that they aren't really failing if they aren't really trying. Despite compelling evidence to the contrary, these children often deny that they have academic problems and argue instead that school is "dumb." Their transparent defense mechanisms and the attendant lack of effort and motivation produce predictable consequences: poor grades, diminished self-confidence, test-taking and learning phobias, and diminished expectations and aspirations.

The downward academic slide of students who have difficulty learning efficiently usually begins in first grade. By fourth grade, many of these children have already acquired an entrenched pattern of self-defeating habits. Described by their concerned and exasperated teachers and parents as lazy and unmotivated, they appear oblivious to the consequences of their behavior. Unless they are provided with effective remedial intervention, their academic fate may be sealed by the time they enter middle school.

As many as 15 percent of American students are wrestling with learning problems. Another 25 percent are working below their full scholastic potential, but only 3–4 percent of these children are typically identified as having specific learning disabilities. The vast majority of these underachieving students haven't a clue about how to learn efficiently and study productively, but because their problems are deemed "nonincapacitating," they are not evaluated or do not qualify for formal learning assistance.

Children who do poorly in school usually bear deep emotional scars. Nonachieving and marginally achieving children quickly learn to devalue their talents and minimize their intellectual capabilities. Skills may never be fully developed. Motivational goals may never be established. Rewarding careers may never be launched. Potential contributions to society may never be actualized.

In the following section, you will learn about the specific academic implications of learning disabilities and about issues that can obstruct the full development of your child's natural aptitude and abilities.

Aptitude

▲

Refers to an inherited ability or natural talent in a specific area.

▲

Often referred to as "natural talent," aptitude is an inherited, genetically based ability that may manifest as a mechanical, scientific, mathematical, musical, creative, expressive, linguistic, athletic, socially interactive, or artistic skill. Although aptitude and intelligence often overlap, children may have superior natural aptitude in a specific area or areas without necessarily possessing superior general intelligence (as measured by an IQ test). Other children may be exceptionally intelligent but may possess no demonstrable specific aptitudes. Some children are doubly blessed. They are bright, and they also possess specialized aptitude. They may be able to solve advanced algebraic equations in fourth grade, and they may also have excellent expository writing skills and a facility for learning foreign languages. Other children may have exceptional mechanical aptitude and be capable of taking apart a malfunctioning engine, identifying and correcting the problem, and rebuilding the engine, but they may

---

INTERPLAY BETWEEN APTITUDE AND INTELLIGENCE

- superior specialized aptitude/high intelligence (e.g., a bright student who is also a highly accomplished musician)
- superior specialized aptitude/low-to-average general intelligence (e.g., a non-learning-disabled student with natural artistic or mechanical aptitude who struggles to comprehend complex material in textbooks)
- limited specialized aptitude/high intelligence (e.g., a student with superior intelligence who possesses a prodigious memory and a highly analytic mind but who demonstrates no artistic, mechanical, or musical talents)

struggle in school because of a learning disability that causes decoding, comprehension, and/or retention deficits.

Children tend to identify, gravitate toward, and develop their natural talents. This impetus is intuitive and instinctual. For example, a child with musical aptitude is likely to begin "fooling around" with a piano or guitar at an early age if an instrument is available. She is also likely to request formal lessons.

Psychologists can administer an IQ test such as the Wechsler Intelligence Scale for Children III (WISC III) to measure overall intelligence and identify specific school-related aptitudes. These tests, however, provide little information about a child's non-school-related natural talents and are not designed to assess mechanical, musical, artistic, athletic, leadership, or interpersonal aptitude. These abilities can be vital self-concept-building resources for students who are not succeeding scholastically. Once identified and developed, nonacademic abilities can provide critically important opportunities for achievement and can help orient children toward vocations that capitalize on their natural talents. This process of figuring out what they are good at can be of critical importance to youngsters who are unlikely to pursue a career requiring an advanced college degree.

Helping children cultivate their natural aptitude is especially important in the case of children who are struggling with learning problems. Often frustrated, discouraged, insecure, emotionally vulnerable, and psychologically defended, many of these children are at risk for giving up and shutting down in school. Encouraging them to develop their abilities in nonacademic areas and urging them to establish short-term and long-term performance goals can provide them with an oasis where they can achieve and experience a sense of pride. Children who attain a black belt in karate or who become accomplished dancers, computer whizzes, or consummate chess players are less likely to become demoralized by the battle to survive academically. Their successes in the nonscholastic arena can significantly build their self-concept and sustain them emotionally while they are working to improve their academic skills.

School psychologists, clinical psychologists, and school counselors can administer a range of tests that can help teenage students better understand themselves and identify their vocational interests. Their identified interests and preferences will usually be congruent with their aptitude and talents.

ASSESSMENT TOOLS THAT IDENTIFY PERSONALITY TRAITS AND VOCATIONAL INTERESTS

- Myers-Briggs-type indicator
- Please Understand Me
- the self-directed search
- DISCOVER
- learning-styles inventory
- the strong-interest inventory
- COPS (Career Occupational Preference System)

SEE: Auditory Memory *(page 322)*; Brain Dysfunction *(page 326)*; Critical Thinking *(page 161)*; Decoding *(page 332)*; Essays and Essay Tests *(page 18)*; Goal Setting *(page 165)*; Identifying Important Information *(page 41)*; I'm Dumb Syndrome *(page 388)*; Intelligence *(page 45)*; Judgment *(page 260)*; Keeping Up with the Class *(page 51)*; Language Arts *(page 58)*; Logic *(page 171)*; Mastery of Academic Content *(page 67)*; Math *(page 72)*; Planning *(page 176)*; Problem Solving *(page 185)*; Reading Comprehension *(page 100)*; Self-concept *(page 410)*; Spelling *(page 112)*; Standardized Tests *(page 116)*; Strategic Thinking *(page 189)*; Teacher-Designed Tests *(page 132)*; Time Management *(page 138)*; Underachievement *(page 143)*; Visual Memory *(page 360)*; Vocabulary *(page 150)*.

Essays and Essay Tests

▲

Refers to the ability to express ideas effectively in writing and specifically in well-written, organized, cogent, and persuasive paragraphs that communicate comprehension and retention of key information about the subject matter.

▲

Students assigned an essay for homework or asked to answer an essay question on an exam must be able to express effectively their ideas, feelings, insights, and knowledge. To get a good grade, they must demonstrate that they have:

- understood key information and concepts
- assimilated relevant data
- tied important facts together
- organized their thoughts
- crafted a powerful topic sentence
- presented the relevant information systematically
- stated their position clearly and cogently
- drawn inferences and conclusions from the data
- supported their contentions with facts and data
- communicated their ideas logically, lucidly, and convincingly
- provided a coherent summarization of their insights in their concluding sentence or sentences

Unfortunately, many children who struggle with learning problems are so preoccupied with overcoming their perceptual-processing difficulties (a *decoding* function) that they often fail to develop good language arts skills (an *encoding* function). Given the limited time that resource specialists spend with students, the priority is usually to help children learn how to decipher written language and written symbols so that they can read their textbooks and do their math assignments. Teaching students how to write grammatically correct sentences may be a component of the remediation program, but decoding skills typically take precedence over encoding skills.

Effective expository writing is a skill that must be methodically developed. As is the case in learning any skill, competency and mastery are a function of systematic instruction, incisive feedback, and repeated practice. Natural writing aptitude can make the process easier for some students, but even children with natural talent must work diligently at honing their skills.

Students start acquiring language-arts skills in first grade, where they are taught how to write simple declarative and interrogatory sentences. As they compose these sentences, they begin to assimilate the basic rules of applied grammar. They discover that there are conventions that govern written language, and they learn that these conventions parallel those that govern acceptable spoken language:

- Sentences must have a verb and a subject.
- There must be agreement between the subject and verb.
- Qualifiers (adverbs and adjectives) can amplify their thoughts and add precision to their observations and feelings.

During the next six years, children learn to use different tenses, create compound sentences, incorporate predicates, and use proper punctuation. They learn that well-chosen adverbs and adjectives can make their sentences more interesting and evocative. They also learn to identify and eliminate common mistakes, which include misspelled words, sentence fragments, run-on sentences, mixed tenses, redundancies, nonparallel constructions, and repetitive syntax.

By the time students enter middle school, they should theoretically be able to express coherently information and ideas in writing. In many cases, their language-arts skills will still be quite rudimentary, but they should be capable of crafting a well-organized and essentially grammatically correct essay, book report, or term paper. Children who cannot do so are at a major disadvantage, and their grades will suffer.

In high school, the bar for expository-writing performance is raised, at least in theory. Good teachers, especially the teachers of advanced-placement classes, expect their students to be capable of logically analyzing issues, accurately "writing up" chemistry, physics, or biology lab experiments, and communicating insightful reactions to historical events, scientific discoveries, and works of literature. Students who want good grades must demonstrate that they can express their ideas effectively and write essays that are convincing, cogent, incisive, and grammatically correct.

High-school students who are asked to answer an essay test question about the factors responsible for the French Revolution may have only twenty minutes to pull together all the pertinent information they have learned and to craft their essay. They must include key facts, but a plethora of disjointed facts does not guarantee a good grade. Students must select information that documents their understanding of the issues, and they must methodically cull, distill, and shape this information into a well-written essay that convincingly demonstrates their knowledge and insight. Those who get good grades on essays follow a similar modus operandi. They typically:

- make a mental or written "thumbnail" outline of key information they want to include
- begin with a powerful and interesting topic sentence
- organize information and ideas
- intentionally vary their sentence style
- write legibly
- tie the information together
- express their thoughts sequentially and succinctly
- make their points convincingly
- end their essay with an effective concluding/summarizing statement
- proofread to correct spelling, grammar, and punctuation errors

There are two basic formats for writing an effective essay. The most common is called the *deductive method*. For example, an essay question on a European history exam might ask: "Why was the French Revolution a time bomb waiting to explode?" A student using the deductive method would present a general overview statement in the opening paragraph such as: "The French Revolution,

which began in 1789 and ended in 1799, was one of the most important events in European history and was sparked by a financial crisis,
a political battle, and a class struggle." The student would then methodically describe the specific historical events and sociological
conditions that triggered the revolution. She would include relevant
facts to substantiate her analysis and document her knowledge. In
her concluding paragraph, she would tie the information together
and concisely summarize her position or conclusion.

The deductive method can best be visualized as a triangle or pyramid. The topic or introductory sentence is represented by the point of
the triangle. Substantiating data are positioned below the tip in expanding layers. The concluding sentence or sentences tie together the
information and are represented by the base of the triangle.

Deductive Format

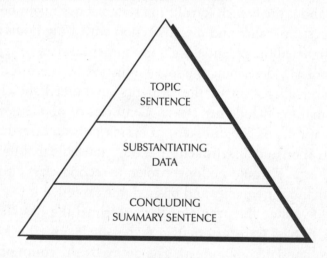

The *inductive method* can be best visualized as an *inverted* triangle or pyramid. The student using this format would methodically
present information and supporting data that lead to the point of
the essay. Information is stacked in *descending layers* that lead to a
logical conclusion and the main point of the essay. This conclusion
that is drawn from the data is expressed in the final paragraph and
represents the inverted point of the triangle.

Inductive Format

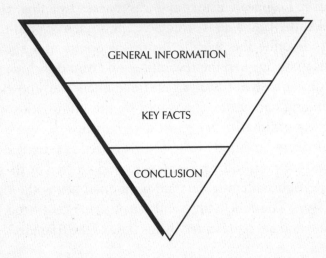

The first sentence in an inductive essay answering the same question about the French Revolution stated above might be: "Great social unrest in France and dissatisfaction with King Louis and the nobility signaled the potential for a monumental class struggle." After methodically describing the social injustices, dire economic conditions, and alienation of the peasants and merchant class, the student might conclude her essay: "Centuries of oppression, social discrimination, and the disregard of basic rights and freedoms created frustration and dissatisfaction. It was inevitable that the second and third estates would no longer tolerate second-class citizenship. Their demand for equality and basic rights exploded into a revolution in 1789 when the people of Paris stormed the Bastille. Thousands of nobles were arrested and executed, and the king was dethroned and later guillotined. The desire by the common people for liberty, democracy, and equality forever changed the course of European history and civilization."

Inductive essays can be very persuasive, but they require careful planning, organization, and advanced expressive language skills. Many teachers never teach the inductive method to their students, or if they do, they do so in a cursory manner. For these reasons, most students choose the deductive model when writing an essay.

Hegelian dialectic is another highly effective expository writing technique. Named after the German philosopher Hegel, this technique is required in most European schools. Students present and document a well-reasoned position on a subject *(thesis)* and a contrasting position *(antithesis)*. They then blend the best components of both positions into a conclusion *(synthesis)*. Because the dialectic acknowledges that issues can be viewed from different perspectives and integrates the best components of the differing perspectives into the conclusion, the dialectic format is usually effective and persuasive. Students, however, must extensively practice this demanding writing technique before they can reasonably be expected to use it effectively.

Whatever expository-writing method is used, students must be provided with repeated opportunities to write if they are to improve and refine their language-arts skills. Ideally, children should be required to write hundreds of essays and reports during the course of their education, and these essays and reports should be meticulously corrected and assessed by their teachers and annotated with incisive feedback and constructive criticism.

Students in elementary and junior high school who are not required to write a weekly essay and a monthly book report are being short-changed. Those who are required to take only multiple-choice, short-answer, and true/false tests (i.e., *objective tests*) and who are rarely, if ever, required to take a timely essay exam (i.e., *subjective tests*) are also being short-changed. These students are likely to become overwhelmed and demoralized in high school if they encounter teachers who assign essays and give essay exams.

Requiring children to memorize facts, circle the correct answer, indicate "true" or "false," or respond to a test question with one or two words does not prepare them for the rigors of having to organize, distill, and communicate what they know about a subject in a two- or three-page essay. Students who are not taught how to write effectively in elementary, middle, and high school and who are not required to practice writing cannot possibly acquire first-rate expository-writing skills. These students will be at a significant disadvantage in college, and their language-arts deficiencies will erect major educational and vocational barriers.

The obstacles posed by poorly developed expository-writing skills are all the more formidable in the case of learning-disabled students. It is vital that the remediation program include a meaningful emphasis on teaching these children functional writing skills.

INDICATIONS OF ESSAY-WRITING DEFICIENCIES

- nonparallel construction (mixing tenses and grammatical forms, such as: "Her dream was to dance and having opportunities to travel.")
- run-on sentences (e.g., "The show pleased her, and she likes to sing, too.")
- sentence fragments
- disorganization
- grammar and syntax mistakes (e.g., mixed tenses, nonparallel construction, lack of subject-verb agreement)
- punctuation and spelling errors
- lack of clarity
- illogical statements and non sequiturs (ideas that do not follow or belong logically in a sentence or paragraph)
- imprecision
- lack of cohesiveness
- wordiness
- redundancies
- monotonous sentence structure
- difficulty developing a cogent topic sentence
- difficulty supporting a stated position with appropriate and convincing facts
- difficulty incorporating precise, accurate, varied, and evocative vocabulary

Grades

▲

Refers to evaluating of students' performance on quizzes, exams, homework, essays, class work, and reports.

▲

The grading process can be a heart-wrenching experience for children struggling with learning problems. Material that may be relatively easy for other children to assimilate can be a nightmare for students with perceptual-processing deficits. These decoding deficits can quickly undermine academic performance and self-confidence. Finding themselves at a major competitive disadvantage, many learning-disabled children resign themselves to poor grades and lower their expectations and aspirations accordingly.

Children who struggle to learn are often entangled in a paradox. They must work more diligently to compensate for their learning deficits, but these deficits derail the desire, motivation, and effort required to overcome their problems.

For learning-disabled children, grades are an initiation into the harsh realities of life where performance is critically evaluated, achievement is contingent on producing quality work, and rewards and praise are allotted to those who work hard and can conform to the standards. These brutal facts of life can crush the spirit of the struggling learner.

In the classroom, teachers are the judge and jury. They are responsible for evaluating their students' skills and mastery of academic content. They establish grading criteria, set deadlines, and provide ongoing feedback and criticism. Students with poor skills, motivation, and attitude are shunted to the bottom rung of the scholastic pecking order. Those who are irresponsible and act out are punished even more severely.

Basic cause-and-effect principles drive the evaluative process. Achieving children recognize and acknowledge that if they are to succeed academically, they must consistently:

- establish short- and long-term goals
- set priorities
- study conscientiously
- identify, understand, and recall key information
- complete their work on time
- write legibly
- proofread carefully and eliminate careless errors
- attend to important details
- develop an effective study strategy
- understand concepts
- relate what they are currently learning to what they have already learned
- apply what they've been taught
- plan ahead
- manage time
- learn from mistakes and miscalculations

- bounce back from setbacks
- persevere

Marginally achieving students may understand these fundamental cause-and-effect principles, but they typically lack the requisite decoding and focusing capacity to put the principles into play. As a consequence, their grades suffer.

The traditional evaluative procedures used by most classroom teachers can pose grave psychological risks for children with learning problems, especially when teachers' performance standards are inflexible and make no accommodations for learning differences. Children who have difficulty processing sensory information, lack good skills, and cannot conform to their teachers' expectations are candidates for becoming frustrated and demoralized. Their poor grades will probably cause them to conclude that they are hopelessly incompetent. As they become increasingly discouraged, their self-confidence and motivation will plummet, and they are likely to resort to an elaborate system of counterproductive defense mechanisms to help them cope with their setbacks and feelings of inadequacy.

Children who regularly receive poor grades have five basic options:

1. They can continue to work diligently despite the negative feedback.
2. They can lower their expectations and resign themselves to marginal performance and achievement.
3. They can give up, go through the motions of being educated, and acquire a range of self-defeating psychological coping mechanisms that include procrastination, blaming, and irresponsibility.
4. They can direct their emotional and physical energies toward nonacademic pursuits, such as sports.
5. They can shut down completely and retreat into daydreams or resort to rebellious behavior.

Most demoralized children select option three, four, or five. Some have already given up academically by the middle of first grade. Lowering their expectations, they unconsciously adjust their self-concept so that it is congruent with the negative feedback they are receiving. Unless these children are provided with effective remedial assistance, their fate is sealed. They are destined to remain nonachievers or underachievers in school and, perhaps, in life.

Despite the potential negative psychological repercussions inherent in evaluating the performance of learning-disabled students, grades are a legitimate and important assessment tool. They provide feedback and can be a catalyst for effort. Children who believe they are capable of succeeding academically will aspire to good grades because they like the payoffs: pride, a sense of accomplishment, acknowledgment, and affirmation from parents, teachers, and classmates. Conversely, children who believe they are incapable of succeeding in school will eschew making the effort.

The conundrum teachers face is how to establish fair performance-evaluation criteria for children who learn differently. Should a hardworking learning-disabled child who is making demonstrable improvement be given a B when a non-learning-disabled child who has better skills and is performing at a higher level is only given a C?

Parents who believe that their child's teacher is using unfair or biased grading criteria should discuss their concerns with the teacher. If the teacher cannot adequately explain her criteria, a conference with the principal may be advisable.

Other factors besides learning disorders may contribute to lower grades. These include attention deficit/attention deficit hyperactivity disorder, study-skills deficits, family problems, emotional problems, rebelliousness, defiance, poor teaching, drug use, and negative peer influences.

Poor school performance can be a primary indicator of an emotional problem. Children who are depressed, hostile, or in conflict with their family and/or society and those who consciously or unconsciously sabotage themselves require the assistance of a mental-health professional before their parents and teachers can realistically expect their grades to improve.

When poor grades on teacher-designed tests and poor classroom performance are compounded by low scores on standardized tests, warning bells should sound. A current assessment of the child's learning efficiency is clearly indicated. If a child is already in a resource program, the remediation strategy may need to be modified. These issues should be discussed at the next scheduled IEP (Individual Educational Plan) conference. Parents who do not want to wait for the next regularly scheduled annual meeting can request an interim conference.

If a learning disability is suspected and the child is not receiving assistance in a resource program, parents should insist that their child be diagnostically tested to determine if he qualifies for participation in the resource program. If the administration refuses to do this assessment and parents believe that an evaluation is justified, they will need to be insistent. As enrollment criteria for a special-education program can vary significantly from district to district, parents may need to assert their child's rights as mandated by specific federal laws:

- *IDEA* (Individuals with Disabilities Education Act—PL105-17)
- *SECTION 504* of the Rehabilitation Act
- *ADA* (Americans with Disabilities Act)
- *FAPE* (Fair and Appropriate Education Act)*

GUIDELINES FOR IMPROVING CHILDREN'S GRADES

- Encourage your child to establish specific short- and long-term goals and targeted grades in each course.
- Help your child develop a study strategy that increases the likelihood of his attaining his objectives.
- Develop a daily study schedule that allocates specific, realistic, and appropriate amounts of study time for each subject.
- Confirm that your child is accurately recording assignments and explicit directions.
- Confirm that the teacher's instructions are being followed.
- Identify your child's specific learning deficits and impediments.

---

*Descriptions of these federal laws that protect children's rights are found in the Appendix.

- Make certain that appropriate learning assistance and focused instruction in study skills is being provided in school and/or after school.
- Have periodic meetings with your child to evaluate his progress and problems.
- Maintain ongoing contact with teachers to gauge improvement and identify specific deficiencies.
- Request reasonable accommodations in grading and in the amount of work being assigned until your child is able to catch up with the class.

SEE: Apathy *(page 208)*; Aptitude *(page 15)*; Attention Deficit/Attention Deficit Hyperactivity Disorder *(page 214)*; Attention to Details *(page 223)*; Auditory Memory *(page 322)*; Bouncing Back from Setbacks *(page 232)*; Brain Dysfunction *(page 326)*; Conduct and Attitude *(page 235)*; Critical Thinking *(page 161)*; Dealing with Consequences *(page 241)*; Decoding *(page 332)*; Defense Mechanisms *(page 373)*; Depression *(page 378)*; Disorganization *(page 251)*; Dyslexia *(page 335)*; Essays and Essay Tests *(page 18)*; Fear of Failure, Success, and/or Competition *(page 383)*; Goal Setting *(page 165)*; Identifying Important Information *(page 41)*; I'm Dumb Syndrome *(page 388)*; Incomplete Assignments *(page 256)*; Intelligence *(page 45)*; Judgment *(page 260)*; Keeping Up with the Class *(page 51)*; Language Arts *(page 58)*; Learning from Mistakes *(page 267)*; Logic *(page 171)*; Mastery of Academic Content *(page 67)*; Math *(page 72)*; Note Taking *(page 79)*; Parent-Child Conflict *(page 393)*; Passive Learning *(page 84)*; Performance Standards *(page 91)*; Planning *(page 176)*; Priorities *(page 180)*; Problem Solving *(page 185)*; Procrastination *(page 278)*; Psychological Overlay and Psychological Problems *(page 399)*; Reading Comprehension *(page 100)*; Reading Fluency *(page 351)*; Recording Assignments *(page 107)*; Resistance to Help *(page 282)*; School Anxiety *(page 406)*; Self-concept *(page 410)*; Self-control *(page 287)*; Spelling *(page 112)*; Standardized Tests *(page 116)*; Strategic

Grammar and Syntax

▲

Refers to the proper use of accepted conventions and rules in spoken and written language.

▲

The mechanics of spoken and written speech are regulated by rules and conventions. Children unconsciously start to assimilate the basic rules of applied grammar during infancy. As they listen to their parents speak, they begin at a genetically predetermined developmental stage to mimic the sounds, words, intonations, and grammatical constructions and to attach meaning to the words they hear and say.

During the early phases of language development, mastering the grammatical constructions of spoken language is painless. Children are motivated to learn how to communicate for a compelling reason: They want to make themselves and their needs understood.

By the time children enter kindergarten, they have acquired relatively sophisticated grammatical skills. They cannot cite the rule for subject/verb agreement but most know that "the boy *goes*" and "the girls *go*" are correct constructions. When communicating, they will use the standardized conventions they have effortlessly assimilated (unless, of course, their particular subculture uses other conventions). By listening and mimicking, they figure out how to use adjectives and adverbs properly. This assumes, of course, that they are exposed to correct grammar in their environment.

Despite their ever-expanding language proficiency, children often make grammatical mistakes. Common examples include: "I feel good." "Him and I went to the park." "He plays better than me." "It's between he and I." Despite these gaffs, children's facility with applied grammar expands as they progress through school. They will shift effortlessly from the present to the past, present-perfect, and future tenses. They will use declarative sentences, interrogative sentences, and compound sentences. They may not know how to identify or define a participle, but they will use participles in their everyday speech.

For many children, their first painful association with grammar occurs when the learning arena shifts from the informal learning context at home to the more formal context of the classroom. In many schools, children are required to learn and practice grammar rules ad nauseam. Understandably, many react negatively and find this rote procedure boring, irrelevant, and excruciatingly painful. Despite ample evidence that the traditional *learn the rules approach* "turns kids off" and often fails to improve applied grammar, the method has endured and is used in thousands of schools.

Most children see little correspondence between the grammar rules they are required to learn and the language they speak at home and with friends. Finding the rules of grammar complex, mysterious, and impenetrable, they often react by actively or passively resisting the repetitive, mind-numbing exercises being imposed upon them.

A persuasive argument can be made for systematically teaching grammar and for reinforcing the rules by having children diagram sentences, but an even more persuasive argument can be made for teaching grammar dynamically and creatively and making the application of grammar rules interesting, relevant, and practical. Children who realize how everyday communication and grammatical conventions are linked are far more likely to be receptive to learning and applying the rules.

INDICATIONS OF GRAMMAR DEFICIENCIES

- incorrect grammar in reports and essays (run-on sentences, non-parallel construction, mixed tenses)
- incorrect grammar when speaking
- difficulty identifying parts of speech
- difficulty citing the rules that govern how written and spoken language is constructed

HELPING CHILDREN IMPROVE THEIR GRAMMAR

- Identify specific grammatical errors that are being made.
- Examine with your child the appropriate rule for correct usage and practice using the rule correctly.
- Apply the grammar rule being learned to other examples to reinforce mastery.
- Resist correcting every grammatical mistake to avoid triggering resentment and resistance.
- Gear your expectations to your child's grade level.
- Demonstrate to your child how much grammar she already knows. (E.g., she knows that it is grammatically correct to say, "While I was watching the movie, I ate popcorn," and incorrect to say, "While I was watching the movie, I eats popcorn.")
- Compose a short essay with intentional and glaring grammatical mistakes and find the mistakes together.
- Have your child compose short essays with intentional grammatical mistakes and find the mistakes together.
- Hire a creative and dynamic tutor if you lack the skills, inclination, or patience to help your child.
- Request supplemental materials from the teacher that reinforce the grammar concepts your child does not understand.
- Have your child check over reports and essays to see if she can correct the mistakes her teacher has identified.

- Encourage your child to experiment with different grammatical constructions for communicating ideas more effectively.
- Rewrite essays together after they have been graded (if your child is willing).
- Be creative and make the sessions enjoyable.
- Stop when your child becomes fatigued, distracted, or resistant.
- Gear duration of sessions to your child's age and maturity.
- Be patient if your child makes a mistake even if you've already gone over a particular rule several times.
- Do not express disappointment.
- Provide positive feedback and affirmation for improvement.
- Remind yourself that children usually require several exposures before they achieve mastery.

GRAMMAR INVENTORY

	Yes	No
My child:		
recognizes subject-verb agreement	____	____
avoids run-on sentences	____	____
uses tenses properly when writing	____	____
uses punctuation correctly	____	____
writes in complete sentences	____	____
knows the parts of speech	____	____
uses parallel constructions when writing (1)	____	____
uses adverbs and adjectives correctly (2)	____	____
uses pronouns correctly (3)	____	____
avoids dangling or misplaced modifiers (4)	____	____
uses transitive and intransitive verbs correctly (5)	____	____

1. Incorrect:	She is singing, dancing, and *likes* to have a good time.
Correct:	She is singing, dancing, and *having* a good time. (parallel construction)
2. Incorrect:	She feels *good*.
Correct:	She is *good*. (Predicate adjective modifies subject.) She feels *well*, or she is *well*. (Adverb modifies verb.)
3. Incorrect:	It is between *she* and *I*.
Correct:	It is between *her* and *me*. (object of preposition)
4. Incorrect:	We learned that Pearl Buck wrote the book *in* class. (dangling modifier)
Correct:	We learned *in class* that Pearl Buck wrote the book.
5. Incorrect:	I want to *lay* down.
Correct:	I want to *lie* down. (intransitive verb) I want to *lay* it down. (transitive verb)

Handwriting

▲

Refers to the ability to write neatly and legibly. This capability is linked to fine-motor control (regulating finger muscles), eye-hand coordination (reproducing accurately what the eyes see), graphomotor skills (being able to use a pencil or pen to draw and write), spatial awareness (recognizing dimensions, positions in space, and relationships), and the capacity to focus attention.

▲

Children in elementary school are expected to write neatly and legibly, and those who cannot are often criticized for their sloppy and illegible handwriting. As they advance in school, the grades these children receive on essays, reports, homework assignments, and exams are likely to be lowered if their teachers cannot read what they have written.

To write legibly, children must be able to control the fine-motor muscles of their fingers when holding a pencil, pen, or chalk. If their fine-motor difficulties and handwriting problems are extreme and what they write is virtually incomprehensible, these students may be classified as having *dysgraphia*. Young children who have significant difficulty using a pencil to draw and reproduce basic shapes may be described as having a *graphomotor dysfunction*. This ability to use and control a pencil or crayon is one of the criteria that is used in determining whether a child should enter kindergarten or remain in preschool or developmental kindergarten.

Other factors besides fine-motor control can contribute to handwriting difficulties. Problems accurately perceiving spatial relationships can cause distortions in shapes, dimensions, and proportions. These perceptual-processing deficits, which are referred to as *figure-ground* deficits, can affect the formation and precision of individual letters, the positioning of letters and words, and the uniformity of the space between letters and words.

Spatial awareness deficits can also cause math problems. Children with these deficits often have difficulty lining up number columns when adding, subtracting, dividing, and multiplying and as a consequence are predisposed to making computational mistakes.

Attention deficit disorder/attention deficit hyperactivity disorder (ADD/ADHD) can be a contributing factor in poor penmanship. Writing words and sentences accurately requires self-regulation, concentration, and attention to details. Children who are impulsive, distractible, and inattentive are clearly at a disadvantage when precision is required. These children often forget to indent, cross their t's and dot their i's, space their letters properly, and write on the line.

Visual-acuity deficiencies can be another source of handwriting problems. Children with *near-point deficits* (i.e., difficulty seeing accurately at a close distance) often make mistakes when copying words and numbers written in textbooks or handouts, and those with *far-point deficits* often make mistakes when copying words and numbers written on the chalkboard.

Children who struggle with visual efficiency are also susceptible to handwriting and copying deficiencies. This inefficiency usually manifests as difficulty with:

- tracking letters and words (i.e., moving their eyes smoothly from left to right when reading and/or writing)
- eye teaming (coordinating both eyes)
- eye convergence (focusing both eyes on words)

Attitude and effort can play significant roles in handwriting problems. Children whose work is sloppy and illegible usually receive a great deal of negative feedback. Once they conclude that the situation is hopeless and that they are incapable of writing legibly, they may be unwilling to make any effort to improve the legibility of their work. The more their parents and teachers complain about their poor penmanship, the more they dig in their heels. Before long, their poor penmanship will become an entrenched habit.

When illegible handwriting is attributable to bad habits and laziness, it usually indicates that children have failed to assimilate a basic fact of academic life: Teachers don't like sloppy work and usually respond to carelessness by lowering students' grades.

A brain dysfunction can also cause poor handwriting. Children who have suffered certain types of cerebral injury or who have even subtle cerebral palsy are likely to have difficulty controlling the movement of their hands. Less acute problems involving crossing the midline (coordinating both hemispheres of the brain) can make writing legibly a major challenge.

The first step in an effective intervention process is to identify and address the specific factors responsible for a handwriting problem. If the legibility deficits are not severe, the classroom teacher may be able to help the child either during or after class. If the deficits are more extreme, the child may require the assistance of a resource specialist, educational therapist, or occupational therapist. These specialists can systematically train youngsters to control the fine-motor muscles of their hands, perceive visual relationships and proportions more accurately, and integrate their visual-motor and fine-motor coordination skills.

When near-point or far-point acuity deficits are suspected, the child's vision should be tested by an ophthalmologist or optometrist, who may prescribe corrective lenses. If visual-efficiency deficits are suspected, an evaluation by a developmental optometrist may be advisable. Although some health professionals consider this intervention of questionable value, visual-efficiency deficits may respond positively to systematic eye-muscle training techniques.

Parents who suspect that ADD/ADHD may be contributing to their child's poor handwriting should consult their pediatrician. If the child's concentration and/or hyperactivity difficulties are severe, the pediatrician may prescribe attention-focusing medication, such as Ritalin, to see if it improves the legibility of the child's handwriting.

Most children can learn how to write more legibly if provided with effective, systematic instruction. Establishing reasonable but demanding standards for legibility can be an important catalyst for more focused effort. Actively encouraging children with poor handwriting to set legibility-improvement goals is vital. Positive expectations from parents and teachers, acknowledgment of progress, and rewards and praise for achievement can dispel negative expectations, build confidence, and stimulate the desire to write more legibly.

COMMON SYMPTOMS OF A HANDWRITING PROBLEM

- misshapen and uneven letters and numbers
- letter crowding
- words that do not sit on the line
- lack of uniformity in letter size and slant
- irregular spacing between letters and words
- irregularities in formatting written work

CAUSES OF POOR HANDWRITING

- fine-motor control difficulty
- eye-hand coordination difficulty
- Attention Deficit/Attention Deficit Hyperactivity Disorder
- visual-acuity deficits
- brain damage or dysfunction
- visual-motor inefficiency
- difficulty crossing midline
- difficulty with spatial awareness
- difficulty with perceptual processing
- peripheral nervous system deficits
- laziness
- inattention to detail

TREATMENT OPTIONS

- methodical training in handwriting skills by a qualified resource specialist, educational therapist, occupational therapist, or tutor
- medication to control ADHD
- glasses to correct visual-acuity deficits
- vision therapy to correct visual efficiency deficits
- firm and reasonable performance standards to address attitude, laziness, and motivation deficits

SEE: Apathy *(page 208)*; Attention Deficit/Attention Deficit Hyperactivity Disorder *(page 214)*; Attention to Details *(page 223)*; Avoiding Responsibility *(page 227)*; Conduct and Attitude *(page 235)*; Brain Dysfunction *(page 326)*; Dealing with Consequences *(page 241)*; Decoding *(page 332)*; Essays and Essay Tests *(page 18)*; Inaccurate Copying *(page 342)*; Language Arts *(page 58)*; Note Taking *(page 79)*; Parent-Child Conflict *(page 393)*; Performance Standards *(page 91)*; Psychological Overlay and Psychological Problems *(page 399)*; Resistance to Help *(page 282)*; Teacher-Child Conflict *(page 293)*; Working Independently *(page 302)*.

Identifying Important Information

▲

Refers to the ability to target key facts and concepts when reading, taking notes, listening to lectures, and studying.

▲

Children with learning problems face formidable academic challenges, especially when they are enrolled in mainstream classes. Despite their learning deficits, classroom teachers generally expect these children to understand, assimilate, and recall information in textbooks, workbooks, handouts, and lecture notes. The information they are expected to assimilate includes facts, historical dates, grammar rules, spelling, formulas, symbols, concepts, and vocabulary definitions.

The difficulties that learning-disabled children encounter when trying to decode written and/or spoken language, pay attention, and master basic skills can be overwhelming. Faced with major challenges and seemingly insoluble problems, these children are at risk for becoming demoralized and resigning themselves to substandard or marginal achievement. Those who receive effective remedial help and emotional support from their parents and teacher may continue to work diligently. Those who are not receiving effective help or making headway may simply give up. Shutting down intellectually, these children are likely to become passive and uninvolved learners who attempt to compensate for their learning problems by simply memorizing information without giving any thought to the importance of what they are learning. Studying translates into little more than a mindless procedure of turning the pages of their textbooks. Their mechanical, unfocused learning produces predictable consequences: deficient comprehension, poor grades, and diminished academic self-confidence.

In contrast, successful students think about what they are studying. They switch on their radar and try to identify significant information. They are alert to clues from their teacher, and they look for concepts, facts, and procedures that have been emphasized or underscored in class. Realizing that they cannot learn and retain everything, they create a hierarchy of what they need to assimilate. If their teacher is oriented toward facts, historical dates, and science formulas, they adjust their study procedures accordingly. If their teacher emphasizes concepts, they make certain that they identify and understand the key concepts. Their ability to target key information, prioritize what's important, and learn selectively allows them to maximize their study efficiency.

Intelligent children clearly have a competitive advantage when they study. This advantage notwithstanding, virtually all children of normal intelligence can be methodically trained to identify important information, learn more discerningly, and study more effectively.

The first step in helping children learn how to think and learn actively is to train them to ask four key questions:

- What is this material about?
- Why is it important to my teacher that I read or learn this material?
- What does the teacher specifically want me to know and remember?
- How can I best understand, learn, and recall the important information?

In the real world, getting good grades requires that students not only identify what *they* consider important but also what *their teachers* are likely to consider important. Students must factor into their study strategy their teacher's stated and implied predilections; develop highly focused and individualized study procedures that capitalize on their learning strengths; think about why information is significant; differentiate important facts from those less important facts; and consider such issues as relevance, implications, and repercussions. They must also take effective notes from textbooks and lectures, develop the habit of methodically identifying and highlighting key information, manage their study time efficiently, relate what they're currently learning to what they've already learned, anticipate what's likely to be asked on tests based on previous experience with a particular teacher, and develop practical methods of retaining the key information.

The value of the preceding commonsense recipe for academic achievement is indisputable. Unfortunately, helping children acquire these learning skills is easier said than done. This is especially true in the case of children who are struggling to master basic academic skills, such as being able to read with fluency, spell accurately, follow directions, express ideas in writing, and solve math problems.

Helping learning-disabled children acquire basic skills is only one step in a comprehensive and effective remediation process. Once the fundamentals are mastered, the focus of the learning-assistance program must shift to teaching more advanced learning and study skills. These skills are not only requisites for success in middle school, high school, and college; they are also requisites for developing academic self-confidence. It is axiomatic that children who possess the tools they need to learn will be motivated to learn.

It is unrealistic to expect students with a history of learning problems to develop first-rate study skills on their own. The skills must be systematically taught and methodically practiced under the supervision of a qualified resource specialist, educational therapist, or tutor. Before struggling students can realistically be expected to identify, comprehend, and recall important information, they must be taught how to get the job done.

CHARACTERISTICS OF SUCCESSFUL STUDENTS

Achieving students:

- think actively (versus passively) about what they are reading or studying
- establish personal performance goals
- critically evaluate the significance of the information they are learning
- target key data based on their teachers' clues and statements
- take effective notes from textbooks and during lectures
- seek common denominators between information in textbooks and information presented in class
- relate and link what they are currently learning to what they have already learned
- think strategically and attempt to identify while studying what is likely to be covered on a test

- review previous tests when studying to identify the types of information the teacher has emphasized
- identify clues, statements, and hints in study guides that suggest what the teacher considers important (facts, details, concepts, formulas, principles, issues, ideas)
- analyze the teacher's testing style (multiple-choice, short-answer, essay questions)
- carefully consider what they need to understand or memorize in order to master the course content
- adjust their study techniques to the teacher's content emphasis and the type of tests the teacher typically gives
- identify how they learn most effectively (visual, auditory, or kinesthetic preference)
- develop a practical, effective, and individualized study system that capitalizes on their learning strengths
- gear their study strategy and methods to their teacher's testing style and content emphasis
- adjust their study methods for each class and each teacher

SEE: Apathy *(page 208)*; Aptitude *(page 15)*; Attention to Details *(page 223)*; Auditory Memory *(page 322)*; Avoiding Responsibility *(page 227)*; Bouncing Back from Setbacks *(page 232)*; Critical Thinking *(page 161)*; Goal Setting *(page 165)*; Grades *(page 25)*; I'm Dumb Syndrome *(page 388)*; Incomplete Assignments *(page 256)*; Intelligence *(page 45)*; Judgment *(page 260)*; Keeping Up with the Class *(page 51)*; Learning from Mistakes *(page 267)*; Logic *(page 171)*; Mastery of Academic Content *(page 67)*; Note Taking *(page 79)*; Passive Learning *(page 84)*; Priorities *(page 180)*; Problem Solving *(page 185)*; Reading Comprehension *(page 100)*; Self-concept *(page 410)*; Standardized Tests *(page 116)*; Strategic Thinking *(page 189)*; Study Skills *(page 127)*; Teacher-Designed Tests *(page 132)*; Test Anxiety *(page 420)*; Underachievement *(page 143)*; Visual Memory *(page 360)*; Working Independently *(page 302)*.

Intelligence

▲

Refers to the capacity to comprehend, apply, and recall what is being learned, solve problems, understand abstractions, generate innovative ideas, perceive underlying issues, draw inferences and conclusions, think analytically and critically, create strategies, acquire insights, make associations, recognize subtle relationships, and link what has already been learned to what is currently being learned.

▲

Intelligence plays a pivotal role in the academic-achievement equation. Bright children generally have little difficulty recalling what is said in class, answering the teacher's questions, and remembering what they have read in their textbooks and have written in their notes. They can grasp concepts, master procedures, identify important issues, apply what they have learned, analyze data, perceive relationships, make accurate deductions and conclusions, draw inferences that are implied but not necessarily stated, understand and assimilate abstract, complex, or obtuse ideas, integrate new information with what has already been learned, solve problems, and think creatively. These capabilities clearly provide intelligent children with a distinct competitive advantage in school.

Children who are intelligent, motivated, and conscientious and who possess first-rate academic skills typically get A's on their spelling quizzes, math tests, book reports, and essays. When they study, they methodically identify what they need to learn and intuitively develop an individualized, efficient, and effective method for assimilating the information and mastering the specific skills being taught.

A child's intelligence is measured by an IQ test. The most common test, the Wechsler Intelligence Score for Children III (WISC III), is designed to assess the child's potential to succeed academically and to measure the child's capabilities relative to other children of the same age. The test, which consists of a number of specific subtests, is predicated on the principle that the higher a child's measured IQ, the better the child's academic performance. In theory, children with a superior IQ are expected to master academic skills with facility, assimilate concepts, comprehend and retain important information, receive good grades, earn coveted scholarships, attend the best universities, enter the most glamorous, prestigious, and remunerative professions, and make the most significant contributions to our society.

In practice, the cause-and-effect model that correlates intelligence and academic achievement often breaks down. As most front-line educators can attest, the scores on intelligence tests do not always correlate with school success. Some children with a high IQ perform marginally, while others with a lower IQ are remarkably successful in school and in life. Every teacher has encountered intelligent children who are lazy and unmotivated and perform marginally in school. They have also encountered less-than-brilliant, highly conscientious, and intensely goal-directed students who rank among the highest achievers in their class. The explanation for this discrepancy between IQ and performance is obvious: Grit and determination can in many instances compensate for intellectual limitations.

Clearly, the academic-success formula is more complex than the simplistic belief that a high IQ equals superior achievement. Environmental, psychological, temperamental, and educational components must also be factored into the equation.

Some professionals consider IQ tests to be of limited value because they do not take into consideration two critically important elements: motivation and effort. IQ tests have also been faulted for other reasons. The tests:

- do not measure critically important capabilities, such as creativity, leadership, motor coordination, interpersonal skills, communication skills, and musical or artistic aptitude.
- are biased against children from disadvantaged backgrounds who do not receive equivalent levels of intellectual stimulation and educational instruction as their middle-class counterparts.
- can be skewed by cultural factors, language deficits, emotional problems, perceptual processing deficits, ADD/ADHD, anxiety, and poor rapport with the examiner.

IQ tests are not administered to all students. They are typically used by school psychologists* to determine eligibility for gifted-students programs and for special-education programs. In the latter instance, a discrepancy between ability (as measured by an IQ test) and school performance is one of the primary criteria for classifying students as learning disabled.**

In spite of the aforementioned limitations, flaws, and concerns about validity, IQ tests do provide a relatively objective, albeit imperfect, measurement of a child's level of intellectual functioning. Parents and educators, for instance, might consider the scores in determining fair and reasonable expectations and defining fair and reasonable performance standards and guidelines for a child. If the scores indicate that a child's intelligence is in the average-to-superior range, encouraging the child to raise his level of expectations and aspirations and establishing fair but demanding standards at home and in school can be important catalysts in intellectual, academic, and character growth. Conversely, the fact that a child scores below average on an IQ test such as the Wechsler might reasonably be factored into parents' expectations, especially if observations of performance by parents and teachers tend to confirm the accuracy of the testing data.

That parents and teachers should encourage all children to "stretch" intellectually and develop their talents to the fullest is indisputable. This encouragement must be differentiated, however, from making unreasonable or excessive demands on a child with demonstrated intellectual limitations. These demands can cause stress, undermine self-esteem, and trigger emotional damage. Conversely, making too few demands and erroneously discounting a child's potential can have an equally destructive psychological impact. In establishing expectations, parents must make a judgment call that relies not only on testing data but also on their intuition and observations.

---

*Private, licensed clinical psychologists, educational psychologists, and neuropsychologists also administer IQ tests.

**Some professionals believe that IQ tests are biased against minority students and argue that these tests should not be used with these children to determine special education eligibility. They contend that an inordinate number of minority children are being classified as mentally challenged and are being warehoused in special education programs.

The contention that *inherited intelligence* is the primary determinant in school success clearly discounts the crucial role of *applied intelligence* in the academic-achievement equation. To succeed in school, children must be capable of thinking and acting strategically. Irrespective of their IQ, they must be capable of using their intelligence pragmatically to get the job done. They must discipline themselves to sit down and learn the irregular verbs in their Spanish class, the important dates in their history class, and the key formulas in their chemistry class.

Perhaps as many as 40 percent of the students in American schools work below their full scholastic and intellectual potential. These underachieving children perform marginally for reasons that may include identified or unidentified learning disabilities, poor teaching, inadequate study skills, emotional problems, family problems, and little or no support and affirmation for academic achievement from their parents or peers. Some intelligent but marginally performing children become indifferent to their academic responsibilities and choose not to study. Some submit incomplete, late, or shoddy work. Others focus their intellectual and emotional energy on sports, music, skateboarding, or video games. The net effect is wasted potential. Capable children who become habituated to marginal performance in elementary school are at risk for underachieving throughout their lives. Once they lower the performance bar, they will function congruently with this standard.

Learning disabilities can obviously erect significant barriers to functioning at a level commensurate with one's ability. Bright children can just as easily be dyslexic as children with average or below-average intelligence. They can have difficulty following directions, staying focused, writing cogently, attending to details, and reading with fluency. Yes, intelligent children can often compensate more successfully for their learning problems than children who are less intelligent. A child with a high IQ may struggle to decode words and read with fluency, but she may somehow still be able to comprehend the content of the material she is reading.

Because bright learning-disabled children often function academically in ways that belie their intelligence, teachers may underestimate their capabilities. This phenomenon is especially prevalent when underlying learning problems have not been accurately identified and classroom teachers do not understand the dynamics and implications of learning differences.

Although test scores generally do not fluctuate significantly when IQ tests are readministered, there are notable exceptions. Children with ADD/ADHD or emotional problems may perform better on an IQ test when medicated, and children with learning problems may receive higher scores once their perceptual-processing deficits are remediated. At the same time, IQ test scores may drop if children experience an emotional trauma or become discouraged, demoralized, and depressed in school.

Parents and teachers who perceive a discrepancy between a child's intelligence and academic performance should make every effort to identify and address the impediments that could be causing the discrepancy. A comprehensive evaluation by a school psychologist, educational psychologist, clinical psychologist, or neuropsychologist can often pinpoint specific underlying causal factors, and the tests may suggest effective intervention strategies. Educational therapy and/or counseling can play a key role in helping underachieving children learn more efficiently and perform at a level commensurate with their ability.

INDICATIONS OF POSSIBLE INTELLECTUAL LIMITATION*

This child has difficulty:

- comprehending verbally communicated information
- comprehending written information
- recalling verbally communicated information
- recalling written information

---

*These descriptions may also be symptomatic of a learning disability. Some children present as having below-average intelligence because they are seriously learning disabled. With effective intervention, many of these children can be helped to compensate successfully for their deficits. Once they do, they will begin to perform congruently with their actual ability.

- grasping concepts
- understanding abstractions
- mastering operations and procedures
- identifying important issues
- applying what has been learned
- analyzing information
- making astute observations
- solving problems
- developing strategies
- understanding cause-and-effect principles
- learning from mistakes
- perceiving relationships
- recognizing subtleties
- attending to details
- drawing conclusions
- handling multiple tasks concurrently
- centering, decentering, and recentering (being interrupted and then being able to refocus on the task)
- drawing inferences that are implied but not necessarily stated
- understanding and assimilating abstract, complex, or obtuse ideas
- integrating new information with previously learned information
- thinking creatively and innovatively

GENERAL GUIDELINES FOR INTERPRETING INTELLIGENCE QUOTIENT (IQ)

70 and below:	mentally challenged
70–85:	below average
85–115:	average range
115–130:	high average
130 and above:	gifted

SEE: Aptitude *(page 15)*; Attention Deficit/Attention Deficit Hyperactivity Disorder *(page 214)*; Attention to Details *(page 223)*; Auditory Memory *(page 322)*; Bouncing Back from Setbacks *(page 232)*; Critical Thinking *(page 161)*; Dealing with Consequences *(page 241)*; Essays and Essay Tests *(page 18)*; Goal Setting *(page 165)*; Grades *(page 25)*; Identifying Important Information *(page 41)*; I'm Dumb Syndrome *(page 388)*; Judgment *(page 260)*; Keeping Up with the Class *(page 51)*; Language Arts *(page 58)*; Learning from Mistakes *(page 267)*; Logic *(page 171)*; Mastery of Academic Content *(page 67)*; Math *(page 72)*; Planning *(page 176)*; Priorities *(page 180)*; Problem Solving *(page 185)*; Reading Comprehension *(page 100)*; Self-concept *(page 410)*; Standardized Tests *(page 116)*; Strategic Thinking *(page 189)*; Study Skills *(page 127)*; Teacher-Designed Tests *(page 132)*; Underachievement *(page 143)*; Verbal Directions *(page 356)*; Visual Memory *(page 360)*; Vocabulary *(page 150)*; Working Independently *(page 302)*; Written Directions *(page 364)*.

Keeping Up with the Class

▲

Refers to the ability to handle grade-level curriculum, complete assignments, do well on teacher-designed and standardized (nationally normed) tests, and assimilate grade-level material.

▲

When students of average or above-average intelligence struggle to keep up with their class, their difficulties are often directly attributable to a learning disability and/or deficient academic skills. Deficiencies in reading, math, or language arts can obviously erect major barriers to academic achievement, and these deficits are especially problematic when children are in classes in which the majority of the students have superior academic skills.

It is axiomatic that teachers raise their expectations and performance standards in fast-track classes. This can be demoralizing to students with less advanced skills who are placed in such classes and find themselves desperately battling to keep up. Having to compete with efficient learners can cause struggling students to become increasingly discouraged and demoralized. If these children conclude that their academic situation is hopeless, they are likely to choose the path of least resistance and shut down academically.

Teachers who are not knowledgeable about learning disorders tend to latch onto simplistic explanations for why students cannot keep up with the class. They often label these academically deficient students "immature." Certainly, there are children in preschool who are not developmentally ready to enter kindergarten, and there are kindergartners who are not developmentally ready to advance into first grade. Most struggling learners, however, are neither immature nor developmentally delayed. Nor are they intellectually deficient. The majority of these youngsters have specific perceptual-processing and/or concentration deficits that interfere with their ability to learn efficiently.

Labeling learning-disabled students "immature" and recommending that they repeat a grade is rarely an effective long-range solution to the underlying problem. Retaining them is a stopgap measure that simply puts off the "day of reckoning." If they repeat first or second grade, they may do better initially, but unless their learning deficits are accurately identified and effectively remediated, these children will remain at risk scholastically. Their unresolved learning problems are a ticking time bomb that is likely to detonate in third or fourth grade or in middle school.

Other factors besides learning disorders and deficient academic skills can also cause children to have difficulty keeping up with their class. These include:

- poor study skills
- poor time-management skills

- attention-deficit hyperactivity disorder
- family or emotional problems
- inadequate goal orientation
- an inadequate understanding of basic cause-and-effect principles
- a pattern of self-defeating behavior

Children may also lag behind academically if their parents devalue educational achievement and do not provide encouragement and affirmation for progress. Negative peer pressure can also cause students to eschew educational achievement and become unmotivated. Students who perform poorly in school tend to gravitate toward other students who are also doing poorly. To defend themselves from feelings of inadequacy and incompetence, their peer group may denigrate academic achievement and substitute other pursuits (e.g., video-game, athletic, or skateboarding prowess) as substitutes for school success. In extreme cases, nonachieving youngsters may become socially alienated, hostile, rebellious, delinquent, nihilistic, and/or self-mutilating.

Before students with learning problems can realistically be expected to keep up with their class, the impediments must be accurately diagnosed. The first step in this evaluative process is for parents to request precise information from their child's teachers about any specific deficits or issues that might be causing their child to struggle academically. If the teacher and the parents suspect that the child has a learning disability, the next step is to refer the child to the child-study team and to request a comprehensive evaluation by the school psychologist.

Enlisting information and assistance from upper-grade teachers can be problematic. Whereas elementary-school teachers work with twenty-five or thirty students each day, middle-school and high-school teachers may teach as many as 150. Because of this student-teacher ratio, teachers in the upper grades usually cannot monitor their students as closely as elementary-school teachers, nor can they provide as much substantive academic support for students who are falling behind.

Another factor may inhibit middle- and high-school teachers from providing the same degree of support and assistance as their elementary-school counterparts. Many teachers in grades seven through nine believe that students should be responsible for requesting assistance. Focused on teaching their content area, these teachers often profess an unwillingness to serve as "nursemaids" for unmotivated teenagers.

Many middle- and high-school teachers are also resistant to the idea of modifying their curriculum and academic demands despite federal laws that mandate that accommodations be made for children with special learning needs. When students appear lazy or irresponsible, these teachers may construe the behavior as a personal affront and as a rejection of what they are teaching. They may not realize that the student who is falling behind and not submitting his assignments may lack the basic skills to do the work. What they perceive as the *source* of the problem—a bad attitude and lack of motivation—may actually be *symptoms* of the student's underlying perceptual-processing deficiencies. These symptoms are often attributable to frustration and demoralization.

Unfortunately, many teachers in middle school and high school have a relatively limited understanding of learning disabilities and their psychological implications. Whereas elementary-school teachers are usually required to take one or more courses in identifying and dealing with learning problems to be certified, teachers at the secondary level may not be required to take these courses in some states.

Often overworked and overwhelmed by their many teaching responsibilities, teachers in upper grades may contend that they have neither the time nor the training to identify why students are having difficulty keeping up with the class. Many may conclude that nonperforming students simply lack the requisite intelligence to do the assigned work, and they may argue that it is the responsibility of school psychologists and counselors to deal with such issues. Writing off students who appear lazy and irresponsible, these teachers react punitively and penalize with low grades those who fail to study, do the assigned work, and meet deadlines.

Economics can also play a role. Many school districts lack the funds to provide assistance to the vast pool of students who are performing marginally in school. Enrollment in resource programs is often severely restricted, and only students with significant learning disabilities usually qualify for assistance. Compounding the challenge of meeting the needs of children who are failing to keep up is the fact that school counselors, trained to deal with psychological overlay, are frequently assigned many more students than they can realistically handle. Limited funding has caused some districts to severely restrict their counseling program, thus forcing students who desperately need guidance and psychological support to fend for themselves.

Ironically, learning-disabled children who qualify for learning assistance may find themselves in a double bind. When they leave class to work with the resource specialist, they usually miss a great deal of in-class work. Although resource specialists may prefer to address their students' underlying learning deficits, they may be forced to devote most of their remedial time to helping students complete their class work and homework. This prioritization leaves little or no time for actually addressing the specific underlying learning deficits that are impeding academic progress. The resource specialist is thus forced into the role of a tutor.

Some classroom teachers resent the time that struggling students spend out of the classroom working with the resource specialist. These teachers may actually "punish" students by holding them strictly accountable for everything covered in class while they were in the resource room.

Children who are struggling to keep up with their class are at significant risk. The more they fall behind, the greater the danger of demoralization and academic shut-down. If lasting scholastic and psychological damage is to be avoided, it is vital that parents, teachers, resource specialists, tutors, and educational therapists work together to develop and implement a practical and effective catch-up plan.

FACTORS THAT MAY PREVENT STUDENTS FROM KEEPING UP WITH THE CLASS

- learning disabilities
- academic-skills deficits
- study-skills deficits
- ADHD
- emotional and/or family problems
- negative peer or environmental influences
- poor teaching
- lack of interest in the subject matter
- lack of parental oversight
- denial of access to formal learning assistance in school
- restricted availability of school counseling
- poorly defined family behavioral guidelines and expectations
- family values that deemphasize educational achievement
- psychological problems

INDICATIONS OF DIFFICULTY KEEPING UP WITH THE CLASS

- frustration
- demoralization
- negative expectations
- reduced aspirations
- deficient academic skills
- inefficient study procedures
- inadequate effort
- deportment problems
- difficulty understanding material presented in class
- difficulty completing homework assignments independently
- general confusion about what is expected
- incomplete assignments

- missed deadlines
- deficient academic self-confidence
- counterproductive behavior
- dislike of school
- resistance to learning
- procrastination
- rebelliousness
- chronic irresponsibility
- identification with other nonachieving students

SEE: Apathy *(page 208)*; Aptitude *(page 15)*; Attention to Details *(page 223)*; Auditory Discrimination *(page 317)*; Auditory Memory *(page 322)*; Brain Dysfunction *(page 326)*; Conduct and Attitude *(page 235)*; Critical Thinking *(page 161)*; Decoding *(page 332)*; Defense Mechanisms *(page 373)*; Developmental Immaturity *(page 246)*; Disorganization *(page 251)*; Essays and Essay Tests *(page 18)*; Fear of Failure, Success, and/or Competition *(page 383)*; Grades *(page 25)*; Identifying Important Information *(page 41)*; I'm Dumb Syndrome *(page 388)*; Incomplete Assignments *(page 256)*; Intelligence *(page 45)*; Language Arts *(page 58)*; Logic *(page 171)*; Mastery of Academic Content *(page 67)*; Note Taking *(page 79)*; Parent-Child Conflict *(page 393)*; Passive Learning *(page 84)*; Peer Pressure *(page 272)*; Performance Standards *(page 91)*; Phonics *(page 346)*; Planning *(page 176)*; Priorities *(page 180)*; Problem Solving *(page 185)*; Procrastination *(page 278)*; Psychological Overlay and Psychological Problems *(page 399)*; Reading Comprehension *(page 100)*; Reading Fluency *(page 351)*; Recording Assignments *(page 107)*; Resistance to Help *(page 282)*; School Anxiety *(page 406)*; Self-concept *(page 410)*; Spelling *(page 112)*; Standardized Tests *(page 116)*; Strategic Thinking *(page 189)*; Study Interruptions *(page 122)*; Study Skills *(page 127)*; Teacher-Child Conflict *(page 293)*; Teacher-Designed Tests *(page 132)*; Test Anxiety *(page 420)*; Time Management *(page 138)*; Underachievement *(page 143)*; Working Independently *(page 302)*.

Language Arts

▲

Refers to the ability to express clearly in writing ideas, information, and feelings. Language-arts proficiency encompasses both expository and creative-writing skills.

▲

The capacity to express ideas, insights, and feelings in writing is a requisite for academic success. Unfortunately, learning-disabled children are typically so preoccupied with assimilating basic reading and math skills that they often fail to develop first-rate expository writing skills.

Children who are enrolled in a learning-assistance program spend limited time each day with the resource-program specialist (RSP), who must establish priorities in allocating this precious instructional time. If a student has significant perceptual-decoding deficits and is struggling to master basic skills, resource specialists will usually focus on providing remedial instruction in phonics, auditory and visual discrimination and memory, word attack, blending, spelling, handwriting, vocabulary development, and/or math. This prioritization often allows little or no time for the RSP to work with the student on developing language-arts skills.

The ranking of reading skills over writing skills is not capricious. Children must be able to decode written language to survive academically and avoid psychologically devastating frustration and demoralization. Their most compelling need is to learn how to decipher and comprehend the content of their textbooks, workbooks, and teacher handouts. For many of these children, acquiring grade-level reading skills poses a monumental challenge. Although the resource specialists may devote a limited amount of time to teaching students how to write simple, grammatically correct declarative and interrogatory sentences and to helping them correct the grammar, punctuation, and syntax errors in their written work, these endeavors usually assume secondary importance.

Given the limited student–resource-specialist instructional time that is available, a persuasive argument can be made for prioritizing reading. A steep price, however, must be paid for the de-emphasis of language-arts instruction. Learning-disabled children who cannot write a well-constructed essay will be at a severe disadvantage as they progress into the upper grades. Their deficient writing skills are a ticking time bomb. Those who go on to college will discover that instructors require students to write cogently and persuasively. Those with poor expository writing skills are destined to receive poor and, perhaps, failing grades in courses in which essays and reports are assigned. When these students ultimately enter the workforce, those on a professional career track will find that their bosses expect them to write sound, convincing, and grammatically correct business letters and reports. Employees who cannot do so are likely to find their career advancement blocked.

To write effectively, children must find the words that can accurately communicate their ideas, feelings, observations, and experiences. The selection of precise, descriptive vocabulary and the process of crafting these words into written language involve two overlapping neurological functions: the *decoding* (or deciphering) of sensory data and the *encoding* (or expression) of responses to this sensory data.

As the brain receives input from the external world (facts in a textbook, information in a lecture, and observations in a biology lab) or from the internal world (ideas and emotions emanating from within the mind), it instantaneously deciphers the sensory stimuli. The brain then makes associations with previously stored information and selects words that can communicate the student's perceptions, impressions, feelings, insights, conclusions, and knowledge.

Eight critically important factors can affect the quality of children's writing:

- the complexity of the stimuli being processed by the brain
- intelligence
- natural language aptitude

- the quality of the language-arts instruction
- desire and effort
- self-confidence
- attention to details
- self-criticism/self-editing

An essay or report represents the distillation of literally thousands of conscious and unconscious choices of vocabulary, syntax, grammar, perceptions, data, ideas, organization, expressive style, and imagery. The ultimate effectiveness and aesthetics of what a child writes is a function of these choices and the child's intention to communicate persuasively.

NEUROLOGICAL PROCESSING AND WRITTEN EXPRESSION

- *input:* receiving external and internal stimuli that trigger a neurological response
- *decoding:* interpreting and processing stimuli and making associations with stored neurological data
- *encoding:* selecting words to communicate information, ideas, feelings, reactions, and interpretations

---

Children's writing skills are continually being evaluated in school, and their grades reflect the teacher's objective and subjective assessment of the content, quality of language, and efficacy with which the student has crafted his or her words into sentences and paragraphs. Teachers give the best grades to students who use precise, varied, and evocative vocabulary, write cogent sentences, spell accurately, consistently apply grammatical conventions, develop a pleasing, engaging, and dynamic writing style, and produce cohesive, organized, and well-conceived essays and reports.

The neurological decoding/encoding process that generates written language can be represented graphically:

Written Communication

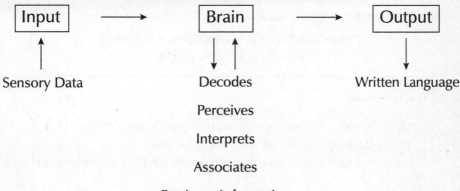

Input → Brain → Output

Sensory Data   Decodes   Written Language

Perceives

Interprets

Associates

Retrieves Information

Generates Reactions, Thoughts, and Emotions

Selects Words

Applies Language Conventions

(Grammar, Syntax, Punctuation, Spelling)

Expository and creative writing demand more conscious thought, focused effort, meticulous care, self-discipline, and diligence than verbal communication. Translating thoughts into words and creating clear and comprehensible sentences and paragraphs can be a major challenge to any child. The challenge is compounded in the case of students who have learning problems and/or ADD/ADHD. Having to apply stringent rules of grammar, punctuation, and usage and attend to exacting spelling requirements can significantly increase the trials and tribulations of these youngsters.

With good instruction, sufficient practice, and incisive teacher feedback, virtually all children of normal intelligence can improve their writing skills. This systematic instruction should begin with teaching the fundamentals in the first three years of elementary school (e.g., systematically teaching how to write powerful declarative sentences and effective topic sentences) and should expand as children advance into the upper grades.

FUNDAMENTALS OF IMPROVING STUDENTS' LANGUAGE-ARTS SKILLS

Teachers must:

- flag students' spelling, grammar, and punctuation errors
- train students how to self-edit and proofread
- teach students easy-to-use methods to identify and eliminate errors
- encourage students to search for more effective ways to communicate their ideas and insights
- identify students' syntax, organization, word choice, and grammatical mistakes
- examine in class the common expository writing errors (i.e., mixed tenses, dangling modifiers, improper subject-verb agreement, nonparallel constructions, run-on sentences, etc.)
- model how to create powerful topic and concluding sentences
- teach students a range of expository-writing techniques that include the deductive, inductive, and Hegelian* methods
- teach students techniques for organizing and clarifying their ideas
- encourage students to assess their writing style critically so that they can eliminate repetitive declarative sentences and redundancies and develop a more textured writing style
- encourage students to expand their vocabulary
- provide repeated opportunities for practice
- affirm progress

---

*This highly effective method of presenting the thesis, antithesis, and synthesis is described in Essays and Essay Tests (page 18).

The mind-numbing practice of requiring students to insert the correct adverb, adjective, or verb tense in language-arts handouts is not the equivalent of teaching effective expository and creative-writing skills. Children in fourth grade and above should be assigned daily writing exercises, weekly essays, monthly book reports, and semester term papers. Teachers should meticulously grade this material and underscore the errors with a red pencil. Students should then be required to rewrite the assignment and eliminate the errors. The consequences of teachers circumventing these essay-grading conventions are distressingly apparent: Millions of potentially capable American students are graduating from high school with abysmal language-arts skills.

Unfortunately, the tradition of assigning and correcting students' writing projects has fallen into disfavor. Many teachers no longer want to spend hours every day grading thirty essays. Some younger teachers are actually incapable of finding the mistakes in their students' written work because their own expository writing skills are dreadful. Because of their own deficiencies, these teachers haven't a clue about how to teach language arts effectively.

Expectations and standards for written work should be age-appropriate, but by fourth grade students should be regularly practicing the fundamentals of expository and creative writing. The goal is for them to be able to:

- create powerful topic and concluding sentences
- vary syntax and sentence structure
- use active versus passive constructions
- avoid redundancies
- apply appropriate grammar conventions
- proofread for spelling and punctuation mistakes
- apply age-appropriate reason and logic
- organize ideas and information
- draw insightful conclusions
- argue issues persuasively
- incorporate effective examples, analogies, imagery, and metaphors

- substantiate ideas with facts
- make points clearly
- produce interesting, engaging, aesthetically pleasing, thought-provoking prose

Students who conclude they're incapable of writing well are at risk of becoming writing-phobic. Once they become convinced that they are incompetent and that the situation is hopeless, they are likely to make minimal effort and minimal progress, and their expectations of disaster are likely to become self-fulfilling.

REQUISITES TO EFFECTIVE LANGUAGE-ARTS INSTRUCTION

1. a well-conceived language-arts program
2. an emphasis on writing skills in the curriculum
3. an enthusiastic and competently trained teacher
4. practice (regularly assigned essays, journals, diaries, book reports, and term papers)
5. methodical grading of students' writing and the flagging of errors
6. an emphasis on training students to develop self-editing skills
7. parental support, monitoring, and when appropriate, assistance (Parents, however, should not actually write their child's essays and reports.)

BEHAVIORS AND ATTITUDES INDICATING
LANGUAGE-ARTS DEMORALIZATION

My child:

- puts off doing writing assignments to the last moment
- is inattentive to explicit instructions
- chronically submits late or incomplete work

- is inattentive to details
- does not do assignments
- is unenthusiastic
- complains
- expends minimum effort
- disregards indicated errors on graded assignments
- repeats the same mistakes
- does not critically evaluate own work
- is unwilling to take the time to edit and proofread carefully

Encouraging children with language-arts deficits to read their essays and reports aloud can be very productive in helping them catch spelling, punctuation, grammar, and syntax mistakes (e.g., sentence fragments, run-on sentences, poorly organized ideas) that might otherwise be overlooked. Ideally, the child will recognize that a phrase or a sentence doesn't "sound right." Actually hearing the words can also help children identify redundancies and sentences that need to be revised because they are unclear.

Highly effective and innovative programs for teaching language arts have been developed, and there's no excuse for schools to have an inadequate writing-skills program. Some programs have computer-based components. Others are remedial and are designed to help children master the fundamentals. Voice-recognition software, which allows students to "speak" their essays into the computer and see the material on-screen, can be very effective in building self-confidence and in helping children who have negative associations with writing get unblocked.

The following language-arts inventory is designed to identify specific language-arts deficits. Students in the lower grades obviously cannot be expected to have mastered some of the skills listed. Be concerned only about skills relevant to your child's grade level. Your child's teacher can tell you which skills have been taught and practiced.

INDICATIONS OF DEFICIENT LANGUAGE-ARTS SKILLS

	Yes	No
Inconsistent use of capital letters	___	___
Incorrect or inconsistent punctuation	___	___
Sentence fragments (sentences without verbs)	___	___
Run-on sentences (too many ideas included in the sentence)	___	___
Incorrect subject/verb agreement ("I goes.")	___	___
Inaccurate spelling	___	___
Sloppy or illegible handwriting	___	___
Ineffectual topic and concluding sentences	___	___
Mixed tenses (mixing of future, present, and past tenses)	___	___
Nonsequential presentation of ideas	___	___
Inconsistent or improper use of paragraphs	___	___
Difficulty summarizing	___	___
Poorly organized stories, essays, and reports	___	___
Difficulty expressing ideas within a reasonable time frame	___	___
Difficulty finding blatant grammatical and syntax errors	___	___
Difficulty writing interesting, creative stories	___	___
Difficulty identifying parts of speech	___	___
Redundancies	___	___
Lack of clarity	___	___

SEE: Apathy *(page 208);* Aptitude *(page 15);* Attention to Details *(page 223);* Critical Thinking *(page 161);* Disorganization *(page 251);* Dyslexia *(page 335);* Essays and Essay Tests *(page 18);* Goal Setting *(page 165);* Grades *(page 25);* Grammar and Syntax *(page 31);* Handwriting *(page 36);* Identifying Important Information *(page 41);* Incomplete Assignments *(page 256);* Intelligence *(page 45);* Judgment *(page 260);* Language Disorders *(page 433);* Learning from Mistakes

Mastery of Academic Content

▲

Refers to mastering skills, understanding and recalling information and concepts, and consistently applying what has been taught.

▲

Learning problems and the attendant perceptual processing deficits can erect major barriers to understanding and recalling information introduced in class and in textbooks. Students who have decoding and auditory and visual memory difficulties often require repeated explanations and extensive practice before they master new concepts and procedures. This mastery and assimilation process is referred to as *achieving closure.*

Attempting to help children who struggle to understand, assimilate, and retain information and who require multiple explanations can be frustrating and puzzling for teachers and parents. A sixth-grade teacher may carefully explain to the class that before adding mixed fractions students must find the common denominator. She might then model the procedure several times on the chalkboard and have students refer to examples in their math textbook. Children who learn differently may appear to understand the procedure and may practice it several times in class. That evening, however, when they sit down to do their homework, they may have no idea about how to add mixed fractions. Despite having seemingly understood the methodology in class, it is clear that they did not achieve closure.

When new material is presented children may have difficulty mastering academic content for several reasons. These may include:

- inadequate instruction
- poor academic skills
- passive learning (e.g., lack of enthusiasm and active involvement)
- inattentiveness and distractibility
- perceptual-processing dysfunction (e.g., visual- and auditory-memory deficits)
- a tendency to become easily overwhelmed and confused
- lack of confidence
- inefficient study skills
- negative associations with learning
- negative expectations
- chronic school-related stress and anxiety that interfere with concentration, comprehension, and retention

Habituated to poor performance and frustration and convinced in advance that they won't be able to understand what they are being taught, many struggling students shut down mentally whenever something new is presented. Their apprehension triggers confusion, and the confusion, in turn, exacerbates their apprehension and magnifies the challenge of assimilating and retaining information. Their expectation of disaster becomes self-fulfilling. This phenomenon can be graphically represented:

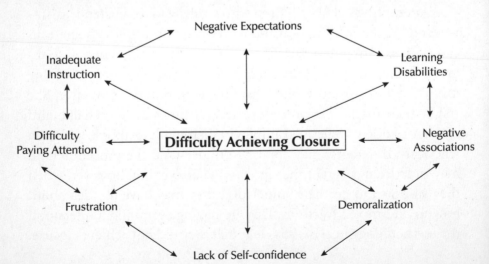

As can be seen in the preceding graphic, each factor in the "Difficulty Achieving Closure Loop" can affect the other factors and trigger a counterproductive chain reaction.

Unfortunately, many children who have difficulty achieving closure have not figured out how they learn best and do not know how to capitalize on their learning strengths.* A child who is a visual learner may not realize that she can most effectively assimilate new material, concepts, or procedures by translating the information into a diagram or visual representation. The kinesthetic or tactile (hands-on) learner may not realize that for her to understand part/whole relationships and add mixed fractions, she needs to manipulate concrete number units or fraction tiles.

Unfortunately, many teachers insist on teaching the way that they themselves learn best. ("I've been teaching fractions this way for twenty years, and I'm not about to change my method!") These teachers may be incapable of, or uninterested in, identifying their students' preferred learning styles and may refuse to make instructional modifications to accommodate students who are having academic difficulty and learn differently than their classmates or the teacher.

Patience and creative, systematic instruction that capitalizes on students' abilities are the most potent resources for helping struggling children achieve closure. Other effective techniques include:

- breaking instruction and explanations down into small chunks (the *divide-and-conquer* principle)
- providing repeated opportunities for practice
- modeling the correct way to solve a problem or do an assignment using different modalities (auditory, visual, tactile/kinesthetic)
- controlling the level of difficulty of newly introduced material
- providing consistent supervision until mastery is attained
- carefully orchestrating success
- providing effusive affirmation of progress and success

---

*It is the role of a master teacher or resource specialist to help children identify their learning strengths and preferences and to show classroom teachers how to help students make use of these learning strengths.

Creativity can be a powerful instructional resource for assisting students who are not "getting it." Experimenting with innovative, alternative teaching strategies to help the struggling children comprehend, retain, and apply new information often produces dramatic improvements in academic performance.

The parents and teachers of a child who has difficulty achieving closure are frequently caught in a dilemma. If they provide too much supervision and assistance, they risk creating dependency and unwittingly encouraging helplessness. If they provide too little supervision and assistance, they risk allowing their child to flail helplessly and suffer academically and psychologically.

Children who believe that they are incapable of understanding what they are being taught and who conclude that their situation is hopeless are emotionally vulnerable and likely to become defensive and demoralized. Unless the instructional delivery system is creatively modified, these youngsters are at risk for shutting down in school.

Patience when giving instructions and explanations is vital, especially when children are wrestling with learning problems. To expect children who learn differently to master newly introduced information the first or second time the material is introduced is generally unrealistic. These youngsters are likely to require multiple exposures to new material and extensive opportunities to practice and apply what they have been taught; they will also need periodic and systematic review. This review is especially important when the information or procedures have not been recently used.

BEHAVIORS AND LEARNING DEFICITS COMMONLY ASSOCIATED WITH DIFFICULTY MASTERING ACADEMIC CONTENT

- confusion when verbal or written explanations are given
- difficulty decoding (processing) auditory and visual information
- difficulty focusing
- difficulty identifying key information

- difficulty retaining information
- need to have instructions repeatedly explained and clarified
- frustration
- difficulty comprehending concrete and/or abstract concepts
- difficulty remembering procedures
- inefficient studying and test preparation
- anxiety when new material is presented
- feelings of inadequacy
- expectations of disaster
- low academic self-confidence
- deficient effort and motivation
- difficulty understanding symbolic language
- deficient receptive language skills
- difficulty recalling and properly sequencing auditory and visual information
- difficulty forming mental visual pictures that reinforce understanding and retention
- difficulty perceiving the link between newly presented and previously learned information
- difficulty thinking logically
- difficulty keeping up with the class
- chronic disorganization
- poor time management
- difficulty planning
- difficulty analyzing and solving problems
- chronic test anxiety
- chronic underachievement
- difficulty working independently

SEE: Apathy *(page 208)*; Aptitude *(page 15)*; Attention Deficit/Attention Deficit Hyperactivity Disorder *(page 214)*; Auditory Memory *(page 322)*; Avoiding Responsibility *(page 227)*; Brain Dysfunction *(page 326)*; Conduct and Attitude *(page 235)*; Critical Thinking *(page 161)*; Decoding *(page 332)*; Defense Mechanisms *(page 373)*; Disorganization *(page 251)*; Essays and

Essay Tests *(page 18)*; Grades *(page 25)*; Identifying Important Information *(page 41)*; I'm Dumb Syndrome *(page 388)*; Incomplete Assignments *(page 256)*; Intelligence *(page 45)*; Keeping Up with the Class *(page 51)*; Logic *(page 171)*; Passive Learning *(page 84)*; Problem Solving *(page 185)*; Psychological Overlay and Psychological Problems *(page 399)*; Reading Comprehension *(page 100)*; Resistance to Help *(page 282)*; School Anxiety *(page 406)*; Self-concept *(page 410)*; Self-control *(page 287)*; Standardized Tests *(page 116)*; Strategic Thinking *(page 189)*; Study Interruptions *(page 122)*; Study Skills *(page 127)*; Test Anxiety *(page 420)*; Underachievement *(page 143)*; Verbal Directions *(page 356)*; Visual Memory *(page 360)*; Working Independently *(page 302)*; Written Directions *(page 364)*.

Math

▲

Refers to the ability to comprehend how numbers work, perform computations using numbers, and understand and apply concepts and formulas.

▲

Math deficiencies can erect formidable barriers in school and can be as psychologically damaging to a child's self-concept as a reading problem. Children who struggle with math in elementary school and whose deficiencies are not remediated are at risk for becoming math-phobic. Unpleasant associations with doing math problems, continual embarrassment, and negative expectations often trigger anxiety, stress, and feelings of inadequacy whenever math skills are required. This fear of, and aversion to, math can persist throughout life and have serious educational and vocational consequences.

Some children have relatively minor math difficulties. They may be careless when adding columns of numbers or forget to move the decimal point when dividing. These operational and computational errors can usually be quickly resolved with extra help from the classroom teacher or a tutor.

Students with serious math deficiencies require more intensive and systematic intervention. Chronic errors when copying from the chalkboard (far-point copying) or from textbooks and handouts (near-point copying) and chronic column alignment errors usually indicate a spatial-awareness, visual-acuity, and/or visual-efficiency difficulty. Children who manifest these types of precision mistakes should be evaluated by an optometrist, developmental optometrist, or ophthalmologist.

Math skills are acquired sequentially, and proficiency must be attained at each instructional level if subsequently introduced skills are to be understood and mastered. Students who never learn how to add or subtract accurately in first and second grade are destined to struggle later when they do two-place multiplication problems or division problems and must align and add columns of numbers. Those who never memorize their multiplication tables are destined to struggle with division and word problems. Those who do not understand part-whole relationships are destined to struggle with fractions and percentage and decimal conversions. Those who never learn how to divide are destined to struggle with finding common denominators, multiplying fractions, and doing algebraic equations. The consequences when students do not systematically and sequentially master basic math skills are predictable: poor grades, confusion, embarrassment, feelings of incompetence, and diminished self-confidence.

The first step in addressing a significant math problem is to figure out *where* and *why* a student is "stuck." Is the child struggling because of intellectual and math-aptitude limitations? Is he struggling because he doesn't understand math concepts or because he cannot perform math operations and computations accurately. Does the student have difficulty with both concepts and operations? Diagnostic math tests can provide this important information.

The child who understands the concepts but who makes careless computation errors is actually less vulnerable than the child who does not understand the concepts. The carelessness may be attributable to difficulty concentrating and staying on task (ADD/ADHD), perceptual-processing deficits (number reversals), fine-motor deficits (controlling the muscles of the hand that hold a pencil), and/or memory deficits (recalling the multiplication tables). Focused remediation can reduce these deficiencies. Children predisposed to carelessness can be methodically trained to be more vigilant and conditioned to anticipate, identify, and correct careless computational errors.

Children who struggle with conceptual deficits have difficulty grasping how numbers "work" and "interact." In some cases, the difficulty may be attributable to deficiencies in math aptitude or intelligence. In many cases, however, children have the intellectual wherewithal to understand math, but they cannot learn the material the way it is being taught. They may require tangible manipulatives (plastic or wooden units that represent numbers or geometric shapes that represent part-whole relationships) to help them assimilate fundamental relationships.

Children who have not mastered the concepts may be able to do some of the assigned math problems using a mechanical methodology, but at some point their lack of understanding will cause them to falter. For example, their teacher or textbook may provide a model for reducing fractions or finding common denominators, and they may be able to follow this model and complete their homework with few, if any, mistakes. If, however, they don't grasp the basic part-whole concept that fractions represent, they might be unable to do problems involving fractions on a math quiz two days after having completed the homework problems. Youngsters with conceptual deficits will almost invariably encounter substantive problems in the upper grades and will have trouble transitioning from arithmetic to algebra, trigonometry, geometry, and calculus.

Teachers can use in-class quizzes and tests to ascertain students' skills mastery and identify their deficiencies. Another option for identifying specific deficits is to analyze the errors on standardized (nationally normed) math tests. This process, called *item analysis,* will indicate the specific type of problems that are causing confusion and difficulty. For example, a child who is in the third month of fifth grade (5.3) may achieve test scores that indicate her math skills are at the 37° (37th percentile), and her G.E. (grade expectancy), based on her number of correct answers, may be 3.9 (third grade, ninth month). These scores would place her almost one and a half years below grade level. This is useful information, but the scores only provide an overview of the student's relative level of performance. They do not indicate the student's specific deficits.

Although some standardized tests provide a breakdown of a student's specific deficits, some do not. If a teacher or resource specialist has access to the child's answers on the test, he or she could do an item analysis. This might indicate, for example, that a child is able to do addition, subtraction, multiplication, and one-place division problems but struggles with word problems, long division, decimals, and fractions.* The information could then be used by a teacher, resource specialist, tutor, or educational therapist to design a focused and individualized remediation strategy that methodically addresses the student's underlying deficiencies.

Some children have deficiencies in several different areas. They may have conceptual and computational deficiencies as well as concentration and near-point copying deficits. To address one problem without addressing the others is usually ineffectual. The following information must be considered when designing a well-conceived math-remediation strategy:

- the specific nature of the deficiency (i.e., computational or conceptual)
- the causative factors (i.e., near-point copying or spatial orientation)

---

*Standardized math and reading-achievement tests are typically sent to the publisher for scoring. Many schools, however, have older versions of tests and hand-scoring templates. These vintage tests can be selectively administered to children who are struggling in math, and an item analysis can be performed that will indicate specific computational and conceptual deficits.

- the specific types of errors the student is making (e.g., adding or aligning numbers improperly when doing two-place multiplication or long division)

The traditional prescription for helping students who have difficulty mastering the basics is to assign pages of additional addition or subtraction problems and to require children to recite the multiplication tables ad nauseam. Even though these children may improve their computational accuracy through repetitive practice, they often remain confused and insecure about their math ability. The often ineffectual learn-by-rote procedure has contributed to the angst (and swelled the ranks) of legions of frustrated and demoralized math-deficient and math-phobic students in American schools.

Repetitive practice, of course, has value. Children must learn how to add and subtract in their heads, and they must learn their multiplication tables by rote. Practice is vital, and repetition may be the only recourse for children who have intellectual limitations. To insist that a struggling child of normal or above-normal intelligence drill number facts without addressing the underlying confusion and/or mental block is ill conceived. Rote learning and repetitive practice will not resolve a conceptual math problem. Children who are guided to an understanding of the underlying concepts that govern math computations will have far less difficulty learning and retaining their number facts, and they will find higher-level math less challenging than students who have simply memorized facts and procedures.

The increasing use of calculators in elementary-, middle-, and high-school classrooms could camouflage math deficiencies. Students must, of course, become proficient in using calculators and computers, but they must also understand the concepts and be able to perform the computations manually. Those who do not understand the concepts and who become dependent on a calculator to solve math problems could face disaster if their calculator crashes while they're taking a college entrance exam. These students are also likely to face disaster in advanced math courses that require sound basic skills.

INDICATIONS OF MATH DIFFICULTY

- chronic errors and inaccuracies
- incomplete assignments
- difficulty understanding newly introduced concepts and operations
- difficulty applying what has already been learned to what is currently being learned (e.g., using multiplication to do long division)
- need for repeated explanations and clarifications
- need for continual help and prodding when doing homework
- negative statements (e.g., "I hate math." "Math is dumb, boring, etc.")
- negative expectations (e.g., "I know that I'm going to flunk this test.")
- procrastination when doing homework
- chronic stress and anxiety when doing math
- aversion to and avoidance of any situation that requires applied math skills
- concentration deficits (e.g., difficulty staying focused, filtering out distractions, attending to details, such as plus and minus signs)
- perceptual decoding deficits (e.g., reversing number sequences ["79" perceived or written as "97"] or confusing "6" with "9")
- near-point or far-point copying deficits (e.g., difficulty accurately copying problems from the chalkboard or from a textbook)
- spatial deficits (e.g., difficulty accurately perceiving size, orientation, and angles of geometric shapes, etc.)
- ocular inefficiency (e.g., visual inaccuracies involving errors aligning columns of numbers or of placing decimal points, etc.)

FACTORS THAT CAN CAUSE MATH DIFFICULTIES

- computational deficits (e.g., difficulty accurately performing mathematical operations, such as subtraction or multiplication)
- conceptual deficits (e.g., difficulty understanding the part-whole relationships represented by fractions)

- concentration deficits (e.g., difficulty staying focused, filtering out distractions, attending to details such as plus and minus signs)
- perceptual decoding deficits (e.g., reversing number sequences ["79" perceived or written as "97"] or confusing "6" with "9")
- near-point or far-point copying deficits (e.g., difficulty accurately copying problems from the chalkboard or from a textbook)
- spatial deficits (e.g., difficulty accurately perceiving size, orientation, and angles of geometric shapes, etc.)
- visual efficiency deficits (e.g., visual inaccuracies involving errors tracking numbers, aligning columns of numbers, or placing decimal points with precision, etc.)
- intellectual and aptitude limitations

COMMONLY USED NORMED MATH TESTS*

- Key Math
- Wechsler Intelligence Score for Children III (WISC III)
- Brigance Diagnostic Inventory of Basic Skills
- Wide Range Achievement Test (WRAT-3)
- Peabody Individual Achievement Test—Revised (PIAT-R)
- California Achievement Test
- Stanford Achievement Test
- Stanford 9 Test

SEE: Apathy *(page 208)*; Aptitude *(page 15)*; Attention Deficit/Attention Deficit Hyperactivity Disorder *(page 214)*; Attention to Details *(page 223)*; Auditory Memory *(page 322)*; Bouncing Back from Setbacks *(page 232)*; Defense Mechanisms *(page 373)*; Goal Setting *(page 165)*;

---

*These tests contain components that measure math aptitude and/or applied math skills.

Note Taking

▲

Refers to the ability to identify and record succinctly important information from textbooks and lectures.

▲

Being able to take good notes is essential to effective studying and test preparation. Students who cannot identify and succinctly record key information from textbooks, lectures, and class discussions will find themselves at a severe academic disadvantage, especially in upper-level classes. Those who are unable to distinguish, extract, distill, organize, retain, and condense key data will usually perform marginally in school.

Taking effective notes in class and from textbooks requires concentration, efficient perceptual processing, listening comprehension, reading comprehension, short-term auditory- and visual-memory skills, and judgment. Children must be able to identify and prioritize not only what they consider important but also what their teachers are likely to consider important.

Just as some children can essentially learn to read on their own, so, too, can some students intuitively figure out how to take notes on their own. Most children, however, require systematic instruction, extensive practice, and ongoing teacher feedback before they can master the exacting procedure of concisely transferring information from textbooks and lectures onto paper.

Unfortunately, many identified learning-disabled students never learn how to take effective notes because their resource specialist must usually prioritize the fundamentals during time-constrained remedial sessions. These basic skills include phonics, reading fluency, reading comprehension, spelling, handwriting, expository writing, and math. Resource specialists may recognize that teaching students how to take notes is critically important, but they may be forced to forgo this instruction in favor of a more compelling obligation to teach demoralized learners how to read.

Learning-disabled students are not the only ones who are not being taught how to take effective notes. Many mainstream students never develop proficiency because their schools are not committed to incorporating note-taking instruction into the curriculum. The neglect of formal training in this vital area can usually be traced to two factors: flawed assumptions and miscommunication. Many elementary-school teachers assume that their students will figure out on their own how to take notes and consequently provide little or no hands-on instruction in how to flag and record vital information. Others assume that their students will be taught note-taking skills when they enter middle school.

Teachers in the upper grades usually have a radically different set of assumptions. They expect that their students have been taught how to take notes in elementary school. The consequences of this miscommunication are predictable: Hundreds of thousands, perhaps millions, of students enter high school without having a clue about how to identify, extract, distill, and record key information on paper.

The two basic note-taking functions must be differentiated. When taking notes from a textbook, children have the time to evaluate information thoughtfully and selectively. When they take notes in class, however, they do not have the luxury of being able to consider carefully the content of what they are hearing. The recording procedure must be virtually instantaneous. Their teacher explains something or makes a comment, and they must immediately decide if the information is important and needs to be written down. They must then do so quickly or they will fall hopelessly behind and become confused and overwhelmed.

Motivated, goal-directed students intuitively recognize the value of taking notes. They realize that the procedure will help them understand and retain what they are studying. They also realize that although note taking initially requires extra time, their notes can significantly reduce the total amount of time that they must spend to do a first-rate job of preparing for tests. Instead of having to reread an entire chapter several times, they can review their notes.

Intellectually passive students have a very different mind-set. Habituated to taking the path of least resistance, these children will scrupulously avoid any steps that might involve additional time and effort.

The ideal time to teach note-taking skills is before counterproductive study habits have become entrenched and before poor grades have produced frustration, demoralization, diminished academic self-confidence, and lowered expectations and aspirations. Fourth-, fifth-, and sixth-grade teachers who incorporate methodical note-taking instruction into their lesson plans and who structure ample opportunities for practice are providing their students with an invaluable resource that they will be able to use throughout their education.

Unfortunately, in far too many instances note taking is taught mechanically, and the instruction is often boring. Some teachers simply write their own notes on the chalkboard and require their students to copy them. These teachers usually defend this mind-numbing practice by arguing that by having students copy their notes, they are providing a good model and ensuring uniformity and quality. These teachers do not realize that by doing all the work, they are encouraging passive thinking and passive learning. Students essentially become scribes and quickly learn to dread the ordeal.

Students who perceive note taking as a useless mechanical exercise intentionally designed by their teachers to make their lives miserable are likely to become resistant to taking notes. This is unfortunate, as taking notes does not have to be a boring or painful ordeal. By demonstrating how the procedure can be easily mastered and immediately applied to preparing for the next history or science test, creative teachers can actually make the procedure relevant, interesting, and even enjoyable.

Taking notes is only one component in an effective learning methodology. Students must also be taught how to use their notes. They must be trained to ask questions about what they have written in their notebooks. They must practice connecting important facts to underlying concepts and relating what they're currently learning to what they've already learned. Simply taking notes mechanically and reviewing them mindlessly is not the equivalent of effective studying. Achieving students use their notes as a springboard for delving into the substance of what they are studying and for organizing key ideas and information. They seek relevance and highlight important information when they use their notes to study. This systematic process of seeking relevance produces superior comprehension, recall, and mastery.

Note taking should not be confused with outlining. Many children intensely dislike the traditional procedure of outlining because the method appears contrived. Whereas outlining is a highly formatted and formularized technique for organizing and recording information, note taking is less structured. Both procedures can help children "digest" and retain information, and in the appropriate contexts, both can be powerful study tools. Outlining can be especially useful in organizing information when preparing written reports and making oral presentations. As a general rule, however, note taking should be taught before outlining.

Children who are taught how to take notes and how to use them when they study will usually see a demonstrable improvement in their schoolwork. As they begin to recognize the connection between good notes and good grades and realize that effective note taking will produce desirable academic payoffs, their resistance to spending the initial extra time will usually disappear.

STANDARD NOTE-TAKING PROCEDURES

- Identify key information, concepts, and relevance.
- Differentiate main ideas from details in textbook and lectures.
- Record data quickly using a consistent format.
- Link what is currently being learned with what has already been learned.
- Highlight information that the teacher is likely to incorporate on tests.
- Develop a personalized system for retaining important information.

SEE: Apathy *(page 208)*; Aptitude *(page 15)*; Attention Deficit/Attention Deficit Hyperactivity Disorder *(page 214)*; Attention to Details *(page 223)*; Auditory Memory *(page 322)*; Avoiding Responsibility *(page 227)*; Brain Dysfunction *(page 326)*; Conduct and Attitude *(page 235)*; Critical Thinking *(page 161)*; Disorganization *(page 251)*; Dyslexia *(page 335)*; Essays and Essay Tests *(page 18)*; Goal Setting *(page 165)*; Grades *(page 25)*; Handwriting *(page 36)*; Identifying Important Information *(page 41)*; I'm Dumb Syndrome *(page 388)*; Inaccurate Copying *(page 342)*; Incomplete Assignments *(page 256)*; Intelligence *(page 45)*; Judgment *(page 260)*; Keeping Up with the Class *(page 51)*; Learning from Mistakes *(page 267)*; Logic *(page 171)*; Mastery of Academic Content *(page 67)*; Parent-Child Conflict *(page 393)*; Passive Learning *(page 84)*; Performance Standards *(page 91)*; Planning *(page 176)*; Priorities *(page 180)*; Problem Solving *(page 185)*; Reading Comprehension *(page 100)*; Recording Assignments *(page 107)*; School Anxiety *(page 406)*; Self-concept *(page 410)*; Self-control *(page 287)*; Strategic Thinking *(page 189)*; Study Skills *(page 127)*; Teacher-Child Conflict *(page 293)*; Teacher-Designed Tests *(page 132)*; Test Anxiety *(page 420)*; Time Management *(page 138)*; Underachievement *(page 143)*; Visual Memory *(page 360)*; Working Independently *(page 302)*.

Passive Learning

▲

Refers to the lack of active and enthusiastic intellectual involvement in what is being learned.

▲

Most children enter kindergarten with a boundless curiosity about life and a ravenous appetite to acquire new skills and assimilate new information. This desire to learn is instinctual and is infused into their DNA. If effectively taught, these youngsters will enthusiastically learn to read, add, subtract, and write. They will eagerly develop their talents, and their academic achievements will generate satisfaction, pride, self-appreciation, and self-confidence.

When children become passive learners, something is profoundly amiss. The natural impetus to absorb new skills and information has been impacted. The indifference is a red flag, and parents and teachers have legitimate and compelling cause for concern.

Children who learn passively may appear to be studying, but their studying is rarely more than a mechanical process of mindlessly turning the pages in their textbooks. These children perceive minimal relevance in what they are being taught and feel little motivation to master the content. Functioning on automatic pilot, their main preoccupation is to finish their homework as quickly and painlessly as possible so that they can watch TV, surf the Internet, or talk with their friends on the telephone. The overriding priority is to avoid anything that might require additional time and effort. To apathetic learners, comprehension, retention, and mastery are essentially inconsequential.

Learning-disabled children are particularly at risk for becoming passive learners. Consumed by the continual effort to process sensory data efficiently, recall information, follow directions, read with fluency, and comprehend what they hear and read, these children often find school arduous and unpleasant, and their negative experiences undermine their eagerness to learn. To protect themselves from feelings of incompetence, struggling learners often latch onto a pattern of maladaptive coping behaviors and defense mechanisms. Some shut down in school. Others simply go through the motions and become intellectually lethargic and indifferent. They may act out, or they may retreat into a comfort zone where they expect little and where little is expected from them.

Unlike their intellectually engaged classmates, passive learners rarely establish personal-performance goals. They do not take pride in honing their academic skills, nor do they revel in knocking down the barriers that stand in their way. Disinterested in searching beneath the surface for underlying issues and concepts, these students are content to memorize facts without understanding the meaning or significance of the information they are ostensibly studying. Their superficial learning produces predictable consequences: deficient comprehension, retention, test performance, and grades.

Not all children with learning problems become passive learners. In fact, many continue to work diligently despite their academic trials and tribulations. Their remarkable grit and determination can usually be directly attributed to the quality of the academic and emotional support they receive from their parents, teachers, and resource specialists. Children who can see that they are making substantive progress are far more likely to retain their enthusiasm for learning than those who are bruised and defeated by their experiences in school. Fortified by concrete evidence that their skills are improving, these children will remain optimistic that they can ultimately prevail over the challenges. This optimism will translate into motivation and effort.

Unfortunately, some learning-disabled students who are provided with remedial support and encouragement from their parents and teachers remain discouraged and fatalistic. Acutely aware that they are falling further and further behind, these children are at risk for becoming increasingly demoralized, passive, and apathetic. Once they capitulate to a sense of hopelessness, they are destined to spend twelve years treading water in school. Lacking goals and motivation, their learning will be perfunctory, unfocused, and ineffectual, and their academic accomplishments will be minimal.

The likelihood of children becoming passive learners increases significantly when their underlying learning deficits are undiagnosed, misdiagnosed, and/or inadequately remediated. Frustration and discouragement are at the core of their resistance to becoming actively engaged in learning. Concluding, either consciously or unconsciously, that if they don't try, they aren't really failing, these students become habituated to expending minimal effort and construe education as something *being done to them* and not something that they are *doing for themselves.*

Students who feel overwhelmed by seemingly insurmountable scholastic obstacles have five basic options. They can:

- continue to work conscientiously
- express their frustration and anger by acting out
- blame others, make excuses, and act irresponsibly
- find surrogates for academic achievement
- withdraw into a shell and become academically uninvolved

Passive learners are rarely willing to spend the requisite extra time and effort proofreading their assignments for careless errors. They typically miss deadlines, submit shoddy, incomplete work, and fail to study adequately for tests. They then rationalize their irresponsibility by arguing that school is dumb and a waste of time.

In some cases, attention deficit/attention deficit hyperactivity disorder (ADD/ADHD) may play a central role in the passive learning of some children. Youngsters who tune out, daydream, and become distracted in class are unlikely to be intellectually engaged when they learn and study. If their inattentiveness and distractibility are chronic, these children should be evaluated by a physician or mental-health professional.

The effects of passive learning in tandem with reduced effort, motivation, and academic zeal are predictable. They include poor grades, diminished academic self-confidence, parental despair, teacher distress, and psychological overlay (behavior, attitudes, and feelings attributable to poor performance). The overlay may manifest as blaming, irresponsibility, procrastination, denial, and/or misbehavior in class.

Not all passive learners develop overt behavior or attitude problems. Many remain cooperative, compliant, and well behaved. They do the assigned work, but the switch for their mental propulsion system remains in the OFF position.

Poor teaching may also be a causal factor in passive learning. Children who are required to endure boring, mind-numbing lectures and memorize and regurgitate irrelevant facts ad nauseam are at risk for ending up cerebrally anesthetized. Continual fill-in-the-blanks handouts and repetitive drilling can dull the mind and destroy the enthusiasm of even the most motivated child. Teachers who resort to these brain-dulling materials may not have taught a dynamic, creative lesson in years, if ever. Despite this inferior teaching, some remarkably resilient children remain motivated and enthusiastic about learning. Others simply withdraw into a cerebral fog.

Parent-child and teacher-child conflict are common by-products of passive learning. Children who appear nonchalant or cavalier about their schoolwork are bound to elicit negative reactions from adults. These reactions often include lectures, sermons, threats, and punishment. Many parents and teachers believe that the solution to undesirable behavior is vigorous negative reinforcement. This strategy seldom works, and the criticism (e.g., "You need to work harder and think about what you are doing!") often causes passive learners to become resistant and resentful.

The starting point in effectively reorienting passive learners is to identify *why* they are indifferent. Those with underlying perceptual-processing deficits must be accurately diagnosed and provided with effective learning assistance. Those who do not know how to study efficiently must be taught practical, hands-on methods for actively engaging their brains when they learn. They must be taught how to ask penetrating questions and how to look beneath the surface and seek the relevance and meaning of what they are learning. They must be taught methods of identifying and memorizing important information and ferreting out key concepts. They must be taught how to express their ideas cogently in writing and verbally. They must have repeated opportunities to practice these critically important skills, and they must be provided with on-going teacher feedback.

Passive learners must also acquire other skills that are essential to academic survival and success. They must be systematically taught how to:

- manage time and meet deadlines
- record assignments properly
- get organized
- identify important information
- take notes
- prepare for tests

In addition, it is critically important that passive learners be encouraged to establish specific, realistic short-term goals, such as a B− on the next math quiz, and long-term payoffs, such as a B in math. They must also be prodded to raise the bar each time they attain a targeted objective.

Helping passive learners identify and capitalize on their natural learning strengths can play a major role in stimulating their effort and enhancing their motivation and performance. As they begin to achieve in school, they should be effusively acknowledged and affirmed for their progress. Success can be a powerful catalyst for effecting positive changes in the attitude and behavior of intellectually lethargic and unmotivated children. Once indifferent learners begin to experience success and the attendant satisfaction and pride, most will voluntarily raise the level of their expectations and aspirations.

When parents or teachers suspect that emotional or family problems may be causing or contributing to a child's passive learning, a psychological assessment is vital. To hope that psychological problems will simply go away is at best risky and at worst foolish. The symptoms may change as a child matures, but the unresolved underlying issues are likely to endure in one form or another.

Children who lose their natural enthusiasm for learning are

ringing warning bells. Unless help and guidance are provided, a pattern of passivity and intellectual lethargy could persist throughout their lives.

Children who are content to coast mindlessly through school are likely to be content coasting mindlessly through life. If not reoriented, their prospects for developing their full potential are virtually nil. Like unused muscles, unstimulated minds quickly wither. Without productive intervention, this atrophy could be permanent.

CHARACTERISTICS ASSOCIATED WITH PASSIVE LEARNING

- apathy and complacency
- irresponsibility
- poor judgment
- difficulty keeping up with the class
- difficulty thinking logically
- resistance to establishing personal short- and long-term goals
- immaturity
- manipulative behavior
- difficulty accepting performance standards
- lack of perseverance
- poor planning skills
- difficulty establishing priorities
- procrastination
- resistance to help
- school anxiety
- maladaptive and counterproductive behavior
- poor self-concept
- lack of self-discipline
- difficulty focusing and filtering out distractions
- inattention to details
- negative behavior and attitude
- difficulty bouncing back from setbacks
- poor problem-solving skills
- disregard of consequences

- denial of responsibility
- denial of problems
- frustration and demoralization
- depression
- chronic underachievement
- reluctance to establish personal goals
- poor grades
- self-sabotaging behavior
- test anxiety
- difficulty understanding concepts
- poorly developed critical thinking skills
- poorly developed strategic thinking skills
- difficulty decoding auditory and visual symbols
- poor reading comprehension
- poor study skills
- difficulty identifying and recalling important information
- difficulty taking notes
- difficulty with standardized tests
- difficulty with teacher-designed tests
- excessive study interruptions
- resistance to recording assignments
- disorganization
- difficulty expressing ideas verbally and in writing
- fear of competition
- fear of failure or success
- incomplete, inaccurate, and/or late assignments
- poor time management
- difficulty working independently
- difficulty following verbal and written directions
- identification with other students who are indifferent learners

SEE: Apathy *(page 208)*; Aptitude *(page 15)*; Attention Deficit/Attention Deficit Hyperactivity Disorder *(page 214)*; Attention to Details *(page 223)*; Avoiding Responsibility *(page 227)*; Conduct and Attitude *(page*

Performance Standards

▲

Refers to establishing clear guidelines about how school responsibilities are to be handled, defining an acceptable work ethic, and establishing fair and reasonable achievement expectations.

▲

Parents face a monumental challenge in attempting to define fair and reasonable academic performance standards for children who are struggling in school. They may recognize the value of encouraging their children to "stretch" for goals slightly beyond their grasp, and they may fully appreciate the benefits of encouraging children to work conscientiously, knock down barriers, and attain coveted pay-offs. They may also realize the cause-and-effect link between prevailing over challenges and developing determination, acquiring character, building self-confidence, and experiencing the exhilaration, pride, and satisfaction of a job well done. Translating these insights into an acceptable system of guidelines and expectations, however, is easier said than done.

The dilemma the parents of learning-disabled children confront is how to define performance standards that are fair, reasonable, and attainable. Parents who make excessive and unreasonable demands on a child can cause emotional stress and undermine their child's self-confidence. When children conclude that they cannot possibly fulfill their parents' expectations, they are likely to feel oppressed and resentful. They may react to the perceived unfairness of their parents' demands by shutting down in school or by becoming increasingly depressed, withdrawn, resistant, and alienated.

Parental expectations are a double-edged sword. If too little is expected, children are likely to perform commensurately with these diminished expectations. Conversely, if too much is expected, children are likely to become frustrated and demoralized.

In attempting to define performance guidelines for children, parents must base their standards on a realistic assessment of their child's capabilities and potential. This is a risky procedure, as there is a complex mix of variables that can affect a child's school performance and achievement potential. The variables include:

- intellectual ability
- aptitude
- perceptual-processing efficiency
- concentration
- academic skills
- emotional stability
- self-concept
- motivation
- inherited personality traits and temperament

- family, peer, and cultural influences
- educational opportunities
- role models

Some parents and educators consider a child's performance on an IQ test the most reliable determinant of ability and potential. This may be a flawed assumption, as the variables enumerated above can skew IQ scores and undermine the predictive value of this supposedly reliable and objective assessment of a child's intelligence and potential.

The challenge of establishing realistic expectations and standards for children is significantly compounded when children have learning deficiencies. Developing fair and reasonable performance standards requires a careful evaluation of all the available data. To conclude on the basis of an IQ test score, standardized achievement scores, and classroom performance that a learning-disabled child lacks potential may not only be erroneous; it may also be psychologically destructive.

Every day tens of thousands potentially capable children are "written off" by teachers, administrators, and school psychologists, and their abilities are discounted. Many of these children then perform in a manner consistent with these flawed assessments.

Children are genetically programmed to learn. When they shut down academically, the behavior is invariably linked to underlying issues that must be accurately identified and effectively addressed. Parents who conclude that their child is not working up to his potential must do some serious detective work and figure out how to rectify this situation. The alternative is to accept continued marginal performance, abdicate the obligation to define guidelines, standards, and expectations, and allow the child to tread water in school for twelve years.

When a clear and persistent pattern of underachievement is evident, a comprehensive evaluation of the child's skills, learning efficiency, and intellectual ability is vital. The scores, however, must be cautiously and judiciously interpreted, and the recommendations of the professional doing the evaluation must pass the litmus test of parental instincts. If the conclusions do not intuitively *feel* right, parents should seek another professional opinion, just as they would if a physician recommended that they undergo major surgery.

Parental expectations and performance standards must not only be carefully calibrated to a child's current level of functioning but also to a realistic assessment of the child's potential level of functioning. This determination requires an informed judgment call based upon all available data. This includes the observations of parents, teachers and resource specialists, test scores, classroom performance, and the results of diagnostic assessments. If parents believe they cannot effectively interpret the data and make an informed judgment, they should seek counsel from a qualified professional. A school psychologist or a private educational psychologist or educational therapist should be able to help them analyze their child's test scores and class work, understand the issues, and evaluate the options.

After all the input is considered, parents, in the final analysis, may need to rely on their intuition as to what's fair and realistic. They may conclude: "My child is working as conscientiously as she can. I am not going to push her any harder." Or they may conclude: "My child is goofing off and doing the minimum possible. It's time to intervene, lay down the law about effort, pride, and motivation and clearly define what's expected."

KEY ISSUES WHEN ESTABLISHING PERFORMANCE GUIDELINES

- Can we reasonably expect our child to do what's being required? ("If he is reading two years below grade level, can we realistically require him to complete all the assigned homework? Should we ask the teacher to make adjustments in the quantity and difficulty of these assignments?")
- Are learning, focusing, and self-confidence deficits skewing his performance on an IQ test and undermining his schoolwork? ("How can we get an accurate assessment of our child's intellec-

tual potential if he appears incapable of focusing for more than forty-five seconds at a time?")

- Is our child unmotivated because he anticipates failure, fears competition, or is afraid of succeeding? ("Is our child unwilling to work diligently because she's convinced that effort is futile? Is she afraid to succeed because she fears that this will lead to more demands?")
- Has our child acquired a set of counterproductive psychological coping mechanisms to deal with frustration, poor self-confidence, low self-esteem, and negative expectations? ("Is our child misbehaving, acting irresponsibly, and procrastinating because he lacks self-esteem and doesn't feel deserving of success?")
- Does our child appear lazy and irresponsible because underlying learning problems make it difficult for him to sustain his effort, meet expectations, and achieve at a level commensurate with his ability? ("Is our child phobic about accepting academic challenges because he lacks the requisite skills to do the required tasks?")
- What is our role in determining reasonable academic performance expectations and standards for our child? ("Should we accept the school's assessment of our child's problems and ability, should we seek an independent assessment, or should we rely on our intuition?")
- Should we be more stern and demanding, or should we back off and reduce the pressure? ("Are we dealing with a child who is intrinsically lazy or legitimately struggling to process information, get the work done, and keep up with the class? How can we best serve this child?")

SEE: Anger *(page 201)*; Apathy *(page 208)*; Attention Deficit/Attention Deficit Hyperactivity Disorder *(page 214)*; Attention to Details *(page 223)*; Avoiding Responsibility *(page 227)*; Conduct and Attitude *(page 235)*; Brain Dysfunction *(page 326)*; Critical Thinking *(page 161)*; Defense Mechanisms *(page 373)*; Depression *(page 378)*; Disorganization *(page 251)*; Fear of Failure, Success, and/or Competition *(page 383)*; Goal Setting *(page 165)*; Grades *(page 25)*; Identifying Important Information *(page 41)*; Incomplete Assignments

Punctuation

▲

Refers to the proper use of accepted conventions and rules for inserting standardized marks in written material to clarify the meaning and separate structural units.

▲

By the time children enter fourth grade, they are expected to be able to use commas, periods, question marks, and quotation marks correctly when punctuating simple declarative sentences, interrogatory sentences, compound sentences, and quotations. The basic rules are repeatedly pounded into them:

- "All declarative sentences begin with a capital and end with a period."
- "All interrogatory sentences end with a question mark."
- "Compound sentences require a comma before the conjunctions *and, but,* and *or.*"
- "You must use quotations marks whenever you write something that someone else has said."

By sixth grade, children are expected to know how to punctuate introductory prepositional phrases, series, and restrictive and non-restrictive clauses. They will make occasional mistakes, of course, and it is the function of the teacher to correct students' assignments and indicate these punctuation errors. The ultimate goal is for students to acquire effective self-editing skills so that they can recognize and eliminate the errors themselves.

In middle school, students are destined to make a key discovery: Their teachers expect them to apply the rules of punctuation accurately and consistently in reports and essays. Those who do not punctuate correctly will find red marks on their papers and will usually be negatively reinforced with lowered grades.

Children must understand the fundamental rules of English grammar to punctuate correctly. Those who cannot identify a compound sentence or a restrictive clause are likely to play Russian roulette with punctuation marks. As they write their essays and reports, they will say to themselves: "Gee, I guess I'll put a comma here. . . ."

Learning problems and punctuation mistakes often go hand in hand. Preoccupied with acquiring basic decoding, reading comprehension, and language-expression skills, many learning-disabled students are either oblivious to the rules or disregard them when doing their assignments. Simply getting the essay written is a major accomplishment for these children. Reviewing the essay to make certain that it is properly punctuated is beyond the pale. Since correctly punctuating essays or reports requires attention to details, highly distractible and/or impulsive children with ADD/ADHD are also likely to be oblivious to, or cavalier about, using correct punctuation in their written work.

Although some teachers are not exacting about the consistent use of correct punctuation, other are sticklers for strict adherence to the rules. Students must be prepared to meet the demands of those who are sticklers. Children who learn how to punctuate properly and diligently check over their work to find their errors are certainly on safer ground than those who never learn how to punctuate properly or are nonchalant about using the conventions. A well-written but poorly punctuated essay or term paper that may deserve a B on the basis of content and expository writing style may receive a C if it is poorly punctuated. Successful students recognize and accept this fact of life. They carefully proofread their work and make certain that the correct punctuation marks are in place.

Parents of children who have poor punctuation skills should ask the teacher if they should proofread their child's work to find mistakes. Some teachers do not want parents to assume this role, but others encourage the practice. Parents who do check over their child's work may need to review the rules first.

If parents decide to provide help, they should be aware of the risks in allowing their child to become overly dependent on them. Showing a child where punctuation marks should be inserted, succinctly explaining why, and then having the child insert the marks is preferable to actually doing the corrections, creating a dependency, and becoming the child's on-call editor. To reinforce mastery, parents could write a similar sentence (e.g., compound sentence, series, introductory phrase, etc.) and leave out the punctuation marks. Using the previously corrected sentence as a model, the child would then punctuate the new sentence properly.

Creative at-home procedures can help children assimilate punctuation rules while avoiding the drudgery of memorizing them. For example, parents could make two photocopies of a very short, interesting article written at their child's comfort reading level. The child and the parent would then count all the punctuation marks in the article. Setting one copy aside, the parent would then carefully "white out" *all* the punctuation marks on the second copy and make *two* photocopies of this page. The parents and the child would then systematically go through the page with no punctuation, discuss where the commas, periods, and quotation marks should be placed, and insert the appropriate punctuation marks. The parent would *patiently* explain that when conjunctions such as *and, or,* or *but* are followed by a second subject (predicate nominative) and a second verb, the result is a compound sentence, and a comma is required before the conjunction that separates the two independent clauses. After methodically going through the article together (spending no more than ten minutes), the child would then be asked to punctuate independently the second copy that has no punctuation marks. Parents would tell their child how many total punctuation marks there are in the article and challenge the child to see how many he can replace. The more practice, the better. Parents, however, should know when to stop for the day! "Overkill" can trigger resistance and resentment.

The same procedure could be used with written work the child has *already* submitted. Parents could count the child's original punctuation marks, white out corrections by the teacher, photocopy the report, and then go through the report together. The number of punctuation marks in the child's original written work would then be compared with the second edited version. Parents who lack the skills or patience to work with their child in this way should consider hiring a qualified tutor, especially if their child's punctuation is chronically poor.

Helping children learn how to punctuate need not be a painful experience for the child or parent. The key to defusing resistance and facilitating mastery is to make the self-editing process as interesting as possible. By demonstrating that punctuating an assignment properly can actually be an enjoyable challenge, parents can "reframe" a potentially negative experience and make it a positive one. Children who become convinced that they can win the "punctuation contest" handily will be far more receptive to spending the requisite time and effort to make sure they have punctuated their assignments correctly.

STRATEGY FOR IMPROVING CHILDREN'S PUNCTUATION

- Ask the teacher to identify your child's specific and recurring punctuation deficits.
- Request supplemental instructional materials that might be used in school and/or at home to reinforce the rules and improve mastery.
- Request that the teacher provide individualized help after class.
- At a teacher supply store purchase material (workbooks or software) specifically designed to teach and reinforce punctuation rules.

- Model and demonstrate how to punctuate properly.
- Acknowledge and affirm progress.
- Consider hiring a professional tutor to work with your child if you feel incapable of providing effective help.

▼

SEE: Apathy *(page 208)*; Attention Deficit/Attention Deficit Hyperactivity Disorder *(page 214)*; Attention to Details *(page 223)*; Auditory Memory *(page 322)*; Avoiding Responsibility *(page 227)*; Conduct and Attitude *(page 235)*; Essays and Essay Tests *(page 18)*; Grades *(page 25)*; Grammar and Syntax *(page 31)*; Handwriting *(page 36)*; Inaccurate Copying *(page 342)*; Language Arts *(page 58)*; Learning from Mistakes *(page 267)*; Performance Standards *(page 91)*; Resistance to Help *(page 282)*; Self-control *(page 287)*; Standardized Tests *(page 116)*; Teacher-Designed Tests *(page 132)*; Underachievement *(page 143)*; Visual Memory *(page 360)*; Working Independently *(page 302)*.

Reading Comprehension

▲

Refers to the ability to understand and recall information that is read silently or aloud.

▲

Reading instruction during the first two years of elementary school focuses primarily on teaching children how to decode words accurately. As challenging as learning how to decipher letters and words can be for some children, this is only the first phase of an extended process of acquiring effective reading skills.

By the middle of first grade, children begin the transition from primarily learning how to decode words to comprehending and remembering the content of what they are reading. Many youngsters make this segue painlessly. Others, especially those who have perceptually based learning disabilities, frequently find the transition a nightmare. Physically and emotionally depleted by the continual challenge to decipher words accurately, many of these struggling children lack the residual cerebral stamina to make sense out of what the words actually mean.

Although the focus of reading instruction shifts as children advance beyond second grade, decoding skills are still, of course, emphasized in grades three and four. The gradual transition from decoding to comprehension, recall, and application of written information is reflected in textbooks that become increasingly cognitive and content oriented as students progress into the upper grades.

The most basic level of reading comprehension—the *literal level*—emphasizes the basic recall of information. For example:

Written Statement:	The man carried the piece of wood into the shop, tightened it in the vise, and picked up the saw.
Literal Question:	What did the man do?

On the second level of reading comprehension—the *inferential level*—children are required to recognize and understand information that is implied but not directly stated. For example:

Written Statement:	The man carried the piece of wood into the shop, tightened it in the vise, and picked up the saw.
Inferential Question:	What do you think the man was going to do?

On the highest level of comprehension—the applicative level—children are required to use the information they read. For example:

Written Statement:	The man carried the piece of wood into the shop, tightened it in the vise, and picked up the saw.
Applicative Question:	If you were building something, what tool would you probably need after you measured the material?

By the time students enter fifth grade, they are expected to be able to answer questions that gauge their understanding on all three levels of comprehension. The requirement that they comprehend written information accelerates in high school. Students who are able to remember, evaluate, infer, and apply what they read receive the best grades and are on a track that leads to college and, ideally, satisfying and remunerative careers. Those who do not acquire good reading-comprehension skills will find their advancement impeded or blocked and are likely to lower their expectations and aspirations accordingly.

In upper-level classes, especially in accelerated, college-preparatory courses, the capacity to memorize facts and formulas is not sufficient to guarantee good grades. Teachers of advanced-placement (AP) courses require that their students not only understand and recall what they read but that they also be able to evaluate critically the information. These teachers want students to dig below surface appearances for underlying issues, themes, and implications. They want them to link what they are currently learning to what they have already learned. They require insight, and they reward students who are capable of thinking analytically and perceptively with A's.

That advanced reading-comprehension skills and intelligence are linked is indisputable. It is axiomatic that the brighter the child, the easier it is for the child to understand complex issues and derive superior insights. There are, however, notable exceptions. Factors such as learning disabilities, family dysfunction, psychological problems, and negative social influences can undermine comprehension, divert and deplete mental and emotional energy, and cause intelligent children to function in school at a level considerably below their potential.

Concentration deficits can also play a major role in undermining reading comprehension. To understand what they are reading, children must be able to stay on task, control impulsivity, and filter out distractions. Attention deficit/attention deficit hyperactivity disorder (ADD/ADHD) can obviously impede the ability to stay focused, and the net effect is often diminished comprehension and retention. Even extremely bright ADD/ADHD students who have good decoding skills may struggle to comprehend what they read because they are unable to concentrate for more than a few seconds at a time.

Children who have difficulty forming visual pictures when reading are also likely to have poor reading comprehension. A high-school student may be required to read a unit in his science textbook that describes nuclear fission and fusion. To understand the concepts and retain the salient information, the student must be able to form a mental picture of the atomic-fission process and see in his mind an atom of enriched uranium or plutonium splitting and releasing vast amounts of nuclear energy. He must also be able to form a mental picture of the hydrogen-fusion process in which multiple atoms of enriched uranium are subjected to extreme heat, combine, initiate a chain reaction, and release huge quantities of nuclear energy. Some students form visual images naturally when they read, and this capacity enhances their comprehension. Others must be methodically trained to form these images.* If not provided with this systematic instruction, these students are likely to struggle with reading comprehension throughout life.

The development of critical-thinking skills is also a requisite of advanced reading comprehension. Students who study and learn actively, search for relevance in the material they are reading, pose questions about the content, and relate new information to previously learned information invariably have better comprehension than those who read, study, and think passively.

Despite the concerns of parents, educators, and politicians about the quality of reading instruction in the United States, millions of students are continuing to graduate every year from our high schools with glaringly deficient comprehension skills. These deficiencies are affirmed by the decline in standardized test scores in many areas of the nation.

The explanation for the deterioration of children's reading skills is complex and involves overlapping pedagogical and sociological factors. These include undiagnosed or misdiagnosed learning disabilities, inadequate teaching, English-language deficiencies, negative

---

*A program called Visualizing/Verbalizing, developed by Nanci Bell, has been specifically designed to help students learn how to form and imprint visual images when reading. See Bibliography.

cultural influences, ineffective remedial assistance, insufficient school funding, and lack of parental involvement in children's education.

The starting point in improving children's reading comprehension is to identify any underlying perceptual-processing problems that may be interfering with efficient learning. If a learning disability is suspected, children should be referred to the child-study team and then evaluated by the school psychologist. Students with decoding problems attributable to visual and auditory memory, sequencing, and discrimination deficits should be provided with intensive remedial assistance. Once their perceptual-processing difficulties have been resolved, systematic instruction to improve their reading-comprehension skills should be provided. Remedial teaching materials specifically designed to develop these skills are generally available to all resource specialists.

ADD/ADHD children with poor reading comprehension should be evaluated by a physician. Irrespective of whether medication is prescribed, classroom teachers and resource specialists must make every effort to help these children compensate for their focusing problems. High-interest material and creative, dynamic, and textured teaching methods can often provide a potent antidote for chronic inattentiveness and distractibility.

Multimodality teaching can also be a highly effective tool for improving reading comprehension. This instructional model acknowledges that children have different learning styles and learning preferences. The multimodality method intentionally incorporates visual, auditory, kinesthetic/tactile, and experiential learning into the curriculum. For example, the previously described student who is studying nuclear energy and is struggling to form visual images in his mind might be encouraged to manipulate (or build) models that represent the fission and fusion processes. This kinesthetic/tactile learning experience could play a key role in helping the student to improve his comprehension.

By helping students to identify their learning preferences and by encouraging them to capitalize on their preferred learning modality, or combination of modalities, teachers can stimulate motivation and enhance academic self-confidence. Children who are convinced they can understand and recall what they are reading are far more likely to assimilate academic content successfully than those who feel demoralized and defeated.

Teachers can urge auditory learners to hear important material in their minds as they read and study, and they can encourage visual learners to create diagrams, charts, and pictures and to take notes. They can show students who have poor reading comprehension how to reinforce and enhance their understanding and retention by forming visual pictures or recording imaginary "audiotapes" of the information they are studying. They can encourage tactile/kinesthetic learners to build (or imagine) models that create a three-dimensional representation of key information.

Effective teachers expressly integrate into the curriculum opportunities for active and engaged learning (e.g., debates, journals, cooperative study groups, putting on historical plays, etc.). They ask probing questions that stimulate thinking. They praise students for their insights and acknowledge effort and improvement. They provide extra help for struggling learners and make reasonable homework and in-class accommodations for students who are reading below grade level. They team achieving students with nonachieving students. They present course content dynamically and creatively and encourage students to develop a personalized system of deriving meaning from printed words.

SYMPTOMS OF READING-COMPREHENSION DEFICIENCIES

- passive learning
- difficulty focusing
- labored reading
- preoccupation with decoding words at the expense of understanding the meaning of the words
- difficulty forming mental visual images
- difficulty identifying what is important

- inattention to detail
- difficulty with visual memory and sequencing
- difficulty drawing inferences
- difficulty applying information
- poorly developed critical intelligence
- discouragement
- avoidance of reading
- defensiveness
- feelings of inadequacy in reading situations
- negative attitude about school and learning
- procrastination
- irresponsibility
- incomplete assignments

STEPS FOR IMPROVING READING-COMPREHENSION SKILLS

Students must be taught how to:

- identify key information and facts
- differentiate main ideas from details
- ferret out underlying issues and concepts
- form visual pictures to help recall information
- take notes whenever feasible
- capitalize on preferred learning modality or modalities
- relate what is currently being learned to what has already been learned

SEE: Apathy *(page 208)*; Aptitude *(page 15)*; Attention Deficit/Attention Deficit Hyperactivity Disorder *(page 214)*; Attention to Details *(page 223)*; Avoiding Responsibility *(page 227)*; Brain Dysfunction *(page 326)*; Conduct and Attitude *(page 235)*; Critical Thinking *(page 161)*; Decoding *(page 332)*; Defense Mechanisms *(page 373)*; Depression

Recording Assignments

▲

Refers to having and using a systematic procedure for writing down homework instructions, assigned pages and problems, due dates, and test dates.

▲

Many learning-disabled children never establish the habit of methodically and consistently recording their homework assignments. Some do not have a designated assignment sheet in their notebook. Some choose not to use an assignment sheet, preferring instead to jot down haphazardly occasional page numbers or due dates. Others delude themselves into thinking that they can remember what has been assigned and when the work is due without having to write down the information. These students usually hand in work that is late and incomplete, forget to do important tasks, or submit homework that does not conform to the teacher's explicit instructions.

Learning disabilities can play a major role in deterring children from systematically recording their homework. Conditions such as dyslexia, visual-memory and visual-sequencing problems, and far-point copying deficits can magnify the challenge of transferring assignments written on the chalkboard to an assignment sheet. Auditory-memory and auditory-sequencing difficulty can interfere with recording assignments that are communicated orally by the teacher. Even if children make a genuine effort to write down their assignments, their handwriting may be so illegible as a result of fine-motor or graphomotor deficiencies that they cannot decipher what they have written.

Some children with learning problems may struggle to record key information because they cannot understand the directions or recall the verbally communicated specifics. For example, a teacher may remind the class to reduce all fractions after finding the common denominators and adding and subtracting the mixed fractions problems on page 52. As she writes down her math assignment, the learning-disabled student may be so confused that she may fail to record this important instruction. Even if her teacher distributes a weekly assignment sheet to each student, the child with a reading problem may not accurately register vital information in her mind.

Because the procedure of recording assignments requires self-discipline, organization, intention, and concentration, children with ADD/ADHD are at a significant disadvantage. Their minds may wander when specific instructions are given. They may be distracted and miss essential points or omit writing down critical details. They may record something that doesn't make sense and then be bewildered when they sit down to do their homework. Some children with ADD/ADHD are so impulsive that they may begin to do their homework without even bothering to look at their assignment sheet. The consequences are predictable: incomplete work that doesn't conform to the teacher's explicit instructions, missed deadlines, inadequate test preparation, and lowered grades.

Children with learning problems may be quite cavalier about completing their homework and submitting assignments on time. This nonchalant behavior is invariably a defense mechanism. Convinced in advance that they will perform poorly, they do the minimum possible and unconsciously rationalize that if they don't really try, they can't really fail.

The prospect of doing homework can be intolerable to children who feel academically incompetent, frustrated, demoralized, and incapable of doing the assigned work. After having spent a miserable day in school, their teachers and parents now insist that they go home and spend an additional two or three hours being miserable. That many of these children try to evade their academic responsibilities is understandable. There is little incentive for children to record their assignments diligently when they believe that they will receive poor grades on their homework no matter how hard they try and that studying for tests is a futile exercise.

Of course, not all children who fail to record their assignments have learning problems. In many instances, the explanation for the maladaptive behavior is quite simple: No one has ever taken the time to teach them how to record assignments properly, and no one is monitoring them to make certain that they know what they are expected to do.

Some chronically self-sabotaging students may appear quite willful about disregarding what their teacher asks them to do. A pattern of poor judgment, denial of basic cause-and-effect principles, active or passive resistance to authority, oppositional behavior, and self-defeating attitudes places these youngsters on a collision course with the educational system. Unless their attitudes and behavior are reoriented, these children are likely to get failing grades and become increasingly demoralized and resistant to help and authority. Once they conclude that their situation is hopeless and that school is "dumb," they are at risk for dropping out of school or failing to meet the requirements for graduation. These youngsters clearly require counseling before the damage becomes irreversible.

Students who lack intuitive organizational skills will require explicit, systematic instruction and a simple and practical system for getting the job done. If provided with clear, easy-to-follow models and guidelines for recording their assignments and an easy-to-use assignment sheet, most children can quickly learn the procedure. They will need to practice and to be monitored until the process becomes an imprinted habit. Once they master the assignment-recording methods and experience the payoffs of knowing each evening precisely what they are required to do for homework, they will be far more likely to use the system voluntarily. Positive reinforcement in the form of parent and teacher encouragement, affirmation for progress, improved grades, and reduced stress and anxiety are powerful incentives for altering maladaptive behavior.

THE CONSEQUENCES OF FAILING TO RECORD ASSIGNMENTS

Students typically:

- "forget" to do homework
- "forget" to study for tests
- "forget" to hand in homework
- miss deadlines
- study the wrong material
- fail to follow explicit directions
- submit incomplete, inaccurate work
- are poorly prepared for class
- frustrate and alienate their teachers
- frustrate their parents
- receive negative feedback and poor grades
- become increasingly demoralized

COUNTERPRODUCTIVE BEHAVIOR ASSOCIATED WITH FAILURE TO RECORD ASSIGNMENTS

- deficient motivation
- negative attitudes about school
- general disorganization
- difficulty with time management

- difficulty with planning
- deficiencies in auditory and/or visual memory
- inattentiveness to details
- disregard of consequences
- difficulty establishing priorities
- difficulty establishing goals
- helplessness
- difficulty working independently
- denial of responsibility and blaming
- auditory and/or visual sequencing, discrimination, and memory deficits
- irresponsibility
- learning inefficiency
- poor judgment
- active or passive resistance to meeting academic obligations
- difficulty accepting rules, guidelines, and performance standards
- resistance to authority
- procrastination
- poor self-discipline

SEE: Apathy *(page 208)*; Attention Deficit/Attention Deficit Hyperactivity Disorder *(page 214)*; Attention to Details *(page 223)*; Auditory Memory *(page 322)*; Conduct and Attitude *(page 235)*; Dealing with Consequences *(page 241)*; Decoding *(page 332)*; Defense Mechanisms *(page 373)*; Disorganization *(page 251)*; Goal Setting *(page 165)*; Grades *(page 25)*; Handwriting *(page 36)*; Identifying Important Information *(page 41)*; Incomplete Assignments *(page 256)*; Judgment *(page 260)*; Keeping Up with the Class *(page 51)*; Note Taking *(page 79)*; Parent-Child Conflict *(page 393)*; Passive Learning *(page 84)*; Performance Standards *(page 91)*; Priorities *(page 180)*; Procrastination *(page 278)*; Psychological Overlay and Psychological Problems *(page 399)*; Resistance to Help *(page 282)*; School Anxiety *(page 406)*; Self-control *(page 287)*; Strategic Thinking *(page 189)*; Study Skills *(page 127)*; Teacher-Child Conflict *(page 293)*; Teacher-

Spelling

▲

Refers to difficulty recalling accurately the written symbols that comprise phonetic and nonphonetic words.

▲

Chronic spelling problems can make life miserable for children. Having to study for and take weekly spelling tests can be a nightmare. Despite their best efforts to memorize the assigned words and despite help from their parents, children who spell poorly are likely to be greeted by a sea of red marks when their test is handed back.

Some students with spelling problems actually have little difficulty memorizing words for a spelling test. For them, the nemesis is spelling correctly when writing a report or essay. And, of course, there are children who spell poorly on tests *and* writing assignments.

Spelling problems are generally attributable to perceptual decoding dysfunctions in two key areas: auditory discrimination (i.e., being able to hear the difference between sounds) and visual memory (i.e., being able to remember what is seen). Children who cannot differentiate the words *sand* and *send* and those who cannot visualize the spelling of nonphonetic words such as *thorough* are destined to spell poorly.

Phonetic rules (e.g., *i* before *e* except after *c*) may help with some words, but most children, especially those with learning disabilities and attention deficit/attention deficit hyperactivity disorder

(ADD/ADHD), have difficulty recalling and consistently applying these rules when taking a test or writing a report. Because so many words in English fail to conform to the phonetic rules, children discover that there are countless spelling exceptions. For example, "alibi" is spelled with one "l," whereas "alligator" is spelled with two, even though both words have similar pronunciations. To the dismay of poor spellers, there is no facile explanation for this divergence, nor are there phonetic rules to help them recall the correct spelling of these words.

As they progress through elementary school, children will also discover that there are other disconcerting phonetic exceptions. Foreign words such as *lieutenant, colonel,* and *sergeant* can make life miserable for students with spelling problems. Despite the English pronunciation, these words are spelled as they would be in the language of origin. The only recourse students have is to memorize the correct spelling, and those who have difficulty memorizing are at a distinct disadvantage.

The challenge of spelling correctly is compounded by the fact that many common words are often mispronounced. For example, the word *prerogative* is often misspelled because most Americans pronounce the word as "perrogative." There are many other examples of imprecise American pronunciation. Few people differentiate the pronunciation of words ending in "ant" (e.g., *reliant*) and "ent" (*dependent*) or between words ending in "able" (e.g., *readable*) and "ible" (e.g., *edible*). Other mispronunciations magnify the challenge of spelling certain words accurately. For example, the word *delectable* is often pronounced "dillectible." In addition, words such as *caught* and *taught* are pronounced the same as *bought,* and *fought,* and the word *tough* is spelled the same as the word *through. Calf* is pronounced the same as *laugh,* and *although* is pronounced the same as *flow. Construe* is pronounced like *flew,* and *please* is pronounced like *trees* and *seize.* Given these common pronunciation errors and overlaps, it should not surprise us that many children (and many adults!) have difficulty spelling words that are pronounced imprecisely or that do not conform to phonetic rules.

A unique characteristic of the English language further contributes to confusion of students with spelling problems. Whereas the pronunciation of spoken English has evolved, the spelling of many words has not. During the era of Chaucer, words such as *thought, through, should, tough, fought, although, enough,* and *bough* were pronounced precisely as they were spelled. (In Middle English, these *ough* words were pronounced with a guttural sound similar to German.) Linguists have concluded that the pronunciation of the *ou* sound was once the same in all words. Because there is no longer a consistent relationship between the spelling and pronunciation of these words, the nonconforming words are classified as nonphonetic, and children are required to memorize the correct spelling.

For the reasons cited above, the simple drilling of assigned spelling words does not guarantee improved spelling performance in written work. Because children with perceptually based learning problems usually spell words the way the words are pronounced (i.e., *phonetically*), their corrected papers and essays are typically covered with red marks indicating their spelling errors. Those with poor visual memory who cannot visualize how words are spelled will find the spelling of nonphonetic and commonly mispronounced words especially problematic.

The first step in designing an effective spelling-improvement program is to identify why children are misspelling words. A school psychologist or resource specialist can administer a simple diagnostic test to identify the specific types of spelling errors being committed. This information is an invaluable resource in designing a focused remediation strategy.

Poor spellers who struggle to discriminate the sounds of phonetic words and to visualize the spelling of nonphonetic words can be systematically trained to improve their spelling skills. With methodical instruction and sufficient practice, their phonemic awareness, auditory discrimination, and visual-memory skills can be enhanced, and they can be taught to compensate for their lack of "natural" spelling talent.

The Lindamood Auditory Conceptualization (LAC) test provides a quick and effective diagnostic tool for identifying auditory-discrimination deficits. Systematic programs such as the Lindamood LIPS program and the Fast Forward program are specifically designed to enhance auditory discrimination and phonemic awareness.* These programs address the basic decoding skills that are required for accurate reading and spelling, and they can be particularly useful in helping children handle words that are phonetically consistent. The Orton Gillingham and Slingerland methods* have also proved to be highly effective, especially with dyslexic children.

Most special-education teachers are aware of a range of methods of analyzing spelling deficits and enhancing auditory-discrimination and visual-memory skills. Parents are advised to consult with the specialist or school psychologist at their child's school.

SEE: Apathy *(page 208)*; Aptitude *(page 15)*; Attention Deficit/Attention Deficit Hyperactivity Disorder *(page 214)*; Attention to Details *(page 223)*; Auditory Discrimination *(page 317)*; Auditory Memory *(page 322)*; Brain Dysfunction *(page 326)*; Decoding *(page 332)*; Dyslexia *(page 335)*; Essays and Essay Tests *(page 18)*; Frustration *(page 378)*; Grades *(page 25)*; I'm Dumb Syndrome *(page 388)*; Keeping Up with the Class *(page 51)*; Language Arts *(page 58)*; Performance Standards *(page 91)*; Psychological Overlay and Psychological Problems *(page 399)*; Phonics *(page 346)*; Resistance to Help *(page 282)*; School Anxiety *(page 406)*; Self-concept *(page 410)*; Self-control *(page 287)*; Standardized Tests *(page 116)*; Study Skills *(page 127)*; Teacher-Designed Tests *(page 132)*; Test Anxiety *(page 420)*; Underachievement *(page 143)*; Visual Memory *(page 360)*; Word Attack *(page 318)*; Working Independently *(page 302)*.

---

*See Bibliography.

Standardized Tests

▲

Refers to achievement and diagnostic tests that are administered to large populations of students and are statistically normed.

▲

Children are regularly given standardized achievement tests in school that measure the level of their skills in areas such as reading comprehension, math, spelling, and vocabulary. The statistical norms for these standardized tests are derived by administering the tests to large populations of students and compiling extensive data about the number of correct answers attained by children at different grade levels and at different chronological ages. A student's raw score (or number of correct answers) can then be statistically correlated with the scores of hundreds of thousands of other students in the same grade and/or of the same age, and comparative levels of performance are generated. Some standardized tests provide additional data that include the comparative performance of students living in specific geographic and socioeconomic areas and the comparative performance of students attending private schools versus public schools and private schools versus other private schools.

A wide range of tests have been standardized and are regularly used by school districts, resource specialists, speech and language therapists, school psychologists, and clinical psychologists. Common standardized tests include IQ tests, general-reading and math-achievement tests, specific diagnostic tests for learning disabilities, content-area tests in subjects such as American history and English, and college-admissions tests. The scores can provide important information about students' academic strengths and weaknesses. School psychologists and resource specialists use specialized standardized tests to measure perceptual-processing efficiency, identify deficits, and determine eligibility for special-education programs. The scores on these tests can play a key role in helping classroom teachers and resource specialists develop an effective remediation strategy, target goals for improvement, and create reasonable criteria for evaluating educational progress.

During the last decade, a major controversy has emerged over the use of standardized testing to assess students' general academic skills. These achievement tests are being used by schools to evaluate the efficacy of their instructional programs and to compare a school's performance to that of other schools in the same district, the same county, and in other districts throughout the state and the nation. Extensive media scrutiny has placed intense political pressure on principals, district superintendents, school boards, mayors, and governors. Virtually every elected and appointed official appears fixated on being able to demonstrate improvement in student scores. Because of this intense political pressure, many school administrators have directed teachers to focus primarily on raising their students' standardized test scores. At the core of this *teach-to-the-test* phenomenon are six critical issues:

- What constitutes academic achievement and educational excellence?
- What skills should be taught?
- How should teachers teach?
- What are appropriate educational objectives and priorities?
- How do you measure academic achievement?
- Should teachers significantly modify their curriculum to improve their students' scores and their school's overall test performance?

The answers to these questions have the potential to alter the nature, direction, and quality of American education. Two countervailing forces are driving the debate: the need to assess the efficacy of school instruction and create a uniform standard for measuring students' skills versus the need to allow teachers to teach creatively and without artificial pressure being imposed on them.

The distorted application of standardized testing procedures, the misinterpretation of statistically derived scores, a poorly conceived and myopic philosophy of education, and an inadequate educational delivery system can cause students to become pawns in a political chess game. Once school districts succumb to the political pressure and adopt a simplistic teach-to-the-test mentality, they risk leaching the joy, creativity, and dynamism from the instructional process and making school a drudgery for millions of children who might otherwise be enthusiastic and actively engaged learners.

Insightful parents and educators recognize that good teaching is the most effective way to stimulate academic effort and enhance students' scholastic abilities. Clearly, children are far better served when school districts focus less on elevating test scores and more on strengthening teachers' instructional skills and meeting students' individual learning needs. The most effective formula for improving student performance on standardized tests is: better teaching = better learning = better scores.

Despite the misuse of standardized testing, test scores can provide useful information if parents understand the jargon, statistical terms, and classifications. Unfortunately, most test-report forms are often confusing to parents because the results are sent home without any easy to understand explanations. Parents who do not know the definition of terms such as stanine, grade equivalency, percentile, mean, and standardized deviation are going to perplexed by what the scores mean.

Many of the common testing terms represent multiple methods of comparing students' performance and presenting essentially the same statistical data. The following definitions are intended to clarify the meaning of the most common testing terminology.

COMMON DESCRIPTIVE TERMS
USED WITH STANDARDIZED TESTS

Grade Equivalent: a test-performance ranking based on the total number of correct answers. This *raw score* is used to compare statistically a student's correct answers with those of other children in the same grade. The score is correlated with a grade level and expressed in terms of years and months, with nine months in each school year. For example, a grade-equivalent (G.E.)

score of 2.8 means that a student's test performance compares with that of other children in the eighth month of second grade. If the child's actual grade level in school is the third month of third grade (3.3) and her grade equivalency score on a standardized test is second grade, eighth month (2.8), the child is testing four months below grade level.

Mean Score: the mathematical average of all students' test scores on a particular test. One-half of the students taking the test score above the mean, and one-half score below.

Mental Age: a score on a *mental-abilities test* that statistically compares a student's performance level to that of other students. The score differentiates actual chronological age from performance-based mental age. The score differentiates actual chronological age from performance-based mental age. For example, a student's chronological age may be 10-2 (10 years, 2 months), but the number of her correct answers on the test may compare statistically with that of other children whose age is 10-9. Her test performance statistically generates a mental-age score that is seven months above the student's actual chronological age. The student would in this case be considered to have higher-than-average intelligence.

Norms: a statistical frame of reference derived from a comparison of the test performance by pupils of specific ages and in specific grades in school. The norms on a test allow students' scores to be compared to the scores of other students of the same age or in the same grade. Some tests offer very precise comparisons, such as the norms for children living in specific geographic areas or the norms for children attending private schools.

Percentile: a score that indicates a student's relative position within a defined group by ranking all those who have taken the test. A score at the fiftieth percentile is generally considered to be at grade level. A score at the fortieth percentile indicates that 39 percent of the children taking the test scored below the student and 59 percent of the children scored above the student. A score at the fortieth percentile is generally approximately one year below grade level. A score at the sixtieth percentile is generally approximately one year above grade level. The highest percentile that can be achieved is ninety-nine.

Raw Score: the total number of correct answers on a test.

Reliability: a statistical representation of how well a test consistently produces the same results.

Scaled Score: a ranking system chosen by the test publisher that is derived from the raw scores obtained by students taking the test. A different scale is established for each test. One particular test may have a scale from 1 to 19, while another may have a scale from 1 to 70. To interpret a scaled score accurately, you must know the mean score and the standard deviation for that test.

Standard Deviation: a measure of how much a student's score varies from the mean score of all the students taking the test.

Standard Score: a statistical ranking of a student's performance on a standardized test based on the raw score the student achieved relative to the performance of a large sample of students of the same age and/or grade level.

Standardized Test: a test with specific and uniform instructions for administering, timing, and scoring that is given to large numbers of children at one time. The test may be an achievement test that evaluates students' skills in specific areas, an IQ test, or a diagnostic test. The testing instrument statistically compares a student's performance with that of a large sample of students of the same age and/or grade level. On some tests, local norms are also provided for comparing students' scores with those of other children of the same socioeconomic background. The norms established by standardization process are used by teachers and school psychologists to determine students' relative level of performance and achievement.

Stanine: a statistical ranking of students' performance on a standardized test on a scale of 1 through 9. The mean score is 5, and a score from 3 to 4 is generally considered low average. A score from 6 to 7 is considered high average. Frequently, the results on a standardized test will be reported in both a stanine score and a percentile score. The higher the stanine score, the higher the percentile score.

Validity: the accuracy with which a test measures that which it has been designed to measure.

SKILLS AND ABILITIES COMMONLY MEASURED BY STANDARDIZED TESTS

- intelligence and aptitude
- reading comprehension
- vocabulary
- word recognition
- spelling
- grammar
- punctuation
- math problem solving and computational skills
- math conceptual skills
- reasoning
- perceptual efficiency (decoding of auditory, visual, and kinesthetic sensory data)
- visual and auditory memory
- visual-motor skills

SEE: Aptitude *(page 15)*; Attention Deficit/Attention Deficit Hyperactivity Disorder *(page 214)*; Attention to Details *(page 223)*; Auditory Memory *(page 322)*; Avoiding Responsibility *(page 227)*; Bouncing Back from Setbacks *(page 232)*; Brain Dysfunction *(page 326)*; Conduct and Attitude *(page 235)*; Critical Thinking *(page 161)*; Decoding *(page 332)*; Defense Mechanisms *(page 373)*; Depression *(page 378)*; Developmental Immaturity *(page 246)*; Dyslexia *(page 335)*; Essays and Essay Tests *(page 18)*; Fear of Failure, Success, and/or Competition *(page 383)*; Goal Setting *(page 165)*; Grammar and Syntax *(page 31)*; Identifying Important Information *(page 41)*; I'm Dumb

Syndrome *(page 388)*; Intelligence *(page 45)*; Judgment *(page 260)*; Keeping Up with the Class *(page 51)*; Learning from Mistakes *(page 267)*; Logic *(page 171)*; Mastery of Academic Content *(page 67)*; Math *(page 72)*; Performance Standards *(page 91)*; Phonics *(page 346)*; Problem Solving *(page 185)*; Psychological Overlay and Psychological Problems *(page 399)*; Punctuation *(page 96)*; Reading Comprehension *(page 100)*; Reading Fluency *(page 351)*; School Anxiety *(page 406)*; Self-concept *(page 410)*; Self-control *(page 287)*; Spelling *(page 112)*; Strategic Thinking *(page 189)*; Study Skills *(page 127)*; Test Anxiety *(page 420)*; Time Management *(page 138)*; Underachievement *(page 143)*.

Study Interruptions

▲

Refers to taking excessive breaks when studying and not sustaining focus and effort.

▲

Children who repeatedly interrupt their studying rarely learn effectively, and their behavior is usually a source of continual parent-child conflict. Most parents have traditional attitudes about studying. They want their children to sit down at their desks and work conscientiously until they complete their homework.

Children who repeatedly interrupt their studying have a different perspective. They typically argue that visiting the kitchen every ten minutes, picking up the telephone whenever it rings, playing a video game for a few moments, or periodically checking out what's on TV has no effect whatsoever on the quality of their studying. Most parents and teachers strenuously disagree with these contentions. They see a direct and unequivocal link between focus, sustained effort, and efficient learning, and they can usually support their position with compelling data at report-card time. These data usually confirm that children who study and learn inefficiently and intermittently receive lower grades than those who maintain their concentration and work diligently and without continual interruptions.

Children with attention deficit/attention deficit hyperactivity disorder have an especially difficult time staying on task when they study (unless they are taking and responding positively to medication to control the ADD/ADHD). Because of their chronic distractibility, inattentiveness, and deficient impulse control, these youngsters have difficulty focusing for more than a few moments (or even, in some cases, for a few seconds) on subjects that do not keenly interest them. Any environmental stimulus has the potential to divert their attention. They might spontaneously start playing with a pencil, become absorbed in tapping their fingers on the table, drift off into a daydream, or attempt to participate in a conversation taking place in another room. Those who are hyperactive will fidget, repeatedly drop objects and retrieve them, and continually get up from or fall out of their chairs. These children will use any pretext to turn on the TV, go into the kitchen for a snack, make gratuitous comments to others in the room, ask irrelevant questions, daydream, or wander about the house. The consequences are predictable: disjointed effort, inattentiveness to details, incomplete assignments, shoddy work, and poor grades.

Learning disabilities can be another source of excessive study breaks. Children who have difficulty processing sensory data efficiently are likely to find their homework challenging, discouraging, and unpleasant. Frustrated by the continual struggle to decode, comprehend, and complete their assignments, these youngsters often grasp at any opportunity to stop working. For a demoralized child, repeated study interruptions can be an enticing relief from drudgery.

Poor study skills and imprinted passive learning habits can also play key roles in children interrupting their studies. Students who do not know how to learn efficiently are often disorganized and have difficulty with managing time, planning, and preparing for tests. Because they do not understand the fundamental cause-and-effect relationship between sustained, focused effort and good grades, their studying is often fragmented.

There are exceptions, however, to the *sustained-studying-equals-good-grades* equation. Many children in our society have become seemingly inured to handling intrusive sensory stimuli and distractions emanating concurrently from multiple sources. Conditioned to a world of frenetic video games, pulsating music, and intense, fast-moving TV programs, some of these youngsters have demonstrated in research studies that they can, in fact, do their homework while watching TV or with music blaring from a boom box. In spite of this seeming capacity to work amid distractions, most parents, teachers, and resource specialists would argue that children, and especially learning-disabled children, require a quiet environment when they study and that repeated interruptions only add to the already formidable challenges these struggling students face.

Before intervening, parents must ask some key questions:

- Is my child's learning efficiency suffering because of too many interruptions?
- Is intervention appropriate?
- Are learning deficits, concentration deficits, or frustration and demoralization responsible for the excessive interruptions?
- How much sustained effort is realistic and reasonable before my child needs to take a break?

To answer these questions, parents should first review their child's test performance and homework assignments. If a child is doing well in school despite taking a great many study breaks, the child may be able to learn effectively with short bursts of intense studying. The cliché "Don't fix it if it isn't broken" would apply in this situation. To impose study-break guidelines when there is no apparent need could be counterproductive and precipitate unnecessary showdowns.

Poor grades, careless mistakes, incomplete assignments, missed deadlines, and sloppy work, on the other hand, clearly indicate inefficient study habits. If parents conclude that their child's marginal performance is attributable, at least in part, to repeated study interruptions, concern is legitimate, and parents would be justified in establishing fair, reasonable, and age-calibrated study-break guidelines.

Children's capacity to sustain their concentration and study without a break will vary according to their age and the nature of their learning difficulties. As a general rule, children with no presenting underlying learning problems or attention deficit disorder should be able to study for the following periods without interruptions:

first- and second-graders	10 minutes
third- and fourth-graders	15 minutes
fifth- and sixth-graders	15–20 minutes
sixth–eighth-graders	20–25 minutes
eighth–twelfth-graders	25–35 minutes

These numbers should be used only as a general guideline. Some second-graders can sustain their concentration for twenty minutes without an interruption, and some sixth-graders can study for forty-five minutes or more without a break.

The preceding suggested guidelines may be unreasonable for learning-disabled children and especially for those with ADD/ADHD. A chronically distractible eleven-year-old may only be able to focus for five minutes before legitimately needing a break. It is also important to note that children may require more frequent breaks when assignments are particularly challenging and they are required to expend intense effort.

Parents should request suggestions from their child's teacher about appropriate study-break guidelines. Chronological age, academic deficits, and concentration span must be factored into the study-break equation. Insisting that a seven-year-old study for thirty-five minutes without a break is as unreasonable as insisting that a twelve-year-old with ADD/ADHD or a learning disability study independently for thirty-five minutes without a break.

Study time should be increased in small increments, and children should be involved in the process of establishing realistic parameters and working toward mutually agreed upon standards. Acknowledgment, praise, and incentives should be integral components in any systematic effort by parents to modify their child's counterproductive study behavior.

SUGGESTIONS FOR REDUCING STUDY INTERRUPTIONS

- Explain to your child why you feel repeated study breaks can reduce his learning efficiency and undermine concentration.
- Set up an experiment to see if increasing the amount of study time between breaks improves your child's schoolwork.
- Involve your child in the process of establishing a reasonable and realistic, sustained studying standard (for example, studying for fifteen minutes between breaks).
- Increase sustained study sessions in two–five-minute increments per week, working up to the defined studying goal. (For example, have your child set an egg timer for ten minutes and encourage him to work without a break until the bell rings.)
- Create an incentive program. (For example, reward your child with points that can be used toward earning a prize or special treat when he can study for the agreed-upon time without an interruption.)
- Acknowledge, affirm, and praise your child for progress and express positive expectations that he can achieve his performance and study goals.

SEE: Apathy *(page 208)*; Avoiding Responsibility *(page 227)*; Bouncing Back from Setbacks *(page 232)*; Conduct and Attitude *(page 235)*; Critical Thinking *(page 161)*; Dealing with Consequences *(page 241)*; Defense Mechanisms *(page 373)*; Developmental Immaturity *(page 246)*; Disorganization *(page 251)*; Essays and Essay Tests *(page 18)*; Fear of Failure, Success, and/or Competition *(page 383)*; Goal Setting *(page 165)*; Grades *(page 25)*; I'm Dumb Syndrome *(page 388)*; Incomplete Assignments *(page 256)*; Irresponsibility *(page 256)*; Keeping Up with the Class *(page 51)*; Learning from Mistakes *(page 267)*; Logic *(page 171)*; Parent-Child Conflict *(page 393)*; Passive

Study Skills

▲

Refers to the ability to prepare effectively for tests, organize academic efforts efficiently, and complete homework assignments competently.

▲

Few teachers would deny that good study skills are an invaluable scholastic resource for children, and yet, ironically, teaching students how to study more effectively is not an especially high priority in many schools. Far too many teachers simply assume that capable children will "naturally" acquire efficient learning skills and somehow figure out how to record assignments, identify important information, take notes, recall facts, create a schedule, and prepare for tests. These assumptions are naive and could have terrible scholastic repercussions. Without methodical instruction, millions of potentially capable children will never acquire first-rate study skills or function scholastically at a level commensurate with their ability. The academic, psychological, and vocational consequences include poor grades, lowered expectations, diminished aspirations, and damaged self-confidence.

The risk of never acquiring effective study habits is especially high in the case of children who are struggling with learning problems. Inadequate study skills compound the disheartening academic challenges these children face every day in school. Addressing their underlying perceptual-processing deficits and helping them acquire adequate reading, writing, and math skills are, of course, vital, but unless these children are also systematically taught how to learn more efficiently, they are likely to continue performing marginally in school.

Most special-education teachers spend approximately forty-five minutes each day with a student. Their immediate priority is to help children process sensory information more efficiently and to help them acquire the basic skills they need to handle the demands of their mainstream classes. For many children who learn differently, the challenge of keeping up with the class can be monumental. Given the academic demands these children face, the emphasis in most resource programs is justifiably on improving basic skills—reading fluency, reading comprehension, recall, spelling, handwriting, math, and language arts skills. Teaching struggling learners how to read their textbooks clearly takes precedence over teaching them how to take notes or prepare for a multiple-choice exam.

In many cases, RSP (resource-specialist program) is essentially tutorial. Resource specialists typically explain and reinforce content-area subject matter taught in mainstream classes and help students understand and complete in-class work and homework assignments.

Despite gains in basic academic skills, many "graduates" of special-education programs enter middle school woefully unprepared to handle the demands of the regular curriculum. They may have the requisite reading and comprehension skills to do the work and survive academically, but they may still lack the higher-level thinking, planning, time-management, organizational, and memorization skills essential to meeting the demands of the curriculum and working up to their full academic potential. A significant percentage of these children haven't a clue about how to prepare properly for multiple-choice, short-answer, true-false, or essay tests. They do not know how to record their assignments accurately, take notes from lectures and textbooks, prioritize their academic obligations, or develop a practical study schedule. Most of are not in the habit of establishing short- and long-term goals. They don't know how to identify important information or memorize facts, foreign-language verb conjugations, and math formulas. Nor do they know how to figure out what questions are likely to be asked on a test. Lacking effective study procedures, these students are at an extreme disadvantage. Many are destined to struggle in middle school and high school and get poor grades. As the academic demands increase, they are also likely to become discouraged and demoralized.

The challenges that students exiting special-education programs face are formidable. The daily battle to survive academically in mainstream classes without academic assistance, assimilate the information in their textbooks, and take notes from lectures can be overwhelming.

Some students with deficient study skills continue to work diligently after being mainstreamed. Others essentially coast through school. They don't complete their homework or submit their assignments on time. They don't check their work for careless mistakes. Many don't even bother to study at all, or if they do, they simply go through the motions. For these children, studying means little more than mechanically and mindlessly turning the pages in their textbooks. Ineffectual effort, frustration, poor grades, discouragement, demoralization, reduced motivation, self-concept damage, lowered expectations and aspirations, and limited career options are the predictable and inevitable consequences.

Non-learning disabled children can also be victimized by ineffectual study skills. Because they do not know how to learn efficiently, these students are at serious risk for becoming underachievers.

Children with deficient study skills who muddle through twelve years of school often bear deep emotional scars. Poor grades, chronic frustration, unpleasant associations with test taking, school phobias, and diminished self-confidence are the common by-products of their negative school experiences. These children quickly learn to devalue their talents, minimize their potential, and lower their educational and career expectations and aspirations.

Academically defeated students typically choose the path of least resistance and do everything they can to avoid studying. Deluding themselves into thinking that they aren't really failing if they aren't really trying, they deny that they have academic problems and contend that school is "dumb." These rationalizations are usually transparent to their teachers and parents.

Ironically, students with the greatest need to study are often the most unwilling to do so. They procrastinate, submit sloppy, incomplete work, blame others for their difficulties, and refuse help. These counterproductive behaviors, of course, accentuate the very deficiencies they are attempting to camouflage, but self-sabotaging children are usually so enmeshed in their psychological defenses that they cannot see this obvious paradox.

Parents who conclude that their child requires study-skills instruction should request that it be provided at school. If they conclude that it is unlikely that this instruction will be offered, they may have no other option but to buy a good study-skills workbook at a teacher supply store and provide the instruction themselves. If parents anticipate that their child will resist and resent their attempts to intervene, they should consider hiring a qualified tutor.

SYMPTOMS OF DEFICIENT STUDY SKILLS

Students typically do not:
- define short- and long-term academic goals
- establish priorities
- focus their efforts
- develop a study schedule
- record assignments accurately
- manage study time efficiently
- plan ahead

- organize themselves and their materials
- study for reasonable periods of time without taking excessive breaks
- read with good comprehension
- know how to identify important information when they study
- know how to memorize important information
- take effective notes from textbooks and lectures
- anticipate what's likely to be asked on tests
- learn actively
- identify and capitalize on their preferred learning strengths
- proofread carefully and check for errors
- meet deadlines
- write effectively
- learn from their mistakes and miscalculations
- develop a comprehensive test-preparation procedure

SEE: Apathy *(page 208)*; Auditory Memory *(page 322)*; Avoiding Responsibility *(page 227)*; Conduct and Attitude *(page 235)*; Bouncing Back from Setbacks *(page 232)*; Critical Thinking *(page 161)*; Decoding *(page 332)*; Defense Mechanisms *(page 373)*; Developmental Immaturity *(page 246)*; Disorganization *(page 251)*; Essays and Essay Tests *(page 18)*; Fear of Failure, Success, and/or Competition *(page 383)*; Goal Setting *(page 165)*; Grades *(page 25)*; Identifying Important Information *(page 41)*; I'm Dumb Syndrome *(page 388)*; Incomplete Assignments *(page 256)*; Judgment *(page 260)*; Keeping Up with the Class *(page 51)*; Learning from Mistakes *(page 267)*; Logic *(page 171)*; Mastery of Academic Content *(page 67)*; Note Taking *(page 79)*; Parent-Child Conflict *(page 393)*; Passive Learning *(page 84)*; Performance Standards *(page 91)*; Planning *(page 176)*; Priorities *(page 180)*; Problem Solving *(page 185)*; Procrastination *(page 278)*; Psychological Overlay and Psychological Problems *(page 399)*; Reading Comprehension *(page 100)*; Reading Fluency *(page 351)*; Recording Assignments *(page 107)*; Resistance to Help *(page 282)*; School Anxiety *(page 406)*; Self-concept *(page 410)*; Self-control *(page 287)*; Standardized Tests *(page 116)*; Strategic Thinking *(page*

Teacher-Designed Tests

▲

Refers to tests that assess mastery of content taught in class and in textbooks. These tests may also be referred to as criterion-referenced, or mastery, tests.

▲

Teacher-designed tests are the primary mechanism for grading the quality of children's work. They are designed to measure students' skills and to identify those who have mastered content that the teacher considers important.

Because the questions on teacher-designed tests are directly linked to material contained in textbooks and presented in class, educators refer to the tests as *criterion referenced.* This course-content focus differentiates teacher-designed tests from *standardized tests* that are administered to hundreds of thousands of students, are statistically normed, and contain a broader range of questions.

Many teachers consider the multiple-choice and short-answer formats the most objective means of measuring what students have learned. Although described as objective, these tests are also subjective in two key regards: Teachers decide what information should be covered on the test, and teachers select the test questions.

Many teachers argue that well-designed multiple-choice and short-answer tests are the most effective means of assessing students' skills and course content mastery. They contend that such tests can quickly and efficiently determine if their students have learned what they consider important. There is, of course, another obvious advantage in using these tests: Objective tests are considerably easier to grade than essay tests. A teacher with an answer key can usually evaluate thirty tests in a relatively short period of time. The process is mechanical, and little or no thought is required. In contrast, a great deal of thinking and evaluative decision making is required to read and grade thirty essays, and the procedure can require hours of the teacher's time.

Essay tests are considered a subjective assessment tool because teachers must evaluate multiple factors in determining a student's grade. They must judge content (i.e., facts and supporting information) as well as appraise expository writing skills, organization, topic-sentence quality, concluding-sentence quality, grammar and pronunciation, overall insight, persuasiveness, and cogency. Teachers who favor essay tests contend that they can judge with fairness the quality and relevance of the included information and can make an objective determination of insight and content mastery. They also argue that evaluating a student's ability to craft an essay that summarizes the child's knowledge about a subject has more educational relevance than assessing the child's retention of minutiae on a multiple-choice test. These teachers will usually point out that most facts are quickly forgotten, whereas insights are likely to be imprinted, retained, and utilized. Teachers favoring essay tests also support their position by underscoring two additional key points:

- Students must be provided with repeated opportunities to organize, synthesize, and summarize their insights and express their ideas cogently if their expository writing skills are to improve.
- Students planning on attending college must learn how to take essay tests.

Such arguments notwithstanding, subjectivity clearly plays a role in determining a student's grade on an essay exam. One teacher may consciously or unconsciously prioritize the inclusion of a great many facts and condensed information, and another may prioritize a cohesive overview of the subject, writing style, and persuasiveness. A student submitting the same essay to two different teachers might conceivably receive a B+ from one and a C from another.

Whether teachers prefer the objectivity and convenience of multiple-choice or short-answer tests or the expression of ideas and insights emphasized on essay tests has little bearing on two central facts of academic life: Children can expect to be evaluated continually in school, and their test performance will have a profound and lasting impact on their self-concept, educational and vocational choices, income, expectations, and aspirations. Those who test well are far more likely to acquire academic self-confidence and to have more educational and vocational options.

Irrespective of the teacher's preferred assessment method, children with learning problems are especially vulnerable when they are tested. Perceptual-processing deficits, such as dyslexia, can make studying for, and taking, teacher-designed tests a nightmare. Difficulty with reading fluency, comprehension, visual memory, auditory memory, concentration, expository writing skills, math, and study skills clearly places children who learn differently at a severe competitive disadvantage. Those who lack the requisite skills to do what is expected of them are destined to get poor grades on tests.

Sensitive teachers realize the challenges that learning-disabled students face, and many will do everything reasonable to "level the playing field." They may allow extra time to complete the test. They may administer the test at a different time and read the questions aloud and perhaps allow the student to answer the questions orally. They may allow the resource specialist to administer the test and to provide reasonable prompting.

Some teachers, however, are sticklers for conformity and are highly resistant to making accommodations for students with learning problems. These teachers are often inflexible and have acquired entrenched attitudes about how "things should be done." Other have a minimal understanding of human psychology and are incapable of empathizing with students who have legitimate learning problems and who require fair and reasonable accommodations until they are able to overcome or successfully compensate for their learning problems.

Federal law (Section 504 of the Rehabilitation Act of 1973) mandates that schools make reasonable accommodations for children with learning difficulties so that discrimination, if not completely eliminated, is, at least, significantly reduced. The adjustments spelled out by most guidelines for Section 504 compliance include permitting extra time for tests, providing a separate room for testing, allowing children to use a computer, allowing children to take oral tests, and having the teacher read test instructions and test questions aloud to students.

School districts cannot claim that they are unable to meet the requirements of Section 504 because of financial problems, but they can attempt to prove that the adjustments would cause undue hardship for the district. This argument rarely prevails, for most reasonable accommodations are inexpensive.

Under the provisions of Section 504, school districts are mandated to develop a grievance procedure. Schools are also required to appoint a Section 504 official to assure compliance with the regulations, and they are prevented from passing on any associated costs to the student's family.

Parents should be reasonable in requesting testing accommodations. They should be prepared to negotiate, and they should make every effort to be diplomatic. Helping the skeptical or unwilling teacher understand why certain testing modifications are fair and reasonable and discussing how the adjustments could be implemented without causing an undue burden or hardship for the teacher or other students can be instrumental in defusing resistance. If the teacher is unyielding, parents should ask that the principal, school psychologist, or resource specialist participate in the dissuasion. Although federal law requires that reasonable accommodations be made for students with disabilities, voluntary cooperation is certainly preferable to a confrontation. If parents cannot reach agreement with the school, they should speak with the school district's Section 504 compliance/grievance officer. Children with legitimate learning problems should not be psychologically scarred by their test-taking experiences, and their parents have a compelling responsibility to do everything possible to prevent profound and lasting emotional damage from occurring.*

---

*See Appendix I for a more comprehensive description of federal laws that apply to children with learning disabilities and a more complete list of accommodations.

FACTORS THAT CAN IMPROVE GRADES ON MULTIPLE-CHOICE AND SHORT-ANSWER TESTS

- identifying what the teacher is likely to consider important when studying
- anticipating questions that are likely to be asked
- gearing study methods to the type of questions the teacher typically asks
- making up practice tests when studying
- being able to recall information (facts, dates, and minutiae)
- eliminating clearly flawed options on multiple-choice tests
- using strategic thinking and logic to deal with "tricky" questions
- attending methodically to details when considering choices
- being able to sustain concentration
- trusting one's judgment when selecting an answer
- practicing relaxation techniques to reduce anxiety before taking tests

FACTORS THAT CAN IMPROVE GRADES ON ESSAY EXAMS

- beginning essay with a powerful topic sentence
- ending essay with a powerful concluding sentence (or sentences)
- organizing and sequencing information effectively
- incorporating substantiating facts
- supporting a position persuasively
- expressing ideas in an aesthetically pleasing style
- using proper grammar and pronunciation
- spelling correctly
- writing legibly

Time Management

▲

Refers to the ability to plan ahead, establish priorities, schedule obligations, and budget adequate time to complete short-term and long-term projects.

▲

Children must manage time effectively if they are to succeed academically. They must be capable of accurately estimating how much time they need to complete their homework assignments and study for tests. They must also be capable of developing a methodical plan for researching and writing a science or history report. They must determine the required steps for completing the project, establish a sequence, organize their efforts, and create a schedule or flowchart that allows them to finish the report and meet the deadline.

Some children intuitively figure out how to manage time. They make a mental note of how long it takes to do a particular task and use this information as a frame of reference when confronted with similar tasks. Over time, their database expands, and they are able to make instantaneous judgments about how much time they need to complete most school-related projects and obligations. They know that it usually takes them twenty-five minutes to do a typical math homework assignment and approximately an hour to read and take notes on the ten pages their teacher assigned in their science textbook. From experience they also know that it will take two weeks to read a book for the next book report. They budget their time accordingly and perhaps schedule twenty minutes of reading time each evening.

Being able to coordinate strategic planning and effective time management is a skill that some learning-disabled children never acquire. These children are usually preoccupied with mastering the fundamentals: decoding words, comprehending content, retaining information, following written and verbal instructions, writing comprehensible sentences, understanding mathematical operations, and proofreading for careless mistakes. Learning how to manage time effectively is usually not a high priority when children are struggling every day to understand the information they read in their textbooks and hear in class.

Because of continual academic challenges they face, youngsters with learning problems may become reliant on assistance and supervision. To make things easier, their teachers, parents, and resource specialists may do the planning and scheduling for them without realizing that by taking ownership of these responsibilities, they are unwittingly encouraging helplessness and dependence. As a consequence, many learning-disabled children may never develop an appreciation for time constraints and exigencies, and they may become habituated to being told what they need to do and how much time they have to get the work done. They are expected to work until told to stop, and if they cannot finish the work within the allotted time, there are few, if any, consequences.

Children with attention deficit/attention deficit hyperactivity disorder usually have an especially difficult time managing the clock. The challenge of simply staying on task consumes much, if not all, of their physical and mental energy. The most pressing concern of most ADD/ADHD children is to get the immediate task completed as quickly and painlessly as possible. Scheduling multifaceted projects and making predictions about time requirements eclipse their self-discipline resources. Managing a long-range project, such as a term paper or a book report, can be overwhelming. The typical "solution" of the ADD/ADHD child is to put off dealing with the project for as long as possible. This avoidance of responsibility produces predictable consequences: repeated crises, chronic stress and anxiety, incomplete assignments, and lowered grades.

The need for effective time-management skills increases as students progress into the upper grades. Having to plan for five different subjects and handle assignments from five different teachers can cause students with learning problems, compounded by poor planning and time-management skills, to go into meltdown. These children are at grave risk for becoming not only overwhelmed and academically incapacitated but also discouraged, demoralized, and depressed. Faced with responsibilities they cannot handle, many of these children will shut down academically. Those who do not will often compensate by becoming increasingly dependent on their parents to help them complete their work.

Children who have poor time-management skills can generate tension in everyone in the family. They are usually in a continual crisis mode. Ironically, students with the greatest need to improve their time-management skills are the ones who are often most resistant to doing so. Some are oblivious to the obvious consequences of inefficient time management. Others are in denial and do not want to confront the implications of their poor planning and disorganization.

Children as young as six can be systematically taught time-management skills. The first step in the process is to show them how to define and prioritize their academic obligations and how to allocate sufficient time to meet these obligations. Children who require extra time to complete projects should be encouraged to build a buffer into their schedule. They must practice making "best guess" predictions of the time requirements based on a careful assessment of the particular task and on past experience with similar tasks. If their predictions prove inaccurate, they must be taught how to analyze what went wrong and make expedient adjustments in their future planning.

By incorporating short- and long-term planning and scheduling exercises as integral components in the curriculum, teachers can play a key role in helping children improve their time-management skills. For example, students might plan a class project and design a schedule that requires careful time management. They might prioritize the necessary steps to complete the task and estimate the time requirements for each step. These data could then be plotted into a flowchart. Miscalculations could be discussed, and appropriate changes could be made. To reinforce the time-management principles and practices that they have learned, each student could then be required to develop a formal step-by-step schedule for completing a long-range project, such as a term paper.

By showing their child how to analyze tasks, break projects down into manageable parts, and make realistic estimates about how much time will be required to complete each component of a particular project, parents can play an instrumental role in reinforcing time-management principles at home. They might examine the steps and time requirements involved in preparing effectively for a midterm science exam or in writing a book report. They could then show their child how to set up a schedule and how to budget the time required each day to complete the work by the deadline.

Parents can also improve their child's time-management skills by doing nonacademic planning activities with that child that require the practical application of time-budgeting principles. For example, they might involve their child in planning a home-improvement project. Working together, they could establish realistic target dates for completing each step, create a list of priorities, and project the amount of time required to complete each step. They could then make up a schedule that indicates a final completion date and the amount of time that needs to be spent each day.

As is the case with mastering any skill, time management will improve with effective instruction, patient guidance, empathetic feedback, repeated opportunities for practice, and effusive praise and affirmation for progress. Once children see the value of managing their time more efficiently and experience the payoffs, they will be far more receptive to incorporating these critically important planning and scheduling skills into their modus operandi.

BEHAVIORS SYMPTOMATIC OF POOR TIME MANAGEMENT

- procrastination
- difficulty making accurate time estimates and projections
- failure to allocate sufficient time for studying, preparing for tests, completing assignments and projects, and proofreading
- irresponsibility
- difficulty planning

- disregard of cause-and-effect principles
- poor study skills
- excessive study interruptions
- poor organization
- dependence on others
- inattention to details
- failure to establish goals and priorities
- failure to record assignments properly
- failure to create a study strategy
- chronic stress and anxiety
- failure to complete assignments
- failure to meet deadlines

SEE: Apathy *(page 208)*; Attention to Details *(page 223)*; Avoiding Responsibility *(page 227)*; Bouncing Back from Setbacks *(page 232)*; Conduct and Attitude *(page 235)*; Defense Mechanisms *(page 373)*; Dealing with Consequences *(page 241)*; Developmental Immaturity *(page 246)*; Disorganization *(page 251)*; Essays and Essay Tests *(page 18)*; Goal Setting *(page 165)*; Grades *(page 25)*; Incomplete Assignments *(page 256)*; Judgment *(page 260)*; Keeping Up with the Class *(page 51)*; Learning from Mistakes *(page 267)*; Logic *(page 171)*; Parent-Child Conflict *(page 393)*; Passive Learning *(page 84)*; Performance Standards *(page 91)*; Planning *(page 176)*; Priorities *(page 180)*; Problem Solving *(page 185)*; Procrastination *(page 278)*; Psychological Overlay and Psychological Problems *(page 399)*; Recording Assignments *(page 107)*; Resistance to Help *(page 282)*; School Anxiety *(page 406)*; Self-control *(page 287)*; Standardized Tests *(page 116)*; Strategic Thinking *(page 189)*; Study Interruptions *(page 122)*; Study Skills *(page 127)*; Teacher-Child Conflict *(page 293)*; Teacher-Designed Tests *(page 132)*; Underachievement *(page 143)*; Working Independently *(page 302)*.

Underachievement

▲

Refers to a discrepancy between potential ability and actual performance.

▲

Hundreds of thousands of children in American schools have specific learning deficits, are classified as learning disabled or "learning different," and participate in special-education programs. These identified learning-disabled students represent approximately 3–5 percent of the student population. Millions of other children with less severe and/or harder-to-define learning difficulties do not meet the rigid standards for official designation. These children are clearly functioning below their full academic potential but are rarely provided with formal assistance in school. Left to their own devices, they must sink or swim on their own.

Despite marginal rewards, some tenacious and highly motivated underachieving children continue to work diligently. Others are less resilient and less persistent. Defeated by their repeated negative school experiences, these children are likely to conclude that they are academically and intellectually inadequate. Once they resign themselves to doing poorly, they will lower their expectations and aspirations accordingly, and their scholastic fate will be sealed.

Some educators (and many parents) are distressed by the narrow criteria that are generally used by school districts to identify children who learn differently. Contending that as many as 30 percent of the school population have performance-diminishing learning deficits, they argue that schools should expand their special-education programs to include marginally performing students with less severe and less incapacitating learning deficiencies. At present, very few of these children are ever formally evaluated by school psychologists, and of those that are evaluated, most fail to qualify for RSP (resource specialist program). The vast majority slip through the diagnostic screen and are provided with no substantive help.

The implications of this disregard of the legitimate educational needs of marginally performing students are self-evident: Millions of children are not functioning in school at a level commensurate with their true ability. The consequences are also self-evident: damaged academic self-confidence, diminished expectations and aspirations, and wasted human talent.

By disavowing any responsibility to provide learning assistance for marginally performing students, the educational system, in effect, holds these underachieving children exclusively accountable for their academic plight. Perplexed teachers who have not been trained to deal with underachieving students may conclude that these children lack scholastic ability or are simply lazy, unmotivated, and immature. They may attribute the underachievement to counterproductive behaviors and attitudes when in fact these maladaptive behaviors and attitudes are actually *symptoms* of subtle and often puzzling underlying learning deficiencies that have never been properly identified or addressed.

Some frustrated and discouraged learners will compensate for their difficulty achieving in the academic arena by choosing other venues in which to excel. They may spend as much time as possible playing music, shooting baskets, learning how to program computers, or driving golf balls. Others may react to their academic plight by shutting down, becoming passive and withdrawn, acting irresponsibly, developing behavior problems, and/or becoming rebellious and antisocial.

Marginally performing children who receive no substantive assistance in school typically muddle through twelve essentially unproductive years of school. Every year, legions of these academically demoralized students arrive at the end of the educational production line without the requisite skills, motivation, and self-confidence to compete in a harsh, demanding, technologically driven workplace. Most are destined to continue underachieving, perhaps throughout their entire life.

In some instances, the learning deficits that cause underachievement may manifest exclusively in only one academic subject. In other cases, the learning deficits may manifest concurrently in several content areas. One child may read aloud without difficulty but may have poor comprehension. Another may read inaccurately but may miraculously have good comprehension. A third child may get decent grades in science and social studies but may spell atrociously and do poorly in math. Although these students struggle academically and work below their potential, their learning deficiencies may not be considered sufficiently debilitating to warrant formal learning-assistance intervention.

To cope with their negative school experiences and defend themselves emotionally, underachieving children often resort to counterproductive, self-sabotaging behaviors. These behaviors typically include:

- procrastination
- resistance to doing homework
- having a cavalier attitude about studying for tests
- submitting sloppy, illegible assignments
- failing to meet deadlines
- daydreaming in class
- misbehaving
- blaming
- complaining
- resistance to accepting help from teachers and parents
- manifesting a negative attitude about school and learning

In reaction to these behaviors and attitudes, teachers, administrators, and even school psychologists may proffer simplistic and inaccurate explanations and solutions that include:

- "He's immature."
- "He should repeat the grade."
- "What do you expect? He's a boy, and boys are more immature and less serious about schoolwork."
- "Stop trying to save her. Let her sink or swim on her own."
- "She just needs to be more motivated and serious about her work."
- "Be patient. He'll ultimately come around."
- "Maybe you have to accept the fact that he's not cut out to be a good student."

Arguing that underachievement can be resolved if a child becomes more conscientious is essentially meaningless. Certainly, diligence plays a key role in the academic-achievement equation, but the preceding observations and recommendations do not address the source of the problem, nor do they provide any substantive functional solutions. A far more productive strategy would be to figure out why a child is "stuck" in school and help the child get "unstuck." This may involve assistance from a resource specialist, a modified instructional methodology that capitalizes on the student's natural learning strengths, tutorial assistance, study-skills instruction, educational therapy, and/or counseling.

Underachieving children with significant reactive behavioral problems (i.e., psychological overlay) triggered by their learning problems will require intervention by a mental-health professional. Those who shut down in school because of emotional or family problems will need to be professionally evaluated. Defiance, oppositional behavior, rebelliousness, hostility, depression, and drug use are red flags that clearly indicate that a child is in trouble. These problems must be addressed, and appropriate counseling must be provided.

Children who chronically underachieve are at serious risk academically and emotionally. If they are to succeed in school, they must acquire basic skills that will allow them to do the required work, and they must apply these skills consistently. They must be capable of reading with good comprehension, doing grade-level math, writing legibly, spelling correctly, expressing their ideas, and writing cogent, grammatically correct essays and book reports. They must know how to take notes from lectures and textbooks, retain important information, and prepare effectively for tests. Those who lack these essential skills and who become demoralized and unmotivated could ultimately end up at the bottom of the food chain.

The desire to learn is infused into human DNA. When children acquiesce to marginal performance, something is profoundly wrong. Unless the causative factors are identified and effective intervention is provided either in school or after school, these children may never fully actualize their abilities.

SOLUTIONS TO UNDERACHIEVEMENT

- Identify specific learning deficits that are impeding academic progress.
- Show children how to solve problems, analyze and learn from mistakes, and neutralize obstacles.
- Teach children how to study more effectively.
- Encourage children to establish short- and long-term goals.
- Teach children how to set priorities.
- Teach children how to plan, get organized, and manage time.
- Establish clear performance and behavior guidelines.
- Employ creative, dynamic instructional strategies.
- Identify and capitalize on students' natural learning strengths (auditory, visual, kinesthetic, tactile, experiential).
- Affirm progress.
- Provide guidance, emotional support, and appropriate supervision.
- Provide intervention by a mental-health professional if red-flag behaviors persist (e.g., defiance, depression, rebelliousness, etc.).

CAUSES OF UNDERACHIEVEMENT

- inefficient learning
- difficulty concentrating
- difficulty with cognitive processing
- emotional problems
- family problems
- fear of competition
- fear of failure
- unwillingness to establish goals
- resistance to doing homework
- immaturity
- incomplete assignments

- irresponsibility
- poor judgment
- flawed logic
- poor organization
- passive learning
- perceptual processing deficits
- unwillingness to accept performance standards
- lack of perseverance
- difficulty planning
- difficulty establishing priorities
- difficulty managing time
- difficulty solving problems
- difficulty thinking strategically
- repeated study interruption
- study-skills deficits
- difficulty managing time
- difficulty working independently
- poorly defined family values
- poorly defined behavior and performance guidelines
- emotional or family problems

SYMPTOMS OF UNDERACHIEVEMENT

- apathy
- absence of short- and long-term goals
- diminished effort
- absence of pride in accomplishments
- inattentiveness to details
- disorganization
- complacency
- lack of perseverance and follow-through
- elaborate coping and psychological defense mechanisms
- frustration
- demoralization

- helplessness
- feelings of inadequacy
- difficulty keeping up with the class
- resistance to accepting performance standards
- manipulative behavior
- poor motivation
- negative attitude
- procrastination
- resistance to help
- depression
- self-sabotaging behavior
- diminished self-confidence
- self-esteem deficits
- teacher-child conflict
- parent-child conflict

SEE: Apathy *(page 208)*; Aptitude *(page 15)*; Attention Deficit/Attention Deficit Hyperactivity Disorder *(page 214)*; Attention to Details *(page 223)*; Avoiding Responsibility *(page 227)*; Brain Dysfunction *(page 326)*; Conduct and Attitude *(page 235)*; Critical Thinking *(page 161)*; Decoding *(page 332)*; Defense Mechanisms *(page 373)*; Depression *(page 378)*; Developmental Immaturity *(page 246)*; Disorganization *(page 251)*; Fear of Failure, Success, and/or Competition *(page 383)*; Goal Setting *(page 165)*; Grades *(page 25)*; I'm Dumb Syndrome *(page 388)*; Incomplete Assignments *(page 256)*; Judgment *(page 260)*; Keeping Up with the Class *(page 51)*; Learning from Mistakes *(page 267)*; Logic *(page 171)*; Parent-Child Conflict *(page 393)*; Passive Learning *(page 84)*; Peer Pressure *(page 272)*; Performance Standards *(page 91)*; Planning *(page 176)*; Priorities *(page 180)*; Problem Solving *(page 185)*; Procrastination *(page 278)*; Psychological Overlay and Psychological Problems *(page 399)*; Reading Comprehension *(page 100)*; Reading Fluency *(page 351)*; Recording Assignments *(page 107)*; Resistance to Help *(page 282)*; School Anxiety *(page 406)*; Self-concept *(page 410)*; Self-control *(page 287)*; Spelling *(page 112)*; Standardized Tests *(page*

Vocabulary

▲

Refers to the ability to use words that accurately express thoughts, feelings, and insights.

▲

To communicate effectively, children must be able to retrieve the words that express with precision what they want to say or write. Those who have a rich vocabulary are far more likely to express themselves effectively than those who have a limited vocabulary.

Every year, hundreds of thousands of bright, potentially capable teenagers graduate from high school with abysmal oral and written expressive language skills and woefully deficient vocabularies. These students are virtually incapable of communicating their thoughts and feelings coherently. Their deficiencies are the legacy of a society and an educational system that do not place a particularly high priority on the development of language proficiency.

Deficient expressive language is especially prevalent among children who are struggling with learning problems. Students who have difficulty with decoding, phonics, reading, auditory memory, visual discrimination, and/or visual memory are at a severe disadvantage when trying to assimilate new words. These children are usually preoccupied with developing basic reading fluency, reading-comprehension skills, math proficiency, and writing fundamentals. Acquiring an expanded vocabulary is seldom very high on the list of remedial priorities. These students face far more compelling challenges: passing the next spelling test, completing their book report, answering the questions in their social-studies textbook, and understanding how to divide fractions.

Learning-disabled children may go through the motions of attempting to learn newly assigned vocabulary words, but they usually do so without a great deal of enthusiasm. The consequences of their passive involvement in the vocabulary-enhancement process are predictable: inadequate skill development and minimal retention.

The traditional method of developing vocabulary skills is mind numbing. Many teachers assign a list of new words at the beginning of the week and require students to look up and memorize the definitions. Children are instructed to use the words in sentences or paragraphs and are given weekly vocabulary tests to measure their mastery. Once they have ostensibly "learned" the new words, they are rarely required to use them again, and the words and their definitions are quickly forgotten.

Research has unequivocally proved that to learn and recall the definitions of unfamiliar words, students require multiple exposures to these words. Before they can assimilate new vocabulary, they must also have repeated opportunities to practice using the words. Periodic review is an equally vital component in the mastery process.

The mechanical, time-honored ritual—memorize the new word, use it in a sentence, and take a test—deprives children of an opportunity to experience the beauty, precision, and grace of the English language and the richness of its words. Most students do little more than go through the motions of enhancing their vocabulary. They never learn to use language dynamically and creatively, and all joy is leached out of what could be an exciting educational experience.

There are, of course, exceptional teachers who do a superb job of developing their students' linguistic skills. Their enthusiasm is contagious and their teaching, inspirational. Unfortunately, far too many teachers consider vocabulary development a painful chore. Discerning their teacher's lack of zeal, students respond accordingly and derive little or no benefit from the process.

In many school districts, the primary concern of administrators, teachers, parents, and school boards is to improve scores on standardized reading, vocabulary, and math tests. In an annual ritual, the scores of the local school are compared to those of other schools in the same district, in other districts, in the state, and nationally. These test results have become the major criterion for gauging the efficacy of a school's educational programs, and because of the political implications of how students perform, teachers are being overtly or covertly pressured to "teach to the tests." In the frenzy to raise scores and demonstrate teaching "excellence," the educational priority in many schools has become: "Memorize as many definitions as you can so that you can get a good score on the vocabulary section of the test." Qualitative language development is inconsequential.

The effects of this orientation are abundantly evident. Listening to many American children express their thoughts and feelings can be an excruciating experience. Reading their essays can be equally distressing. In all but college-prep and advanced-placement classes, effective written and verbal language skills are virtually nonexistent. The typical high school graduate has a working vocabulary of perhaps two thousand words. In daily communication, most teenagers employ fewer than one thousand words, and the two most common words in their lexicon are "you know."

Our educational system cannot be held exclusively responsible for the sorry state of children's language development. Insufficient encouragement, limited opportunities to use communication skills at home, ineffective modeling by parents, inadequate guidance and feedback, and pervasive social pressure to use the current argot are major deterrents to vocabulary development.

In our society, especially in many teenage subcultures, having and using a rich vocabulary is equated with pretentiousness. Youngsters are often reluctant to use "big" words for fear of social rejection. Even well-educated adults may hesitate to use precise vocabulary because they do not want to be considered pedantic.

Language mastery requires continual practice and application both in school and at home. Children who hear their parents use language effectively around the dinner table, who are encouraged to express their feelings, perceptions, and ideas, and who are acknowledged and affirmed for developing their communication skills and for expanding their vocabulary invariably become more articulate than children who are permitted to coast through life with a working vocabulary of one thousand words.

Yes, intelligence and language aptitude play a role in the development of expressive language skills. Children who are blessed with good auditory- and visual-memory capabilities have a distinct advantage when learning new words. Nevertheless, virtually all children of normal intelligence can improve their vocabulary and communication skills if provided with first-rate instruction, sufficient opportunities to practice, empathetic feedback, and affirmation for progress.

As is the case with the development of any skill, communication skills must be practiced and critiqued. If parents and teachers want children to acquire a precise and effective vocabulary, they must encourage children to use newly learned words in their daily communication in school and at home. It may not be realistic to expect a teenager to use the words *convoluted, protracted,* or *irrepressible* when conversing with friends, but it certainly would be realistic and desirable to encourage children to use such words when discussing issues in class or around the dinner table. By providing guidance, modeling, systematic instruction, encouragement, and sensitive and selective feedback, parents and teachers can play a significant, proactive role in enhancing children's vocabulary and communication skills. These skills will prove to be an invaluable resource for children throughout life.

METHODS FOR DEVELOPING YOUR CHILD'S VOCABULARY SKILLS

- Intentionally introduce one new "difficult" word each evening at the dinner table, define the word, and have each person at the table make up a sentence using the word. (Be supportive and affirming and provide empathetic feedback if your child uses the word incorrectly. Your goal is to create positive associations with language!)

- Encourage your child to incorporate the new word during the dinner conversation. (You might set up a point system. One point for the sentence and one point for using the word in the conversation. Keep track of the points on a chart. Perhaps provide a reward when a certain number of points are attained. Make the process fun!)
- Introduce another word after dinner that your child is expected to look up in the dictionary and use in a sentence. (Make certain that a dictionary is always handy. If your child's dictionary skills are deficient, provide instruction. Make this a fun activity!)
- Play word games with your child. (Show your child a list of twenty-five words and definitions. Say: "I'm thinking of a word that begins with 'de' and ends with 've.' and means 'to get.'" Your child would get one point for selecting the word "derive" and one point using the word correctly in a sentence.)
- Play synonym and antonym games with your child. (For example, you might say "verbose," and your child might say "talkative" or "wordy.")
- Encourage your child to use the thesaurus function on the computer (or a thesaurus in book format) when writing an essay or report.
- Intentionally use precise words when communicating. (Do not associate using words such as *restrictive* or *formulate* in your conversation with being pedantic. When appropriate, discuss the "big" words briefly but avoid expansive explanations that could trigger resistance and inhibit communication.)

SEE: Apathy *(page 208)*; Aptitude *(page 15)*; Attention to Details *(page 223)*; Auditory Memory *(page 322)*; Brain Dysfunction *(page 326)*; Essays and Essay Tests *(page 18)*; Grades *(page 25)*; I'm Dumb Syndrome *(page 388)*; Intelligence *(page 45)*; Keeping Up with the Class *(page 51)*; Language Arts *(page 58)*; Language Disorders *(page 433)*; Mastery of Academic Content *(page 67)*; Peer Pressure *(page*

APPLIED
INTELLIGENCE

The commonly held belief that intelligence is the primary determinant in school success discounts the critical role that focused effort, strategic thinking, and efficient thinking, and efficient study skills play in the academic-achievement equation. A critical distinction must be made between inherited intelligence (IQ) and applied intelligence quotient (AIQ).* Certainly a superior IQ and the ability to grasp concepts, understand abstractions, perceive relationships, and recall information can facilitate learning and enhance school performance, but a superior IQ does not guarantee superior academic achievement. Brilliant children may perform marginally in school, while less intellectually gifted children may excel.

Children who have developed their applied intelligence share certain traits that set them apart from their underachieving and non-achieving classmates. These achieving students:

- make wise decisions
- solve problems
- handle challenges
- learn from mistakes
- bounce back from setbacks
- define personal goals
- establish priorities
- record assignments accurately
- manage time efficiently
- plan ahead
- meet deadlines

---

*The term AIQ (applied intelligence quotient) has been coined by the author to describe distilled wisdom and insight, strategic thinking, and the pragmatic application of intelligence in handling challenges.

- identify important information when they study
- develop effective methods of identifying, understanding, and retaining key information when they study
- take good notes from textbooks and lectures
- involve themselves actively in learning
- organize their materials
- attend to details by proofreading carefully and checking for errors
- anticipate what's likely to be on tests

Children struggling with learning disabilities are less likely to acquire these pragmatic thinking, studying, and homework skills. Their priorities are far more basic: academic survival and being able to process and retain written and/or verbal information. Many of these children are physically, emotionally, and intellectually exhausted by the demands of simply keeping up with the class. Developing applied intelligence and learning how to think more strategically and prepare more effectively for tests is a luxury generally beyond their reach. These students may go through the motions of studying, but their learning is usually ineffectual, and they assimilate and retain little of what they have studied.

The vast majority of children who exhibit deficient applied intelligence can be taught *how* to think, reason, study, and learn more effectively. Even those with significant learning problems can be methodically trained to attend to details, identify important information, take notes, and record their assignments. They can be taught practical and easy to assimilate methods for recalling key facts, proofreading their work for careless errors, and preparing for tests.

The requisites for helping children with learning problems develop their applied intelligence include:

- accurate identification of the underlying learning deficits
- effective remediation
- focused, systematic instruction in how to define and solve problems and meet challenges
- guidance and supervision
- fair and consistently applied performance standards and guidelines

- repeated opportunities to practice efficient and effectual learning
- acknowledgment and praise for progress

In the following sections you will learn more about specific symptoms that indicate poorly developed applied intelligence and the specific learning deficits that can impede the development of your child's AIQ.

Critical Thinking

▲

Refers to the use of analytic abilities and, specifically, to identifying both the obvious and underlying issues, evaluating the merits and weaknesses of an argument or contention, and arriving at a reasoned conclusion.

▲

Students who have learning problems are typically preoccupied with the grueling task of decoding, comprehending, and recalling the information presented in class and in their textbooks. Their struggle to decipher and assimilate basic written and/or spoken content is often physically and intellectually exhausting. Depleted by the demands of trying to keep up with their class, these children are unlikely to spend a great deal of time and thought critically evaluating the veracity of what they are learning. While students who learn differently legitimately require extra assistance and reasonable accommodations, there is a potential downside to providing too much help. Some struggling children may become excessively reliant on adults to do their work and to think for them. Despite the best of intentions, parents, teachers, resource specialists, tutors, and/or educational therapists may unintentionally encourage these children to become passive learners and passive thinkers, and in the process unwittingly discourage them from fully developing their critical thinking capabilities.

Achieving students who are dynamically involved in learning have a very different modus operandi. They learn and think actively.

They are inquisitive. They probe and question. They examine not only the apparent issues but also the underlying issues until they have understood and assimilated the material they are studying. They challenge ideas that aren't logical or reasonable and resist shallow or facile explanations. During class discussions, they dispute illogical statements and refute data they believe are inaccurate. This "convince me" attitude can be nettlesome for teachers who don't like to be challenged, but the analytic evaluuative process forms the underpinning of critical thinking and invariably produces superior comprehension, retention, and insight.

In contrast, children who do not think analytically and critically attempt to assimilate information, ideas, and arguments at face value without examining or questioning the validity and without considering obvious contradictions or misrepresentations. Even ludicrous lies—"The Holocaust never really happened"—may be accepted without being challenged. Operating in cerebral neutral, these students are at risk for being easily influenced, led, and controlled by others. In extreme cases, youngsters who never develop critical judgment might conceivably become influenced by cults or hate groups run by charismatic or demonic leaders who radiate self-assurance and harangue their followers with simplistic truths and outright falsehoods.

Because they are generally oblivious to basic cause-and-effect principles, children with poorly developed critical intelligence are apt to disregard the potential implications of their attitudes and behavior. ("If I do this, what are the likely present and future consequences?") Not having developed effective evaluative skills, they often arrive at flawed conclusions, make judgment errors, and repeat their mistakes. Their chronic miscalculations are likely to produce disastrous repercussions throughout life.

The capacity to think critically is a left-brain function that requires applied logic and reasoning. This capability is also clearly linked to intelligence and developmental maturity. Nonetheless, critical thinking skills can be methodically taught to virtually any child who possesses a normal IQ. With appropriate guidance and effective instruction, children as young as six can be trained to challenge flawed reasoning. They can be taught how to question the validity of ideas and arguments, assess problems and temptations, evaluate options, add the pluses and minuses of a course of action, and consider in advance the potential implications of their attitudes and behavior.

During the last decade, many schools and many textbook publishers have climbed aboard the currently popular critical-thinking bandwagon. For pragmatic reasons, however, the methodical teaching of higher-level critical-thinking skills to children with learning problems is not generally deemed a high priority in many schools. Teachers and resource specialists are preoccupied with helping struggling learners acquire fundamental decoding and comprehension skills, and they usually have little time left to devote to teaching Socratic reasoning skills. Certainly, prioritizing academic fundamentals in special-education programs can be justified, but there is a price to be paid for neglecting critical-thinking skills.

Despite the many demands and challenges inherent in helping children with learning problems acquire basic skills and keep up with the class, teachers and resource specialists must also somehow find time to teach academically deficient students to think and reason. Without these vital skills, these children will not be able to function and compete in a technologically advanced society.

SYMPTOMS OF DEFICIENT CRITICAL-THINKING SKILLS

Difficulty in one or more of the following areas:
- analyzing and evaluating information
- identifying key ideas and concepts
- asking penetrating questions that uncover the underlying issues
- applying reason and logic
- considering the pluses and minuses of a position, statement, or choice
- applying cause-and-effect principles
- appreciating the future implications of attitudes and behavior
- questioning the validity of assumptions
- identifying contradictions, inconsistencies, fallacies, flaws, and deceptions
- seeing matters from different perspectives

- relating new information to previously learned information
- assessing issues, ideas, arguments, and contentions
- making judgments based on substantiated data

DIAGNOSTIC TOOLS

There are tests that measure general intelligence and subsets of intelligence, but few diagnostic instruments are specifically designed to measure critical intelligence per se. Those that assess certain components of critical intelligence include:

- **Test of Language Competence** (Psychological Corporation): assesses the ability to understand ambiguous sentences, make inferences, re-create sentences, and understand metaphoric expressions.
- **Adolescent Test of Problem Solving** (**TOPS**; LingulSystems): evaluates students' inferential reasoning, understanding of cause and effect, planning, and powers of deduction.

TREATMENT PROTOCOLS

Many reading programs contain critical-thinking components, and some schools have incorporated critical-thinking curriculum modules at the elementary, middle, and secondary levels. Few schools, however, actually offer a specific course in *critical thinking*.

Classroom teachers and resource specialists can utilize a range of books and supplemental teaching materials specifically designed to develop analytic- and critical-thinking skills. Publishing companies offering these materials include Fearon/Globe, Frank Schaffer Publications, and the Learning Works.

Goal Setting

▲

Refers to defining specific desired objectives and implementing a systematic plan for attaining these objectives.

▲

The concerns of most learning-disabled children are rooted in the present. Preoccupied with academic survival, their foremost challenge is somehow to get through another day in school, ideally without feeling inadequate, becoming demoralized, or being humiliated.

Struggling children seldom think about what might happen in the future and are rarely attuned to the basic cause-and-effect principles that link the establishment of personal goals and achievement. When self-preservation is the overriding priority, down-the-road expectations and aspirations are little more than abstractions. The immediate consuming objective is to be able to read aloud in class, do a math problem at the chalkboard, or recall information when their teacher asks them a question in class.

The failure to target long-term performance and achievement goals—compounded by the tendency to learn passively—magnifies the formidable challenges that learning-disabled students face in school. Because these children rarely manifest goal-directed motivation and effort, their learning is often disjointed and ineffectual.

In contrast, achieving students are typically highly goal-directed. They define their specific short- and long-term objectives, formulate a practical plan for getting what they want, and focus their mental and physical energy on attaining the desired payoff. Realizing that interim goals are stepping-stones to attaining their long-term goals, they strategically plot a course that allows them to proceed from point A to point B to point C, and they persevere until they ultimately arrive at their destination.

Learning-disabled students usually follow a very different trajectory. Unlike their achieving classmates who intuitively figure out how they learn best and consistently capitalize on their learning strengths, struggling students are consumed with acquiring basic academic skills. Few know how to develop a methodical plan for learning and studying with maximum efficiency and minimum pain. They do not know how to identify important information when they study, nor do they know how to devise effective ways to understand and remember this information. They also do not know how to budget adequate time to complete their homework or meet deadlines. That these children are often frustrated, discouraged, unmotivated, emotionally vulnerable, psychologically defended, and lacking in self-confidence, and that they typically resist establishing personal performance goals should come as no surprise. To establish demanding goals would simply expose them to the likelihood of more failure and more demoralization.

A paradox becomes quickly apparent: Students with learning

problems don't reach for the brass ring because they don't believe they can capture it, and they don't capture the ring because they're unwilling to risk reaching for it. This paradox can be graphically represented:

IMPLICATIONS OF FAILURE TO ESTABLISH GOALS

The arrows point in both directions to underscore how each

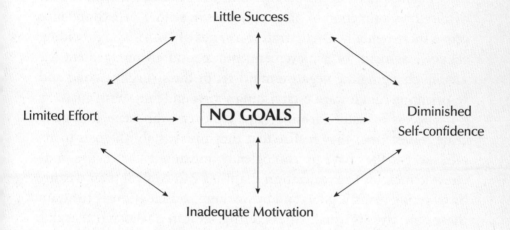

component in the loop affects the others. For example, little success produces low self-confidence, and low self-confidence produces little success.

Whereas achieving, goal-focused children want to test the limits of their abilities and determine what they are capable of achieving, learning-disabled children are often consumed with protecting themselves. They want to reduce the challenges, not expand them.

The first step in the process of orienting learning-disabled children toward establishing goals is to identify accurately their specific learning deficits. The second step is to provide effective remediation. The third step is to involve struggling students actively in their remediation program and insist that they participate in setting priorities, establishing short- and long-term objectives, and determining performance standards. The final step is to require that they work conscientiously to attain their defined goals and to affirm them effusively for their progress and accomplishments.

Parents and teachers should urge children who are struggling in school to establish modest and attainable goals initially. A child reading two years below grade level who targets as a long-term goal an A in history on his next report card is probably setting himself up for disappointment and failure. Aiming for a C or C+ (depending on the grading criteria) would be more realistic. Once this initial goal is achieved, the child can then establish more exalted objectives.

A child's faith in his abilities and his capacity to achieve academically is a function of his experiences in school. Self-confidence grows incrementally. Orchestrating a series of "wins" and providing acknowledgment for achievement, praise, and encouragement are vital in changing the negative mind-set of the struggling child and re-orienting him toward establishing short- and long-term goals.

Success is habit-forming, and children who taste it usually crave more. Once they realize that they must establish goals to attain success, they have psychologically imprinted a key cause-and-effect principle. The realization that they can control their destiny by targeting realistic goals and by working conscientiously to attain these objectives is usually life-altering. Children who arrive at this crucial insight can begin to participate proactively in the process of overcoming their learning difficulties and attaining what they want in life.

CHARACTERISTICS OF GOAL-DIRECTED STUDENTS

- They select their desired targets. ("I want a minimum of B+ on my science report.")
- They are motivated. ("Getting that scholarship is more important than anything!")
- They identify the challenges and barriers standing between them and their goal. ("My handwriting needs to improve.")
- They weigh the pros and cons, calculate the odds, and think ahead. ("Taking advanced-placement classes will require a lot more work, but it will improve my chances of getting into a first-rate college.")

- They examine and assess options. ("I think taking Spanish is more practical than taking German.")
- They plan meticulously and do what needs to be done to attain their objectives. ("I need to spend a minimum of five hours doing library research to complete this social-studies term paper.")
- They manage time effectively. ("To get the book report done on time, for the next two weeks I'll need to spend a minimum of thirty minutes each night reading the novel.")
- They analyze the obvious and underlying issues. ("The teacher is tough and makes us work hard, but she does this because she wants to prepare us for high school.")
- They capitalize on their learning strengths. ("I'll learn the new vocabulary words by recording each definition and a sentence using the word on a cassette, and I'll replay the recording on the way to school.")
- They consider the potential consequences. ("If I don't complete this essay on time, I may not get an A in the course.")
- They are disciplined and work diligently. ("I'll have to study at least six hours to get a B on the science test.")
- They bounce back from setbacks. ("I didn't study hard enough. I'll do better next time.")
- They can make sacrifices and suspend immediate gratification. ("I'll go to the movies with my friends next week. I've got to study for the math test.")
- They persevere. ("I'll have to work extra hard in practice so that I can convince the coach to put me on the varsity.")
- They learn from mistakes. ("I now realize that she asks tricky multiple-choice questions. I'll have to adjust my study strategy if I am going to improve my grade on the next test.")
- They methodically analyze and solve problems. ("I have to change the coach's attitude about me. I'll have to work harder in practice.")
- They identify resources and accept help and guidance. ("My sister got straight A's in math. I'll ask her to help me with these tricky algebra problems.")
- They are proud of their accomplishments. ("I said I'd get a B in science, and I did!")

CHARACTERISTICS OF NON-GOAL-DIRECTED STUDENTS

- They have little sense of purpose or direction.
- They disregard, deny, rationalize, or are oblivious to the consequences of their counterproductive attitudes and behavior.
- They make excuses.
- They blame others for their difficulties.
- They procrastinate.
- They act irresponsibly.
- They lack self-discipline.
- They learn passively.
- They do not plan ahead.
- They fail to attend to the details.
- They are not driven to excel.
- They prioritize immediate gratification over deferred gratification.

SEE: Apathy *(page 208)*; Avoiding Responsibility *(page 227)*; Bouncing Back from Setbacks *(page 232)*; Conduct and Attitude *(page 235)*; Critical Thinking *(page 161)*; Dealing with Consequences *(page 241)*; Defense Mechanisms *(page 373)*; Depression *(page 378)*; Developmental Immaturity *(page 246)*; Disorganization *(page 251)*; Fear of Failure, Success, and/or Competition *(page 383)*; Grades *(page 25)*; I'm Dumb Syndrome *(page 388)*; Incomplete Assignments *(page 256)*; Judgment *(page 260)*; Keeping Up with the Class *(page 51)*; Learning from Mistakes *(page 267)*; Logic *(page 171)*; Parent-Child Conflict *(page 393)*; Passive Learning *(page 84)*; Peer Pressure *(page 272)*; Performance Standards *(page 91)*; Planning *(page 176)*; Priorities *(page 180)*; Problem Solving *(page 185)*; Procrastination *(page 278)*; Psychological Overlay and Psychological Problems *(page 399)*; Resistance to Help *(page 282)*; School Anxiety *(page 406)*; Self-concept *(page 410)*; Self-control *(page 287)*; Strategic Thinking *(page 189)*; Study Skills *(page 127)*; Time Management *(page 138)*; Underachievement *(page 143)*; Working Independently *(page 302)*.

Logic

▲

Refers to the ability to reason and think rationally and analytically.

▲

Children must be capable of thinking logically in order to solve problems, understand concepts, analyze and evaluate issues, make predictions, perceive relationships, make associations, and communicate ideas effectively. If they are studying about global warming, they must be able to recognize the potential repercussions of rising global temperature. If they cannot grasp the logical implications, they will not understand the significance of the phenomenon and the inherent risks, and they are unlikely to remember important information when they take a test covering the material.

Because most children with learning problems are preoccupied with mastering basic scholastic skills, they may never fully develop their ability to apply logic when they study. For students whose energy is focused on decoding letters, reading with comprehension, and recalling information, acquiring reasoning skills is not a high priority. Their consuming concern is basic academic survival.

Logic and language are processed in the left hemisphere of the brain. Feelings, intuition, and artistic and creative functions are processed in the right hemisphere. This differentiation is, however, somewhat misleading, as is the contention that American schools prioritize left-brain functions over right-brain functions. That school curricula and textbooks emphasize analytic and critical thinking, recall, and expository language facility is indisputable. No child, however, is exclusively right-brained or left-brained, and students are continually required to use *both* hemispheres of the brain. Artistic children must be able to plan a project in science class, and logical thinkers with scientific aptitude must be able to draw a diagram and think creatively.

Students who think logically do have a significant competitive advantage in upper-level and advance-placement classes. Because logic is a key element in the range of abilities that are assessed on IQ tests and university admission tests, children with superior reasoning skills typically receive the highest scores on these exams.

The capacity to analyze and evaluate issues, link previously learned information with new information, think rationally, draw inferences, make associations, and arrive at balanced, reasonable conclusions is driven by a fundamental cause-and-effect principle: *Action produces reaction.* Children who think logically have imprinted this principle and continually apply it as a guide and standard for their behavior and attitudes.

Children who think logically not only consider what's happening in the present but also what might happen in the future, and they consistently factor this future-time consideration into their decisions. This capacity to zoom from the micro to the macro produces strategic goal-directed thinking. Carefully defined short-term goals are seen as stepping-stones to attaining carefully defined long-term goals.

Children who think logically can also make deductions and draw inferences and conclusions from both *direct* and *indirect* experience. They don't need to try drugs in order to decide whether or not to take them. Reading about and/or discussing the consequences is enough to deter them from experimentation.

Intelligence plays a key role in logical thinking. Nevertheless, some intelligent children never fully develop their reasoning powers. They may be affected by emotional or family problems that cause them to think and act illogically or be unduly influenced by peers who act impetuously and mindlessly. The failure of bright children to develop and apply sound reasoning skills usually produces predictable consequences that may include underachievement, repeated errors in judgment, self-sabotaging behavior, and excessive risk taking.

When a child's thinking and behavior are chronically irrational, underlying psychological factors can usually be identified. These factors, which may include fear, anger, insecurity, and poor self-esteem, can undermine the child's ability to reason and cause the child to "self-destruct." Children manifesting these behaviors should be evaluated by a mental-health professional.

With systematic instruction and repeated opportunities for practice, virtually all children can be taught to think more logically. This instruction should be a focal component in all well-conceived curricula.

CHARACTERISTICS OF LOGICAL THINKING

Children who think logically:

- carefully consider the possible consequences of their behavior and attitude
- plan ahead
- think strategically (macroperspective)
- think tactically (microperspective)
- think independently
- establish short- and long-term goals
- establish priorities
- organize their efforts and their materials
- manage time effectively
- think critically
- evaluate the pros and cons of choices
- develop pragmatic methods and techniques for attaining their objectives
- think and function sequentially
- draw reasonable conclusions from data
- react rationally to setbacks
- learn from their mistakes
- analyze problems and challenges
- search for underlying issues
- apply divide-and-conquer principles when solving problems

INDICATIONS OF DEFICIENCIES IN LOGICAL THINKING

- difficulty understanding concepts
- difficulty making predictions
- difficulty communicating ideas
- difficulty understanding cause-and-effect principles
- difficulty planning
- difficulty with organization
- difficulty managing time
- difficulty evaluating the pros and cons of choice
- difficulty establishing goals
- difficulty setting priorities
- difficulty identifying and analyzing underlying issues
- difficulty developing strategies
- difficulty evaluating issues critically
- difficulty perceiving how concepts and issues are linked
- difficulty making associations
- difficulty solving problems
- difficulty learning from mistakes and miscalculations
- difficulty handling setbacks
- difficulty perceiving the sequential progression of ideas
- difficulty drawing reasonable conclusions and inferences from direct and indirect information
- difficulty relating to future time
- use of non sequiturs (conclusions or inferences that do not follow from the premises or evidence) when expressing ideas verbally or in writing

ENHANCING THE ABILITY TO THINK LOGICALLY

- Play logic games that encourage your child to make associations and respond to "mind-teasers." (For example: "Why do you think Boy Scouts are taught how to make rope knots?")

- At a teacher supply store purchase developmentally appropriate materials, games, and software designed to stimulate logical thinking.
- From your child's teacher or resource specialist request materials designed to develop logical thinking.
- Encourage your child to analyze issues and problems encountered in everyday life and to develop logical solutions. (For example, "What would be a good strategy for preventing kids from experimenting with drugs?")
- Encourage your child to establish specific goals and priorities and to develop strategies for attaining the goals. (For example, "What would you need to do to make the varsity soccer team?")
- Encourage your child to evaluate critically relevant real-world issues. (For example, "Why is it important that we preserve our nat-

SEE: Apathy *(page 208)*; Aptitude *(page 15)*; Attention to Details *(page 223)*; Avoiding Responsibility *(page 227)*; Bouncing Back from Setbacks *(page 232)*; Conduct and Attitude *(page 235)*; Critical Thinking *(page 161)*; Dealing with Consequences *(page 241)*; Disorganization *(page 251)*; Essays and Essay Tests *(page 18)*; Fear of Failure, Success, and/or Competition *(page 383)*; Goal Setting *(page 165)*; Grades *(page 25)*; Identifying Important Information *(page 41)*; I'm Dumb Syndrome *(page 388)*; Intelligence *(page 45)*; Judgment *(page 260)*; Learning from Mistakes *(page 267)*; Mastery of Academic Content *(page 67)*; Math *(page 72)*; Passive Learning *(page 84)*; Planning *(page 176)*; Priorities *(page 180)*; Problem Solving *(page 185)*; Procrastination *(page 278)*; Reading Comprehension *(page 100)*; Strategic Thinking *(page 189)*; Teacher-Designed Tests *(page 132)*; Test Taking *(page 000)*; Time Management *(page 138)*; Underachievement *(page 143)*.

Planning

▲

Refers to the ability to create a practical and systematic strategy for attaining defined goals.

▲

School can be a nightmare for children with poor planning skills. To achieve academically, they must be able to define their objectives and develop a practical strategy for getting the job done. They must regulate themselves, work efficiently and effectively, manage time, and meet deadlines. These procedures require careful planning.

Learning-disabled students frequently have difficulty planning because their deficient academic skills can make it impossible for them to predict realistically how much time they need to complete their assignments and projects. Estimating whether it will take one hour or three hours to answer questions 1–9 at the end of chapter 4 in their science textbook can be an exercise in futility when children are struggling to decode words and retain information.

Children with learning problems are usually on the receiving end of a great deal of assistance. This support can make the difference between whether or not they master essential skills and are able to survive academically. The well-intentioned help and supervision, however, can also cause learning-disabled children to become excessively reliant on their parents, teachers, resource specialists, and tutors to do their planning for them. Continually supported children may never establish the habit of targeting their own personal goals or develop and execute a well-conceived plan for getting from point A to point B to point C.

Children who do not learn how to plan are at a distinct competitive disadvantage in school. Those who do not practice strategic thinking and tactical planning are at risk for becoming dependent on others to help them function. This learned helplessness cannot help but compound the already formidable academic challenges they face. Their reliance on others will undermine their self-confidence and encourage irresponsibility that could persist into adulthood, with disastrous educational, psychological, and vocational consequences.

CHARACTERISTICS OF CHILDREN WITH GOOD PLANNING SKILLS

Children who have learned how to plan consistently:

- establish personal short- and long-term goals
- set priorities
- manage time efficiently
- analyze and resolve problems and setbacks
- learn from mistakes and miscalculations
- anticipate and handle contingencies
- manage time effectively
- develop task-directed schedules
- sequence efforts
- meet deadlines
- organize themselves and materials
- apply basic cause-and-effect principles (e.g., If I do this, then this will happen.)
- discipline themselves
- attend to details
- fulfill the stated requirements and standards
- check for accuracy
- work independently
- think independently

Children who lack effective planning skills cannot possibly work up to their full potential. The consequences are predictable: disjointed effort, disorganization, incomplete assignments that do not conform to the teacher's explicit direction, missed deadlines, passive learning, irresponsibility, disinterest, and poor motivation.

In some instances, poor planning skills may be attributable to attention deficit/attention deficit hyperactivity disorder (ADD/ADHD). Children who have deficient impulse control and who are chronically distractible typically struggle with organization and time management. Unable to regulate themselves effectively, they spin their wheels but produce little or no forward momentum.

Many children who lack effective planning skills have not internalized a fundamental cause-and-effect principle: Academic achievement demands thorough preparation, careful scheduling, focused effort, good organization, and efficient management of time and materials. These students either fail to perceive, or consciously or unconsciously deny, the obvious link between poor planning and poor grades.

With systematic instruction, effective modeling, practice, patient feedback, and encouragement, all children can acquire better strategic-planning skills. They can learn how to create pragmatic strategies for completing their assignments and for creating more order in their lives. Even those who appear hopelessly disorganized and scattered can acquire more efficient planning skills if they receive good instruction and are guided toward the realization that effective planning can reduce their workload and produce pleasurable payoffs. The objective is to help children recognize that school success hinges on their being able to juggle the many demands they face every day. To meet these demands, they must be able to define their obligations, determine the time restraints, and prioritize and sequence their efforts.

As children become more adept at planning, their ability to handle challenges and problems and complete their work on schedule will improve. With achievement will come enhanced academic performance as well as enhanced motivation, effort, self-confidence, and self-reliance. The ultimate goal is for careful planning to become an imprinted, automatic response.

PROCEDURES FOR ENHANCING CHILDREN'S PLANNING SKILLS

1. Encourage your child to establish specific short- and long-term goals. Example: Create a form for recording targeted test, homework, and report-card grades for each subject.

2. Encourage your child to establish priorities. Example: Model how to create a hierarchy of what is most important in planning a trip.

3. Help your child develop a schedule. Example: Create a time-management form that allocates a specified time each day to defined school and at-home responsibilities, such as homework, Scouts, chores, etc.

4. Demonstrate methods for effective time-management. Example: Model how to estimate time required to complete pending projects.

5. Demonstrate how strategic planning is relevant to real-life situations. Example: Examine and list the steps required to complete a term paper, plan a party, or prepare for a vacation.

6. Encourage experimentation with different strategies for getting the job done. Example: Model how to create a task/time flowchart.

7. Encourage the use of checklists. Example: Demonstrate how to create a check-off form that indicates when each step of a project is completed.

8. Encourage the analysis of why a particular strategy worked or didn't work. Example: Develop a systematic plan for preparing more efficiently and effectively for tests.

9. Encourage the identification and analysis of strategies in content-area studies. Example: Examine the reasons why the colonialists' battle strategy was more effective than that of the British.

10. Encourage the incorporation of strategic thinking and planning skills into daily life. Example: Develop a plan for earning money for new skates.

SEE: Apathy *(page 208);* Attention Deficit/Attention Deficit Hyperactivity Disorder *(page 214);* Attention to Details *(page 223);* Avoiding Responsibility *(page 227);* Conduct and Attitude *(page 235);* Critical Thinking *(page 161);* Dealing with Consequences *(page 241);* Defense Mechanisms *(page 373);* Developmental Immaturity *(page 246);* Disorganization *(page 251);* Essays and Essay Tests *(page 18);* Fear of Failure, Success, and/or Competition *(page 383);* Goal Setting *(page 165);* Grades *(page 25);* I'm Dumb Syndrome *(page 388);* Incomplete Assignments *(page 256);* Judgment *(page 260);* Keeping Up with the Class *(page 51);* Language Arts *(page 58);* Learning from Mistakes *(page 267);* Logic *(page 171);* Parent-Child Conflict *(page 393);* Passive Learning *(page 84);* Performance Standards *(page 91);* Priorities *(page 180);* Problem Solving *(page 185);* Procrastination *(page 278);* Psychological Overlay and Psychological Problems *(page 399);* Recording Assignments *(page 107);* Resistance to Help *(page 282);* Self-concept *(page 410);* Self-control *(page 287);* Strategic Thinking *(page 189);* Study Interruptions *(page 122);* Study Skills *(page 127);* Teacher-Child Conflict *(page 293);* Teacher-Designed Tests *(page 132);* Test Anxiety *(page 420);* Time Management *(page 138);* Underachievement *(page 143);* Working Independently *(page 302).*

Priorities

▲

Refers to creating a hierarchy of what is important and a practical order for completing tasks and meeting obligations.

▲

Academic achievement is contingent on children being able to rank their responsibilities and obligations in order of descending or ascending importance. To attain their short- and long-term objectives, they must prioritize.

Successful students may not always be consciously aware that they are establishing priorities, but they intuitively apply this ordering principle whenever they are confronted with projects that require careful planning. Those who are conscientious and goal directed will rank studying for a science test ahead of going to a movie with their friends. They will also define and logically sequence the steps required to write a term paper or prepare for a final exam. They will prioritize how they allocate their free time and how they spend their money.

Children who have learning problems often do not develop the capacity to sequence their obligations. Everything is likely to seem like a priority when children feel overwhelmed by monumental academic challenges. They must complete their in-class work, pay attention, record their assignments, write neatly, check over their math problems for careless computational errors, proofread their essays for spelling and grammar errors, finish their homework, and submit their work on time. They must also somehow set aside sufficient time to read books for their book reports, study for their social-studies tests, and finish their term papers. To learning-disabled children, these are staggering obligations, and many of these children react by becoming anxious, emotionally stressed, and in some cases, scholastically dysfunctional. From their vantage point, being selective about what to do and when to do it is a luxury. Preoccupied with basic academic survival, these children are too enmeshed in the day-to-day struggle to recognize that by systematically prioritizing their responsibilities, they can make their lives easier.

Children who do not learn how to rank their obligations in a logical order are at risk for becoming reliant on their parents to monitor them. Seeing that their child is overwhelmed by his or her obligations, many of these justifiably concerned parents react by attempting to take ownership of their child's responsibilities. This intervention, albeit well intentioned, is likely to cause the child to become excessively dependent and increasingly dysfunctional. The consequences are predictable: Parents become enablers, and their children become helpless.

Given the formidable challenges that learning-disabled students face every day, it is vital that they be taught how to develop a practical and efficient plan for doing their work. This translates into showing them how to:

- define what needs to be done
- identify important and/or urgent obligations
- rank responsibilities and tasks in order of importance and/or urgency
- sequence commitments and effort strategically
- create a schedule
- establish realistic deadlines
- manage time efficiently

Children are faced with a myriad of in-school and at-home responsibilities. Those who cannot create a logical and practical system for sequencing these obligations and who cannot create a strategy for getting from point A to point B are going to be thwarted in school. They are also likely to be thwarted in life.

Children must be guided to two key insights: Some things are more important than others, and some things need to be done first. The integration of these two fundamental principals into their academic modus operandi will play a major role in determining whether or not they are successful in school. If they are to achieve in the scholastic arena, they must be clear about priorities. They must realize, and accept the fact, that studying for a science exam is more important than watching a TV sitcom or playing basketball with friends after school.

Prioritization skills can be easily taught if parents and teachers take the time to discuss, demonstrate, and model practical procedures for creating a rational order for successfully completing tasks. Showing children how to handle projects involving multiple components that must be carefully ordered provides invaluable hands-on experience. Helping them organize the steps involved in writing a term paper (i.e., doing library or on-line research, taking notes, putting information on index cards, organizing index cards, writing a first draft, making revisions, writing a second draft, and proofreading) provides another invaluable instructional opportunity. Planning at-home projects, such as building a birdhouse or making a quilt, also provides a context for children to practice prioritizing. Involving children in the process of planning a vacation, packing the car for a trip, or organizing a party can sharpen their sequencing skills. With effective and patient instruction, sufficient opportunities for practice, and affirmation for progress, children can assimilate the planning, organizational, and prioritization skills that are requisites to their being able to function in school at a level commensurate with their ability.

INDICATIONS OF DIFFICULTY ESTABLISHING PRIORITIES

- frustration
- confusion
- demoralization
- stress
- procrastination
- irresponsibility
- disorganization
- difficulty planning and scheduling
- difficulty with time management
- missed deadlines
- incomplete assignments
- resistance to doing homework
- complacency
- apathy
- helplessness
- defensiveness
- denial
- blaming
- difficulty learning from mistakes
- resistance to establishing goals
- incomplete assignments
- lack of motivation

- inattention to details
- difficulty studying efficiently
- difficulty working independently
- difficulty with problem solving
- inefficient learning
- difficulty keeping up with the class
- underachievement

SEE: Apathy *(page 208);* Avoiding Responsibility *(page 227);* Conduct and Attitude *(page 235);* Critical Thinking *(page 161);* Dealing with Consequences *(page 241);* Defense Mechanisms *(page 373);* Developmental Immaturity *(page 246);* Disorganization *(page 251);* Fear of Failure, Success, and/or Competition *(page 383);* Goal Setting *(page 165);* Grades *(page 25);* Identifying Important Information *(page 41);* I'm Dumb Syndrome *(page 388);* Incomplete Assignments *(page 256);* Judgment *(page 260);* Keeping Up with the Class *(page 51);* Learning from Mistakes *(page 267);* Logic *(page 171);* Parent-Child Conflict *(page 393);* Passive Learning *(page 84);* Performance Standards *(page 91);* Planning *(page 176);* Problem Solving *(page 185);* Procrastination *(page 278);* Recording Assignments *(page 107);* School Anxiety *(page 406);* Self-concept *(page 410);* Self-control *(page 287);* Strategic Thinking *(page 189);* Study Interruptions *(page 122);* Study Skills *(page 127);* Teacher-Child Conflict *(page 293);* Teacher-Designed Tests *(page 132);* Test Anxiety *(page 420);* Time Management *(page 138);* Underachievement *(page 143);* Working Independently *(page 302).*

Problem Solving

▲

Refers to the ability to handle and resolve rationally and constructively challenges, setbacks, mistakes, failures, and conflicts.

▲

Children who struggle with learning difficulties can easily become overwhelmed by the myriad problems they face every day. The challenge is especially acute when they cannot define their problems accurately, identify the causal factors, and develop viable solutions. The negative impact of continually receiving bad grades on essays is significantly magnified when children have no idea as to why the teacher is dissatisfied with their work or how to improve their performance. Can the problem be traced to careless errors that might be eliminated by taking the time to proofread more carefully? Do they need help with grammar and punctuation? Is their syntax boring? Do they have difficulty writing a powerful topic sentence, organizing their thoughts, or drawing convincing conclusions from the information they present? Because these students do not understand why things are "going wrong," they cannot address the issues and resolve the problem. This inability to get a handle on the underlying causal factors invariably produces frustration, demoralization, feelings of inadequacy and helplessness, damaged self-confidence, minimal effort, and diminished motivation.

Children who conclude that their problems are insurmountable are at risk for becoming academically and emotionally dysfunctional. To cope with their frustration and discouragement and to protect themselves from feeling incompetent, they often resort to maladaptive coping and defense mechanisms that may include apathy, procrastination, irresponsibility, denial, blaming, misbehavior, and deficient effort and motivation.

Whereas children who believe they can prevail over their problems are likely to continue battling, those who believe that their academic situation is hopeless are likely to shut down. They may lower their expectations and aspirations, throw in the towel, or substitute surrogates for academic achievement that may include sports, video-game competency, or gang associations. Others will become angry, depressed, and resistant. In extreme cases, these demoralized children may become rebellious, defiant, and delinquent.

A child who is experiencing difficulty in math and is convinced he cannot do the work might attempt to handle the problem by chronically "forgetting" to do his homework, hand in his assignments, or study for tests. He may attempt to camouflage his inadequacies by becoming the class clown. He may escape into daydreams when the teacher is explaining how to do problems that he cannot understand. He may complain of a stomachache or a sore throat and plead to stay home on days when he has to take a math test. These solutions are, of course, ineffectual, but most highly defended, emotionally vulnerable children are too enmeshed in their coping mechanisms to recognize the contradiction.

The common defense mechanisms to which most children resort actually call attention to the problems they are attempting to flee, but most struggling youngsters are so intent on protecting themselves that they do not recognize this irony. The illusion of having successfully defended themselves invariably shatters at report-card time.

Many parents and teachers believe that counterproductive behavior, such as laziness, procrastination, and irresponsibility, is the primary cause of poor school performance. Statements such as "If only she would do her work, she would do better in school" or "If he stopped daydreaming and concentrated in class, he would understand what he's expected to do" may appear accurate, but the statements are deceptively simplistic. In most instances, children's counterproductive behaviors are actually *symptoms* of specific underlying deficiencies that frequently include academic or study-skills deficits, learning disabilities, attention-deficit disorder, poor time management, disorganization, and diminished self-confidence. The detrimental behavior undoubtedly exacerbates the problem, but it is not the cause of the problem.

Demoralized children who cannot devise solutions to their problems often gravitate to other children who are struggling with similar issues. These youngsters may band together into a socially alienated and, in extreme cases, delinquent subculture that may signal its disaffection, frustration, and anger with distinctive and frequently grotesque clothing, hairstyles, tattoos, body piercing, and nihilistic behavior.

The antidote to allowing children to become overwhelmed and defeated by problems is to take the time to teach them how to:

- define their problems accurately
- identify the underlying causal factors
- brainstorm logical potential solutions
- experiment with solutions until one works

This divide-and-conquer procedure eliminates wheel spinning and reduces stress and anxiety. When children define the difficulty, identify the causative factors, and experiment with solutions, challenges that appeared overwhelming and insoluble become manageable.

Problems are an inescapable fact of life. Children who can step back, rationally analyze the situation, determine the factors responsible for the glitch, and implement a practical corrective strategy have a significant advantage over those who react mindlessly and impulsively. Their ability to solve problems logically and systematically is an invaluable asset that they will be able to use throughout life.

INDICATIONS OF DEFICIENT PROBLEM-SOLVING SKILLS

When confronted with a problem, my child:

- becomes overwhelmed
- attempts to run away
- blames others
- denies responsibility

- reacts defensively
- struggles to identify underlying causal factors
- thinks irrationally
- repeats the same mistakes
- has difficulty devising reasonable and rational solutions
- becomes frustrated and demoralized
- becomes paralyzed by stress and anxiety
- resorts to counterproductive compensatory behavior (procrastination, irresponsibility, lack of effort)
- makes chronically flawed decisions
- gives up easily
- works inefficiently
- becomes resigned to being inept
- loses self-confidence
- lowers expectations and aspirations

SEE: Apathy *(page 208)*; Aptitude *(page 15)*; Attention to Details *(page 223)*; Avoiding Responsibility *(page 227)*; Bouncing Back from Setbacks *(page 232)*; Conduct and Attitude *(page 235)*; Critical Thinking *(page 161)*; Dealing with Consequences *(page 241)*; Defense Mechanisms *(page 373)*; Disorganization *(page 251)*; Fear of Failure, Success, and/or Competition *(page 383)*; Goal Setting *(page 165)*; Identifying Important Information *(page 41)*; I'm Dumb Syndrome *(page 388)*; Incomplete Assignments *(page 256)*; Intelligence *(page 45)*; Judgment *(page 260)*; Keeping Up with the Class *(page 51)*; Learning from Mistakes *(page 267)*; Logic *(page 171)*; Math *(page 72)*; Parent-Child Conflict *(page 393)*; Passive Learning *(page 84)*; Planning *(page 176)*; Priorities *(page 180)*; Procrastination *(page 278)*; Psychological Overlay and Psychological Problems *(page 399)*; Reading Comprehension *(page 100)*; Resistance to Help *(page 282)*; School Anxiety *(page 406)*; Self-concept *(page 410)*; Self-control *(page 287)*; Strategic Thinking *(page 189)*; Teacher-Child Conflict *(page 293)*; Time Management *(page 138)*; Underachievement *(page 143)*; Working Independently *(page 302)*.

Strategic Thinking

▲

Refers to the ability to establish a logical and practical plan for attaining defined objectives, analyze and solve problems, apply cause-and-effect principles, handle setbacks, and learn from mistakes.

▲

Children with significant identified learning problems usually receive a wide range of assistance in school and at home. Empathetic classroom teachers make an extra effort to help them master skills, comprehend course content, and keep up with the class, and resource specialists provide remediation as well as practical assistance with assigned class work and homework. Most parents also furnish homework assistance at home, and in some cases, private tutors, educational therapists, and learning centers provide additional remedial support after school.

A steep price may be paid for supplying children with these overlapping safety nets. Struggling children who continually receive help and support can become academically and emotionally reliant on others to rescue them, solve their problems, manage their time, and take ownership of their obligations. These children are at risk for becoming passive and dependent learners who never develop their full range of intellectual abilities and problem-solving resources. The phenomenon of children becoming reliant on their parents, teachers, resource specialists, and tutors to help them handle life's challenges and conundrums is called *learned helplessness.*

Academic achievement hinges on children not only having the requisite skills to do their work and the willingness to expend the necessary effort but also on their being capable of using their intelligence strategically to get the job done. If a book report is due in two weeks, children who think strategically realize that they must schedule adequate time to read the book, write a first draft, edit, write a second draft, and proofread. To complete the assignment, they may have to forgo watching a favorite TV show or playing baseball in the park after school. This self-discipline and pragmatic, tactical utilization of intelligence are usually the fulcrum in the scholastic-achievement equation.

Successful students who think strategically share key traits. They consistently:

- handle challenges
- solve problems
- think analytically
- define their goals
- establish their priorities
- focus their efforts
- neutralize obstacles
- discipline themselves
- study effectively
- develop an efficient plan for getting from point A to point B

Being intelligent does not guarantee that a child will think and act smart. Bright children may be capable of doing advanced algebra problems in fourth grade, but they may receive poor grades in math because they don't submit their homework assignments on time or take the time to check over their work for computational errors. This nonstrategic behavior underscores the essential difference between *inherited intelligence* and *applied intelligence*.

Students who think strategically may not be the brightest children in their class, but they often rank among the highest achievers. They use to the fullest advantage their inherited abilities, and they get the job done.*

When confronted with a problem or challenge, children who think strategically will, on either a conscious or unconscious level, ask themselves seven key questions:

---

*Whereas IQ is for the most part inherited, strategic thinking is primarily acquired through observation and by modeling behavior. Many educators believe that IQ is 80 percent inherited and 20 percent influenced by environmental factors. Neurological research strongly suggests that mental stimulation during the formative years can play a significant role in enhancing IQ.

1. What am I trying to achieve?
2. What possible problems might I face?
3. What do I already know about dealing with this?
4. How can I break this problem down into manageable pieces? (the divide-and-conquer principle)
5. How can I avoid mistakes?
6. How can I increase my chances of success?
7. If I need help, whom should I ask?

These questions usually become an automatic, conditioned response to any presenting problem or challenge, and in many cases, children are not even aware that they are asking the questions.

The strategic student whose goal is to get an A on a social-studies test would automatically apply time-management, organization, and test-preparation skills that have proved effective in the past. If her study methods have not produced the desired payoffs, she would objectively analyze and evaluate the procedures, learn from her past experience and miscalculations, and either modify her test-preparation strategy or develop a new and more effective strategy.

Children who think strategically realize that the shortest distance between two points is a straight line, but they also recognize that the path to their objective is not always straight and direct and that they may need to make detours and interim stops along the way. They understand, and accept the fact, that basic cause-and-effect principles govern what happens in school and in life. They also recognize that goal setting and achievement are intrinsically linked and that a short-term goal such as an A on the next math test is a stepping-stone to achieving their long-term goal, which might be a grade-point average sufficient to be accepted at UCLA or Notre Dame.

Having defined their goals, strategic students voluntarily commit the time and effort required to attain the objectives. If they suffer a setback, they assess the situation rationally and make the requisite strategic adjustments so that they can avoid repeating the mistake. This capacity to think analytically and learn from miscalculations is a distinctive benchmark of strategic thinking.

A strategic high-school student studying for a biology exam would recognize that her teacher has stressed ecology in class lectures. When preparing for the test, she would focus on understanding relevant environmental issues and she would link information in her notes and textbook with the ecological issues her teacher has emphasized. She would review her previous tests and quizzes, carefully consider the teacher's "hints" about what is important, and anticipate the questions that are likely to be asked on the test, target the grade she wants, and allocate the time required to study effectively and comprehensively.

Non-strategic students handle academic challenges very differently. When preparing for a test, they would probably not carefully consider information that their teacher has emphasized in class, and they would probably disregard her hints. They might forget to attach a bibliography to a history term paper, check over their math problems for errors, or review newly assigned vocabulary words before a Spanish test.

Underachieving students characteristically manifest a significant discrepancy between their IQ (intelligence quotient) and their SIQ (strategic intelligence quotient).* Whereas an IQ test is designed to measure the *potential to succeed academically,* it does not assess the *practical application of intelligence,* nor does it indicate whether students are actually utilizing their full intellectual abilities. In fact, the phenomenon of underachievement reflects an incongruity between *potential ability* and *applied ability.*

Unfortunately, many bright, capable students never fully develop their strategic intelligence. Students who float through school in a *cerebral haze* quickly become habituated to passive, ineffectual thinking. The long-term academic and vocational implications of this cerebral dulling can be disastrous. Such students are on a collision course with the grading system and will be jolted by an immutable fact of academic life: Teachers give A's and B's to those who think effectively, study consciously, learn actively and enthusiasti-

---

*This is a term coined by the author. No formal test of SIQ currently exists.

cally, handle challenges, solve problems effectively, and consistently produce quality work.

Children with learning problems are at particular risk for failing to develop their strategic thinking skills. Strategic intelligence requires an awareness of not only *present time* but also of *future time*. Preoccupied with handling constant and immediate academic crises and challenges, many learning-disabled children never learn how to plan ahead. This is especially true when the adults providing them with assistance do all the planning and fail to involve them actively in the process of identifying and handling academic challenges.

The antidote for deficient strategic thinking is obvious: Parents and teachers should encourage children with learning problems to define personal short-term goals, such as a B on the next spelling test, and long-term goals, such as a B− in math, and they should then help them create pragmatic strategies for attaining their goals. Parents and teachers must also teach children how to define their problems accurately and how to develop a logical plan for solving these problems. With sufficient practice and effective guidance, children can acquire more effective strategic-thinking skills. Once they begin to experience the many benefits of their possessing such skills, they will begin to perceive themselves as more competent, and their self-confidence, expectations, and aspirations will expand commensurately.

CHARACTERISTICS OF CHILDREN WHO THINK STRATEGICALLY

These children typically:

- focus on getting the job done efficiently and with a minimum amount of grief
- establish short- and long-term goals
- establish priorities
- focus intellectual and physical energy on attaining defined objectives
- calculate the odds
- plan ahead

- manage time effectively
- meet deadlines
- create a logical and practical strategy for attaining their goals
- establish new goals once they attain an objective
- accept responsibility for their actions
- analyze and neutralize challenges and obstacles
- consider the potential consequences of their actions
- have positive expectations and aspirations
- anticipate potential problems
- handle glitches and setbacks
- bounce back from defeats
- learn from mistakes and successes
- utilize available resources
- accept help when appropriate
- are motivated and enthusiastic
- weigh the pluses and minuses of options
- avoid unnecessary risks
- make wise choices

BEHAVIORAL INDICATIONS OF DEFICIENT STRATEGIC THINKING

- repetition of the same mistakes
- disorganization
- procrastination
- unclear thinking when upset or frustrated
- failure to analyze the pros and cons of choices
- failure to develop rational strategies for solving problems
- difficulty bouncing back from setbacks
- passive learning
- difficulty working independently
- defensiveness
- denial of responsibility for actions
- failure to establish long-term goals
- failure to establish interim goals
- failure to set priorities

- failure to plan ahead
- failure to manage time effectively
- difficulty estimating time required to do work
- unrealistic expectations
- procrastination
- failure to use a schedule
- failure to record assignments consistently
- submission of incomplete assignments
- submission of late assignments
- excessive stress when confronted with problems and challenges
- unrealistic scheduling of too many things to do at once
- chronic lateness

ATTITUDINAL INDICATIONS OF DEFICIENT STRATEGIC THINKING

Students typically:

- do not think in terms of cause and effect (consequences)
- are unmotivated
- deny problems
- deny responsibility
- resist help
- avoid confronting problems
- blame others
- avoid challenges
- resist developing new skills and talents
- lack faith in their ability to succeed and prevail over problems
- give up easily
- do not take pride in doing a first-rate job
- do not take pride in accomplishments
- are unwilling to suspend immediate gratification in order to attain their long-term objectives

SEE: Apathy *(page 208)*; Aptitude *(page 15)*; Attention to Details *(page 223)*; Avoiding Responsibility *(page 227)*; Bouncing Back from Setbacks *(page 232)*; Conduct and Attitude *(page 235)*; Critical Thinking *(page 161)*; Dealing with Consequences *(page 241)*; Developmental Immaturity *(page 246)*; Disorganization *(page 251)*; Fear of Failure, Success, and/or Competition *(page 383)*; Goal Setting *(page 165)*; Grades *(page 25)*; Identifying Important Information *(page 41)*; Incomplete Assignments *(page 256)*; Intelligence *(page 45)*; Judgment *(page 260)*; Keeping Up with the Class *(page 51)*; Learning from Mistakes *(page 267)*; Logic *(page 171)*; Mastery of Academic Content *(page 67)*; Parent-Child Conflict *(page 393)*; Passive Learning *(page 84)*; Peer Pressure *(page 272)*; Planning *(page 176)*; Priorities *(page 180)*; Problem Solving *(page 185)*; Procrastination *(page 278)*; Psychological Overlay and Psychological Problems *(page 399)*; Resistance to Help *(page 282)*; Self-concept *(page 410)*; Self-control *(page 287)*; Study Interruptions *(page 122)*; Teacher-Child Conflict *(page 293)*; Time Management *(page 138)*; Underachievement *(page 143)*; Working Independently *(page 302)*.

BEHAVIOR

Exasperated teachers and desperate parents who lack a precise understanding about why an academically deficient child is acting out often resort to labels such as "unmotivated," "immature," "poorly prepared," "irresponsible," "having an attitude," or "oppositional." These descriptions may be quite accurate, but the labels offer little insight into what needs to be done to reorient the struggling child's counterproductive behaviors and attitudes.

Despite compelling evidence that effective learning assistance can significantly reduce the incidence of acting-out behavior, many struggling children are essentially left to their own devices in school because they do not qualify for special-education programs. When these children are deprived of needed help, their learning deficiencies often become increasingly debilitating and intractable. Resistance to help, self-concept damage, frustration, discouragement, depression, hostility, truancy, and antisocial behavior are common consequences of this neglect.

Children struggling with significant learning problems who are not provided with effective remedial help are destined to spend twelve agonizing, nonproductive years in school. Every day, these children are forced to confront their inadequacies. By fourth grade, many have already been so badly scarred and demoralized by their repeated negative school experiences that they essentially shut down in school and simply go through the motions of being educated. The damage to their self-image is often profound and in some cases irreversible.

Once children conclude that they're "dumb" and that their situation in school is hopeless, they are on a track that leads to limited educational advancement and ultimately menial, nonrewarding jobs or no jobs at all. In some cases, this track can also lead to encounters with the criminal-justice system. That 90 percent of the adult inmates in American prisons have learning problems underscores the potentially disastrous repercussions of failing to address the legitimate educational needs of children who are being psychologically maimed by school failure.

Defeated learners who become emotionally defended, school-phobic, and resistant often vent their demoralization and anger through self-sabotaging behavior. They may decide not to study because they are convinced that effort is futile. They may not complete their homework or submit their assignments on time. They may act out and become disruptive and disrespectful. They may become the class clown or the class bully. Those who are less overt and demonstrative about expressing their pain and frustration may simply retreat into their daydreams until the bell finally rings at the end of the school day.

Understanding the factors responsible for the maladaptive attitudes and actions of an academically demoralized child is the critical first step in reorienting the counterproductive deportment. In most instances behavior problems that are linked to learning problems will diminish once struggling children begin to experience success in school. As their academic performance and self-confidence improve, their conduct will also usually improve.

There are no iron-clad formulas for dealing with behavior and attitude problems, but there are steps parents can take to discourage the misconduct. These steps include making certain that:

- underlying learning problems are accurately identified
- adequate remedial support is provided in school and/or after school
- reasonable classroom and homework accommodations are made until the child is able to catch up with the class
- reasonable and consistently applied performance, behavior, and attitude guidelines and standards are established at home

- repeated opportunities for success are carefully orchestrated
- praise, affirmation, and encouragement for even small accomplishments are provided in school and at home

Specific behavior and attitude issues that might be magnifying your
child's academic difficulties are examined in the following section.

Anger

▲

*Refers to upset activated by an emotional or situational trigger. When
openly expressed, anger may manifest as frustration, hostility, resentment, tantrums, rebelliousness, rage, bullying, antisocial behavior, or
resistance to authority. When repressed, anger may cause depression,
social alienation, isolation, or fantasized violence.*

▲

Struggling children who are embarrassed by their classroom performance and grades and who are identified and segregated because
of their learning inadequacies are at risk for becoming frustrated,
discouraged, upset, and angry. Those who believe that their academic situation is hopeless are likely to conclude that effort is futile.
Some may react to their frustration and discouragement with periodic outbursts and tantrums. Others may become actively or passively resistant to help or authority. Those who cannot handle the
setbacks and demoralization are at risk for becoming increasingly
dysfunctional. As their emotional resilience is stretched to the breaking point, they may also become increasingly angry.

Occasional outbursts in reaction to frustration can be cathartic.
Children who sporadically erupt after experiencing a setback and
whose anger then quickly dissipates may actually be handling their
upset better than those who warehouse their upsets and are unable

to acknowledge or express their anger. Recurring rage and persistent hostility, however, are red flags signaling that a child's psychological coping mechanisms are being overwhelmed.

Many children express their anger through counterproductive behavior. They may shut down emotionally and academically and refuse to study or do homework assignments. They may act irresponsibly, procrastinate, blame others, complain, whine, resist authority, or strike out at siblings. As the frustration takes its toll, their self-confidence will erode, and their pain will warp their perceptions about themselves and their abilities.

Children enmeshed in a cycle of upset, frustration, and chronic explosive anger may be described as having a short fuse, a nasty temper, or a volatile personality. Those who cannot manage their anger and express it nondestructively are at risk for making flawed, impulsive decisions that could cause problems throughout life and ultimately cost them their jobs, marriages, and friendships.

Not all academically demoralized children become overtly angry. Some are able to handle the challenges and stress they face in school better than others. Despite setbacks and discouragement, these youngsters continue to work diligently. The likelihood of perseverance in the face of adversity obviously increases when students who learn differently are provided with effective remedial assistance and ongoing emotional support from their parents, teachers, and resource specialists.

Unless the academic deficiencies of struggling students are addressed, the sense of despair and the potential for anger will increase, as will the incidence of defensive, nonadaptive, and self-sabotaging behavior. Ironically, children who feel hopelessly inadequate often act in ways that reinforce their negative perception of themselves. They may flagrantly break the rules, associate with counterculture youngsters, dress in ways that set them apart from the mainstream, and become increasingly alienated from their families and society. In extreme cases, these youngsters may express their hostility through antisocial or delinquent behavior.

Angry children tend to gravitate toward other angry children for the same reasons that achieving children band together. They seek out those who share the same experiences and can relate to their feelings. Their peer group offers comfort, support, and a sense of identity.

Anger is not always explosive. When frustrated and demoralized children deny, repress, or disown their negative feelings, their anger implodes. These imploding emotions are highly toxic, emotionally corrosive, and academically debilitating and typically trigger depression.

Angry children often unconsciously express the warehoused hostility through passive aggression. Common manifestations of repressed or camouflaged anger include:

- teasing or sarcasm
- sabotaging or striking out at others in nonobvious ways
- camouflaged acts of cruelty

Whether expressed, repressed, or disguised, chronic anger can immobilize children psychologically and academically, and the negative emotions invariably create stress and unpleasantness for everyone who interacts with these youngsters.

BEHAVIORS AND ATTITUDES ASSOCIATED WITH IMPLODING ANGER

- depression
- listlessness
- social isolation or alienation
- fearfulness
- chronic fatigue
- defensiveness
- chronic irresponsibility
- chronic self-consciousness
- unwillingness to communicate
- academic immobilization
- negative expectations
- chronic fearfulness
- emotional withdrawal

- lowered aspirations
- diminished motivation and effort
- fear of failure, success, and/or competition
- self-sabotaging actions and attitudes
- diminished self-confidence
- diminished self-esteem
- acting out
- blaming
- irresponsibility
- sarcasm
- resistance to authority
- resistance to help
- complaining
- academic immobilization
- diminished self-confidence
- excessive sensitivity
- diminished effort
- reduced expectations and aspiration
- passive resistance
- passive aggression
- rebelliousness
- violent fantasies
- self-pity
- manipulative behavior

Some children cope with their anger by escaping into a violent fantasy world. (Video games offer a highly accessible means of acting out brutal fantasies.) Those who are preoccupied with violence are signaling that their rage could detonate, with catastrophic consequences. The danger signals must be recognized and addressed by parents and teachers before children become violent. Intervention by a mental-health professional is imperative.

To hide feelings of ineptitude, angry, academically demoralized children often acquire elaborate compensatory behaviors that may include procrastination, complaining, and dependency. Because intense negative emotions are disconcerting to acknowledge, these children can become so adept at hiding, denying, or disowning their underlying feelings that even mental-health professionals may not recognize their inner turmoil.

Children who feel guilty about their anger often perceive themselves as being "bad." Unless there is effective mental health intervention, the pattern of upset and frustration followed by either explosions or implosions of anger and self-sabotaging behavior and guilt could persist into adulthood.

Chronic anger rarely disappears of its own accord. It may assume different forms—hitting, bullying, self-sabotage, vandalism, sadism, violent fantasies, depression, stealing, cutting school, lying—but the hostility will usually continue to manifest itself in one way or another until the feelings and causative factors have been identified, examined, and resolved.

Children who have a genetically based predisposition toward anger may require intensive behavior-modification therapy and/or pharmacological controls. Whatever the source of the anger, the sooner intervention is provided, the lower the risk that the child will make tragically flawed life-altering decisions.

Anger attributable to learning problems can be exacerbated by other factors, which include:

- poor family communication
- continual dissension at home
- divorce
- inadequately defined values, performance guidelines, and expectations
- belittling parental feedback
- physical or psychological abuse
- inconsistently enforced family rules
- unrealistic expectations and standards
- sibling rivalry

When children are struggling concurrently with family problems and learning issues, such as dyslexia or attention deficit hyperactivity disorder, the potential for frustration, demoralization, exploding or imploding anger, and depression increases. To treat the learning problem exclusively without addressing the psychological and family issues is likely to be ineffectual.

COMMON SOURCES OF ANGER

- learning problems
- academic frustration
- repeated setbacks
- feelings of inadequacy
- feelings of despair and hopelessness
- family dysfunction
- emotional conflict and turmoil
- excessive or unrealistic parental expectations
- inadequate coping mechanisms
- temperamental, genetically based predisposition

COMMON RED-FLAG MANIFESTATIONS OF ANGER

- highly aggressive behavior
- tantrums
- rage
- profanity
- belittling of others
- prejudice
- jealousy
- teasing
- sarcasm
- cruelty
- stress and anxiety
- active or passive resistance to authority
- rebelliousness

- preoccupation with violence
- rigid judgmental values
- intolerance
- paranoid behavior (lurking enemies)
- bullying
- sadism
- chronic fighting
- prejudice
- vandalism
- stealing
- cutting school
- lying
- obsessive-compulsive behavior (rigid and ritualistic mannerisms)
- warped perceptions
- identification with antisocial groups

SEE: Apathy *(page 208)*; Avoiding Responsibility *(page 227)*; Bouncing Back from Setbacks *(page 232)*; Conduct and Attitude *(page 235)*; Dealing with Consequences *(page 241)*; Defense Mechanisms *(page 373)*; Depression *(page 378)*; Fear of Failure, Success, and/or Competition *(page 383)*; Grades *(page 25)*; I'm Dumb Syndrome *(page 388)*; Judgment *(page 260)*; Keeping Up with the Class *(page 51)*; Logic *(page 171)*; Parent-Child Conflict *(page 393)*; Performance Standards *(page 91)*; Problem Solving *(page 185)*; Psychological Overlay and Psychological Problems *(page 399)*; Resistance to Help *(page 282)*; School Anxiety *(page 406)*; Self-concept *(page 410)*; Self-control *(page 287)*; Strategic Thinking *(page 189)*; Teacher-Child Conflict *(page 293)*; Underachievement *(page 143)*.

Apathy

▲

Refers to a lack of motivation and goal-directed behavior. Character-ized by passive thinking and learning, reduced effort, diminished self-confidence, negative associations with learning, and possible depression.

▲

Children are genetically programmed to learn and assimilate infor-mation. To function effectively in the world, they must develop skills that are valued by society and be able to use their intelligence to solve problems and attain their goals. The basic instinct to acquire knowl-edge is infused into their DNA.

When children become apathetic about learning and perceive no payoff for academic achievement, red flags are flapping. Apathy is unnatural and symptomatic of an underlying problem that needs to be identified and addressed.

Skills and knowledge are acquired sequentially and in conform-ity with genetically programmed developmental stages. Children learn to count in preschool. They make their first tentative efforts at writing their names in kindergarten and typically learn to read words and simple sentences in first grade. The progression from the basic decoding of isolated letters, sound blends, and words to advanced reading-comprehension skills follows a predictable timetable. If the schedule breaks down, parents and teachers have a legitimate cause for concern.

As children acquire new skills, they acquire confidence in them-selves. Their academic accomplishments generate pride, which in turn stimulates the desire to acquire additional skills and experience more success. When children become apathetic, the causative factors must be identified and addressed, or the complacency could become an entrenched habit that persists throughout life.

Several factors can cause children to become apathetic learners. These include:

Inferior Teaching

Parents should be on the alert if their child begins to lose enthusiasm for learning. The first step in addressing the problem is to observe in the classroom and assess the quality of instruction.* Unfortunately, some teachers haven't a clue about how to teach dynamically and creatively and do little more than hand out an endless stream of worksheets that they require their students to complete robotically. Mind-numbing instruction can obviously cause children to become passive, apathetic learners.

Parents who conclude that their child's apathy is attributable to deficient teaching should discuss their concerns with the principal. If the situation cannot be rectified, they should request that their child be transferred to a different class.

Family Values

The impetus to learn can be undermined when a child's family, sub-culture, and peers ascribe little importance to academic achievement. Parents who do not read to their children, encourage discussions of current events and the day's experiences at the dinner table, express interest in what is being taught in school, and affirm academic successes are clearly communicating that they devalue education.

Learning Problems

Identified or unidentified learning problems can cause children to become apathetic. Children who struggle to read, comprehend, recall, and express their ideas are clearly at risk for becoming discouraged and demoralized. Dispirited learners who believe they are incapable of learning often counterproductively compensate by tuning out and

---

*Most teachers do not object to having parents observe their class, assuming that the proposed observation is approved and scheduled in advance. If the teacher is resistant, parents should consult the principal and explain their concerns and reasons for wanting to observe their child in class.

daydreaming. Some may misbehave and actively resist doing their work. Others may simply shut down and become passive and complacent. These children may not actively rebel, but they often lower their expectations and aspirations. Appearing lazy, uninvolved, and intellectually dulled, they become habituated to expending minimal effort. These behaviors are red flags. If an apathetic child is suspected of having a learning disability and if the child has not yet been diagnostically evaluated to determine eligibility for special-education resources, the child's parents should insist on an assessment.

Psychological Factors

Emotional conflict and/or family problems can also trigger apathy. Children who cannot handle the crises and stresses at home may attempt to cope with their pain, anger, unhappiness, and depression by shutting down emotionally, tuning out in school, and retreating into a world of fantasies or daydreams.

Angry, guilt-ridden, alienated, insecure, and/or depressed children can become consumed by their personal problems. Academic achievement becomes secondary. As these children rarely feel deserving of success, they often acquire self-defeating attitudes and behavior that impede academic achievement.

Whereas children who have a positive self-concept are typically enthusiastic learners who delight in acquiring new skills and learning new information, children who don't feel good about themselves are often preoccupied by protecting themselves psychologically. They may express their pain by striking out at others, sabotaging themselves, or walling off their feelings. Enthusiasm for learning is an emotion that academically demoralized children rarely experience.

Cultural or Environmental Factors

Children crave their peers' acceptance and praise. Most children, especially teenagers, desperately want to identify with a group. They may want to be perceived as athletes, skateboarders, surfers, scholastic achievers, musicians, or outcasts. If a child's peer group values scholastic effort and skill acquisition, the child is likely to share these values. Conversely, if a child's peer group demeans academic success, the child is likely to disavow achievement in school. This usually leads to complacency and, in extreme cases, apathy or rebellion.

The *academic apathy loop* can be represented graphically:

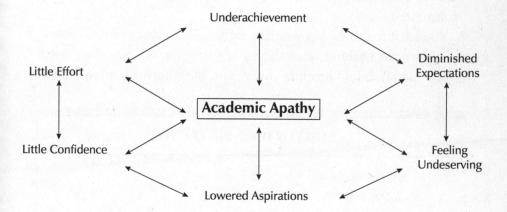

The arrows in this diagram point in both directions to underscore how each component in the loop can reciprocally affect the others.

The most effective way to break this negative cycle is for parents and teachers to orchestrate repeated successes for unmotivated, marginally performing children. The earlier this process begins, the better. This intervention strategy is predicated on six basic principles of human behavior:

- Satisfaction and pride in a job well done produce pleasant feelings.
- Success enhances a child's self-concept.
- Success is habit-forming and stimulates the desire for more success.
- Achieving students identify with and seek out other achieving students to be their friends and peers.
- Peer group support for scholastic achievement motivates scholastic achievement.

- Parents and teachers can play a pivotal, proactive role in positively altering a child's self-concept.

When children become apathetic, the underlying academic and/or psychological issues that are undermining their enthusiasm for learning and impeding their academic achievement must be resolved. Children who remain chronically apathetic and who consciously or unconsciously act in ways that guarantee underachievement may require both learning assistance and counseling from a mental-health professional.

Academic apathy is a warning signal. The crossing gate is down, red lights are flashing, and alarms are ringing. Disregarding these danger signals could produce disastrous, life-altering consequences.

CAUSES OF LEARNING APATHY

- inadequate teaching
- learning problems
- emotional problems
- family problems
- poor self-esteem
- family values that deemphasize educational achievement

SYMPTOMS OF ACADEMIC APATHY

- minimal effort
- passive thinking and learning
- procrastination
- chronic forgetfulness
- resistance
- absence of personal short- and long-term goals
- lack of enthusiasm and zest
- frustration

- discouragement
- demoralization
- poor planning
- irresponsibility
- difficulty prioritizing
- difficulty with time management
- inattention to details
- inaccurate work
- rationalizations for poor performance
- avoidance of challenging situations
- lack of pride
- deficient self-confidence
- low self-esteem
- lethargy
- resistance to help or advice
- helplessness and excessive dependency
- resistance to working independently
- blaming
- complaining
- excessive time spent watching TV or socializing
- reduced curiosity
- feelings of worthlessness and being undeserving of success
- rejection of family values
- resistance to accepting reasonable performance standards and guidelines
- identification with a peer group that belittles scholastic achievement
- emotional detachment
- contention that school is dumb
- contention that skills being taught are irrelevant
- depression
- reluctance to accept challenges
- fear of competition
- fear of failure or success
- lowered expectations and aspirations
- diminished self-confidence
- retreat into daydreams or fantasies

SEE: Attention to Details *(page 223)*; Avoiding Responsibility *(page 227)*; Conduct and Attitude *(page 235)*; Critical Thinking *(page 161)*; Defense Mechanisms *(page 373)*; Depression *(page 378)*; Developmental Immaturity *(page 246)*; Disorganization *(page 251)*; Fear of Failure, Success, and/or Competition *(page 383)*; Goal Setting *(page 165)*; Grades *(page 25)*; I'm Dumb Syndrome *(page 388)*; Incomplete Assignments *(page 256)*; Judgment *(page 260)*; Keeping Up with the Class *(page 51)*; Note Taking *(page 79)*; Parent-Child Conflict *(page 393)*; Passive Learning *(page 84)*; Peer Pressure *(page 272)*; Performance Standards *(page 91)*; Planning *(page 176)*; Priorities *(page 180)*; Procrastination *(page 278)*; Problem Solving *(page 185)*; Psychological Overlay and Psychological Problems *(page 399)*; Resistance to Help *(page 282)*; School Anxiety *(page 406)*; Self-concept *(page 410)*; Self-control *(page 287)*; Strategic Thinking *(page 189)*; Study Interruptions *(page 122)*; Study Skills *(page 127)*; Teacher-Child Conflict *(page 293)*; Time Management *(page 138)*; Underachievement *(page 143)*; Working Independently *(page 302)*.

Attention Deficit Disorder/Attention Deficit Hyperactivity Disorder (ADD/ADHD)

▲

Refers to difficulty filtering out distractions, controlling one's body, staying on task, inhibiting impulses, and focusing attention.

▲

Children who have difficulty staying focused and controlling their bodies are at a major disadvantage in a highly structured and regimented academic environment. These children are rarely able to function in school at a level commensurate with their ability. Some are chronically inattentive and distractible. Others are also hyperactive (frenetic, seemingly purposeless body movements).

The terms attention-deficit disorder (ADD) and attention deficit hyperactivity disorder (ADHD) were created to differentiate the two conditions. This terminology has recently been modified in the *Diagnostic Statistical Manual* (DSM4), a reference book that describes medical and psychological conditions and provides diagnostic codes for physicians, psychologists, and health-care providers. The following terms are currently used to describe concentration deficits:

- ADHD Inattentive Type
- ADHD Hyperactive-impulsive Type
- ADHD Combined Type
- ADHD NOS (Not Otherwise Specified)

In effect, the diagnostic description ADD has been replaced by ADHD with specific descriptive qualifiers.

In many cases, ADHD is compounded by specific learning disabilities linked to the inefficient neurological processing of sensory data. The concentration deficits may affect academic performance in all subjects or may manifest exclusively in one or two specific areas. For example, a child with ADHD may be able to focus when doing math because of a natural aptitude or interest in the subject area. The same child, however, may be chronically inattentive when reading a textbook or writing an essay. If the child has dyslexia, the ADHD is likely to exacerbate reading and writing problems by making it difficult for the child to concentrate when decoding (deciphering sounds, letters, and words) and encoding (using words to express ideas and communicate verbally or in writing).

Children with ADHD who continually struggle in school frequently develop negative associations with learning, and their frenetic and impulsive behavior often presents as misconduct. Their behavior can disturb the class and create significant stress for teachers and parents. Because children with ADHD are frequently censured, they are at risk for becoming frustrated and demoralized and, in some cases, angry and resentful. The anger may explode in the

form of acting-out behavior, resistance to authority, or rebelliousness. The anger may also implode and trigger depression.

ADHD children are frequently intelligent and creative but
rarely function in school at a level commensurate with their ability.
Their marginal academic performance often triggers feelings of inadequacy that could persist throughout life. Continual criticism,
reprimands, and punishment may cause these youngsters to conclude that they are intrinsically "bad."

Whereas ADHD can magnify perceptual-processing difficulties,
learning problems can, in turn, magnify the effects of ADHD. Reading problems are invariably compounded when children have chronic
difficulty in sitting still and staying on task.

Conversely, the struggle to sit still may be compounded by
chronic difficulty decoding words efficiently. In effect, one condition
exacerbates the other. This interplay can be graphically represented:*

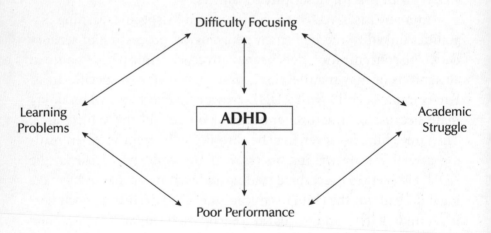

The arrows in the diagram point in both directions to underscore how each condition can reciprocally affect the others.

---

*ADHD is included as a dysfunction covered under the ADA (Americans with Dis-
abilities Act) and Section 504 of the Rehabilitation Act and may warrant special in-class accommodations. See Appendix I for a brief description of these laws. Parents are advised to
request the school district's Parents' Rights Manual. They may also refer to *Finding Help
When Your Child Is Struggling in School* (Lawrence J. Greene, Western Publishing, 1998) for a
more complete discussion of federally mandated children's rights and parents' legal options.

It is estimated that from 5 to 10 percent of the children in American classrooms have ADHD in one form or another. The figures vary depending on the diagnostic criteria, perceptions, and biases of those making the diagnosis. Some professionals in the fields of education, psychology, and medicine contend that ADHD is overdiagnosed and that perfectly normal children are being medicated to treat a condition they may not actually have. These professionals argue that many bright children are naturally exuberant and that these children can easily become distracted and bored in school, especially when the instruction is inadequate. Daydreaming, playing with a pencil, or disturbing others may simply be coping mechanisms that children use to handle mind-dulling teaching and curriculum.

Behaviors commonly associated with ADHD include:

- impulsivity
- distractibility
- deportment problems
- inattention to details
- difficulty understanding and following written and verbal directions
- disorganization
- procrastination
- improperly recorded assignments
- missed deadlines
- sloppy, incomplete, or inaccurate work

Chronic concentration deficits can obviously create major impediments when children are required to do work they find uninteresting or difficult. Attempting to keep distractible, inattentive, and impulsive children on task while they complete a page of repetitive math problems or diagram sentences can be a major challenge for teachers and for parents monitoring homework.

There are ironies associated with ADHD. Some children are unable to sustain their attention for more than a few seconds when doing schoolwork but can concentrate for hours when playing a video game. This selective capacity to stay focused suggests that high-interest, engaging activities can, in some cases, offset the effects of ADHD.

Most ADHD children have significant difficulty handling challenging, repetitive, detail-oriented academic tasks that demand sustained, focused concentration, effort, and self-discipline. A traditional "prescription" for controlling ADHD in the classroom is to impose additional structure and external control and create a learning environment with few distractions. A teacher might, for example, place the ADHD child near her desk or designate a "quiet place" where the child is sent when he becomes excessively hyperactive or unmanageable. Some teachers use hand signals to alert ADHD children when they are becoming inattentive.

Children with concentration deficits generally function more productively when:

- external stimulation and distractions are kept to a minimum
- behavior guidelines are clearly defined and consistently enforced
- appropriate and reasonable performance standards are established
- immediate feedback is offered in a nondemeaning manner
- affirmation for improved performance and behavior is provided
- individualized, creative, and dynamic teaching strategies are employed
- academic requirements are calibrated to the child's individual needs
- concentration expectations and demands are calibrated to the child's individual needs

Limiting stimulation, however, is not always an effective solution in handling ADHD. Some students drift off and become even more distracted and inattentive when deprived of stimulation. These children, who are often very bright, creative, and intellectually curious, actually do better in an interactive, dynamic classroom context that is not tightly controlled and rigid. They are able to focus because their brains are actively engaged in learning, and they become inattentive when they're required to do repetitive, mindless work. Nonetheless, ADHD students must be able to handle tedious assignments that require perseverance and self-discipline. To work up to their full potential, they must be capable of regulating themselves, staying on task, and attending to details even when the instruction and curriculum are not particularly stimulating.

Chronic inattentiveness and hyperactivity can create major stress in the classroom, and even dedicated teachers who are supportive and empathetic can be overwhelmed by this stress. In a room of thirty students, each child should receive approximately 3 percent of the teacher's time. The ADHD child who acts out, fidgets, distracts other students, disrupts lessons, disregards instructions, acts foolishly, forgets to do assignments, requires repeated admonishments and explanations, and demands 10 percent of the teacher's energy clearly undermines the teaching equation.

Because ADHD children typically have difficulty conforming to demands and standards that are reasonable for other children, teachers often find themselves thrust into the role of police officers. The extra supervision required by the ADHD student can deprive classmates of their fair share of instructional time, and teachers may begin to feel resentful and guilty. If they express their frustration as anger, they may unwittingly further stigmatize the already self-conscious and emotionally fragile ADHD student.

To protect themselves emotionally, ADHD students on the receiving end of continual disapproval from frustrated teachers and parents may resort to a range of counterproductive behaviors that include procrastination, irresponsibility, rebelliousness, and resistance to help. These behaviors, of course, offer no protection from criticism and feelings of inadequacy and, in fact, only call attention to the ADHD.

The *New England Journal of Medicine* (November 1990) pinpoints a brain abnormality that could explain why children develop ADHD. The report indicates that the brain of a hyperactive adult (50 percent of hyperactive children become hyperactive adults) uses 8 percent less glucose (the brain's main source of energy) than normal. The research suggests that hyperactivity results when specific regions of the brain that control attention, handwriting, motor coordination, and inhibited responses function improperly. The new findings, in tandem with previous research that found that approximately 30 percent of all children with ADHD have at least one parent with ADHD, appear to confirm that hyperactivity is genetically and biologically based. The research may pave the way for developing a precise diagnostic test for ADHD and new methods for treating the condition.

Currently, the diagnosis of ADHD is usually based on the observations of teachers, parents, and physicians that are recorded on rating scales such as the Conner. A diagnosis based on this type of anecdotal information lacks the precision of a quantitative biochemical assessment. A computer-based test called the TOVA purports to diagnose ADHD with accuracy, but some physicians question the accuracy of this instrument.

Physicians treating ADHD children often prescribe stimulants or antihistamines, such as Ritalin, Aterol, Cylert, and Benadryl, to control the symptoms. The medications have clearly demonstrated their effectiveness in treating concentration disorders.

Despite the evidence of efficacy, some parents and professionals are concerned about the potential long-term physical and emotional consequences of extended use of attention-focusing medication and particularly about possible depression after children stop using the drug, as well as sleeplessness, inhibited growth, reduced appetite, accelerated heart rate, and drug dependency. Physicians who regularly prescribe medication to control ADHD argue in rebuttal that drugs such as Ritalin have been used safely and effectively for over twenty-five years with no conclusive, documented, long-term side effects.

To treat ADHD, some physicians are now prescribing antidepressant medication that addresses neurotransmitter functions. Doctors using this protocol claim ADHD is linked to an imbalance in the cerebral hormone levels and that drugs such as Epramin, Prozac, and Desyrel act for more extended time periods and do not produce many of the negative side effects associated with stimulants and antihistamines.

Parents who have concerns about the use of medication in treating ADHD should question their child's pediatrician, neurologist, or psychiatrist closely about the pluses and minuses of the recommended treatment. A great deal of information about ADHD and medication can also be gleaned from the Internet. If the concerns are not allayed, parents should seek a second opinion and/or explore alternative strategies for helping their child.

Overt hyperactivity may, in some cases, ostensibly diminish with the onset of puberty, but the associated distractibility and impulsivity may persist in less obvious forms. Teenagers or adults who no longer appear overtly hyperactive may still have difficulty staying on track, following instructions, maintaining interest, remaining motivated, disciplining themselves, completing projects, and filtering out distractions. The academic and vocational challenges these teenagers and adults face can be formidable. Unless the focusing and associated perceptual-processing deficits are addressed and successfully treated, ADHD could pose a significant barrier to achievement and self-actualization throughout life.

COMMON SYMPTOMS OF ADHD

- short attention span
- disregard of consequences
- disturbing other students
- appearance of immaturity
- overactivity
- impulsivity
- fidgeting
- distractibility
- resistance to discipline
- predisposition to having accidents
- forgetfulness
- daydreaming
- slowness in completing tasks
- excitability

- unpredictability
- procrastination
- disorganization
- inattentiveness to details
- chronically sloppy and inaccurate work
- difficulty accepting responsibility
- difficulty following oral directions
- difficulty following written directions
- difficulty planning
- incomplete work

POSSIBLE INTERVENTIONS FOR ADHD

- physician-prescribed medication
- consistently imposed structure at home and in school
- clearly defined behavior guidelines and performance standards
- behavior-modification methods (positively rewarding acceptable behavior and negatively rewarding unacceptable behavior)
- relaxation methods, such as yoga or meditation, when children become agitated or distractible
- biofeedback procedures (electronic equipment that trains children to regulate neurological functioning)
- diets that eliminate food additives and sugar
- creative, intellectually stimulating teaching strategies
- disciplined athletic training (gymnastics, karate, ice-skating, etc.)

SEE: Attention to Details *(page 223)*; Brain Dysfunction *(page 326)*; Conduct and Attitude *(page 235)*; Critical Thinking *(page 161)*; Dealing with Consequences *(page 241)*; Decoding *(page 332)*; Disorganization *(page 251)*; Inaccurate Copying *(page 342)*; Incomplete Assignments *(page 256)*; Judgment *(page 260)*; Keeping

Up with the Class *(page 51)*; Logic *(page 171)*; Mastery of Academic Content *(page 67)*; Parent-Child Conflict *(page 393)*; Performance Standards *(page 91)*; Planning *(page 176)*; Procrastination *(page 278)*; Psychological Overlay and Psychological Problems *(page 399)*; Reading Comprehension *(page 100)*; Reading Fluency *(page 351)*; Recording Assignments *(page 107)*; Resistance to Help *(page 282)*; Self-concept *(page 410)*; Self-control *(page 287)*; Study Interruptions *(page 122)*; Study Skills *(page 127)*; Teacher-Child Conflict *(page 293)*; Time Management *(page 138)*; Underachievement *(page 143)*; Verbal Directions *(page 356)*; Working Independently *(page 302)*; Written Directions *(page 364)*.

Attention to Details

▲

Refers to the care and scrutiny requisite to submitting timely, accurate, complete, and legible work that conforms to teachers' explicit directions.

▲

Academic achievement requires effort, self-control, concentration, and precision. Students must be capable of disciplining themselves and attending to important details. This translates into consistently:

- eliminating spelling, grammar, and punctuation mistakes in essays and reports
- finding careless errors in homework and tests
- following explicit instructions
- meeting deadlines
- writing legibly
- submitting complete and properly formatted assignments

Children with learning disorders often appear to be unconcerned about details that can make the difference between receiving a good grade or a poor one. The most plausible explanation for their cavalier attitude is that the continual struggle to decode words, comprehend information, express ideas in writing, and stay focused is exhausting. Depleted by this effort, many academically deficient students have little physical and emotional energy left to devote to dotting i's, inserting commas, checking grammar, spelling words accurately, and making sure number columns are properly aligned when they multiply or divide.

Psychological factors can also affect a child's willingness to attend to details. Demoralized children who are convinced that their scholastic situation is futile usually feel profoundly inadequate. Preoccupied with insulating themselves from failure and embarrassment, they may adopt an "I don't care attitude." Although this mind-set and the associated counterproductive attitudes and behaviors call attention to the deficiencies and vulnerabilities the child is attempting to hide, struggling, emotionally defended children are unlikely to perceive this irony.

Some children with learning problems remain highly motivated and spend long, grueling hours diligently doing their work. Others become resigned to poor grades and do the minimum possible. Effort, quality, and precision are not a high priority for defeated learners. Many unconsciously rationalize that they are not really failing if they do not really try. This "not trying/not really failing" delusion invariably produces profound consternation in their teachers and parents.

Children who chronically disregard important details frequently become resentful when their parents or teachers censure them and attempt to modify their maladaptive attitudes about precision. Unfortunately, if not reoriented, these attitudes are likely to become habit-forming and may persist throughout life.

In some cases, the chronic disregard of details can be directly attributed to attention deficit hyperactivity disorder (ADHD). Because children with chronic concentration problems typically have poor impulse control and struggle to stay on task, filter out distractions, and monitor themselves, they often rush through their assignments. The consequences are predictable: substandard work replete with errors.

Visual-acuity and visual-efficiency deficits can also cause inaccurate, imprecise work. Children who struggle to see letters, numbers, and words accurately are at a significant disadvantage. Those who have difficulty tracking words efficiently when they read or write are bound to make mistakes. They may have difficulty aligning columns when they add, subtract, and divide. They may not see blatant spelling mistakes, and they may leave out words when writing or overlook key details on a homework-assignment sheet.

Most children who disregard important details can be systematically trained to be more attentive and work with greater precision. Using cognitive behavior-modification techniques,* they can be conditioned to compensate for their perceptual decoding problems by carefully and methodically checking over their work for accuracy. Teachers and parents should be prepared, however, for resistance. Emotionally defended children are often reluctant to relinquish their entrenched habits. To reorient them successfully, parents and teachers must clearly model what is expected (i.e., showing a child how a first-rate book report must look), and they must establish reasonable and consistent performance standards and guidelines. The objective is to condition children to take responsibility for finding and correcting their mistakes and to convince them that with extra diligence they can produce quality work that makes them proud.

BEHAVIOR THAT INDICATES INATTENTIVENESS TO DETAILS

- difficulty focusing
- passive learning
- disregard of consequences

---

*A systematic method of negatively reinforcing counterproductive behavior and positively reinforcing productive behavior while at the same time helping children understand the reason why their maladaptive behavior must change.

- poorly developed strategic thinking skills
- rushing through classwork and homework
- chronic spelling, grammar, and punctuation mistakes
- carelessness
- sloppiness
- poor handwriting
- errors when copying from textbooks and chalkboard
- missed deadlines
- failure to follow explicit directions
- poor organization
- poor time management
- poor planning skills
- incomplete assignments
- diminished academic self-confidence
- diminished expectation
- lack of personal-performance standards
- minimal effort and motivation
- lack of pride
- procrastination
- resistance to establishing short- and long-term goals
- difficulty setting priorities
- refusal to accept responsibility for shoddy work
- cavalier attitude about school and at-home responsibilities

SEE: Apathy *(page 208);* Attention Deficit/Attention Deficit Hyperactivity Disorder *(page 214);* Auditory Discrimination *(page 317);* Auditory Memory *(page 322);* Avoiding Responsibility *(page 227);* Conduct and Attitude *(page 235);* Critical Thinking *(page 161);* Dealing with Consequences *(page 241);* Decoding *(page 332);* Disorganization *(page 251);* Essays and Essay Tests *(page 18);* Goal Setting *(page 165);* Handwriting *(page 36);* Inaccurate Copying *(page 342);* Incomplete Assignments *(page 256);* Judgment *(page 260);* Language Arts *(page 58);* Mastery of Academic Content *(page 67);* Parent-Child Conflict *(page 393);* Passive Learning *(page 84);* Performance Standards *(page 91);* Planning *(page 176);*

Avoiding Responsibility

▲

Refers to acquiring a pattern of passive and/or manipulative behaviors designed to avoid challenges, reduce stress, and deflect responsibility.

▲

Children who struggle in school and who feel inadequate and demoralized may conclude consciously or unconsciously that their academic situation is hopeless. To protect themselves from frustration, negative feedback, and feelings of inadequacy, some of these children may act out and become resistant, rebellious, or antisocial. Others may respond passively and attempt to insulate themselves from their pain, stress, and feelings of futility. These children may retreat into a comfort zone where they expend minimal effort and become dependent on others to help them do their work and prop them up emotionally and academically. In their attempt to avoid frustration and failure, they lower their expectations and aspirations and adopt a pattern of passive behavior that allows them to evade taking responsibility for themselves.

Children who retreat into an escapist comfort zone typically perceive themselves as helpless. The boundaries of the haven they create are clearly marked. The sign at the gate says, "This is as far as I am prepared to venture. Don't ask more from me. This the best I can do." These children are, in effect, proclaiming, "I'm not prepared to risk trying hard and possibly failing."

Responsibility-adversive children can be masterful at manipulating their environment. They typically require constant monitoring and prodding to do their homework. They may demand repeated explanations from their teachers and parents. They may insist that their parents continually sit at their side while they do their homework. They may coerce their parents into checking over their work for careless mistakes and even into typing their essays. They may need to be continually reminded to take their assignments to school. Ensconced in their sheltered world of dependency, these children are likely to become enfeebled, dispirited, unmotivated, and resigned to minimal success. Once their parents "buy into" their manipulative behavior and resign themselves to being an on-call 911 rescue service, helpless children no longer have a reason to accept accountability for their own actions.

The severity of children's learning problems does not necessarily determine the extent of their dependency and diminished motivation. Some children with significant deficits remain highly motivated and relatively self-reliant. Others with less incapacitating problems become complacent, passive, reliant, and emotionally defended.

Inherited temperament may play a role in determining how children respond to their learning difficulties and whether or not they seek the protection of a comfort zone. Certain children appear to be by nature more passive than others.

Parents, of course, may play an unwitting, but pivotal, role in encouraging irresponsibility and dependency. Some may feel guilty because their child is struggling in school and they cannot find an immediate solution. Others may have an unconscious need to be helpers and enablers. They may feel that the only way they can validate themselves and assuage their conscience is to continually protect and rescue their child.

Nudging children out of a comfort zone that fosters irresponsibility requires fortitude, perseverance, and astute planning. The challenge can be monumental when children are struggling with significant learning problems. These children may be convinced that they cannot possibly do the work that is expected of them, and this perception could be correct. Given their deficient skills, the teacher's expectations and the curriculum demands may be unrealistic and unfair. Determining how much help to provide without encouraging excessive dependency requires insight into children's legitimate academic needs and a clear understanding of the severity, dynamics, and implications of their learning dysfunction.

The starting point is to have the reliant child's learning strengths and weaknesses accurately assessed. If specific learning disorders are identified, the child must be provided with effective remedial assistance. The child must also be guided to the realization that he has other options besides helplessness and that he can survive and achieve in school if he is willing to work diligently, relinquish his defense mechanisms, and venture outside of his comfort zone. This is, of course, easier said than done. Success hinges on helping struggling children resolve, or compensate successfully for, their learning problems and discover that they are far more capable than they ever thought possible. Defended children who are addicted to avoiding responsibility will not emerge from their comfort zone unless they are convinced that they possess the requisite resources to meet the challenges they must face every day.

Parents are destined to pay a steep price if they allow their child to become manipulative, irresponsible, and lazy. Once maladaptive behavior becomes imprinted, their child could remain helpless throughout life. The parents of a highly dependent eight-year-old may discover that their child is still helpless and dependent at thirty-eight.

Children with learning problems legitimately require extra help, explanations, and supervision. Providing selective assistance, however, is not the equivalent of encouraging dependency, laziness, and marginal effort. A parent helping a child with a math assignment might say: "I'll show you how to do one problem. We'll practice doing another together, and then you're on your own." Certainly, there are times when more help is needed, but providing an unconditional rescue service is not in any child's best interests.

To discourage children from becoming ensconced in an academically and emotionally debilitating comfort zone, parents must establish fair, reasonable, realistic, and consistently applied performance standards that take into consideration their child's current skills and the severity of the child's learning problems. Parents must also clearly define an acceptable and responsible work ethic that emphasizes effort, diligence, and pride and firmly resist manipulative behavior that encourages helplessness. At the same time, parents must effusively affirm and praise their child when he begins to assume increasing responsibility for his academic obligations and at-home chores and demonstrates expanding independence.

The process of cutting the umbilical cord can tug at parents' heartstrings, as the natural instinct is to protect and nurture the child who is vulnerable. Excessive protection, however, can work at cross-purposes with the child's emotional and cognitive development and can undermine the child's ability to cope with life and prevail in a demanding, competitive, and often harsh and unforgiving world.

BEHAVIORS SIGNALING ADDICTION TO A COMFORT ZONE

- diminished effort and motivation
- excessive dependency
- absence of personal goals
- difficulty working independently
- avoidance of challenges
- manipulative behavior
- passive learning
- lowered expectations and aspirations
- irresponsibility
- fear of success, failure, and/or competition
- apathy
- complacency

- capitulation whenever obstacles are encountered
- chronic rationalizations for marginal performance
- blaming others
- disregard or denial of consequences
- lack of perseverance
- self-sabotaging behavior
- chronic underachievement

▼

SEE: Apathy *(page 208)*; Attention to Details *(page 223)*; Bouncing Back from Setbacks *(page 232)*; Conduct and Attitude *(page 235)*; Critical Thinking *(page 161)*; Dealing with Consequences *(page 241)*; Defense Mechanisms *(page 373)*; Depression *(page 378)*; Fear of Failure, Success, and/or Competition *(page 383)*; Goal Setting *(page 165)*; Grades *(page 25)*; I'm Dumb Syndrome *(page 388)*; Incomplete Assignments *(page 256)*; Judgment *(page 260)*; Keeping Up with the Class *(page 51)*; Learning from Mistakes *(page 267)*; Logic *(page 171)*; Mastery of Academic Content *(page 67)*; Parent-Child Conflict *(page 393)*; Passive Learning *(page 84)*; Performance Standards *(page 91)*; Planning *(page 176)*; Priorities *(page 180)*; Procrastination *(page 278)*; Psychological Overlay and Psychological Problems *(page 399)*; Resistance to Help *(page 282)*; School Anxiety *(page 406)*; Self-concept *(page 410)*; Self-control *(page 287)*; Strategic Thinking *(page 189)*; Study Interruptions *(page 122)*; Study Skills *(page 127)*; Teacher-Child Conflict *(page 293)*; Underachievement *(page 143)*; Working Independently *(page 302)*.

Bouncing Back from Setbacks

▲

Refers to handling glitches and reversals effectively, applying produc-
tively the insights derived from negative experiences, and responding
with emotional resiliency to disappointments.

▲

All children make mistakes and experience setbacks. These two inescapable facts of life have particularly significant implications for
children struggling with learning problems. For many of these students, poor grades, negative feedback, frustration, demoralization,
and feelings of incompetence are everyday occurrences, and their
repeated negative school experiences invariably exact a psychological toll.

If children with learning problems are to prevail in school and
in the competitive world they will face when they complete their education, they must learn how to handle glitches and setbacks, analyze the challenges and problems they encounter, and rebound from
disappointments and failures. They must also learn how to make the
appropriate strategic adjustments so that they can avoid repeating
their mistakes. Those who do not acquire effective analytic thinking
skills, problem-solving skills, and emotional resiliency are destined
to suffer greatly.

Achieving students don't like to fail. If they receive a poor grade
on an exam, they react pugnaciously. They analyze what went wrong
so that they can do better the next time. Convinced that they deserve
to prevail, fortified by a positive school track record, and driven by
ego (a positive sense of self and one's own power), these children
typically persevere until they overcome the problem or become ab-
solutely convinced that the problem is insoluble.

Unfortunately, many learning-disabled children lack this quin-
tessential self-confidence, ego strength, and emotional resiliency. If
they receive a poor grade, they often respond passively or stoically.
They may become discouraged, depressed, and resigned to doing

poorly, and they may present as being unperturbed and nonchalant. Rather than rationally and proactively figuring out what went wrong, these children are likely to plow ahead mindlessly and use the same flawed study strategy. This inevitably produces the same dismal results.

As repeated setbacks and failures take their toll, struggling students usually become increasingly frustrated, demoralized, insecure, defended, and psychologically fragile. Those who become convinced that effort is futile and failure inevitable will shut down academically, mentally, and emotionally. They will then spend their remaining time in school treading water.

Children's confidence in their ability to handle predicaments directly reflects their life experiences. Positive experiences produce self-confidence, the desire to compete, the will to win, and elevated expectations and aspirations. Children who have proved to themselves that they can overcome obstacles and survive occasional failures, disappointments, and rejections will acquire faith in themselves and confidence in their ability to handle problems.

Chronic failure, on the other hand, produces the opposite effect. Repeated defeats in school are psychologically corrosive. They undermine self-confidence and trigger anxiety, anger, despondency, and counterproductive behavior.

Many struggling children are understandably fearful about revealing their inadequacies, experiencing more failure, and exposing themselves to real or imagined ridicule. Preferring flight to fight, they would rather accept defeat than deal with the stress of having to confront problems that appear unsolvable. To protect themselves, they may blame others, resist help, procrastinate, manipulate, act irresponsibly, become withdrawn, or feel sorry for themselves. On the surface they may appear unconcerned, lazy, resistant, and unmotivated, but underneath their affected *I don't care* image, these children are driven by profound feelings of incompetence. From the perspective of a defeated learner, routine academic challenges often appear monumental. Convinced that they will simply fail once again if they continue trying, these children often cope with their insecurities by becoming apathetic.

All children of normal intelligence can be taught methods of analyzing their miscalculations objectively. They can also be taught how to develop a logical and pragmatic strategy for handling setbacks and solving problems. Teaching these survival skills is as important as teaching students how to read, write, and do math.

Children who are crushed by setbacks and who react thoughtlessly or irrationally are at risk for becoming emotionally and academically incapacitated. A poor grade on an exam or a mistake when reading aloud in class can be distressing to any child, but when these setbacks are perceived as unequivocal confirmation of inadequacy, intervention is vital. If the child has learning problems, remedial assistance must be provided. Should the resource or tutoring program prove ineffectual, then the program must be reexamined and appropriately modified so that the child can see demonstrable progress. If these interventions fail to effect changes in the child's capacity to handle setbacks, a psychological assessment is imperative. Children who lack emotional resilience and who do not respond to their parents' efforts to help them develop more effective problem-solving and coping skills are vulnerable to becoming depressed and dysfunctional. These children require help from a well-trained mental-health professional.

INDICATIONS OF DIFFICULTY HANDLING SETBACKS

- lack of emotional resiliency
- expectations of disaster
- lack of self-confidence
- extreme sensitivity to others' opinions and reactions
- frustration
- demoralization
- depression
- explosive anger
- poor problem-solving skills
- procrastination
- obstinacy
- denial
- blaming others (i.e., "The test didn't cover the assigned unit.")

- rationalizations (i.e., "I don't care if I do poorly.")
- fear of failure
- unwillingness to examine and analyze failures
- fear of ridicule
- evasion of responsibilities

▼

SEE: Apathy *(page 208);* Attention to Details *(page 223);* Conduct and Attitude *(page 235);* Critical Thinking *(page 161);* Dealing with Consequences *(page 241);* Defense Mechanisms *(page 373);* Depression *(page 378);* Fear of Failure, Success, and/or Competition *(page 383);* Goal Setting *(page 165);* Grades *(page 25);* I'm Dumb Syndrome *(page 388);* Judgment *(page 260);* Learning from Mistakes *(page 267);* Logic *(page 171);* Passive Learning *(page 84);* Planning *(page 176);* Priorities *(page 180);* Problem Solving *(page 185);* Procrastination *(page 278);* Psychological Overlay and Psychological Problems *(page 399);* Resistance to Help *(page 282);* School Anxiety *(page 406);* Self-concept *(page 410);* Self-control *(page 287);* Strategic Thinking *(page 189);* Underachievement *(page 143);* Working Independently *(page 302).*

Conduct and Attitude

▲

Refers to behavior, thoughts, and feelings about school-related responsibilities and performance.

▲

Conduct and attitude problems are common by-products of a learning disability. When struggling children act counterproductively, their negative behavior can usually be directly traced to frustration, demoralization, and feelings of inadequacy.

    Children who are convinced that their situation in school is hopeless are especially vulnerable. To protect themselves emotionally, many of these children adopt an "I don't care" or "School is dumb" attitude. At the core of their rationalizations and justifications is a simplistic and flawed logic: If I don't really try, then I'm not really failing, and if I'm not really failing, then I'm not really dumb.

Youngsters who feel incompetent may procrastinate, act irresponsibly, misbehave, reject authority, and resist help. Not only does this behavior offer no real protection from feelings of inadequacy; it actually calls attention to the very inadequacies they are desperately trying to hide. Because these children are so intensely invested in defending themselves, they rarely recognize this obvious irony.

Self-defeating attitudes and behavior can significantly compound the difficulty of getting children with learning problems on track in school. Their conduct can also sorely test the patience and resolve of their parents and teachers. Helping students who are functioning two years below grade level and who are acting out in class, being disrespectful, refusing to do their homework, and getting into fights on the playground can pose a formidable challenge.

Counterproductive conduct often becomes scripted, and many parents can predict with relative certainty how their child will react to particular situations. Homework and studying will be put off until the last minute. Essays will be sloppy and illegible. Papers will be stuffed haphazardly into a backpack and strewn around the room. Assignment sheets will be left at school, and homework will disappear on the way to school. This modus operandi may be attributable in part to attention deficit hyperactivity disorder, handwriting problems, and/or fallout from intractable learning problems. Nonetheless, the underlying maladaptive attitudinal issues invariably magnify the scholastic problems.

Struggling children must transcend their instinctual need to defend themselves if they are to overcome their learning problems. They must be willing to work more conscientiously than their classmates. They must discipline themselves to proofread their essays to find spelling and punctuation mistakes, check over their math assignments for computational errors, and stay focused even when doing "boring" assignments. They must force themselves to pay attention when their teacher gives verbal directions, condition themselves to verify that their assignments have been recorded accurately, and after completing their homework, check to make certain they have completed the work as instructed. These educational prescriptions are clearly logical but unfortunately, psychologically defended children who are enmeshed in a system of counterproductive behaviors and attitudes often refuse to take the "medicine."

Maintaining a positive attitude and working conscientiously can represent monumental obstacles for students who must continually battle to process and retain sensory information, concentrate, and stay on task. The temptation to give up and shut down in school can be very inviting.

Lectures and sermons about the value of effort, motivation, diligence, dedication, and follow-through are rarely effective in reorienting maladaptive conduct and behavior. In fact, reproaches and admonishments usually have the opposite effect and typically cause children to become even more defended and self-sabotaging.

Children who become convinced that their learning-assistance program is effective, that they are making progress, and that they can ultimately prevail over their problems are far less likely to resort to counterproductive behavior. Their need to latch onto self-defeating coping mechanisms can be reduced if reasonable in-class and homework accommodations are made until they can handle the regular curriculum.* They will usually relinquish their defense mechanisms if they are protected from feeling hopelessly inadequate. They will be less likely to act out if they are not embarrassed in class or overtly or covertly ridiculed by their classmates. And they will also be less prone to acting irresponsibly or becoming the class clown if they are insulated from continual frustration and demoralization.

Insecure and emotionally vulnerable children desperately need their parents to advocate for them and to take a constructive and proactive role in asserting their legitimate educational rights and

---

*See Appendix II for a comprehensive list of reasonable accommodations.

needs. These rights are guaranteed by federal law, specifically Section 504 of the Rehabilitation Act.*

PARENTAL GUIDELINES FOR DEALING PROACTIVELY WITH CHILDREN'S LEARNING PROBLEMS

- Inform the teacher when your child is confused, discouraged, or overwhelmed.
- Inform the teacher when your child cannot handle an assignment.
- Ask the teacher or resource specialist to provide extra help when the work is too difficult.
- Request less difficult homework or that fewer problems be assigned until your child can catch up.
- Consider hiring a professional tutor.
- Ask the teacher to tell you in advance what sections your child will be asked to read aloud in class and practice at home.
- Request that your child be given extra time when taking tests.
- Ask the teacher to assign your child a "homework buddy."
- Ask the teacher to verify the accuracy of your child's assignment sheet.

Many children with learning problems continue to work diligently, but others, particularly those who are convinced that their situation is hopeless, may express their frustration and demoralization by being disrespectful, disobedient, disruptive, manipulative, or delinquent. They may break the rules, continually challenge the "system" and authority figures, deny responsibility for their actions, rationalize their behavior, or blame others for their problems, transgressions, and mistakes.

The first step in the process of reorienting children with behavior and attitude problems is to procure an accurate and up-to-date assessment of their academic strengths, weaknesses, and learning

---

*See Appendix I for a description of applicable federal laws.

needs. The second step is to make sure that they are being provided with effective remedial assistance. The next step is to establish fair, reasonable, and consistent expectations and performance guidelines.

Unfortunately, some children, especially those who have been struggling for many years with their learning problems, may become addicted to their defense mechanisms and may integrate the maladaptive behavior into their personality. Children manifesting entrenched conduct problems need to be evaluated by a mental health professional and may require counseling as an adjunct to effective learning assistance.

REALISTIC PERFORMANCE GUIDELINES FOR CHILDREN WITH LEARNING PROBLEMS

- Make your best effort.
- Do your homework.
- Take pride in your work.
- Keep your commitments.
- Complete and submit assignments and projects on time.
- Ask for help when you need it.
- Conform to the rules.
- Do your assigned chores at home.
- Attend to important details.
- Use your head.
- Act honorably.
- Treat others with respect and consideration.

Parents who clearly define reasonable and consistent performance and behavior standards are helping their children internalize values that will serve them throughout life. The standards establish what is permissible and nonpermissible, and this certainty provides children with a critically important sense of security and consistency.

Parents must also unequivocally communicate to their child that they value education and that they are determined that their child acquire the academic and thinking skills needed for success in life. They must be consistent and, when appropriate, unyielding. They must resist manipulative behavior and establish and impose firm consequence for noncompliance. They must also effusively affirm and acknowledge effort and successes, however small these achievements may be initially. Finally, they must be aware of and sensitive to the many challenges their child faces, and they must continually communicate their faith in their child's capacity to prevail over these challenges.

The goal of methodical behavior modification is to teach children how to regulate themselves, handle problems constructively, and acquire a productive work ethic. These capacities are vital to the development of self-confidence, self-sufficiency, and self-esteem.

RED-FLAG INDICATIONS OF BEHAVIOR AND ATTITUDE PROBLEMS

- incomplete and/or late assignments
- chronic procrastination
- lack of pride in work
- sloppy and inaccurate work (This may also be symptomatic of visual perception and fine-motor deficits.)
- failure to pay attention to details (This may also be symptomatic of visual-perception deficits and ADHD.)
- inadequate time spent doing homework and studying
- defiance or oppositional behavior
- hostility and aggressiveness (fighting, teasing, belittling others)
- blaming others for difficulties
- making excuses for irresponsibility
- resistance to help
- refusal to study or do homework
- insistence that school is "dumb"
- unwillingness to accept rules
- chronic testing of limits
- anticipation of failure
- lowered expectations and aspirations

SEE: Anger *(page 201)*; Apathy *(page 208)*; Attention Deficit/Attention Deficit Hyperactivity Disorder *(page 214)*; Attention to Details *(page 223)*; Bouncing Back from Setbacks *(page 232)*; Critical Thinking *(page 161)*; Dealing with Consequences *(page 241)*; Defense Mechanisms *(page 373)*; Depression *(page 378)*; Developmental Immaturity *(page 246)*; Fear of Failure, Success, and/or Competition *(page 383)*; Goal Setting *(page 165)*; Grades *(page 25)*; Incomplete Assignments *(page 256)*; Judgment *(page 260)*; Learning from Mistakes *(page 267)*; Logic *(page 171)*; Parent-Child Conflict *(page 393)*; Passive Learning *(page 84)*; Peer Pressure *(page 272)*; Performance Standards *(page 91)*; Planning *(page 176)*; Priorities *(page 180)*; Problem Solving *(page 185)*; Procrastination *(page 278)*; Psychological Overlay and Psychological Problems *(page 399)*; Resistance to Help *(page 282)*; School Anxiety *(page 406)*; Self-concept *(page 410)*; Self-control *(page 287)*; Strategic Thinking *(page 189)*; Study Skills *(page 127)*; Teacher-Child Conflict *(page 293)*; Test Anxiety *(page 420)*; Time Management *(page 138)*; Underachievement *(page 143)*; Working Independently *(page 302)*.

Dealing with Consequences

▲

Refers to recognizing that specific behaviors and attitudes produce predictable repercussions and being guided by cause-and-effect principles when planning and making decisions.

▲

Children who do not consider the potential consequences of their actions and attitudes before they act are destined to experience many painful collisions in school and in life. The disregard of the predictable repercussions of behavior can be particularly problematic for children who are struggling with learning disabilities. Often consumed with academic survival, many of these children operate on automatic pilot. Acting and reacting without forethought about the ramifications of their choices, they may ignore clearly defined rules, guidelines, and standards. They may act out on the playground, disrupt the class, and take unnecessary risks. They may "forget" to record their assignments, proofread their essays, hand in their reports on time, study for important tests, or budget adequate time to complete a term paper. They may arrive late for class or lie to their parents about having no homework. Their maladaptive behavior can significantly compound the already formidable scholastic challenges they face in school.

Children who chronically disregard the consequences of their actions tend to live in the present and have little or no concern about the future. Those who acquire the habit of acting and reacting mindlessly are at risk for making tragically flawed choices. Without considering the potentially disastrous implications of their conduct, they may experiment with drugs, join gangs, have unprotected sex, take weapons to schools, and/or shoplift.

All children miscalculate and misbehave from time to time. When a student studies the wrong material and subsequently gets a poor grade on a test, the setback may reflect a temporary lapse in judgment or an inaccurate recording of the assignment. If, however, the child typically studies the wrong material and is cavalier about accurately writing down his assignments, his behavior signals that he has not assimilated fundamental cause-and-effect principles and is not linking his irresponsible behavior with the predictable consequences.

The child who experiences a setback because of a miscalculation has two basic options. He can shrug his shoulders and say, "So what," or he can analyze the miscalculation and do everything possible to avoid repeating it. The child who thinks strategically and is aware of cause and effect will select the second option.

Lecturing or punishing children who chronically disregard the consequences of their actions is rarely effective. Children become resentful when they are on the receiving end of repeated admonishments and sermons. If they feel oppressed, they may intentionally disregard the admonitions.

Attention deficit hyperactivity disorder (ADHD) can obviously trigger thoughtless and impulsive behavior. Children who have difficulty focusing, handling distractions, and staying on track often lack the requisite self-control to make careful, well-reasoned choices. Reacting spontaneously to internal and external stimuli, they often disturb other students, speak without raising their hands, and disrupt the class without considering the implications of their behavior.

Brain physiology may also play a significant role in the mindless behavior that is characteristic of many juveniles. The frontal lobe of the brain is not fully developed in children and teenagers. This cerebral area controls impulsivity, and its incomplete development could, in part, explain the propensity of children to disregard consequences and take excessive risks.

Brain physiology notwithstanding, with proper training virtually all children are clearly capable of thinking critically and strategically, exerting control over themselves, and considering consequences before they act. Effective parenting and consistently applied rules and guidelines are clearly the antidote for children's neurological penchant to act impulsively and mindlessly.

The most effective method of helping children assimilate cause-and-effect principles is to train them to think logically and to impose clearly defined consequences when they act irresponsibly. ("Do you understand why cheating on that test was a mistake, and do you understand why the teacher gave you an F? Do you also understand why, as a consequence of your behavior, privileges are being taken away?") The goal of this training is to help children imprint the *mental reflex* of asking three simple but critically important questions *before* they act. These questions can significantly reduce the risk of their making tragically flawed judgments:

- What's going on here?
- What are my options?
- What are the potential implications of this decision?

To assume that children will *naturally* learn to factor cause-and-effect principles into their decisions and that they will *automatically* weigh the pros and cons is both risky and naive. Given the frightening temptations and risks that children face every day in our society, failure to consider the potential consequences of their actions and reactions could produce disastrous repercussions.

Children with learning problems are particularly at risk for making flawed choices. Because they are often frustrated, discouraged, and demoralized, these children are apt to choose the path of least resistance. They may decide not to submit a difficult assignment because they are embarrassed by their inability to understand the material, or they may decide not to study for a test because they are convinced that they are going to do poorly no matter how hard they try. In view of the formidable challenges that struggling students face, it is vital that they be trained to compensate for their academic deficiencies by thinking and acting more strategically. To prevail in school, they must be prepared to work harder, and they must create—with the help of their teachers, parents, resource specialists, and/or tutors—a pragmatic system for learning effectively and successfully meeting their academic obligations.

Mindlessness can quickly become an entrenched habit. Children who do not consider the possible or probably implications of their behavior and attitudes could make nonjudicious choices throughout their lives. These flawed choices are likely to have life-altering academic, vocational, economic, and emotional implications. Effective and timely academic intervention and systematic mental conditioning are essential. Children must be trained to recognize when they have arrived at a critical juncture in their lives, and they must be trained to consider *what might happen* if they choose to pursue a particular course of action. Those who are unresponsive to this training and conditioning require professional counseling. This counseling should be provided before a pattern of mindlessness becomes an embedded habit.

COUNTERPRODUCTIVE BEHAVIOR ASSOCIATED WITH THE DISREGARD OF CAUSE-AND-EFFECT PRINCIPLES

- excessive risks
- flawed judgment and choices
- irresponsibility
- procrastination
- poor motivation and effort
- missed deadlines
- repetition of mistakes
- behavior problems
- poor planning
- poor time management
- difficulty with scheduling
- impulsive behavior
- marginal motivation and effort
- disorganization
- ineffective planning
- poor problem solving
- inattention to details
- failure to anticipate predictable outcomes
- failure to weigh the pros and cons
- poor strategic thinking
- chronic crises
- failure to establish short- and long-term goals
- failure to establish priorities
- unwillingness to suspend immediate gratification
- failure to analyze and learn from miscalculations
- failure to make expedient adjustments to setbacks
- tendency to repeat the same mistake
- poor grades

SEE: Apathy *(page 208)*; Attention to Details *(page 223)*; Avoiding Responsibility *(page 227)*; Bouncing Back from Setbacks *(page 232)*; Conduct and Attitude *(page 235)*; Critical Thinking *(page 161)*; Defense Mechanisms *(page 373)*; Developmental Immaturity *(page 246)*; Disorganization *(page 251)*; Fear of Failure, Success, and/or Competition *(page 383)*; Goal Setting *(page 165)*; Grades *(page 25)*; Incomplete Assignments *(page 256)*; Judgment *(page 260)*; Keeping Up with the Class *(page 51)*; Learning from Mistakes *(page 267)*; Logic *(page 171)*; Parent-Child Conflict *(page 393)*; Passive Learning *(page 84)*; Peer Pressure *(page 272)*; Performance Standards *(page 91)*; Planning *(page 176)*; Priorities *(page 180)*; Problem Solving *(page 185)*; Procrastination *(page 278)*; Psychological Overlay and Psychological Problems *(page 399)*; Resistance to Help *(page 282)*; Self-concept *(page 410)*; Self-control *(page 287)*; Strategic Thinking *(page 189)*; Study Interruptions *(page 122)*; Study Skills *(page 127)*; Teacher-Child Conflict *(page 293)*; Time Management *(page 138)*; Underachievement *(page 143)*; Working Independently *(page 302)*.

Developmental Immaturity

▲

Refers to skills and behavior that are incongruent with a child's chronological age.

▲

Most children follow a genetically imprinted timeline as they mature. Despite occasional anomalies, the developmental phases are predictable, sequential, and chronological. At predetermined stages, children learn to smile, babble, talk, crawl, and walk, and the specific developmental milestones generally do not vary significantly.

The term *developmentally immature* (or *developmentally delayed*) is often used by health professionals, psychologists, and educators to describe children who lag behind in acquiring age-appropriate abilities. Some may be late to talk or walk. Some may have difficulty mastering age-appropriate motor and academic skills. Others may behave inappropriately in school and have problems acquiring social skills. Third-graders who act like first-graders are likely to be labeled by their teachers as developmentally immature.

When children do not follow the typical developmental timetable, their subsequent skill acquisition can be derailed. Examples of common developmental milestones include:

Examples of Typical Developmental Milestones

Age	Age-Appropriate Skills	Implications of Delay
5–6 years	Fine-motor/graphomotor coordination	Difficulty using scissors, grasping pencil, writing name legibly, and copying shapes
3–5 years	Gross-motor coordination, balance, bilaterality (ability to coordinate both sides of the body efficiently; also referred to as "crossing the midline?")	Difficulty skipping, hopping, riding a scooter, throwing a ball
5–7 years	Eye-hand and eye-foot coordination	Difficulty catching a ball, kicking a soccer ball, shooting baskets
5–7 years	Directionality (knowing right from left)	Difficulty with visual decoding (letter reversals—a primary symptom of dyslexia)

For often perplexing reasons, some children bypass certain developmental phases. They may never go through the crawling stage and instead scoot around the room, or they may pull themselves upright and begin walking at eleven months. Ironically, the parents of children who skip developmental stages may be quite proud of their child's seeming precocity, but the precocity could produce negative academic consequences. Efficient perceptual-processing and motor-coordination skills are acquired sequentially. In much the same way as a brick wall is built, nature mounts each developmental tier on the preceding tier. If one level is partially missing, it affects the integrity and solidity of the entire structure.

Children learn about their world by crawling, manipulating objects, and placing things in their mouths. When they crawl, they learn about time and space (i.e., how long it takes to crawl from point A to point B).* When they manipulate objects and place them in their mouths, they learn about shapes and about the composition and weight of articles in their environment. Orienting toward an objective and using purposeful movement to get there stimulate and enhance perceptual-decoding functions and cerebral development.

Missing one or more developmental phases could pose major problems down the road. Children who fail to build a solid perceptual-processing and motor-coordination foundation during the formative years may have great difficulty with subsequent skill acquisition.

Children who attain developmental milestones on schedule generally have fewer academic problems than children who are developmentally immature. They are better able to conform to the demands of the classroom and to assimilate age-appropriate skills that are sequentially introduced by their teachers.

In contrast, children who lag behind developmentally often manifest age-inappropriate behavior, have difficulty learning efficiently, and struggle to acquire academic and motor skills. Critically important abilities and talents that are requisites to success in school and in life may never be fully mastered.

---

*There is little parents can do about preventing their child from walking prematurely, but they can encourage their child to experience crawling by getting down on the floor and crawling with her. Parents can bilaterally pattern the child's movement of arms and legs while crawling (i.e., right arm, left leg forward). The child may still want to pull herself up and walk, but at least she will have experienced the developmental phase of crawling, and this may mitigate the possibility of subsequent difficulty with motor coordination and skill acquisition. When motor development, balance, and coordination deficits are significant, parents should inform their pediatrician. The physician may refer them to an occupational therapist who can systematically re-create the normal developmental patterns.

An important distinction must be made between bypassing key developmental phases and progressing quickly through certain skill- and motor-acquisition stages. Some developmentally precocious children attain the milestones early. These children, who are usually very bright and possess exceptional natural aptitude or ability, may begin talking at twelve months, dribbling a basketball at two and a half, playing golf at three, or reading at three.

The reasons why children do not follow the traditional developmental blueprint vary. Some may have been born with special natural abilities that impel them to take developmental shortcuts. Some may have subtle, moderate, or severe genetic anomalies. Others may have experienced a trauma during gestation or at birth or may have had an accident that caused brain damage. In many cases, however, the specific causal factors of minor developmental deviations and delays are difficult to pinpoint.

Concluding that a five-year-old isn't ready to enter kindergarten and placing the child in a developmental kindergarten or keeping her in preschool for an additional year may be a wise decision. This recommendation by preschool teachers is appropriate if the child is having difficulty sitting still (this behavior may also be symptomatic of attention deficit/attention deficit hyperactivity disorder), lacks age-appropriate socialization skills, or has demonstrable gross- and/or fine-motor deficits.

Unfortunately, some children are inaccurately labeled as developmentally immature because their teachers are perplexed by their atypical behavior and by their inability to keep up with the class. These children may procrastinate, misbehave, act irresponsibly, disrupt the class, or have difficulty mastering basic skills. Confusing developmental immaturity with psychological overlay (i.e., emotional reactions to frustration, demoralization, and feelings of inadequacy), defense mechanisms, and coping mechanisms attributable to an improperly diagnosed and/or improperly treated learning disability, these teachers may erroneously conclude that the child is not ready to settle down and learn. Because they themselves are misinformed about the symptoms of developmental immaturity and learning disabilities, they may, in turn, "miss the diagnosis."

   Recommending that a child repeat kindergarten or first grade may be appropriate if the child is truly developmentally immature. This recommendation is inappropriate when children are struggling with a learning disability and are attempting to protect themselves from feelings of incompetence by resorting to maladaptive behavior. Being labeled immature and being retained is not the solution to a learning problem. Retention may provide a temporary fix and reduce the pressure on children for a while, but this prescription only delays the day of reckoning. Unless there is an accurate diagnosis of the underlying learning difficulties and unless effective remediation is provided, the learning problems and the counterproductive behavior will persist and continue to cause grief.

SYMPTOMS OF DEVELOPMENTAL IMMATURITY

- gross-motor coordination difficulty
- fine-motor coordination difficulty
- poor balance
- delayed language development
- difficulty crossing midline (coordinating right and left sides of the body, as in skipping)
- graphomotor deficits (difficulty drawing, reproducing shapes with a pencil)
- figure-ground deficits (perceiving relative proportions of shapes)
- spatial deficits (accurately perceiving the position of the body and other objects in space)
- difficulty with body image (accurately perceiving one's own proportions and position in space)
- delayed academic readiness skills
- difficulty with social interaction and making friends
- tendency to play with younger children
- age-inappropriate behavior (silliness, baby talk, etc.)
- resistance to settling down to work
- excessive dependency

Sᴇᴇ: Apathy *(page 208)*; Articulation *(page 429)*; Attention Deficit/Attention Deficit Hyperactivity Disorder *(page 214)*; Attention to Details *(page 223)*; Avoiding Responsibility *(page 227)*; Brain Dysfunction *(page 326)*; Conduct and Attitude *(page 235)*; Critical Thinking *(page 161)*; Dealing with Consequences *(page 241)*; Decoding *(page 332)*; Defense Mechanisms *(page 373)*; Disorganization *(page 251)*; Fear of Failure, Success, and/or Competition *(page 383)*; Goal Setting *(page 165)*; Grades *(page 25)*; Handwriting *(page 36)*; I'm Dumb Syndrome *(page 388)*; Incomplete Assignments *(page 256)*; Judgment *(page 260)*; Keeping Up with the Class *(page 51)*; Language Disorders *(page 433)*; Learning from Mistakes *(page 267)*; Logic *(page 171)*; Mastery of Academic Content *(page 67)*; Parent-Child Conflict *(page 393)*; Passive Learning *(page 84)*; Performance Standards *(page 91)*; Planning *(page 176)*; Priorities *(page 180)*; Procrastination *(page 278)*; Psychological Overlay and Psychological Problems *(page 399)*; Resistance to Help *(page 282)*; School Anxiety *(page 406)*; Self-concept *(page 410)*; Self-control *(page 287)*; Strategic Thinking *(page 189)*; Study Interruptions *(page 122)*; Study Skills *(page 127)*; Teacher-Child Conflict *(page 293)*; Teacher-Designed Tests *(page 132)*; Time Management *(page 138)*; Underachievement *(page 143)*; Vocabulary *(page 150)*; Working Independently *(page 302)*.

Disorganization

▲

Refers to difficulty creating order and handling responsibilities efficiently and systematically.

▲

Chronically disorganized children rarely function at a level commensurate with their ability. They waste vast amounts of time searching for textbooks, handouts, binders, paper, homework assignments, pencils, dictionaries, pens, calculators, and lecture notes. Energy that should be devoted to studying is dissipated trying to figure out what assignments are due, trying to locate misplaced materials, and scurrying to meet deadlines. Some of these children may spend more time looking for things than actually studying, and their disjointed behavior invariably generates stress for everyone in the family.

Many disorganized students appear cavalier about the consequences of the disorder they create in their lives. They stuff papers haphazardly in their notebooks or book bags. Their desks and rooms are disaster areas with piles of material scattered around. Their school binders are in disarray. This disregard of basic principles of cause and effect produces predictable repercussions: lowered grades, distress for their parents and teachers, and resentment from those negatively affected by the chronic disorganization and the continual crises.

Students with learning problems, especially those with ADD/ADHD, are particularly susceptible to becoming disorganized. Often overwhelmed by the challenges, difficulties, and obligations they face in school, these children are at risk for becoming confused and scattered. The resulting disorder invariable exacerbates their academic difficulties and undermines their efforts to keep up with the class.

Children with the most urgent need to become more organized are often the most resistant to change and the most oblivious to the effects of the disorder in their lives. The ramifications are predictable: inefficient studying, incomplete assignments, missed deadlines, work not submitted, poor grades, and stress for them and for everyone who comes into contact with them.

The parents of chronically disorganized children usually feel compelled to intervene. Unfortunately, the traditional methods of intervention are rarely effective and often trigger active or passive resistance. Recriminations ("What a mess!"), lectures ("You need to get rid of this clutter if you want to be a good student!"), put-downs ("How can anyone live like this?"), and threats ("No TV this weekend if you don't put everything away!") are usually a waste of time. These negative reinforcements—and especially threats—may achieve a temporary change in behavior, but the long-term prospects of meaningful change remain dim. Chronically disorganized children who associate admonitions with nagging will insulate themselves from the negative feedback by tuning out and by insisting on doing it *their* way.

Patterns of chronic disorganization established in childhood are likely to persist throughout life. Before these children can realistically be expected to modify their counterproductive behavior, they must be taught specific, pragmatic, and easy-to-apply techniques to reduce the chaos in their lives. They must then practice these techniques under the patient and affirming supervision of their parents. The goal is to guide them to the realization that by creating order and by functioning more methodically and systematically, they can enhance their efficiency, make school easier, and create more free time for themselves.

Providing a practical model for becoming organized is the first step in helping children acquire new and more productive habits. Children must be taught practical, hands-on techniques for organizing their binders, creating an ordered work area, planning, scheduling time, recording assignments, and making certain they have the necessary materials to study and do their homework. The guiding principle in this *cognitive behavior-modification* strategy (i.e., conditioning and reinforcing improved behavior while guiding children to greater insight) is to create a context in which parents and children work together to develop a practical strategy for creating order and efficiency and then systematically practice implementing the plan. The more active the child's involvement in the organizational process, the more likely the child is to master, assimilate, and apply the organizational procedures.

Once disorganized students begin to derive benefits from the new behavior, they will be less resistant to integrating practical organizational principles into their daily modus operandi. The litmus test of the success occurs when previously disorganized children alter their self-perceptions, begin to see themselves as organized, consistently and voluntarily apply the organizational skills they have learned, and derive satisfaction and pride from their new and more efficient procedures.

INDICATIONS OF DISORGANIZATION

Child has difficulty:
- planning ahead
- establishing priorities
- budgeting time effectively
- meeting deadlines
- recording assignments consistently and accurately
- developing an effective system for checking off completed work
- creating a basic filing system
- designating places for storing school-related materials and supplies
- bringing home the essential study materials needed to do homework (assignment sheet, needed textbooks, and binder)

COGNITIVE BEHAVIOR-MODIFICATION METHODS FOR ENHANCING CHILDREN'S ORGANIZATIONAL SKILLS

- Demonstrate the payoffs for creating order. "Let's see how much time you can save if you organize this project."
- Create a cooperative context. "Let's see how we can organize these note cards for your term paper."
- Model the application of more efficient organization. "Would you help me organize the garage so that we can get to the things we need most?"
- Demonstrate specific techniques for organizing notebooks, study areas, desks, and living areas. "Let's put dividers in your notebook."

- Demonstrate how to plan ahead and schedule time. "How much time do you realistically estimate you'll need to complete this project?"
- Demonstrate techniques for making certain the necessary materials for studying effectively and doing homework are accessible. "Let's make up a simple checklist you can use to make certain you are taking everything you need home from school."
- Experiment with creating individualized organizational procedures. "What do you think about using colored tabs to organize your file folders?"
- Encourage the consistent application of organizational methods until they become habits. "Why don't we organize the workbench in the shop so that we can find the tools, nails, and screws?"
- Provide nonconfrontative monitoring. "Let's see how the project is going."
- Encourage the application of organizational principles in nonacademic areas. "Let's figure out how we want to pack the car for the vacation."
- Affirm progress. "What an improvement! Your desk looks great."
- Reward mastery. "You've done such a great job organizing your room that I think we ought to celebrate by going to the amusement park."

SEE: Apathy *(page 208)*; Attention Deficit/Attention Deficit Hyperactivity Disorder *(page 214)*; Attention to Details *(page 223)*; Avoiding Responsibility *(page 227)*; Conduct and Attitude *(page 235)*; Critical Thinking *(page 161)*; Dealing with Consequences *(page 241)*; Defense Mechanisms *(page 373)*; Goal Setting *(page 165)*; Incomplete Assignments *(page 256)*; Judgment *(page 260)*; Keeping Up with the Class *(page 51)*; Logic *(page 171)*; Parent-Child Conflict *(page 393)*; Passive Learning *(page 84)*; Performance Standards *(page 91)*; Planning *(page 176)*; Priorities *(page 180)*; Problem Solving *(page 185)*; Procrastination *(page 278)*; Psychological Overlay and Psychological Problems *(page 399)*; Recording Assignments *(page 107)*; Resistance to Help *(page 282)*; School Anxiety *(page 406)*; Self-control *(page 287)*;

Strategic Thinking *(page 189)*; Study Interruptions *(page 122)*; Study Skills *(page 127)*; Teacher-Child Conflict *(page 293)*; Time Management *(page 138)*; Underachievement *(page 143)*; Working Independently *(page 302)*.

Incomplete Assignments

▲

Refers to submitting unfinished work.

▲

Teachers expect children to fulfill their academic obligations. They are intolerant of incomplete assignments, especially in the upper grades, and discourage the practice by giving poor grades to students they consider irresponsible.

A chronic pattern of incomplete work is a red flag that signals a problem. The maladaptive behavior not only has immediate scholastic consequences; it can also have serious long-term vocational implications. Counterproductive patterns established in childhood often endure into adulthood. Children who are perceived as unreliable are at a distinct competitive disadvantage in a society that values and rewards effort, diligence, and consistency.

The two most plausible explanations for incomplete assignments are the most obvious: a learning disability and poor academic skills. Children who cannot do the assigned work and who are convinced they will get poor grades no matter how hard they try often have maladaptive work habits. Beset by frustration and negative expectations, they may refuse to do their homework or complete only those sections they can do easily. This behavior is clearly escapist, but to struggling, defeated learners, escape may appear the only solution to their seemingly insoluble academic problems.

Other factors that may cause children to submit incomplete work include:

- difficulty recording assignments accurately
- difficulty following and/or remembering explicit directions
- difficulty understanding the content of assignments
- poor planning skills
- poor organizational skills
- poor time-management skills
- disregard of consequences
- inadequate motivation
- laziness and irresponsibility
- procrastination
- frustration
- confusion about family standards, performance guidelines, values, and expectations
- psychological problems
- psychological overlay (i.e., emotional reactions to chronic difficulty and repeated setbacks)
- family problems
- negative peer influences

Children who attempt to protect themselves from feeling inadequate and from experiencing frustration and discouragement by not completing their work do not recognize, or choose to deny, an obvious irony: Their behavior actually calls attention to the learning deficiencies they're trying to hide. They may be able to deflect pain temporarily, but they will pay the price for evading their obligations when the teacher grades their work. This cause-and-effect reality rarely dissuades them. Most defeated learners choose to evade now and pay later.

The natural parental instinct is to protect children from making mistakes and experiencing failure and pain. Most parents who recognize that their child is manifesting counterproductive behavior will feel a responsibility to intercede. Traditional intervention usually consists of lectures, sermons, threats, punishment, and

showdowns. These admonitions are generally ineffectual and typically trigger denial, defensiveness, resentment, anger, and active or
passive resistance. Children who see no viable alternative to their
self-protecting behavior will tenaciously hold on to their behavior.
Because they are so enmeshed in their defense mechanisms, these
youngsters cannot see, or choose to deny, that the behavior is self-
defeating.

The far more effective alternative to lectures, sermons, and punishment is to identify the underlying factors that are responsible for
the child's incomplete assignments and to provide feasible and tangible alternatives to counterproductive defense mechanisms. The
options might include participation in a school resource program,
private tutoring, peer tutoring, or close parental supervision until
the child demonstrates that he can consistently complete his work
on his own.

In most cases, a child's work ethic is directly linked to the
child's academic skills and self-confidence. If the child requires
help, it must be provided before parents can realistically expect substantive changes in attitude, motivation, and diligence. Once children become convinced they can actually do the required work and
begin to receive better grades, they will be far less likely to submit
incomplete work.

If a child's learning difficulties are being methodically addressed
and the child continues to act irresponsibly, parents must be prepared to provide counseling. Depressed and/or angry children often
resort to self-sabotaging behavior to express their unhappiness, get
attention, and punish their parents. These children require the assistance of a mental-health professional who can help them examine their underlying feelings. The litmus test of the efficacy of the
counseling process is a gradual relinquishment of self-defeating attitudes and behavior and a gradual improvement in academic self-
confidence and self-esteem.

STRATEGY FOR DISCOURAGING INCOMPLETE ASSIGNMENTS

1. Determine if your child has academic-skills deficits.
2. Make certain that appropriate learning assistance is provided in school (the resource program) or privately (tutoring or educational therapy).
3. Gear expectations to a realistic assessment of your child's skills. (If your child cannot do the required work, reasonable accommodations should be requested. As your child's skills improve, the academic demands and expectations can be increased.*)
4. Provide appropriate and reasonable help and supervision while avoiding encouraging learned helplessness.
5. Provide study-skills instruction if appropriate.
6. Develop reasonable and consistent homework and performance guidelines and clearly assert the family's position on effort, commitment, diligence, and follow-through.
7. Establish specific academic goals for each subject (i.e., a B in history) and help your child develop a practical, systematic strategy for attaining these goals.
8. Make certain that an effective system of recording assignments and due dates is being consistently used.
9. Help your child develop an effective study schedule that incorporates planning and time-management principles.

---

*See Appendix II for a comprehensive list of accommodations.

Sᴇᴇ: Apathy *(page 208)*; Attention Deficit/Attention Deficit Hyperactivity Disorder *(page 214)*; Attention to Details *(page 223)*; Avoiding Responsibility *(page 227)*; Bouncing Back from Setbacks *(page 232)*; Conduct and Attitude *(page 235)*; Critical Thinking *(page 161)*; Dealing with Consequences *(page 241)*; Defense Mechanisms *(page 373)*; Developmental Immaturity *(page 246)*; Disorganization *(page 251)*; Fear of Failure, Success, and/or Competition *(page 383)*; Goal Setting *(page 165)*; Grades *(page 25)*; Judgment *(page 260)*; Learning from Mistakes *(page 267)*; Logic *(page 171)*; Mastery of Academic Content *(page 67)*; Parent-Child Conflict *(page 393)*; Passive Learning *(page 84)*; Performance Standards *(page 91)*; Planning *(page 176)*; Priorities *(page 180)*; Problem Solving *(page 185)*; Procrastination *(page 278)*; Psychological Overlay and Psychological Problems *(page 399)*; Recording Assignments *(page 107)*; Resistance to Help *(page 282)*; School Anxiety *(page 406)*; Self-concept *(page 410)*; Self-control *(page 287)*; Strategic Thinking *(page 189)*; Study Interruptions *(page 122)*; Study Skills *(page 127)*; Teacher-Child Conflict *(page 293)*; Time Management *(page 138)*; Underachievement *(page 143)*; Verbal Directions *(page 356)*; Working Independently *(page 302)*; Written Directions *(page 364)*.

Judgment

▲

Refers to the capacity to think rationally, logically, and analytically about issues, draw reasonable conclusions from available information, and make wise choices.

▲

As children mature and consciously and unconsciously process their life experiences, they begin to acquire key insights into the fundamental principles of cause and effect. They discover that temper tantrums will cause their parents either to capitulate to their wishes or dig in their heels. They also discover that misbehavior, lying, and stealing will result in punishment, that diligence and effort will usually produce achievement, and that laziness and irresponsibility will usually result in marginal performance.

Children store the data they experientially acquire about life and begin to form conclusions about what works and what doesn't, what's safe and what isn't, and what's smart and what isn't. These conclusions create a frame of reference that guides their thinking, attitude, and behavior. This frame of reference is called judgment.

Parents and teachers expect children to manifest a level of judgment commensurate with their developmental maturity. They expect a six-year-old to look both ways when crossing a street and an eight-year-old to behave when the teacher leaves the classroom. They expect a sixteen-year-old to resist the temptation to cheat on a test or plagiarize from an encyclopedia.

Children who have acquired good judgment share certain key traits. They are:

- capable of suspending immediate gratification
- in the habit of thinking analytically and strategically
- able to prioritize
- clear about their goals
- aware of their family's values when making choices

These youngsters will usually make astute choices and follow a path that leads them to their defined objectives. If they need to study for a test, they will forgo an opportunity to go to the mall with their friends. They will discipline themselves to proofread their essays carefully. They will meet deadlines and make the extra effort that produces positive results, pride, and a sense of accomplishment.

Children's choices are a window into how they think and how they weigh the pros and cons of their options. Those who are unable to make wise decisions and who think illogically and/or irrationally are at risk. If their judgment is chronically flawed, their defective decisions could profoundly alter the course of their lives.

The failure to develop good judgment is one of the potential downsides to having a learning disability. Because struggling children often require a great deal of assistance and supervision, they may become overly dependent on their parents, teachers, resource specialists, and tutors to make decisions about them and for them. This reliance on others to solve their problems and structure their lives can interfere with the development of the analytic-, strategic-, and critical-thinking skills that are requisites to the formation of good judgment.

All children, including those with learning problems, must be capable of weighing the pluses and minuses of their choices. When they arrive at a critical *decision point* (e.g., "Should I accept a ride to school from this stranger?"), they must be able to assess the risks and potential implications of their actions. Should they climb on a mound of loosely piled rocks? Should they play with a real gun that they find in a vacant lot? Should they cross a rain-swollen stream by jumping from rock to rock, go to a party that gang members are likely to crash, or get into a car driven by an intoxicated friend?

Even choices about non-life-threatening issues can have a significant impact on children's lives. Should they study over the weekend for the biology midterm exam or play basketball in the park with their friends? Should they stay up late to complete a book report that is due the next day? Should they make the extra effort to edit and proofread a term paper or check over their math homework for careless mistakes? Clearly, children who manifest good judgment and consistently make wise decisions have a distinct advantage over those who act impulsively and mindlessly.

Parents play a key role in helping children acquire good judgment. Those who encourage their children to think before they act and to consider the potential repercussions of their decisions are communicating that they value reason and logic, not to the exclusion of expressing feelings but as a necessary complement to expressing feelings. They are, in effect, saying to their children that judgment is the hand brake that prevents the car from rolling down the hill, gathering momentum, and crashing into a wall.

GUIDELINES FOR ENCOURAGING THE DEVELOPMENT OF GOOD JUDGMENT

- Model good judgment. "Crossing this stream here looks too dangerous."
- Share personal experiences that require the application of judgment. "I rejected that job offer because I felt that the company might not survive."
- Establish consistent behavior limits. "We do not want you studying with the TV on."
- Define reasonable performance standards. "We expect you to take the time to check your assignments for careless errors."
- Communicate family values. "We expect you to make your best effort."
- Involve your child in the process of analyzing situations, evaluating challenges, and solving problems. "We're wrestling with the decision about whether or not to buy a new house."
- Examine mistakes and miscalculations in a way that does not trigger defensiveness. "How might you change your study strategy to avoid this problem?"
- Discuss potential situations that require analytic thinking and reasoned decision making. "How would you respond if someone at a party offered you drugs?"
- Acknowledge and affirm good reasoning skills. "I like the way you thought that through."
- Encourage children to contribute to, and participate in, family discussions and family decisions. "What are your thoughts about whether we should visit Yellowstone Park or drive to British Columbia for our vacation this summer?"

Inherent personality traits must be factored into the good-judgment equation. Some children appear to have a hormonal predisposition to taking risks. They are thrill seekers who enjoy testing themselves and the limits of safety. In their pursuit of excitement, these youngsters often place themselves in danger and usually have more accidents.

Neurochemistry can also affect the quality of a child's decision making. Judgment and impulse control are intrinsically linked. Because children with ADD/ADHD have a more difficult time controlling their impulses, they are more likely to make impetuous and often thoughtless choices.

Brain physiology must be factored into the judgment-acquisition equation. In children, the prefrontal lobe that controls impulsivity is not yet fully developed, and this neurological phenomenon may in part explain some of the flawed choices that many children make.

Peers can also have a direct impact on the development of judgment. Children who select and identify with friends who act mindlessly and who manifest maladaptive or self-destructive behavior are likely to adopt these behaviors in order to be accepted.

Emotional problems and family discord can also undermine sound judgment. Children who are chronically angry and who lack self-esteem frequently make flawed choices. They may consciously or unconsciously sabotage themselves because they believe they are undeserving and feel compelled to hurt themselves and/or their parents.

Making chronically poor choices to punish oneself and others can be a powerful weapon. Even if children must suffer the consequences of their flawed judgment, the pain may be offset by the "pleasure" derived from making their parents unhappy. That this unconscious passive-aggressive agenda is self-destructive and will cause them to experience grief is a price that many angry children are willing to pay.

Whatever the source of a child's poor judgment—a personality trait, neurochemistry, brain physiology, peer influences, or emotional problems—children must be trained to think logically and rationally if they are to survive and prevail in a competitive world that is harsh and unforgiving to those who make defective choices. This instructional process should ideally begin during the formative years and continue in age-appropriate form until they leave for college.

Trust is a prerequisite to parents being "invited" to participate in a child's decision-making process. Children will not share the issues they are confronting if they believe they will be admonished, punished, lectured, or belittled. They are far more likely to share their problems, conflicts, and concerns when they are convinced that their parents will respond calmly, patiently, empathetically, supportively, and reasonably.

In some cases, a child's evaluative process is instantaneous. A child riding his bicycle to a friend's house may approach a railroad crossing and see that the gate is down and red lights are flashing. He may hear the train's horn and see the engine approaching. In an instant, he must decide whether to race across the track or wait for the train to pass. The child must be capable of making the right choice even though he is in a hurry to get to his friend's house.

In other cases, the evaluative process may be more complex and require the deliberate and systematic assessment of many factors. A high-school student who qualifies for an advanced-placement class must decide if it is in her best interests to take the course. If she has good judgment, she will carefully and methodically examine the pluses and minuses and ideally arrive at a well-reasoned conclusion.

In situations that demand careful consideration, children with good judgment will factor past experiences with similar situations into their evaluative process. The child who concludes that she didn't do well on the history test because she studied the wrong material and who analyzes her miscalculation and modifies her studying procedure is far more likely to improve her performance on the next test than the child who uses the same study procedure. Just as mindlessness is habit-forming, so, too, is good judgment.

INDICATIONS OF POOR JUDGMENT

- disregard of potential consequences
- irrational reactions to problems and crises
- difficulty assessing the pluses and minuses of a situation
- difficulty analyzing and evaluating information
- difficulty suspending immediate gratification

- difficulty learning from mistakes
- tendency to repeat miscalculations
- chronic irresponsibility
- chronic disregard of family values
- poorly developed impulse control
- difficulty thinking independently
- poorly developed problem-solving skills
- poorly developed analytic and evaluative thinking
- difficulty identifying danger
- difficulty identifying underlying issues
- difficulty establishing goals and priorities
- difficulty relating to future time (considers only what is happening right now)
- difficulty planning
- difficulty managing time
- difficulty with organization
- poorly developed logic
- poorly developed strategic- and critical-thinking skills

SEE: Apathy *(page 208)*; Aptitude *(page 15)*; Attention to Details *(page 223)*; Bouncing Back from Setbacks *(page 232)*; Conduct and Attitude *(page 235)*; Critical Thinking *(page 161)*; Dealing with Consequences *(page 241)*; Defense Mechanisms *(page 373)*; Developmental Immaturity *(page 246)*; Disorganization *(page 251)*; Fear of Failure, Success, and/or Competition *(page 383)*; Goal Setting *(page 165)*; Identifying Important Information *(page 41)*; Intelligence *(page 45)*; Logic *(page 171)*; Parent-Child Conflict *(page 393)*; Passive Learning *(page 84)*; Peer Pressure *(page 272)*; Planning *(page 176)*; Priorities *(page 180)*; Problem Solving *(page 185)*; Procrastination *(page 278)*; Psychological Overlay and Psychological Problems *(page 399)*; Recording Assignments *(page 107)*; Resistance to Help *(page 282)*; Self-concept *(page 410)*; Self-control *(page 287)*; Strategic Thinking *(page 189)*; Study Interruptions *(page 122)*; Study Skills *(page 127)*; Time Management *(page 138)*; Underachievement *(page 143)*; Working Independently *(page 302)*.

Learning from Mistakes

▲

Refers to ability to analyze errors so that miscalculations will not be repeated.

▲

To succeed in school and in life, children must be capable of learning from their mistakes, miscalculations, and failures. Those who do not develop this capacity to evaluate setbacks and apply the insight they derive from these negative experiences when dealing with similar problems and challenges are destined to repeat their mistakes.

Children who do not learn from their missteps are signaling that they have not grasped the basic principles of cause and effect. These children typically disregard, or are oblivious to, the predictable consequences of their behavior. Despite poor grades in English, they may continue to submit essays without proofreading for spelling and grammatical mistakes. They may do poorly on science tests because they repeatedly target the wrong material to study and do not take the time to analyze what went wrong. They may submit late or incomplete homework because they don't record their assignments accurately. This failure to evaluate their miscalculations and make expedient adjustments produces predictable repercussions that include:

- lowered grades
- frustration
- discouragement
- demoralization
- feelings of inadequacy
- reduced motivation and effort
- diminished self-confidence
- lowered expectations and aspirations
- psychological defense mechanisms

All children occasionally make poor decisions and miscalculate. They might forget to do an assignment, procrastinate before starting a difficult project, or occasionally act irresponsibly. These behaviors are not especially significant unless they recur regularly. When mindlessness becomes an integral part of a child's standard operating procedure, parents and teachers have legitimate cause for concern.

The effects of continual poor judgment are cumulative, and children can paint themselves into a corner. The child who falls further and further behind in school because she fails to do her homework and study for tests can reach the point where she cannot salvage the year. Her chronically flawed decisions can have grave and lasting educational and psychological implications.

Mistakes can also serve a positive function in a child's development. When experienced in moderation, miscues and frustration can stimulate intellectual and emotional growth, enhance resourcefulness, and build character. This assumes that the child has the ability and psychological resiliency to be able to reframe a negative experience and convert it into a positive one: "I blew the social studies midterm. I didn't memorize the dates of the Civil War battles. That's not going to happen again. Next time, I'll make flash cards and memorize every date in the chapter!"

The child who has fundamentally good self-esteem will bounce back from a disappointing grade and figure out what he needs to do to avoid another fiasco. Certainly he'll be upset, but he will get over it and focus on how to improve his grade the next time. This reaction dramatically contrasts with that of the struggling child with poor self-esteem who is convinced that his situation is hopeless and that he is irreparably incompetent. When such a child experiences a defeat, he is likely to become even more frustrated and discouraged. If he does not know how to analyze the underlying issues and implement a practical corrective strategy, he will probably do just as poorly on the next exam and in the process further undermine his already tenuous self-esteem.

A setback can, of course, trigger disappointment in any child, even the child with a good self-concept. The critical issue is how the child handles the setback and what she does with the data.

An important distinction must be made between experiencing

an occasional mistake, setback, and frustration and experiencing a demoralizing *pattern* of poor judgment and failures. The cumulative effects of such a pattern are psychologically destructive and can wreak havoc on a child's self-image.

Children with learning problems are especially vulnerable. Often emotionally depleted by their constant struggle to assimilate skills and information, these youngsters typically interpret each new setback as a further confirmation of their inadequacies. Rather than objectively analyzing the mistake and taking corrective action, they are likely to latch onto a self-defeating system of psychological defense mechanisms. They may choose to deny or disregard the blatant, predictable implications of their maladaptive behavior and attitudes. They may act dense. They may misbehave, or they may compensate by seeking surrogates for academic achievement. Their failure to think in terms of cause and effect (e.g., "If I don't want to fail the next test, I have to alter my study strategy") seals their fate. These children are on a collision course with the harsh realities of the academic grading system, and they are likely to be gravely injured. Their maladaptive behavior cannot help but magnify the effects of their learning problems.

The obvious first step in helping learning-disabled children who fail to learn from their mistakes is to identify and address the underlying perceptual-processing deficits that are causing them to struggle academically. Until they have the requisite skills to handle the academic challenges of their mainstream classes, these children will require reasonable accommodations. The amount of work that is assigned and the way in which skill mastery is assessed need to be adjusted. These accommodations are mandated by Section 504 of the Rehabilitation Act. (See Appendix I for a description of federal laws that protect the rights of the learning disabled.)

All children of normal intelligence—including students with learning disabilities—can be taught to think and act more strategically. They can be taught how to analyze and learn from their mistakes and how to make expedient and strategic adjustments that will prevent them from repeating their miscalculations. Obviously, someone needs to take the time to teach them these vital academic survival skills. This person could be their teacher, resource specialist, school counselor, tutor, or parent.

PROCEDURES FOR TEACHING CHILDREN
HOW TO LEARN FROM MISTAKES

- Help the child define the obvious. (e.g., "When I prepared for the test, I didn't accurately identify the information that would be covered, and I made careless mistakes on the true-false questions.")
- Help the child identify the mistake or miscalculation. (e.g., "When I studied for the test, I didn't make a checklist of the key information the teacher emphasized in class.")
- Encourage the child to ask questions and investigate the underlying issues. (e.g., "What specific study-skills techniques could I use to prepare for the next test?")
- Explore corrective options with the child. (e.g., "I'll need to set aside more study time, and I'll need to figure out a system for memorizing key facts.")
- Help the child find common denominators. (e.g., "The teacher usually gives tricky multiple-choice and true-false tests. When I study, I need to make up my own tricky practice test so that I will be prepared for her tricky test.")

BEHAVIORS THAT SIGNAL DIFFICULTY LEARNING FROM MISTAKES

My child:
- becomes discouraged and demoralized after making a mistake
- gives up or shuts down after experiencing a setback
- repeats the same mistakes
- does not take the time to analyze what went wrong
- does not look for common denominators
- resists admitting that he or she has made a mistake

- uses poor judgment
- does not think about consequences
- has difficulty thinking logically
- has difficulty thinking strategically
- has difficulty thinking critically
- is excessively defensive about mistakes
- is unwilling to discuss mistakes
- expects to do poorly or fail upon confronting a challenge
- blames others for mistakes
- tries to avoid projects that are difficult
- interprets a mistake as evidence of inadequacy and/or low intelligence
- regrets having tried something after making a mistake
- is unwilling to ask for or accept help
- quits when something becomes too challenging
- wants to run away and hide after making a mistake

SEE: Apathy *(page 208)*; Aptitude *(page 15)*; Attention Deficit/Attention Deficit Hyperactivity Disorder *(page 214)*; Attention to Details *(page 223)*; Avoiding Responsibility *(page 227)*; Bouncing Back from Setbacks *(page 232)*; Conduct and Attitude *(page 235)*; Critical Thinking *(page 161)*; Dealing with Consequences *(page 241)*; Defense Mechanisms *(page 373)*; Depression *(page 378)*; Disorganization *(page 251)*; Fear of Failure, Success, and/or Competition *(page 383)*; Goal Setting *(page 165)*; Grades *(page 25)*; Identifying Important Information *(page 41)*; I'm Dumb Syndrome *(page 388)*; Incomplete Assignments *(page 256)*; Intelligence *(page 45)*; Judgment *(page 260)*; Keeping Up with the Class *(page 51)*; Logic *(page 171)*; Mastery of Academic Content *(page 67)*; Parent-Child Conflict *(page 393)*; Passive Learning *(page 84)*; Performance Standards *(page 91)*; Planning *(page 176)*; Priorities *(page 180)*; Problem Solving *(page 185)*; Procrastination *(page 278)*; Psychological Overlay and Psychological Problems *(page 399)*; Resistance to Help *(page 282)*; School Anxiety *(page 406)*; Self-concept *(page 410)*; Self-control *(page 287)*; Standardized Tests *(page 116)*; Strategic Thinking *(page 189)*; Study Interruptions *(page 122)*;

Peer Pressure

▲

Refers to the impact of friends and social groups on attitudes, behavior, and values.

▲

The criteria that children use for selecting their friends provide a window into how they perceive themselves. Children are drawn to those with whom they share similar interests, values, talents, feelings, and life experiences. The peer group provides social acceptance, emotional support, and a sense of belonging, and the group synergy buttresses the beliefs, ideals, and customs of the members. By creating a collective sense of identity, the group affirms each child's personal sense of identity. Athletes generally associate with other athletes. Students who enjoy acting or rock music pick friends who share their orientation and talents. Successful students seek out other successful students. This same selection principle applies to students with learning problems. They typically gravitate to children who are also experiencing difficulty in school.

A child's need for peer-group identity, comradeship, and affirmation can be compelling, especially during the teenage years, when parental influence begins to wane and social pressures increase. For children who are struggling academically, a peer group can be a refuge from the trials and tribulations of school, from "unreasonable" expectations of parents and teachers, and from "unfair" pressure to work more diligently. The group may become a surrogate family in which defeated learners find the unconditional acceptance, acknowledgment, empathy, and support that they may be unable to find elsewhere.

The peer-group dynamic can profoundly influence those affiliated with the group. If the dynamic is positive, it can provide a wholesome emotional and social support system. If the dynamic is negative, it can create a maladaptive synergy that encourages struggling students to:

- profess their dislike of school
- resist doing their homework and class work
- act irresponsibly
- resent and resist their parents' supervision
- disobey their teachers
- misbehave
- refuse help
- become rebellious

When a child's peer group encourages and reinforces counterproductive behavior and values, there are predictable repercussions. Groups comprised of underachieving and nonachieving children are likely to denigrate school and academic achievement and to latch onto a litany of shared rationalizations for their deficient performance and negative attitudes. "Everyone hates the teacher and thinks school is dumb" often becomes a standard justification for the lack of motivation and effort. To defend their position, children will argue that all of their friends feel the same way. When their parents refuse to accept this justification for irresponsibility, a major showdown ensues. If this scripted conflict becomes a chronic occurrence, it is likely to cause the resistant or rebellious child to become increasingly resentful and alienated.

Defeated learners who band together to protect themselves from feeling "defective" may create a distinctive social identity that further isolates them from the mainstream. Ironically, this distinctive social identity often confirms the impression of defectiveness.

Negative school experiences, deficient skills, embarrassment and humiliation, diminished self-confidence, and psychological defense mechanisms become the glue that binds these children together. The peer group functions as a buffer that insulates its members from demands and expectations they are convinced they cannot meet. Counterproductive behavior becomes the norm and a requisite of social acceptance.

The need for peer-group identification can be compelling when children are insecure, highly impressionable, and lacking in self-esteem. Peer groups comprised of demoralized and alienated teenagers may express their collective frustration and anger by shutting down academically, acting out, and resisting authority. In extreme cases, they may vent their despair by drinking, taking drugs, and resorting to nihilistic behavior that may include vandalism, graffiti, or more serious misdemeanors, and even felonies.

Children who perceive their friendships as essential to their emotional survival will resist attempts by their parents to limit or forbid their involvement with their friends. Digging in their heels, they will challenge evidence that the group is exerting a negative influence on them, and they will reject documentation of the group's antisocial attitudes, delinquent orientation, or possible gang mentality.

Not all peer groups, of course, exert a negative influence. Many, in fact, serve a wholesome social function. Children who enjoy karate, gymnastics, skateboarding, hockey, scouting, chess, or computers will seek out like-minded friends. These youngsters are likely to be goal directed, achievement oriented, responsible, and conscientious, and the group dynamic reinforces these shared positive values. Religiously oriented peer groups clearly fall into this category.

As children mature, their peer-group value system will increasingly influence their own values. This trend can be represented graphically.

PARENT VERSUS PEER-GROUP INFLUENCE*

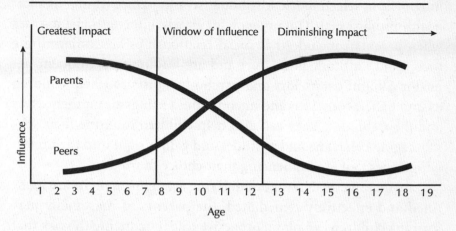

There are exceptions to the *like-minded seek like-minded* selection process. Some learning-disabled children remain highly motivated and conscientious and choose academically successful friends who share their motivation and diligence. If, however, the gap between their performance and that of their achieving friends widens significantly, the friendships may not endure. The contrast in performance may be so demoralizing that these children may begin to avoid contact with their achieving friends. As they become increasingly discouraged and demoralized, they may lower their expectations and aspirations and gravitate to other struggling students with whom they can more easily identify.

Most parents who perceive the negative impact that a peer group is exerting on their child will feel obligated to intervene. Unfortunately, attempts by parents to control their child's selection of friends frequently backfire and trigger resistance, resentment, and showdowns. These confrontations may cause children to become even more enmeshed in their peer group.

---

*Adapted with permission from *Family Wellness Workbook* (George T. Doub and Virginia Morgan Scott, Santa Cruz, 1987). The original concept was adapted from an audiotape by H. Stephen Glen entitled "Dealing with the Hostile Child/Adolescent" (Humansphere Inc., 1981).

Parents who are convinced that their child is manifesting poor judgment in selecting friends should seek guidance from a mental-health professional. The urgency for timely intervention increases when parents conclude that social relationships are undermining their child's attitude and effort and are leading to delinquent behavior. Skillful counselors and psychotherapists can help children examine their conscious and unconscious feelings about themselves and their abilities. They can also help children examine their self-sabotaging behaviors and attitudes and gain insight into the underlying issues that are influencing their choice of friends.

By making certain that underlying academic deficits are identified and effectively remediated, the parents of marginally performing children can play a proactive role in reducing the risk that their children will seek friends who are likely to exert a bad influence. As children begin to feel better about themselves and achieve scholastically, they are likely to choose friends who are on the same track. The better their child's self-concept, the more likely that their child will select friends who will also feel good about themselves.

INDICATIONS OF POSSIBLE NEGATIVE PEER-GROUP INFLUENCE

- resistance to help
- resistance to authority
- unwillingness to study conscientiously
- excessive and inappropriate identification with friends
- alienation from mainstream students
- isolation
- rebelliousness
- justifying of counterproductive behavior by citing similar behavior of friends
- antisocial attitudes and actions
- nihilistic behavior (body piercing, tattoos, extreme attire and hairstyles)

* gang identification
* delinquent behavior
* preoccupation with violence and prejudice

▼

SEE: Anger *(page 201);* Apathy *(page 208);* Avoiding Responsibility *(page 227);* Bouncing Back from Setbacks *(page 232);* Conduct and Attitude *(page 235);* Critical Thinking *(page 161);* Dealing with Consequences *(page 241);* Defense Mechanisms *(page 373);* Depression *(page 378);* Fear of Failure, Success, and/or Competition *(page 383);* Goal Setting *(page 165);* Grades *(page 25);* I'm Dumb Syndrome *(page 388);* Incomplete Assignments *(page 256);* Intelligence *(page 45);* Judgment *(page 260);* Keeping Up with the Class *(page 51);* Learning from Mistakes *(page 267);* Logic *(page 171);* Parent-Child Conflict *(page 393);* Passive Learning *(page 84);* Performance Standards *(page 91);* Planning *(page 176);* Priorities *(page 180);* Problem Solving *(page 185);* Procrastination *(page 278);* Psychological Overlay and Psychological Problems *(page 399);* Resistance to Help *(page 282);* School Anxiety *(page 406);* Self-control *(page 287);* Strategic Thinking *(page 189);* Study Skills *(page 127);* Teacher-Child Conflict *(page 293);* Teacher-Designed Tests *(page 132);* Test Anxiety *(page 420);* Time Management *(page 138);* Underachievement *(page 143);* Verbal Directions *(page 356);* Working Independently *(page 302).*

Procrastination

▲

Refers to avoiding obligations and putting off responsibilities to the last moment.

▲

Chronic procrastination can drive parents and teachers crazy. The behavior invariably creates stress for everyone who interacts with the procrastinating child. The daily after-school confrontations are scripted and predictable. Concerned parents ask: "When are you going to do your homework?" Defended children respond: "Stop bugging me! I'll get it done." Tensions rise, and a blowup ensues. Finally, the exasperated parent bellows: "Turn the TV off, go to your room, and finish your homework right now!"

The temptation to procrastinate is especially appealing when children are required to do something they consider unpleasant, boring, dumb, difficult, or time consuming. For youngsters with learning problems and/or study-skills deficits, virtually every academic assignment falls into one of these categories.

Repeated negative school experiences invariably produce emotional repercussions. Poor grades and continual criticism from parents and teachers cannot help but undermine motivation, damage self-confidence, and trigger phobic reactions to doing homework and studying for tests. After having spent seven painful hours in school, the prospect of returning home and facing two or three grueling hours of homework can be agonizing to learning-disabled children. By procrastinating, children with deficient skills can temporarily evade the unpleasantness and deflect the frustration, demoralization, and feelings of inadequacy. Those who have reading problems are likely to put off reading a book for a book report until the last minute. Those who have language-arts deficits are likely to avoid writing their science term paper. Those who have concentration problems will typically evade any academic task that demands focused, sustained effort. Of course, these "solutions" only put the pain temporarily on hold. The obligations remain, and the piper must ultimately be paid.

Avoiding schoolwork can be an appealing path of least resistance to children who are convinced that effort is futile. The excuses, rationalizations, and complaints that the work is boring or irrelevant are, of course, transparent to most parents and teachers. By procrastinating, academically defeated children can pretend for an hour or two that their obligations do not exist, and they can delude themselves into thinking that they won't have to deal with the repercussions.

Some students procrastinate because they have no personal short- and long-term academic goals and seemingly have no interest in acquiring academic skills. These children may have other interests, such as music, skateboarding, or computers, that provide them with a sense of fulfillment and accomplishment. Completing schoolwork is simply not a high priority. Typically described as lazy and unmotivated by their exasperated teachers and parents, these children essentially coast through school in cerebral neutral.

Procrastination is a common by-product of a poorly internalized appreciation of the basic principles of cause and effect. This counterproductive thinking and behavior can often be traced to a failure by parents to establish fair, reasonable, and consistent performance standards and expectations. Children who habitually disregard the implications and repercussions of their actions and choices essentially disavow the link between their irresponsibility and their poor school performance. Unless their maladaptive thinking is reoriented, denying reality, rationalizing laziness, and conveniently deflecting accountability are likely to become ingrained personality traits.

Self-concept deficits can also cause children to procrastinate. Defeated learners may be terrified by the prospect of failing and having to confront their deficiencies. The alternative is to avoid challenges and responsibilities. These children characteristically rationalize their behavior with excuses such as:

- "The teacher didn't assign any homework."
- "I did my homework in school."
- "Don't worry. I'll get it done."
- "It's boring!"

Once children convince themselves that their rationalizations and self-deceptions are true, they will reject all evidence to the contrary. Poor grades and negative comments from teachers and distressed and exasperated parents will have no impact. The illusion that everything is okay, of course, inevitably shatters when report cards are sent home.

Poor study, time management, and organizational skills can also play a major role in procrastination. Children may have decent academic skills but may not know how to plan projects, organize materials, prioritize the steps required to complete an assignment, or budget time. Their late work testifies to their inefficient study habits, poor planning, and chronic disorganization.

Some children procrastinate because they know their parents will rescue them whenever they get into a bind. The continual parental attention and coddling they receive may become a reward more desirable than any satisfaction they might derive from completing their work independently and submitting it on time. Procrastination is guaranteed to impel their parents to toss them a life preserver, and this payoff encourages them to continue procrastinating.

In some instances, chronic procrastination may be symptomatic of emotional or family problems. Depressed, angry, or resentful children realize—consciously or unconsciously—that their procrastination will press buttons and trigger conflict, and they may use this passive aggressive behavior as a weapon against their concerned parents. The weapon can be especially potent when their parents place great value on diligence, effort, punctuality, and achievement. Children who resort to passive aggression because they believe it is the only way to vent their anger and unhappiness safely and get attention will require professional counseling.

FACTORS THAT CAN CAUSE CHILDREN TO PROCRASTINATE

- poor academic skills
- poor time-management skills
- disorganization
- disregard of cause-and-effect principles
- poor study skills
- inadequate goal orientation
- poor prioritization skills
- passive learning
- poor judgment
- poor planning skills
- difficulty learning from mistakes
- laziness
- poorly defined performance standards
- lack of self-control
- parent-child conflict
- desire for negative attention
- low self-esteem

SEE: Apathy *(page 208)*; Attention to Details *(page 223)*; Avoiding Responsibility *(page 227)*; Bouncing Back from Setbacks *(page 232)*; Conduct and Attitude *(page 235)*; Critical Thinking *(page 161)*; Dealing with Consequences *(page 241)*; Defense Mechanisms *(page 373)*; Depression *(page 378)*; Disorganization *(page 251)*; Fear of Failure, Success, and/or Competition *(page 383)*; Goal Setting *(page 165)*; Grades *(page 25)*; I'm Dumb Syndrome *(page 388)*; Incomplete Assignments *(page 256)*; Judgment *(page 260)*; Keeping Up with the Class *(page 51)*; Learning from Mistakes *(page 267)*; Logic *(page 171)*; Parent-Child Conflict *(page 393)*; Passive Learning *(page 84)*; Performance Standards *(page 91)*; Planning *(page 176)*; Priorities *(page 180)*; Problem Solving *(page 185)*; Psychological Overlay and Psychological Problems *(page 399)*; Recording Assignments *(page 107)*; Resistance to Help *(page 282)*; School Anxiety *(page 406)*; Self-concept *(page 410)*; Self-control *(page 287)*; Strategic Thinking *(page 189)*; Study Interruptions *(page 122)*; Study Skills *(page 127)*; Teacher-Child Conflict *(page 293)*; Teacher-Designed Tests *(page 132)*; Test Anxiety *(page 420)*; Time Management *(page 138)*; Underachievement *(page 143)*; Working Independently *(page 302)*.

Resistance to Help

▲

Refers to an unwillingness to accept academic advice and assistance.

▲

Struggling children are often elaborately defended. Those who are convinced that they are inadequate will usually do everything possible to protect themselves from experiencing pain, embarrassment, and humiliation. They may avoid their academic obligations and resist studying, refuse help, and rebel against authority. If they do their homework, they will often submit assignments that are incomplete, late, shoddy, and replete with careless mistakes.

These defense mechanisms only call attention to the deficiencies defended children are trying to hide. Most of these children, however, are so enmeshed in their self-protecting system that they do not recognize an obvious paradox: In protecting themselves, they are, in effect, sabotaging themselves. This paradox and the predictable consequences of their counterproductive behavior completely elude them.

Parents who become aware that their child is in denial about the implications of their attitudes and actions usually feel compelled to intervene proactively. Typical interventions, however, often prove ineffectual because struggling, emotionally defended children are likely to equate their parents' well-intentioned advice, admonishments, and directives with nagging.

SUGGESTIONS THAT TYPICALLY ELICIT RESISTANCE

- "Spend more time studying."
- "Take fewer study breaks."
- "Don't do homework while watching TV or listening to music."
- "Create a study schedule and maintain it."
- "Make certain you record your assignments in your assignment sheet."
- "Take notes when reading your textbooks."
- "Organize your room and your study area."
- "Plan ahead."
- "Budget your time more efficiently."
- "Establish short- and long-term goals and focus on attaining these goals."
- "Establish priorities."
- "Proofread your assignments carefully."
- "Submit your work on time."
- "Check over your homework for careless errors."
- "Rewrite sloppy or illegible assignments before submitting them."
- "Review previous tests when studying for a new test."
- "Make up practice tests."
- "Ask the teacher for extra help."

The preceding recommendations are, of course, eminently reasonable and logical, but they are virtually guaranteed to trigger resistance and resentment from children convinced that their academic situation is hopeless. Having created a system of coping behaviors that entail minimal effort, irresponsibility, and procrastination, these youngsters are not likely to accept logical solutions to their problems. The more their parents push them to change their modus operandi, the more resistant they usually become.

Children can actively or passively resist help. If the resistance is active, there will be continual confrontations and arguments. Parents will make a recommendation or give a reasonable directive (e.g., "Turn the TV off, and start doing your homework"), and their child will respond with knee-jerk opposition (e.g., "Stop nagging me!"). Over time, the recurring conflicts and showdowns usually become scripted and predictable.

Children who resist passively can be equally exasperating. They may appear to acquiesce to suggestions or directives and then covertly do everything possible to defeat the parents' intentions. Because they are unwilling to risk a direct confrontation, passively resistant children often resort to manipulation and deceit. They may claim that they completed their homework or studied for a test knowing full well that they haven't. In some cases, they may even deceive themselves into believing their own fabrications. Their defense mechanisms, resistance, denial, and manipulative behavior may become so automatic and habitual that these children may not even be consciously aware of what they are doing.

Parents who expect children who have developed maladaptive habits to welcome their commonsense recommendations and guidance are often disillusioned. Resistant children do not respond rationally when they are emotionally entangled in problems and psychologically invested in preserving their coping system. Preferring to blame others for their problems, they typically complain, deny responsibility, evade obligations, and spend their time and energy defending themselves psychologically. They do not want their parents to challenge their rationalizations and justifications, and they certainly do not want unsolicited advice and suggestions.

Frustrated, demoralized children typically acquire very painful associations with learning. As they become increasingly school-phobic, these defeated learners will do anything they can to avoid further discomfort. Many develop an aversion to reading aloud, writing essays, taking notes, doing math, or studying for tests. Selecting the path of least resistance, they do the minimum possible, and their lack of effort essentially seals their academic fate.

The alternative to offering suggestions, advice, and directives that are likely to be rejected is for parents to encourage their child to participate actively in the process of defining and solving their own problems. This direct-involvement strategy is predicated on teaching children systematically how to identify the underlying issues, brainstorm practical solutions, target realistic short- and long-term goals, establish priorities, develop a plan for attaining their objectives, and create a schedule that provides adequate study time and adequate free time.*

Involving the struggling child in the process of proactively resolving his own learning problems can be instrumental in defusing resistance. Parents will no longer be perceived as tyrants by their children, and children will no longer perceive themselves as oppressed.

Parents must be aware of and sensitive to their child's defense mechanisms. As frustrating as these attitudes and behaviors may be, they will be a reality until such time as the child feels sufficiently safe to relinquish the self-protecting conduct and emerge from behind the walls of his emotional fortress. Parents who respond to their child's defense and coping mechanisms by becoming heavy-handed, assertive, and confrontal are likely to cause their child to build even higher walls.

Psychologically defended children will not readily relinquish behaviors that they unconsciously believe are essential to their survival. Support, empathy, patience, carefully orchestrated successes, and effusive praise for even small successes are essential components in the process of modifying maladaptive conduct. Before defended children will accept help, they must become convinced that their parents and teachers are their allies and not their enemies and that the assistance being offered is supportive and not oppressive. Winning their trust is clearly vital.

Struggling children who continue to resist assistance and who are

---

*Methods for actively engaging children in problem solving are described on page 185. Methods for helping children become more goal directed and for teaching them how to manage time, establish priorities, and become more organized are described on pages 138 and 180.

nonresponsive to their parents' efforts to help them get untracked in school are candidates for counseling. These children may be struggling with psychological overlay (emotional reactions to defeat) or psychological problems. In either case, an evaluation by a mental-health professional is essential before the resistance becomes chronic and the counterproductive behavior causes irreparable emotional damage.

BEHAVIORS ASSOCIATED WITH RESISTANCE TO HELP

- unwillingness to accept advice
- unwillingness to confront problems and deficiencies
- insistence on maintaining current modus operandi
- evasion of responsibility for actions
- feelings of persecution and oppression
- automatic opposition to suggestions
- denial that a problem exists
- blaming
- complaining
- secretive behavior
- active or passive aggression
- anger
- manipulative behavior
- contradictory behavior (i.e., saying one thing and doing another)
- lying and distortions of reality
- overt or covert sabotaging of agreements
- unwillingness to accept performance standards and behavioral guidelines

SEE: Anger *(page 201)*; Apathy *(page 208)*; Attention to Details *(page 223)*; Avoiding Responsibility *(page 227)*; Bouncing Back from Setbacks *(page 232)*; Conduct and Attitude *(page 235)*; Critical Thinking *(page 161)*; Dealing with Consequences *(page 241)*; Defense Mechanisms *(page 373)*; Depression *(page 378)*; Disorganization

Self-control

▲

Refers to the ability to regulate emotions and focus efforts on defined objectives.

▲

Fundamental cause-and-effect principles govern academic achievement. Children who are motivated and self-disciplined, have established personal goals, possess good skills, are willing to work diligently, and are able to learn efficiently are destined to be successful in school. Those who lack these traits are destined to perform marginally in school.

The importance of self-control cannot be overemphasized. Children must be capable of focusing in class and paying attention when they study. They must be willing to proofread their essays carefully and check over their math assignments for computational errors. They must be able to plan, create a schedule, complete their assignments, and meet deadlines. The capacity to self-regulate is central to performing these functions.

Children who achieve scholastically consistently:

- record their assignments
- complete their homework
- attend to details
- check over their work for accuracy
- study diligently for tests
- manage their time effectively
- submit their work on time
- confront challenges
- solve problems
- organize their materials

Goal-oriented, pragmatic, and intent on doing well in school, these children are willing to prioritize study over play and to make the extra effort that is often the determining factor in whether or not they get a good grade on a report, homework assignment, or exam.

Some students with poor self-control have specific learning problems or academic-skills deficits that interfere with their capacity to learn efficiently. They may be dyslexic and have perceptual-processing deficits that make learning to read a nightmare. They may have poor study habits. They may have attention deficit/attention deficit hyperactivity disorder (ADD/ADHD), which triggers chronic impulsivity and distractibility. For children wrestling with these conditions, school can be a never-ending, emotionally draining battle. In reaction to their plight, these children may latch onto a pattern of counterproductive compensatory behaviors and attitudes that include procrastination, misbehavior, irresponsibility, denial, and/or resistance to help. To the consternation of their parents and teachers, they may continually sabotage themselves by submitting sloppy, incomplete work, missing deadlines, blaming, and becoming reliant on others to rescue them.

Rather than offer protection, the maladaptive behaviors only exacerbate the learning deficiencies, guarantee continued marginal performance, and intensify the feelings of inadequacy. Emotionally defended children do not, of course, recognize this irony.

Perplexed and frustrated parents and teachers may seize upon convenient and often simplistic explanations for a child's poor school performance. They may attribute the academic deficiencies exclusively to a bad attitude, laziness, deficient effort and motivation, and inadequate self-discipline. Other parents and teachers recognize a more complex cause-and-effect link between attitude and performance: Children's conduct is a barometer of their underlying feelings about themselves and their ability to handle the challenges and demands they face. Counterproductive behaviors are often triggered by learning problems; children frequently become lazy, insufficiently motivated, and lacking in self-discipline in reaction to their school difficulties, and these behaviors exacerbate their academic problems. On the surface, this appears to be an example of the classic conundrum: "Which came first, the chicken or the egg?" Do children perform poorly in school because they lack self-discipline, or do they lack self-discipline because they are doing poorly in school? The answer to *both* questions is *yes*.

To protect themselves psychologically, defeated learners often shift into a passive learning mode. Convinced that they are unintelligent and hopelessly incompetent, they become resigned to marginal performance. If they see no payoff for working diligently, they are likely to divert their emotional, intellectual, and physical energy into other venues, such as sports or music. Other children may react by doing the minimum possible in school and then consciously or unconsciously delude themselves into thinking that *they are really failing because they aren't really trying*. To outward appearances, these children are unmotivated and lack self-discipline, but the actual explanation for their deficient effort is more complex and involves overlapping educational, emotional, and self-esteem factors.

ADD/ADHD is the most plausible explanation for chronic difficulty with self-control. Children with ADD/ADHD lack impulse control and are characteristically inattentive, impulsive, frenetic, easily distracted, disorganized, and oblivious to details. These traits can obviously erect major obstacles to academic achievement.

Ironically, many children who lack self-control compound the problem by surrounding themselves with disorder and distractions. Their room, desk at home and in school, and backpack are usually disaster areas. They stuff papers haphazardly in drawers and binders. They strew their textbooks and worksheets about the room. They do not consistently use an assignment sheet to record their assignments. They do not have at hand the materials they need to complete their homework.

Struggling children who are frustrated because of their learning difficulties or because of emotional or family problems may act out their distress and frustration. Unable to handle problems, challenges, and obligations effectively, they may become angry and aggressive. They may disrupt the class, tease their classmates, or become bullies on the playground. If their behavior is extreme, they may become socially alienated and rebellious. These out-of-control children are clearly at psychological risk, and counseling by a mental-health professional is vital.

Students with poor self-control often develop an elaborate system of rationalizations for their maladaptive behavior. Classic excuses for deflecting responsibility include:

- "The teacher is a jerk."
- "School is boring."
- "The stuff we're asked to learn is stupid."
- "What's the use of studying? I always do poorly on tests because the tests are unfair."
- "I forgot. . . ."
- "I didn't hand in the assignment on time because the teacher didn't tell us it was due today."
- "The teacher didn't explain the assignment."

- "I did check over my work, but . . ."
- "Don't worry. I'll get it done in time."
- "I did my homework in school."

By denying responsibility, blaming, and making excuses, these students delude themselves into thinking that everything is okay. The illusion invariably shatters when report cards are sent home.

Achieving students have a radically different mind-set and operating procedure. They intuitively understand the value of self-regulation. They define their personal short- and long-term goals, establish priorities, plan ahead, develop a schedule, consider consequences, manage time, meet deadlines, organize themselves and their materials, and carefully check over their work. The fruits of their attuned efforts are reflected in superior academic performance.

Focusing exclusively on correcting the behavior of children who lack self-discipline without identifying and addressing the underlying causal factors is usually an exercise in futility.* Children who work inefficiently can be taught practical organizational and time-management techniques that will help them study more effectively. Those who are oblivious to details can be trained and conditioned, using *cognitive behavior-modification methods* (i.e., consistently applied negative reinforcement for counterproductive behavior in tandem with a clear explanation of the rationale for the negative reinforcement), to proofread their essays carefully and check their math assignments for mistakes.

Children who lack self-control may have ADD/ADHD and should be evaluated by a physician. Those who are out of control because of possible emotional or family problems should be evaluated by a mental-health professional. Medication may be a component in the treatment protocol.

---

*Traditional behavior-modification advocates contend that counterproductive behavior can be successfully reoriented using a consistent system of positive and negative rewards without having to examine the underlying emotional issues that may be triggering the behavior. Many psychotherapists take strong exception to this therapeutic model developed by B. F. Skinner.

With appropriate intervention, self-control problems can be corrected, and children can acquire more effective self-regulation skills. The key is to intervene before the maladaptive and self-defeating behavior becomes an entrenched habit.

CHARACTERISTICS OF CHILDREN WITH SELF-CONTROL DEFICITS

- inadequate goal orientation
- lack of motivation
- irresponsibility
- difficulty establishing priorities
- carelessness
- procrastination
- sloppiness
- poor time management
- poor planning skills
- incomplete assignments
- missed deadlines
- disorganization
- resistance to doing homework
- inefficient and/or inadequate studying
- disinterest
- denial and rationalizations for poor performance
- frustration
- explosive anger
- poor judgment
- negative attitude about school
- resistance to help
- poor self-concept
- teacher-child conflict
- parent-child conflict
- difficulty working independently
- underachievement
- resistance to authority
- chronic aggressiveness

SEE: Anger *(page 201)*; Apathy *(page 208)*; Attention Deficit/ Attention Deficit Hyperactivity Disorder *(page 214)*; Attention to Details *(page 223)*; Brain Dysfunction *(page 326)*; Conduct and Attitude *(page 235)*; Critical Thinking *(page 161)*; Dealing with Consequences *(page 241)*; Defense Mechanisms *(page 373)*; Depression *(page 378)*; Disorganization *(page 251)*; Fear of Failure, Success, and/or Competition *(page 383)*; Goal Setting *(page 165)*; Grades *(page 25)*; Identifying Important Information *(page 41)*; Incomplete Assignments *(page 256)*; Judgment *(page 260)*; Keeping Up with the Class *(page 51)*; Logic *(page 171)*; Parent-Child Conflict *(page 393)*; Passive Learning *(page 84)*; Planning *(page 176)*; Priorities *(page 180)*; Problem Solving *(page 185)*; Psychological Overlay and Psychological Problems *(page 399)*; Resistance to Help *(page 282)*; Self-concept *(page 410)*; Strategic Thinking *(page 189)*; Study Interruptions *(page 122)*; Study Skills *(page 127)*; Teacher-Child Conflict *(page 293)*; Time Management *(page 138)*; Underachievement *(page 143)*; Working Independently *(page 302)*.

Teacher-Child Conflict

▲

Refers to tension, discord, and resentment in teacher/student inter-action.

▲

In an ideal world, the relationship between teachers and students would be harmonious, dynamic, productive, and mutually rewarding. Teachers would love their profession and delight in working with children. They would be enthusiastic, skilled, creative, energetic, caring, and nurturing. In this ideal world, students would be eager to learn, motivated, goal directed, diligent, obedient, and cooperative. They would assimilate information effortlessly and master new skills easily.

Unfortunately, the realities of the classroom are not always congruent with this idealized model. Sometimes teachers and students don't get along. From the perspective of most teachers, the conflicts can be directly traced to the students' irresponsibility, misbehavior, laziness, and/or inadequate effort. The transgressions may range from relatively minor issues, such as not raising one's hand or talking in class without permission, to more serious deportment issues, such as cheating, disrespect, defiance, fighting, or lying. Other triggers include procrastination, late and/or incomplete assignments, shoddy work, lack of effort, and excessive dependency.

Students usually have a very different perspective and typically blame their teachers for the conflict. The most popular reproach is that the teacher is unfair and is picking on them. Other complaints include poor teaching, boring subject matter, and preferential treatment of certain students. Of course, these students are usually the ones who are well-behaved, conscientious, motivated, and goal directed. The obvious cause-and-effect link between diligence and effort and preferential treatment is something that "it ain't my fault" children conveniently choose to disregard. That the perspective of students who feel oppressed and tyrannized is often distorted by their compelling need to deflect responsibility for their counterproductive behavior cannot be denied. In some cases, however, their perceptions may be valid. A teacher may, in fact, be consciously or unconsciously biased against certain children.

Teachers are not always faultless in every conflict situation. Certainly, there are tens of thousands of highly competent, enthusiastic, and consummate teachers in American schools who delight in mentoring children, are empathetic, and are able to establish exceptional rapport with their classes. These teachers are obeyed because they are respected. They establish fair and consistent rules, maintain discipline, treat students with respect, demonstrate their love of their profession, express positive expectations, and communicate their faith in their students' capacity to achieve.

At the other end of the rapport/respect spectrum are those teachers who do not particularly like what they are doing and do not particularly enjoy children. They teach primarily because the job provides security and three months' vacation every year. Some have marginal skills. Some are burned out after years of teaching. Others are intolerant of students who require extra effort, guidance, support, and patience. Rather than search for the underlying factors that might be causing students to struggle and might be triggering conflicts and rather than assess their own teaching style and discipline code, they blame the students for their inability to grasp material, master skills, and behave appropriately. In conferences with parents, these teachers are likely to make comments and recommendations such as:

- "He needs to get more serious about his work!"
- "Don't rescue her. Let her sink or swim on her own!"
- "You have to accept the fact that your child is never going to be an academic achiever."
- "He is immature and should repeat the grade."

Having little or no insight into learning problems and the attendant psychological issues, these teachers attribute the lack of progress and maladaptive behavior to students having "an attitude" or having limited intellectual ability. They view a student's misbehavior as a personal affront and a confirmation of their negative appraisal of the child's capabilities.

There are, of course, students with deportment problems whose acting out cannot be traced to learning problems or teacher inadequacies. Some of these children have emotional problems and are oppositional and defiant. Some are the products of dysfunctional families and have been emotionally damaged by inadequately defined rules and values, poor communication, inconsistent performance standards, marital disharmony, a contentious divorce, and/or psychological or physical abuse. That these conditions can distort perceptions, undermine the desire to learn, and warp behavior should surprise no one. The symptoms of the internal discord may manifest as active aggression (e.g., bullying, angry outbursts, fighting, violent fantasies, etc.) or as passive aggression (e.g., teasing, manipulative behavior, complaining, etc.). Frustrated, demoralized, and depressed, these children are likely to act out, show disrespect for their teachers, refuse to cooperate, test the limits of acceptable behavior and performance, challenge authority, deny responsibility for their actions, and precipitate confrontations.

Children who do not recognize or accept that their teachers have the prerogative to define and enforce behavior rules and performance standards in the classroom are on a collision course with the educational system. Seemingly oblivious to the consequences of their attitudes and behavior, they interrupt the class, distract their classmates, pass notes when the teacher's back is turned, talk back, and get into fights on the playground. They also characteristically resist studying, recording their assignments, submitting their homework on time, and accepting help and guidance.

Despite the monumental challenges that difficult students often present in the classroom, many teachers do a masterful job of handling the situation. Unfortunately, others fail miserably. They may become vindictive and confrontational, or they may embarrass and humiliate struggling or misbehaving students. The worst offenders are teachers who are highly opinionated, self-righteous, dictatorial, intolerant, and set in their ways. Some of these teachers have not taught a creative or dynamic lesson in years. They may communicate through word and deed that they prefer girls to boys. They may target specific students as incorrigible troublemakers. They may be insensitive to cultural differences. Their negative attitudes, diminished expectations, lack of rapport and empathy, and deficient insight into child psychology make teacher-child conflict inevitable.

Children with learning disabilities who are preoccupied with compensating and/or hiding their inadequacies and defending themselves psychologically may not realize, or may deny, that their behavior is causing conflict with their teacher. These children are especially vulnerable and reactive to teacher insensitivity, negativity, and inflexibility. To prevail over their learning problems and develop academic self-confidence, they require empathy, extra help, firm, fair, and reasonable standards, and acknowledgment and affirmation for progress. Those who are continually criticized, embarrassed, and humiliated are at significant risk for acting out. They are also at a significant risk for shutting down in school.

Even highly dedicated, conscientious, and competent teachers can be severely challenged by the counterproductive and maladaptive coping behaviors to which some struggling children often resort. Chronic irresponsibility, procrastination, disorganization, helplessness, and incomplete and illegible assignments can sorely test their patience and fortitude. Meeting the legitimate needs of these students to have directions repeated, concepts clarified, and their work closely monitored can generate monumental stress and strain.

The challenges that classroom teachers face increase exponentially when students have ADD/ADHD. Keeping an impulsive, inattentive, highly distractible child on task can be a nightmare when a teacher is responsible for twenty-nine other students. In a class of thirty children, each student should receive approximately 3 percent of the teacher's time. The chronically inattentive or disruptive child who requires 10 percent of a teacher's time undermines this instructional equation. To monitor such a child, teachers may be forced to modify their instructional methodology and lesson plans. If the child's need for continual accommodations and excessive attention begins to elicit resentment, teachers may consciously or unconsciously perceive the ADD/ADHD child as the enemy.

A teacher's reaction to problems in classroom situations directly reflects her values, attitudes, training, teaching philosophy, and feelings about children. Many teachers believe that to instruct effectively and maintain order they must be stern disciplinarians. Prioritizing obedience, decorum, the assimilation of information, and skill mastery, they typically target for punishment any student who obstructs the attainment of these objectives.

Other teachers prefer a less regimented and structured classroom environment. They prioritize active, participatory learning, critical thinking, multisensory instruction, study groups, and learning through discovery, and they believe that when children enjoy learning, they rarely misbehave. Convinced that positive reinforcement (i.e., praise and affirmation) is more effective in productively shaping behavior than negative reinforcement (i.e., threats and punishment), they intentionally engineer repeated opportunities for their students to succeed and effusively praise them for their accomplishments.

When conflicts arise, good teachers model how to use reasoning, strategic thinking, and communication skills to resolve the discord. Rather than continually reprimand students and take away privileges, they seek constructive solutions that actively engage children in the problem-solving process. These teachers have rules, enforce behavior and performance standards, and know when to draw a line in the sand, but whenever possible, they avoid letting soluble problems degenerate into confrontations that they must win a priori because they have all the power. By encouraging students to identify difficulties, examine underlying causal factors, accept responsibility for their actions, and think analytically, they stimulate insight and awareness, and they model for their students how to respond rationally to conflict.

Being reasonable and empathetic certainly does not preclude teachers from establishing academic standards and imposing befitting sanctions. Each situation must be judged on its merits. Interactive problem solving may be appropriate in one context, and punishment may be appropriate in another.

Less insightful teachers wittingly or unwittingly precipitate repeated showdowns with misbehaving children. Failing to recognize that many deportment problems are attributable to insecurity, deficient self-esteem, diminished self-confidence, and inadequate academic skills, they choose to perceive their students' nonadaptive behavior as a challenge to their authority and prerogatives. In so doing, they set the stage for recurring friction, power struggles, confrontations, and conflict.

Certainly, misbehavior can disrupt the class, interfere with teaching, and elicit resentment. Teachers must apprise children of rules, standards, guidelines, and the consequences of breaking the rules. The key issue is whether strictness, reprimands, punishment, and showdowns are the most effective means of reining in children and helping them become better citizens.

Most teachers willingly accept their responsibility to develop their students' academic skills and reinforce the value of diligence, motivation, and attention to details. Some parents, however, have misconceptions about teachers' responsibilities and obligations. These parents must realize that:

- Teachers are not surrogate parents. It is not the teacher's job to impart basic morals, values, and attitudes that should rightfully be taught at home.
- Teachers are not prison guards. It's not the teacher's job to restrain students who are chronically out of control, defiant, hostile, manipulative, disrespectful of authority, or antisocial. Children manifesting these behaviors require psychological counseling and a specialized school environment.
- Teachers are not psychotherapists. It's not the teacher's job to "cure" children who have significant personality or behavioral disorders.

When an entire class loses respect for a teacher, conflict is inevitable. In most cases, the disrespect is earned. Children who are continually reprimanded and yelled at and who perceive their teacher as unfair, inconsistent, prejudiced, or incompetent often respond by misbehaving. This misconduct may be the most accessible means by which students can express their sense of injustice.

Teachers who are unwilling to analyze disagreements objectively and are resistant to making any changes in their preconceptions, attitudes, teaching methodology, and discipline procedures erect major barriers to problem resolution. Those who proclaim, "I've been teaching for twenty years, and I'm not about to change my methods to accommodate your child. When he improves his behavior in my class, the conflict will be resolved," are clearly signaling their intransigence and refusal to engage in a dialogue that might lead to rational problem solving.

Most children lack the insight and communication skills necessary to resolve conflicts with their teachers. Their parents must help them:

- define the issues that are causing conflict
- identify the teacher's values, priorities, and objectives
- recognize that the teacher has the authority to establish rules of behavior and performance standards
- realize that the teacher has the prerogative to punish students who break the rules
- understand the teacher's rationale for insisting that behavior and attitude standards be maintained
- explore ways of making reasonable and expedient accommodations to the teacher's wishes

At the same time, parents may need to help the teacher better understand the underlying factors that are contributing to the conflict without communicating that they are justifying misbehavior. They must also make every effort to see the situation from the teacher's perspective. Having to manage a child who requires an inordinate amount of time and effort could legitimately cause the teacher to feel guilty about depriving the other students of their fair share.

Parents who are unsuccessful in helping their child resolve recurring conflicts with the teacher should request a conference with the school psychologist, counselor, and/or principal. Requesting that the child be transferred to another class is, of course, an option. This transfer may resolve the immediate conflict, but the solution may be only temporary. If a child is chronically misbehaving and if the underlying issues are not identified and addressed, the child may soon find herself in conflict with her new teacher.

Parents who model how to solve problems, handle conflicts, communicate effectively, and think analytically, critically, and strategically are providing their child with invaluable tools. Children who can deal successfully with people in authority and who learn how to resolve disputes possess a vital resource that they will be able to use with great effectiveness throughout their lives.

STRATEGY FOR RESOLVING TEACHER-CHILD CONFLICTS

- Help your child accurately define the problem or conflict.
- Help your child identify the underlying issues.
- Help your child understand the teacher's position, values, goals, and priorities.
- Encourage your child to take responsibility for his behavior and attitudes.
- Discourage your child from blaming the teacher for her problems unless there is compelling evidence that the teacher is at fault.
- Establish open and frank communication with your child's teacher.
- Help the teacher understand your child's feelings, vulnerabilities, and problems.
- Work cooperatively with the teacher to develop mutually acceptable solutions to conflicts.
- Acknowledge your child's feelings (e.g., anger, resentment, exasperation, frustration, discouragement, etc.) while being careful not to project your own feelings onto your child.
- Actively engage your child in the process of finding solutions to problems.
- Establish fair and reasonable behavior, attitude, and performance guidelines.
- Establish fair and reasonable consequences of misbehavior.

SEE: Anger *(page 201)*; Apathy *(page 208)*; Attention Deficit/Attention Deficit Hyperactivity Disorder *(page 214)*; Attention to Details *(page 223)*; Avoiding Responsibility *(page 227)*; Bouncing Back from Setbacks *(page 232)*; Conduct and Attitude *(page 235)*; Critical Thinking *(page 161)*; Dealing with Consequences *(page 241)*; Defense Mechanisms *(page 373)*; Depression *(page 378)*; Developmental Immaturity *(page 246)*; Disorganization *(page 251)*; Fear of Failure, Success, and/or Competition *(page 383)*; Goal Setting *(page 165)*; Grades *(page 25)*; Identifying Important Information *(page 41)*; I'm Dumb Syndrome *(page 388)*; Incomplete Assignments *(page 256)*;

Working Independently

▲

Refers to the ability and willingness to complete assignments without needing continual assistance and prodding from parents and teachers.

▲

A powerful basic instinct compels parents to protect their children. This instinct is especially dominant when children are young, vulnerable, incapable of providing for their own needs, and unable to identify, evaluate, and handle danger.

As children mature, their need for constant safeguarding diminishes. By the time they enter preschool, they are expected to function for several hours each day without parental monitoring. Supervision is delegated to the teacher, who serves as a surrogate parent.

In kindergarten, a second major transition occurs. Children are required to conform to relatively demanding rules. They must raise their hand before speaking, settle down when the teacher tells them to do so, pay attention, and form a line when they leave the classroom. As they advance into the upper grades, the requirements expand exponentially.

By fourth grade, teachers require children to work with relative independence. If they are given an assignment to do in class, they are expected to continue working until they have finished. They must follow explicit verbal and written instructions, complete their in-class assignments within the allotted time, carefully check their work for errors, and stay on task. They must conform to their teachers' behavior rules and performance standards, deal with setbacks and frustration, learn from their mistakes, handle punishment, and interact acceptably with their classmates.

Some children have little difficulty conforming to these demands. Others are overwhelmed by the obligations and struggle to work independently. When directed to do a particular class assignment, these children go into meltdown. In a state of panic and confusion, they desperately look around the classroom and try to figure out what their classmates are doing. They may plow ahead mindlessly, request further explanations and clarification, or shut down.

Children who cannot work independently invariably have difficulty keeping up with the class and are at risk for becoming frustrated and discouraged. Their dependency generates a sense of powerlessness, feelings of inadequacy, and diminished self-confidence.

The ability to transition from dependency to self-sufficiency is vital to the development of a child's self-concept. Realizing this, wise parents actively encourage their children to become increasingly self-reliant. They understand that as their child matures, the power fulcrum will inexorably shift from external parent-based control to internal child-based control, and they correlate their vigilance to their child's developmental age and demonstrated level of maturity. These parents recognize that they must still, of course, supervise and monitor their child and be alert to potential risks, but they also recognize that their overriding objective is to encourage their child to become responsible and to begin to take charge of her own life.

When maturing children remain reliant on their parents to handle all of their problems and responsibilities, something is amiss. Their excessive dependency signals that an imprinted, maladaptive psychological dynamic is preventing them from developing their own autonomous emotional and intellectual resources. This phenomenon is referred to as *learned helplessness.* Parents who wittingly or unwittingly encourage helplessness and continually function as rescuers and enablers are impeding their child's emotional development. The learned helplessness could persist into adulthood with disastrous psychological and vocational consequences.

Excessively reliant children are often confused, disorganized, and forgetful, and their work is typically incomplete, sloppy, and inaccurate. They characteristically procrastinate, miss deadlines, act irresponsibly, and resort to continual "I can't do it" statements whenever they are faced with a challenge or a problem. Their pained facial expressions and gestures clearly communicate insufficiency. To guarantee their parents' concern and attention, some of these children may even affect mildly retarded behavior. Their demeanor sends a clear message to their parents and teachers: "Don't expect much from me!"

Addicted to being rescued and emotionally invested in maintaining the codependent status quo, helpless children typically settle into a comfort zone where they know their needs will be taken care of by others. To perpetuate the support system, they often magnify their difficulties and needs and devise ingenious ways to defeat their parents' attempts to make them more self-reliant. Realizing that if they improve their skills and demonstrate that they can do their work on their own, they will have to assume responsibility for themselves, many of these children become highly resistant to making any improvement. Through skillful manipulation, they may transform every demand, challenge, and setback into a major crisis that they expect their parents to resolve for them. The more their parents urge them to become self-sufficient, the more anxious, insecure, fearful, and resistant they become.

The parents of learning-disabled children with deficient skills are caught in a double bind. If they do not provide help, their child is likely to become defeated and increasingly demoralized. If they do provide help, their child is likely to become increasingly dependent and helpless.

Helplessness is quite common in the case of children who have ADD/ADHD. Chronic difficulty staying on task, filtering out distractions, and completing projects can erect major obstacles to working independently. Realizing that their ADD/ADHD child lacks impulse control, most insightful parents respond by imposing clearly defined behavior guidelines. They know that if they don't closely and vigorously monitor their child's studying and homework, the work will not get done. As is the case with learning-disabled children, the parents of an ADD/ADHD child are also caught in a double bind. Their continual supervision and imposition of external controls may ironically encourage dependency and helplessness.

Reining in a distractible, impulsive, and overactive child can be an emotionally draining experience for parents and teachers. Even medication may not completely resolve the challenge of getting ADD/ADHD children to sustain their effort and work independently. Doing homework can be especially problematic, as the effectiveness of the medication may have worn off by 7:00 P.M., when homework is typically done.

Psychological problems can also play a major role in causing excessive dependency. Children who feel insecure, fearful, ashamed, guilty, or unloved may compensate by manipulating their parents into serving as rescuers. These children often become passive learners who make minimal effort and require constant prodding and support. Some may express their inner turmoil through self-sabotaging behavior. To elicit attention, concern, sympathy, and nurturing, they may pretend that they are incapable of doing what is expected of them. They may refuse to do their homework, study for tests, or submit completed assignments on time. Parents who react by becoming overly attentive and solicitous often send a confusing message to the child: Stay helpless and I will rescue you. To break the cycle of dependency, these children will require counseling from a mental-health professional.

Family dysfunction can also be a primary source of excessive dependency. Marital disharmony, poor communication, health problems, financial problems, continual criticism, or an unpleasant divorce can trigger a range of emotions that include confusion, insecurity, anxiety, sadness, resentment, anger, and guilt. Children whose families are dysfunctional often experience a sense of despair and hopelessness. In reaction, they may become manipulative and controlling and may require continual acknowledgment and assistance. This need for attention and support may be their only means of coping with their pain and insecurity.

Some parents unwittingly encourage dependency by not establishing clearly defined rules, limits, performance standards, and expectations. Children who are not provided with reasonable and consistently applied constraints are invariably confused and often out of control. These youngsters may never fully emerge from the testing phase characteristic of two- and three-year-olds. In their attempt to define the boundaries of what is acceptable and unacceptable, they may continually test and probe and in the process they may become addicted to the concern and negative attention their maladaptive behavior elicits.

Parents may also have an unconscious psychological agenda that discourages their child from becoming self-reliant. They may feel validated and appreciated only when they assume the role of helper, protector, rescuer, and enabler. Emotionally invested in their child's remaining reliant on them, they may construe every problem that their child encounters as a crisis that requires intervention. The consequences of this dynamic can be disastrous. Children who feel they are pleasing their parents by remaining helpless may never become fully functional adults.

When children conclude that their plaintive call for help is guaranteed to bring a concerned parent, teacher, or resource specialist to the rescue, they will be tempted to use this 911 service every time they experience even a minor frustration, setback, or glitch. The reaction they elicit may become more important to them than handling their problems and getting their work done.

Parents who decide to extract themselves from the enabler role and resist their child's manipulative behavior should anticipate triggering stress and unhappiness. Children who have grown habituated to a security blanket are not likely to relinquish it easily. Their parents must draw strength and resolve from the realization that it is in their child's vital self-interest to become self-reliant and that their continual assistance can impede their child's emotional development.

The most potent antidote for dependency is for parents and teachers to encourage children to establish reasonable and attainable short- and long-term goals and to engineer repeated opportunities for children to succeed without help at increasingly difficult tasks. The goal is to help children to reformulate their perceptions about themselves, their abilities, and their need for help. As they become more self-confident, their desire for independence will increase, and they will signal their emancipation by proudly proclaiming: "I don't need help. I can do it on my own!"

COMMON SOURCES OF LEARNED HELPLESSNESS

- learning disabilities
- ADD/ADHD
- emotional problems
- family problems
- poorly defined rules, standards, and expectations
- unconscious parental agenda that encourages dependency

ASSESSING YOUR CHILD'S LEVEL OF INDEPENDENCE

	Yes	No
My child:		
• wants me to sit by her side when she does homework	___	___
• expects me to explain what was taught in class	___	___
• expects me to explain the material in his textbooks	___	___
• expects me to remind her to study for tests	___	___
• expects me to help her study and complete her homework	___	___
• expects me to write and proofread his essays	___	___
• expects me to check over his math problems for errors	___	___
• needs me to prod and coax her to do her work	___	___
• shuts down if I leave her side while she is working	___	___
• tries to manipulate me into rescuing her	___	___
• expects me to help her organize her notebook, desk, and backpack	___	___
• expects me to verify that assignments are completed	___	___
• expects me to help write or type book reports and essays	___	___
• expects me to manage his time	___	___
• expects me to keep him focused and on task	___	___
• expects me to put away his study materials	___	___
• expects me to remind him to hand in his assignments	___	___

A pattern of *yes* answers should be interpreted as a red flag that signals excessive dependency. Unless the maladaptive behaviors are addressed and modified, learned helplessness can become an entrenched, lifelong habit.

ASSESSING PARENTAL ATTITUDES ABOUT INDEPENDENCE

	Yes	No
• I encourage my child to confront reasonable challenges that do not pose a mental or physical threat.	____	____
• I do not take ownership of my child's problems and setbacks, but I do help him understand the issues and examine his emotional responses and options.	____	____
• I allow my child to struggle with reasonable amounts of frustration.	____	____
• I do not attempt to rescue my child every time she encounters a challenge or glitch.	____	____
• I encourage my child to analyze and find solutions to his own problems whenever this is reasonable.	____	____
• I resist being unreasonably guided by my own anxiety or negative expectations when my child confronts a problem or challenging situation.	____	____
• I am willing to seek professional help if my child's helplessness is chronic and emotionally debilitating.	____	____
• I periodically evaluate my parenting style and the appropriateness of my responses to my child.	____	____
• I attempt to understand my child's emotions without projecting my own feelings onto my child.	____	____
• I make every effort to discourage my child from becoming excessively or inappropriately dependent on me.	____	____
• I avoid being overly and unnecessarily protective.	____	____
• I can differentiate my own needs from my child's needs.	____	____

A pattern of *no* answers indicates that parental attitudes about independence and providing assistance need to be examined. Parents who recognize that they are contributing to their child's helplessness have taken the first step in rectifying the situation. Unconscious agendas need to be examined objectively, perhaps with the help of a counselor. Parents who continually assume the role of rescuer are sending their child a psychologically damaging message: "You don't need to grow up. Mommy and Daddy will always be there to save you."

STRATEGIES FOR DISCOURAGING LEARNED HELPLESSNESS

- Encourage the establishment of goals that can be realistically attained.
- Incrementally increase the difficulty of challenges.
- Model how to do an assignment or problem, provide ample opportunities to practice together, and then insist that the assignment be completed without additional help.
- Gradually reduce the amount of time spent proofreading and correcting errors.
- Gradually increase the amount of time allocated for working independently without supervision.
- Resist being manipulated into becoming a rescuer whenever your child confronts a challenge, problem, or setback.
- Create repeated opportunities for success at tasks that do not require continual assistance or supervision.
- Guide your child to the realization that he can prevail over challenges and problems without help.
- Nudge your child from his or her comfort zone.
- Request reasonable accommodations in school if your child cannot do the required work.
- If your child has deficient skills and is not receiving learning assistance, insist on an evaluation to see if your child has learning problems and qualifies for help.
- If your child does not qualify for learning assistance, hire a qualified private tutor or educational therapist.

- Effusively affirm and acknowledge your child for progress and successes.
- Express faith in your child's ability to deal with setbacks and learn from mistakes.
- Urge your child to elevate his goals, expectations, and aspirations.

SEE: Apathy *(page 208)*; Attention Deficit/Attention Deficit Hyperactivity Disorder *(page 214)*; Attention to Details *(page 223)*; Avoiding Responsibility *(page 227)*; Bouncing Back from Setbacks *(page 232)*; Critical Thinking *(page 161)*; Dealing with Consequences *(page 241)*; Decoding *(page 332)*; Defense Mechanisms *(page 373)*; Depression *(page 378)*; Developmental Immaturity *(page 246)*; Disorganization *(page 251)*; Fear of Failure, Success, and/or Competition *(page 383)*; Goal Setting *(page 165)*; Grades *(page 25)*; Identifying Important Information *(page 41)*; I'm Dumb Syndrome *(page 388)*; Incomplete Assignments *(page 256)*; Judgment *(page 260)*; Keeping Up with the Class *(page 51)*; Learning from Mistakes *(page 267)*; Mastery of Academic Content *(page 67)*; Parent-Child Conflict *(page 393)*; Passive Learning *(page 84)*; Performance Standards *(page 91)*; Planning *(page 176)*; Priorities *(page 180)*; Problem Solving *(page 185)*; Procrastination *(page 278)*; Psychological Overlay and Psychological Problems *(page 399)*; Recording Assignments *(page 107)*; School Anxiety *(page 406)*; Self-concept *(page 410)*; Self-control *(page 287)*; Strategic Thinking *(page 189)*; Study Interruptions *(page 122)*; Study Skills *(page 127)*; Teacher-Child Conflict *(page 293)*; Teacher-Designed Tests *(page 132)*; Time Management *(page 138)*; Underachievement *(page 143)*; Verbal Directions *(page 356)*; Vocabulary *(page 150)*; Written Directions *(page 364)*.

PERCEPTUAL PROCESSING

A child's brain is continually being bombarded with sensory data in school. On the most fundamental level, data are comprised of written and spoken symbols: letters, numbers, and words. These symbols constitute the "nuts and bolts" of verbal instructions, written directions, math problems, sentences written on the chalkboard and in textbooks, homework exercises, and class lectures. A child's brain must be able to decode the symbols instantaneously, comprehend the communicated information, retrieve relevant data from memory, and link what is currently being learned with what has already been learned. When this decoding/comprehension/retrieval/linking process functions inefficiently, children are considered to have a learning disability, or to use the more politically correct term, a "learning difference."

Learning problems can wreak havoc on a child's life. The underlying perceptual-processing deficits erect major obstacles to the mastery of fundamental academic skills, and these deficiencies, in turn, impede the acquisition of advanced academic skills.

Learning disorders generally manifest in one or more of the following areas:

- READING:
  Reading can be a nightmare for children who struggle to decipher words. These students typically reverse letters and numbers, omit syllables and words when reading, and lose their place. They also frequently have difficulty copying accurately from the chalkboard and/or from material on their desks.

- SPELLING
  Spelling can confound children with decoding, phonemic awareness, auditory discrimination, and visual memory deficits. Non-phonetic words are usually the most problematic.

- MATH

  Chronic math difficulties may also indicate a learning disability. Students may reverse numbers, align number columns incorrectly, make careless computational errors, have difficulty understanding concepts such as fractions, and have problems performing basic operations, such as adding and subtracting without using fingers, memorizing multiplication tables, finding common denominators, or properly moving decimal points when multiplying or dividing.

- COMPREHENSION AND MEMORY

  Difficulty understanding and recalling information, following verbal and written instructions, and remembering the correct sequence of what is seen or heard places children at a significant academic disadvantage. These deficits are likely to undermine performance in all content areas.

- ENCODING

  Students who have difficulty expressing their ideas verbally and/or on paper are described as having an encoding problem. Their performance on tests, in class discussions, and on essays and reports does not accurately reflect their actual mastery of the academic content.

- MOTOR COORDINATION

  Developmental delays may be a causal factor in inefficient perceptual processing. These delays may manifest as *gross-motor-coordination* deficits. Primary symptoms include difficulty with balance and coordinating both sides of the body. Children with *fine-motor-coordination* deficits have difficulty manipulating their fingers, using scissors, drawing shapes, and writing legibly.

- STUDY SKILLS

  Students who don't know how to identify important information, take notes, and prepare effectively for tests invariably struggle in upper-level courses. Many of these students fail to develop efficient study skills because of underlying perceptual-decoding deficits.

Difficulty concentrating, filtering out distractions, and managing impulsivity can significantly exacerbate perceptual-processing difficulties and magnify specific academic skill deficiencies. Students with chronic attention deficit hyperactivity disorder* are rarely able to function in school at a level commensurate with their true ability.

Diagnostic tests administered by school psychologists can usually identify with great precision and reliability the specific perceptual-processing deficits that are interfering with a child's ability to learn efficiently. Unfortunately, commonly used remediation methods are rarely as precise or reliable as the diagnostic procedures, and significant improvement sometimes proves elusive to children enrolled in special-education programs. For this reason, parents must be prepared to monitor their child's progress closely and intervene proactively when necessary. The more informed parents are about the issues, the more effective their intervention.

In the following section, you will learn about the academic implications of a learning disability and the specific deficits that indicate an underlying perceptual-processing dysfunction.

Auditory Discrimination

▲

Refers to the ability to distinguish the distinct sounds that letters and groups of letters produce. Auditory discrimination is a requisite to being able to read and spell words that conform to the rules of phonics.

▲

The ability to identify and differentiate accurately the vocalized sounds produced by consonants, vowels, and groups of letters is vital to learning how to read and spell phonetically. This phonetic methodology is based on a system of rules that governs the way letters and words are pronounced. Because there are numerous excep-

---

*New terminology has recently been introduced: ADHD inattentive type; ADHD hyperactive-impulsive type; ADHD combined type; and ADHD NOS (not otherwise specified).

tions to the rules of phonics in the English language, many words are considered nonphonetic and must be learned by sight or memorized. Examples include *through, thought, thorough, trough,* and *bread* and foreign words such as *colonel, lieutenant,* and *sergeant.* Despite these anomalies, English is considered a phonetically based language.

In contrast to *sight-reading-programs* that are based on visual recognition of words and *whole-language reading programs* that are based on a less structured acquisition of reading, spelling, and writing skills, all *phonics-based reading programs* systematically teach children how to differentiate sounds. This process, which is called decoding, comprises the foundation of reading instruction in first through third grade, and the acquisition of auditory-discrimination skills is a requisite to progressing successfully.

Students begin the process of learning how to decode basic sounds in kindergarten and first grade. They are methodically taught to break down words into phonetic fragments or phonemes (referred to as *sounding out words*) and to blend the sounds to form words. The phrase *word attack* describes this sounding-out procedure.

Children must be able to hear the difference between the sounds *i* and *e* and *p* and *d* and the consonant-vowel blends *fli* and *fle* if they are to read and spell words such as *did, flip,* and *fled.* Children who struggle to decode sounds are described as having an auditory-discrimination problem. For these children, learning how to read can be a nightmare. Progress is slow and painful, and in some cases, children will remain functionally illiterate unless they receive intensive learning assistance.

Most children with auditory-discrimination deficits do not have an organic *hearing impairment.* Rather, their difficulty deciphering and associating sounds with the letters that comprise sounds is attributable to a perplexing neurologically based *auditory dysfunction.*

Auditory-discrimination problems can be effectively treated and resolved if children are provided with highly specialized, systematic instruction. With early diagnosis and effective intervention—ideally in first grade—children who are making little or no progress in reading and spelling can become fluent readers and competent spellers. They can also be spared the emotional pain and self-concept damage commonly associated with profound reading and spelling problems.

SYMPTOMS OF AN AUDITORY-DISCRIMINATION PROBLEM

- difficulty sounding out and reading phonetic words
- difficulty spelling phonetic words
- difficulty acquiring advanced-reading skills
- frustration and self-consciousness when reading
- negative and/or phobic associations with reading
- diminished academic self-confidence

DIAGNOSTIC TOOLS

Formal Assessment

- Goldman-Fristoe Test of Auditory Discrimination: Using a recorded text, this test measures the ability to discriminate speech sounds against two different backgrounds—quiet and noisy. The test is designed for children ages 3+.
- Lindamood Auditory Conceptualization (LAC) test: This test assesses a child's ability to distinguish the sounds that vowels and consonants produce when isolated and when used in words. The test indicates how many correct answers a child receives out of a possible 100. For example, a third-grade student's score may be 40/100. This score indicates significant auditory-discrimination deficits and strongly suggests that auditory-discrimination training is advisable.
- Woodcock Johnson Psycho-Educational Battery-R: Test of Cognitive Ability (Broad Reading): The letter/word subtest (called

Sound Patterns) asks the student to name letters and sight words, words containing short vowels, and words containing consonant and vowel combinations. The test yields an age score (the student's number of correct answers that corresponds statistically to other children of the same age), a *scaled score* (a statistical ranking of a student's correct answers relative to other children of the same age and grade level), and a *percentile score* (another statistical derivation that ranks a student's score relative to every hundred students taking the test).

- Wepman Test of Auditory Discrimination: measures the ability to discriminate auditorially between two similar words that are presented orally. The rating scale ranges from "very good development" at the top end to "below the level of threshold of adequacy" at the bottom end. The examiner says two words (such as *bid, bit*), and the child is asked if they sound the same or different. The test is for children between the ages of four and eleven.
- Test of Auditory Perceptual Skills-R (TAPS): measures functional level in specific areas of auditory perception and auditory processing, including discrimination.
- Phonological Awareness Test (PAT): measures the ability to progress phonologically from phonemes to syllables to words.

TREATMENT PROTOCOLS

- **Lindamood Phonemic Sequencing (LiPS):** This method, previously called auditory discrimination in depth (ADD), systematically teaches the basic sounds that are central to phonics. Children learn how individual sounds are produced physiologically (called oral-motor feedback); distinguish between sounds (e.g.: "plosives," "tappers," and "poppers"), manipulate colored blocks that represent sounds and form words, and learn how to blend combinations of consonants and vowels. Many schools are now offering this program to children with learning disabilities who require intensive training in auditory discrimination. If taught in its entirety, the program takes at least a hundred hours of intensive instruction to complete.

- **Fast Forward:** This method systematically addresses specific aspects of auditory processing, progressing from the most basic phonemic level (the most fundamental unit of sound) to broader phonological awareness (words and syllables). Some schools offer this program to children with learning disabilities who have serious reading problems that are attributable to inadequate phonemic awareness.

- **Phonological Awareness Kit:** This method, published by the same company that developed the Phonological Awareness Test (PAT), addresses deficient phonological awareness and progress from the basic phonemic level to actual phonics. Some resource specialists and speech-and-language pathologists use this kit.

- **Earobic:** A computer-based auditory-processing, phonemic-awareness, and phonological-processing program. Some resource specialists and speech-and-language pathologists use this program.

- **Speech-and-language therapy:** Speech-and-language clinicians utilize a range of eclectic methods and materials to develop auditory-processing and auditory-discrimination skills. They will often treat clients with both articulation and auditory-discrimination difficulties.

SEE: Articulation *(page 429)*; Auditory Memory *(page 322)*; Brain Dysfunction *(page 326)*; Decoding *(page 332)*; Dyslexia *(page 335)*; Grades *(page 25)*; I'm Dumb Syndrome *(page 388)*; Keeping Up with the Class *(page 51)*; Language Arts *(page 58)*; Mastery of Academic Content *(page 67)*; Performance Standards *(page 91)*; Phonics *(page 346)*; Reading Fluency *(page 351)*; Reading Comprehension *(page 100)*; School Anxiety *(page 406)*; Self-concept *(page 410)*; Spelling *(page 112)*; Test Anxiety *(page 420)*; Underachievement *(page 143)*; Visual Memory *(page 360)*.

Auditory Memory

▲

Refers to the ability to recall accurately verbally communicated information.

▲

Children are required to recall vast amounts of verbally communicated information. Six-year-olds are expected to remember their phone number, address, and teacher's name. They are also expected to be able to recite the alphabet and recall the sounds that individual letters make. In second grade they are required to know how to decode and pronounce blends such as "tr," "th," and "pl" make. (To make these letter/sound associations, children must be able to differentiate sounds—a process called *auditory discrimination.*) As they advance in school, the demands on their ability to retain information increase exponentially. They must remember important historical dates. They must recall the definitions of vocabulary words and their teacher's clues about what will be covered on the next science test. They must recall their teacher's explicit directions about how to format an essay, fill out a test-answer sheet, or solve long-division problems. They must remember which questions in their textbook their teacher told them to answer in class and which they were instructed to answer for homework. Even if they attempt to write down the directions, they must have short-term auditory-memory capabilities or they'll forget the information before they can record it.

Short- and long-term auditory-recall deficits are classified as a perceptual dysfunction. Children with poor auditory memory often have difficulty in other areas of decoding and encoding (verbal and/or written expression). Auditory-memory deficiencies may be compounded by deficits in any or all of the following areas: auditory discrimination, auditory sequencing (difficulty recalling data in the proper order), visual memory, visual sequencing, and/or visual discrimination. These decoding deficiencies are usually attributable to subtle anomalies in the physiology and neurochemistry of the brain where specific cerebral regions are responsible for specific processing functions. It should be noted, however, that relatively few children with perceptual-processing deficits actually have organic brain damage.

Children with significant auditory-memory deficits are at a major disadvantage in school and often become overwhelmed and confused by the barrage of verbal data with which they are bombarded in the classroom. Clueless about what the teacher expects them to do, many will attempt to compensate for their auditory deficits by furtively looking over the shoulder of the closest classmate and desperately trying to divine what he or she is doing.

Chronic short-term and long-term auditory-memory deficits can undermine academic performance in all content areas, and the repercussions are not limited exclusively to the classroom. Children who struggle to recall what they are told in school also typically have difficulty remembering what they are told at home. They might forget to feed the dog or bring in the groceries from the car despite having been explicitly told to do so two minutes previously. They may head for the front door, but by the time they get there, they may have already forgotten what they were asked to do. Because the verbal information is not registering, these youngsters often appear inattentive, distracted, disoriented, and absentminded. Their memory lapses may lead their parents and teachers to conclude that they are inattentive, disinterested, resistant, oppositional, or lacking in intelligence. The excuse typically offered by children with auditory-memory deficits is both simple and accurate: "I forgot."

Children with poor auditory recall usually receive a great deal of negative feedback from their perplexed and frustrated teachers and parents, and their academic self-confidence is often fragile. Because the ability to retain information is so critical in school, many youngsters with poor auditory memory become convinced that they are inadequate and unintelligent. Their anxiety often causes them to become even more dysfunctional.

Auditory-recall deficits can obviously be magnified by

ADD/ADHD. The child who has difficulty filtering out distractions, staying on task, controlling impulsivity, and paying attention is also likely to have difficulty retaining what he is told.

Children who think strategically will often attempt to compensate for their poor auditory recall by writing down instructions and taking comprehensive lecture notes. Some students, however, overcompensate and try to record everything. In their attempt to "get it down on paper," they may not listen to the actual content of what they are hearing, and as a consequence, their comprehension will suffer.

Students who do not think strategically make little effort to compensate for their auditory-memory deficits. Those with the greatest need to record verbally communicated information are often the most resistant to doing so either because they are lazy or because they delude themselves into thinking that they can remember the information. The consequences are predictable: Important details are omitted, assignments are not submitted, instructions are not followed, incomplete work is submitted, and deadlines are missed.

Youngsters with short- and/or long-term auditory-memory deficits are at a particular disadvantage when they have teachers who do a great deal of lecturing. These children are often frustrated and demoralized. By third grade, bright and potentially capable children with severe auditory-memory deficits may have already concluded that they are hopelessly inept. This conclusion can cause them to lower their expectations and aspirations and acquiesce to marginal achievement.

With appropriate intervention and instruction, most children can improve their auditory-recall skills. They can learn a range of memory "tricks" and use other sensory modalities to compensate for their memory deficits. For example, children who are given complex verbal instructions about how to format a report could compensate for their auditory-memory deficits by closing their eyes and visualizing the steps in their mind as they hear them. They might repeat subvocally what has been said while visualizing themselves methodically following the directions. Recording the instructions is, of course, another logical and pragmatic compensation. Teaching children a "speed writing" system that utilizes abbreviations can also help them record the key information more quickly.

These practical strategies can significantly reduce anxiety, improve self-confidence, and enhance retention capacity. Children who learn productive compensatory "tricks" are far less likely to resort to se' sabotaging, counterproductive behavior, such as shutting down, not listening, not paying attention, or disturbing other students.

INDICATIONS OF AUDITORY-MEMORY DEFICITS

- confusion when given verbal instructions
- difficulty following and recalling verbal directions and explanations
- difficulty recalling the content of class lectures
- difficulty remembering verbally communicated information in the correct order
- compelling need to record everything the teacher says in class
- difficulty linking new verbal information to previously given verbal information (e.g., "Move the decimal in these division problems two places in the same way you moved the decimal one place in the preceding problems.")
- panic and stress when information is communicated verbally
- confusion about what the teacher expects
- tendency to tune out when explanations are being given
- feelings of inadequacy in verbally loaded learning contexts
- work that does not conform to explicit directions
- anxiety during oral class discussions
- difficulty taking lecture notes
- discouragement and demoralization
- diminished academic self-confidence

Sᴇᴇ: Attention Deficit/Attention Deficit Hyperactivity Disorder *(page 214)*; Attention to Details *(page 223)*; Auditory Discrimination *(page 317)*; Brain Dysfunction *(page 326)*; Decoding *(page 332)*; Frustration *(page 378)*; Grades *(page 25)*; I'm Dumb Syndrome *(page 388)*; Intelligence *(page 45)*; Keeping Up with the Class *(page 51)*; Mastery of Academic Content *(page 67)*; Math *(page 72)*; Passive Learning *(page 84)*; Phonics *(page 346)*; Reading Comprehension *(page 100)*; Recording Assignments *(page 107)*; School Anxiety *(page 406)*; Self-concept *(page 410)*; Spelling *(page 112)*; Standardized Tests *(page 116)*; Study Skills *(page 127)*; Teacher-Designed Tests *(page 132)*; Test Anxiety *(page 420)*; Underachievement *(page 143)*; Verbal Directions *(page 356)*; Visual Discrimination *(page 343)*; Visual Memory *(page 360)*; Vocabulary *(page 150)*.

Brain Dysfunction

▲

Refers to difficulty accurately perceiving and efficiently processing sensory data.

▲

A child's brain is continually being bombarded with sensory data in the classroom. External stimuli received through the five senses and internal stimuli are processed *(decoded)* neurologically, and the brain then expresses responses in the form of written or spoken words, facial expressions, and/or body movements.

In school the range of sensory data that must be decoded by a child's brain includes teachers' verbal and written directions, explanations, definitions, formulas, and facts as well as information contained in textbooks and verbally communicated during class lectures. With remarkable efficiency these data are assimilated, and the brain either reacts immediately or files the information in memory for future reference.

Thoughts, feelings, and answers to questions are expressed *(encoded)* with equivalent efficiency. The teacher asks a question, and the child's brain instantaneously decodes the question, retrieves relevant previously learned information from memory, and encodes a response, either orally or in writing. In theory, this is how the decoding/encoding process *should* function. Unfortunately, the brains of children who are struggling with learning problems seldom operate with this degree of efficacy.

Two types of problems can interfere with perceptual-processing efficiency and impede the acquisition of auditory, visual, gross-motor, fine-motor, language, and learning skills. The first type is *organic* and can be traced to *measurable deficiencies* in brain function, metabolism, physiology, or visual acuity. Such physiologically based problems are classified as *impairments.* Examples of organic impairments include hearing loss, poor vision, or cerebral palsy.

Certain severe learning disorders are also considered to be organic when they are attributable to brain damage caused by oxygen deprivation, disease, trauma, or genetically based defects. In these cases, actual abnormalities in brain physiology and function can be identified.

The second type of problem that can affect receptive and expressive language, vision, motor coordination, and learning skills is *nonorganic* and is classified as a *dysfunction.* A dysfunction does not involve neurological or physiological damage that can be measured by commonly available medical diagnostic instruments, such as an EEG, MRI, or CAT scan.

Most learning differences are attributable to a perceptual-processing dysfunction and not to an actual organic impairment. The dysfunction typically manifests as deficits in visual or auditory discrimination (accurately differentiating the sounds that letters make), memory, and/or sequencing. These deficits typically cause children to struggle with oral reading, comprehension, math, spelling, handwriting, and/or language arts. Many articulation deficits, gross- and fine-motor coordination difficulties, and expressive language problems are also considered nonorganic and are classified as a dysfunction. More severe deficiencies such as *aphasia* (the inability to communicate effectively with spoken language) are in most cases attributable to organic brain damage and are classified as impairments.

As the diagnostic tools and procedures for analyzing the physiology and metabolism of the brain become increasingly precise, the line separating an organic impairment from a nonorganic dysfunction is beginning to blur. Refined methods can now pinpoint the cerebral origins of anomalies in the brain that are responsible for certain types of learning disorders such as dyslexia.* Using high-tech imaging equipment called functional magnetic resonance imaging (fMRI), neuroscientists can identify specific neurological regions that are malfunctioning when a dyslexic child or adult reads. These brain scans indicate that dyslexics show little activity in areas known to be critically important in linking written words with their phonic components. The new research suggests that many learning problems that were once considered dysfunctions of nonorganic origin may in fact be traced to relatively subtle organically based problems.

Researchers are also beginning to understand how neurotransmitters (cerebral hormones) function and affect learning. This has led to a better grasp of the interrelationship between brain function, brain metabolism, and behavior, to greater insight into the underlying physiological and metabolic factors that can cause learning problems, and to a better understanding of how different types of medication affect neurological functioning.

Neuropsychologists, developmental pediatricians, and pediatric neurologists can administer a range of diagnostic tests that are specifically designed to detect brain dysfunction and organic impairment. These tests assess language development, sensory and motor functions, perceptual decoding, attention, learning efficiency, recall, and learning style.

---

*Currently, these technologically advanced diagnostic tools are generally available only at major medical-research centers.

Since the left and right cerebral hemispheres of the brain have different functions—the left hemisphere being dominant for verbal, sequential, and logical processing and the right being dominant for visual-spatial functions and emotions—a child's preferred hemispheric modes of learning are usually assessed as an integral component of a comprehensive neuropsychological diagnostic workup. The data derived from this assessment can be invaluable in understanding the dynamics of a child's perceptual-processing deficits and in providing insight and guidance to resource specialists and/or educational therapists. The evaluation can be especially useful when the symptoms and origins of the learning problem are complex and confusing and involve multiple, overlapping deficits and causal factors.

Brain dysfunctions can range from subtle to severe. Because many common learning deficits are attributable to the inefficient neurological processing of sensory data, these processing deficits are interpreted by diagnosticians as primary indications of a brain dysfunction. Chronic distractibility, daydreaming, inattentiveness, impulsivity, and hyperactivity—the classic symptoms of ADD/ADHD—are also considered to be anomalies in neurological functioning.

SYMPTOMS OF A POSSIBLE BRAIN DYSFUNCTION

Motor Skills

- clumsiness
- poor handwriting
- graphomotor difficulty (drawing)
- poor gross-motor coordination
- poor balance
- awkwardness
- right/left confusion
- poor eye-hand coordination
- difficulty with spatial awareness and orientation

Behavior (Many of these traits are linked to ADD/ADHD.)

- overactivity
- impulsivity
- short attention span
- distractibility
- excitability
- repeated accidents
- poor self-control
- chronic confusion
- developmental immaturity
- forgetfulness
- slowness in completing work
- unpredictability
- impatience
- daydreaming
- chronic frustration
- causing disturbances to others
- difficulty working independently
- incomplete projects
- difficulty accepting guidelines
- recklessness
- disorganization
- acting out behavior

Academics

- difficulty keeping up with class
- inaccurate assignments
- slow in completing work
- sloppy work habits
- difficulty spelling
- letter or number reversals
- inaccurate reading
- poor phonics
- difficulty following written directions
- poor reading comprehension
- difficulty recalling information

- difficulty following verbal directions
- difficulty blending sounds
- difficulty identifying sight words
- difficulty with word attack
- difficulty with language arts
- difficulty with math concepts
- difficulty with math computations
- inaccurate copying at desk
- sloppy work
- inaccurate copying from chalkboard

SEE: Aptitude *(page 15)*; Attention Deficit/Attention Deficit Hyperactivity Disorder *(page 214)*; Attention to Details *(page 223)*; Auditory Discrimination *(page 317)*; Auditory Memory *(page 322)*; Decoding *(page 332)*; Developmental Immaturity *(page 246)*; Dyslexia *(page 335)*; Essays and Essay Tests *(page 18)*; Grades *(page 25)*; Handwriting *(page 36)*; I'm Dumb Syndrome *(page 388)*; Inaccurate Copying *(page 342)*; Incomplete Assignments *(page 256)*; Intelligence *(page 45)*; Keeping Up with the Class *(page 51)*; Language Arts *(page 58)*; Language Disorders *(page 433)*; Logic *(page 171)*; Mastery of Academic Content *(page 67)*; Math *(page 72)*; Phonics *(page 346)*; Planning *(page 176)*; Priorities *(page 180)*; Problem Solving *(page 185)*; Psychological Overlay and Psychological Problems *(page 399)*; Reading Fluency *(page 351)*; Reading Comprehension *(page 100)*; Recording Assignments *(page 107)*; School Anxiety *(page 406)*; Speech Disorders *(page 429)*; Spelling *(page 112)*; Standardized Tests *(page 116)*; Strategic Thinking *(page 189)*; Study Skills *(page 127)*; Teacher-Designed Tests *(page 132)*; Test Anxiety *(page 420)*; Time Management *(page 138)*; Underachievement *(page 143)*; Verbal Directions *(page 356)*; Visual Discrimination *(page 343)*; Visual Memory *(page 360)*; Word Attack *(page 318)*; Working Independently *(page 302)*; Written Directions *(page 364)*.

Decoding

▲

Refers to the processing of sensory data and specifically the decipher-ing of written and spoken language.

▲

To function effectively in school, children must be able to process immediately the plethora of sensory data that constantly bombard them in the classroom. They must understand and follow direc-tions, decipher phonemes (the basic building blocks of words), blend sounds, sound out words, and assimilate and recall in-formation they see and hear. Under ideal conditions the brain performs these functions with efficiency, and children learn with relative ease.

Children who struggle to decode sensory information may have difficulty visually differentiating letters such as *b* and *d*, hearing the difference between certain vowels or consonants, reading accurately, or recalling what they have heard in class or read in a book. They may reverse letters and numbers and be unable to retain information in the proper sequence. They may struggle to understand written and/or verbal instructions. These perceptual decoding deficits can erect major barriers to academic skill mastery.

Many children with a decoding dysfunction also have deficient reading-comprehension skills. Overwhelmed by the continual strug-gle to decipher written words (a condition called dyslexia), these children are often so emotionally and intellectually depleted by their continual efforts to process sensory information that they have little left to devote to comprehending and retaining the content of what they are reading.

There are anomalies, however. Some children with significant decoding problems are able to understand and retain far more than would normally be expected. Despite their processing deficits and reading inaccuracies, their comprehension is quite good. These chil-dren, who are usually very bright, somehow intuitively figure out how to use their intelligence to offset their decoding deficits. They are, however, the exception rather than the rule.

Most learning-disabled children cannot figure out on their own how to compensate for their auditory- and/or visual-decoding deficits and require intensive remedial assistance if they are to survive academically. Fortunately, highly effective methods of teaching students how to decode auditory and visual sensory data more efficiently have been developed. These programs, which incorporate systematic and sequential training procedures, include Orton-Gillingham, Slingerland, Lindamood, and Fast Forward. Many resource specialists, however, prefer to use less formularized remedial techniques.

The critical first step in developing a productive remediation program is to identify the specific processing deficits that are impeding a child's academic progress. School psychologists, educational psychologists, resource specialists, and educational therapists can administer a range of diagnostic tests that are designed to pinpoint with great accuracy the specific underlying perceptual-processing deficiencies that are interfering with a child's ability to decode sensory data effectively. The information derived from this assessment is vital in developing an effective and focused intervention strategy.

SYMPTOMS OF DECODING PROBLEMS

- difficulty keeping up with class
- incomplete assignments
- inaccurate work (spelling errors, omitted words, poor grammar and punctuation)
- slowness in completing work
- sloppy work
- difficulty spelling
- letter and/or number reversals
- inaccurate reading (transposed letters, flipped words, omissions, etc.)

- poor phonics
- difficulty discriminating sounds (e.g., "a" and "e")
- difficulty with phonemic sequencing (deciphering sounds in the proper order)
- difficulty following written directions
- difficulty following oral directions
- poor reading comprehension
- difficulty retaining information
- difficulty remembering information in the proper sequence
- difficulty with verbal directions
- difficulty blending sounds
- difficulty identifying sight words
- difficulty with word attack
- difficulty with language arts
- difficulty understanding math concepts
- difficulty with math computations
- incomplete assignments
- inaccurate copying at desk
- sloppy and/or illegible work
- inaccurate copying at chalkboard
- poor grades

SEE: Attention Deficit/Attention Deficit Hyperactivity Disorder *(page 214)*; Attention to Details *(page 223)*; Auditory Discrimination *(page 317)*; Auditory Memory *(page 322)*; Brain Dysfunction *(page 326)*; Developmental Immaturity *(page 246)*; Dyslexia *(page 335)*; Grades *(page 25)*; Handwriting *(page 36)*; I'm Dumb Syndrome *(page 388)*; Inaccurate Copying *(page 342)*; Incomplete Assignments *(page 256)*; Intelligence *(page 45)*; Keeping Up with the Class *(page 51)*; Language Arts *(page 58)*; Language Disorders *(page 433)*; Logic *(page 171)*; Mastery of Academic Content *(page 67)*; Math *(page 72)*; Phonics *(page 346)*; Planning *(page 176)*; Priorities *(page 180)*; Problem Solving *(page 185)*; Psychological Overlay and Psychological Problems *(page 399)*; Reading Comprehension *(page 100)*; Reading Fluency *(page 351)*; Recording Assignments *(page 107)*;

Dyslexia

▲

Refers to a reading dysfunction caused by the inaccurate decoding of written symbols. The dysfunction typically manifests as letter and number reversals (example: b/d) and word reversals (example: was/saw).

▲

Human beings have been using oral language to communicate for more than one hundred thousand years, and evolution has hardwired this capacity to communicate with spoken words into the neurology of the species. The progression from cooing to babbling to using single words and, ultimately, multiple words is both natural and automatic.

In contrast, written language is a relatively recent phenomenon that dates back perhaps five thousand years. Because of its belated development, the capacity to read is neither genetically imprinted nor acquired naturally. Most children must be methodically taught how to decipher written words. Some master the requisite skills with relative ease. Others must continually struggle to make sense out of the symbols written on the page and on the chalkboard.

Academic instruction is predicated on students being able to decode, comprehend, and retain what they read. Children with poor reading skills are at a profound disadvantage. Those who cannot read with age-appropriate fluency and comprehension are destined to suffer scholastically and psychologically, and their prospects for self-actualization and rewarding vocations are virtually nil, with a few notable exceptions.*

The term dyslexia is usually used to describe children who have significant reading problems. Some professionals employ the terminology generically to describe all types of serious reading deficiencies. Others use the term to describe a specific neurologically based reading dysfunction the symptoms of which include letter reversals *(b/d)*, number reversals, upside-down letters and numbers *(6/9)*, word reversals *(saw/was)*, and transpositions and/or omissions of letters, syllables, words, and phrases when reading.

Letter and number reversals are quite common in kindergarten, and five- and six-year-olds who confuse *b* and *d* and who write 3s, 7s, and 9s backwards are not necessarily manifesting a reading dysfunction. A red flag should go up, however, when children continue to reverse letters and numbers beyond the first six months of first grade. If the condition persists into second grade, these children are at risk for being dyslexic.

When children cannot make sense out of letters and words, reading is a nightmare. Asking a dyslexic child to read aloud in class is akin to asking a child with a significant physical disability to pole-vault. The child is unwittingly being set up by his teacher to fail. The continual effort to decipher letters and words that are flipped or that dance, wiggle, and tumble across the page and to keep one's place when reading can cause acute embarrassment, undermine self-esteem and self-confidence, generate feelings of inadequacy and hopelessness, and trigger profoundly negative associations with reading.

In reaction to their relentless struggle to decode written language, many dyslexic children become reading-phobic. To protect themselves from feeling incompetent, these children often acquire

---

*The exceptions include Leonardo da Vinci, George Patton, Nelson Rockefeller, Bruce Jenner, and Charles Schwab. All of these luminaries obviously transcended their profound reading problems.

an elaborate system of defensive behaviors that may include laziness, irresponsibility, defensiveness, denial, blaming, dependency, procrastination, acting out, dependency, and manipulative behavior.

There have been many theories about the causes and etiology of dyslexia. These include right/left confusion (directionality deficits), poor ocular-muscle control of the horizontal movement of the eyes across the printed line, difficulty with convergence (getting both eyes to coordinate), poor equilibrium, perceptual-processing deficits, and cranial misalignment (a controversial theory espoused by some chiropractors).

Researchers are now beginning to unravel the neurological physiology and dynamics of dyslexia. Longitudinal studies have clearly established that the condition is genetically based. Dyslexia often afflicts several members of the same family and often spans many generations. A father, his daughter, and her first cousin may all suffer from the problem.

An analysis of the learning patterns of dyslexic children clearly indicates that they must struggle to pull words apart into their constituent sounds. These sounds are called phonemes, and there are more than forty in the English language. For dyslexic children, differentiating the phonemes in a word such as *pat* (i.e., *puh—aah—tuh*) usually represents a monumental challenge. Because dyslexics hear only the entire word and not the phonemes, they cannot break even the simplest of words apart and consequently have difficulty sounding out the words. In addition, dyslexic children also have problems connecting the sounds with the corresponding letters that make the sounds. This linking procedure is referred to as phonics.

Nondyslexic children have little difficulty identifying phonemes and assimilating phonics. The sounding-out process is essentially automatic, and they progress from being able to decode single-syllable words to deciphering multisyllable words with relative ease.

Researchers are currently using brain scans (functional magnetic resonance imaging, or fMRI) to measure cerebral activity when words are being read. The research indicates that when dyslexics try to decipher words, certain areas in the front of the brain where speech production is governed are in overdrive. Other areas in the back of the brain are underactivated. The research suggests that dyslexics may have to work harder to analyze sound patterns because they have faulty cerebral wiring and inefficient cerebral pathways.

Dyslexic children may respond positively to a wide range of remediation techniques. Most resource specialists and reading specialists focus on developing children's visual-discrimination skills (seeing the difference between letters such as *b* and *d*) and improving visual-tracking skills (the effectiveness with which the eyes move from left to right across the printed line). The LiPS program (Lindamood Phonemic Sequencing) has also proved highly effective in helping children learn how to break down words. The program helps students differentiate sounds by methodically training them to identify how sounds feel when they are being pronounced.

That dyslexic children can respond positively to radically different remedial methods suggests that rapport with the teacher and the "halo effect" should be factored into any attempt to substantiate the efficacy of a particular intervention. The halo effect (also referred to as the *Hawthorne Effect*) acknowledges that some skill improvement may be attributable to extra attention and may not necessarily reflect the efficacy of a particular intervention method. A child's reading may improve because he likes his tutor and wants to please her and/or because he's receiving affirmation, encouragement, and individualized help.

Motivation plays a key role in improving the reading skills of dyslexic children. Students who perceive that they are making progress and who become convinced that they can prevail over their reading deficiencies are invariably more willing to work diligently than children who are defeated and demoralized.

Perceptive resource specialists and educational therapists who have been trained in a wide range of remedial techniques will often experiment and combine different methodologies until they discover the most effective remedial prescription for a particular child. Whatever instructional technique is employed, consistent and methodical instruction is vital. Dyslexic children must literally be trained systematically to recognize phonemes, break down words, and link letters with sounds.

Because of more effective learning-assistance programs and better-trained teachers, dyslexic children who might never have learned to read twenty years ago are now successfully compensating for their reading deficits. Many are now able to go on to college, and they are succeeding academically and earning degrees because colleges and universities are now providing learning-disabled students with support services and are making accommodations. These services and accommodations include tutoring, untimed tests, and tutors who take lecture notes for learning-disabled students.*

Despite the improvements in instructional methodology, many schools provide only marginal assistance to dyslexic students. In many districts, children must test at least two years below grade level in order to qualify for remedial help in spite of compelling evidence that early diagnosis and intervention can prevent devastating self-concept damage. Deprived of meaningful help, these stymied students often become convinced that their reading problems are insoluble and that they are hopelessly defective. The consequences are predictable: demoralization, lowered expectations and aspirations, chronic underachievement, and wasted human potential.

When struggling children are deprived of learning assistance or are not making progress, their parents must become their outspoken advocates. They must seek assistance either within or outside the educational system, and they must make certain that the help is provided *before* the window of opportunity slams shut and *before* their child becomes discouraged, turns off to reading, loses academic self-confidence, and shuts down in school.

---

*Many colleges and universities have modified entrance requirements for students with documented learning disabilities. High-school students can also request to take the college entrance exam (SAT) untimed. Qualifying requirements for taking an untimed SAT have recently become far more rigorous, as some families have abused the system and have concocted a learning disability to give their child a competitive advantage on the SAT.

Dyslexic children can learn how to read, and it is essential that parents and teachers find the pedagogical key. The alternative to effective, proactive intervention is unmitigated academic, psychological, and vocational disaster.

SYMPTOMS COMMONLY ASSOCIATED WITH DYSLEXIA

- letter reversals
- word reversals (e.g., *saw/was*)
- number reversals
- omitted syllables when reading aloud
- omitted words
- omitted phrases
- transpositions (i.e., words or syllables read out of order)
- inaccurate reading
- inaccurate spelling
- difficulty reading fluently
- difficulty with phonics
- difficulty blending sounds
- difficulty with word attack
- difficulty tracking words (i.e., child losing place when reading)
- difficulty identifying sight words
- poor reading comprehension
- difficulty with proofreading
- inaccurate copying at desk (near point)
- inaccurate copying from chalkboard (far point)

METHODS FOR TREATING DYSLEXIA

- intensive visual-discrimination training (teaching students how to focus and process sensory data more efficiently)
- methodical visual-tracking exercises (workbooks, handouts, and other remedial materials)

- eye-muscle training (practiced by specialists in developmental optometry)
- kinesthetic/neurological imprinting (incorporated in the Slinger-land and Orton-Gillingham methods)
- colored lenses (used to treat a condition called *scotopic dyslexia* in which letters run together or "fall" off the page)
- intensive auditory-discrimination training (teaching students to differentiate sounds)
- drug therapy for dyslexic students who have ADD/ADHD (Ritalin, etc.)
- cranial adjustments (a highly controversial chiropractic technique)

SEE: Attention to Details *(page 223);* Auditory Discrimination *(page 317);* Auditory Memory *(page 322);* Brain Dysfunction *(page 326);* Decoding *(page 332);* Depression *(page 378);* Essays and Essay Tests *(page 18);* Frustration *(page 378);* Grades *(page 25);* I'm Dumb Syndrome *(page 388);* Incomplete Assignments *(page 256);* Keeping Up with the Class *(page 51);* Language Arts *(page 58);* Mastery of Academic Content *(page 67);* Math *(page 72);* Note Taking *(page 79);* Parent-Child Conflict *(page 393);* Passive Learning *(page 84);* Phonics *(page 346);* Psychological Overlay and Psychological Problems *(page 399);* Reading Comprehension *(page 100);* Reading Fluency *(page 351);* Recording Assignments *(page 107);* Resistance to Help *(page 282);* School Anxiety *(page 406);* Self-concept *(page 410);* Spelling *(page 112);* Standardized Tests *(page 116);* Study Skills *(page 127);* Teacher-Designed Tests *(page 132);* Test Anxiety *(page 420);* Underachievement *(page 143);* Visual Discrimination *(page 343);* Visual Memory *(page 360);* Word Attack *(page 318);* Working Independently *(page 302).*

Inaccurate Copying

▲

Refers to difficulty recording written information with precision.

▲

Children are continually transferring information from one place to another. Typical tasks include recording an assignment written on the chalkboard, copying information from a textbook onto binder paper, reproducing on paper an exercise in a workbook, or writing down a facsimile math problem included in a handout.

The accuracy of children's copying skills can have a profound impact on their scholastic performance in every subject area. Those who inaccurately record the due dates for book reports and term papers are likely to miss an important deadline. Those who copy a science homework assignment from the chalkboard and who write down on their assignment sheet to do the problems on page 69 when they should have written page 67 are going to do the wrong homework assignment. Those who misspell in their binder a newly introduced vocabulary word written on a handout are likely to misspell the word on the next test. Those who do a division problem correctly on a piece of scrap paper and then copy the wrong answer onto their test paper are going to receive a lowered grade. Those who spell the words *perfect* and *further* correctly on the first draft of their essay but copy the words as "prefect" and "father" on their final draft are likely to have many red marks on their graded paper and the initials "Sp" repeatedly written in the margins. These types of copying errors might result in a B+ essay being given a grade of B−.

Children must be capable of performing two types of copying functions. Recording information written on the chalkboard is described as *far-point copying*. Transferring information from a textbook to paper is described as *near-point copying*. Some children have difficulty with one operation and not the other. Other children have difficulty with both procedures.

Being required to copy information can be anathema to children with learning problems. Those who are inattentive to details, distractible, have fine-motor or graphomotor problems (poorly formed and barely legible letters and words attributable to difficulty controlling a pencil), and struggle to concentrate are especially prone to copying inaccurately. Difficulty with visual memory (recalling written information), visual discrimination (recognizing different letters), and visual sequencing (recalling written information in the proper order) can also undermine precision. Because these perceptual-processing deficits hinder effective proofreading, learning-disabled children often have great difficulty identifying their own careless spelling, punctuation, grammar, and math mistakes.

Some students copy inaccurately because they have difficulty with visual acuity. Children who require glasses are likely to make precision errors if they do not have, or refuse to wear, corrective lenses.

The first step in the process of identifying the source of chronic inaccurate copying should be an examination by an ophthalmologist or optometrist. If there is an organic impairment (nearsightedness, farsightedness, astigmatism, etc.), the problem can most likely be quickly resolved by prescribing glasses or contact lenses.

If no visual acuity deficit is identified, the next step in the differential diagnosis procedure (i.e., ruling out what is *not* causing a problem in order to identify what *is* causing the problem) is to have the child evaluated by the school psychologist. This assessment may reveal deficits in perceiving spatial proportions and distinguishing near-ground symbols from the background context. The evaluation may also indicate difficulty decoding letters and words accurately (a visual-discrimination problem linked to dyslexia). Any of these perceptual-processing deficits can interfere with precise copying.

ADD/ADHD can also hinder the ability to copy accurately. Children who have difficulty focusing, filtering out distractions, controlling impulsivity, and/or sitting still in class are likely to be inattentive to details, careless, and prone to making copying mistakes.

Children can acquire more effective self-editing skills. They can be trained to search methodically for the mistakes that they typically make and taught how to create an "error template" that they automatically superimpose on everything that they copy. This personalized template might include the following reminders:

- Check every sentence to make certain there is subject/verb agreement.
- Check every sentence to make certain that all required punctuation marks are inserted.
- Check every sentence to make certain the proper tense has been used.
- Check to make certain there are no letter or number reversals.
- Check every number carefully when copying problems to make certain there are no errors.
- Check the spelling of any word that looks "funny."

With sufficient practice, this systematic verification procedure will become an ingrained habit. Unfortunately, there are no magical cures for carelessness. Children who make chronic careless mistakes when they copy must be conditioned to compensate for their proclivity, encouraged to exert extra effort and diligence, and effusively praised for progress.

COMMON INDICATIONS OF INACCURATE COPYING

- mistakes when transferring information from chalkboard to paper (far-point copying)
- mistakes when transferring information from textbooks and handouts to paper (near-point copying)
- letter transpositions
- reversed numbers and letters
- omission of words and phrases
- omission of key information
- inaccuracies in recording important details
- difficulty with sequencing information accurately
- improperly aligned letters and numbers
- spelling errors
- omitted punctuation marks
- omitted capital letters

POSSIBLE SOURCES OF CHRONIC INACCURATE COPYING

- poor vision (visual-acuity deficit)
- handwriting problems (fine-motor or graphomotor deficit)
- difficulty perceiving the relative size and shape of symbols (spatial-awareness deficit)
- perceptual processing dysfunction (dyslexia)
- visual-efficiency difficulty (inefficient ocular-muscle control when reading)
- concentration difficulty (ADD/ADHD)
- inattention to details
- irresponsibility
- difficulty remembering what is seen (visual-memory deficit)
- difficulty recalling information in the proper sequence (visual-sequencing deficit)

SEE: Attention Deficit/Attention Deficit Hyperactivity Disorder *(page 214);* Attention to Details *(page 223);* Brain Dysfunction *(page 326);* Conduct and Attitude *(page 235);* Decoding *(page 332);* Dyslexia *(page 335);* Essays and Essay Tests *(page 18);* Grades *(page 25);* Handwriting *(page 36);* I'm Dumb Syndrome *(page 388);* Incomplete Assignments *(page 256);* Keeping Up with the Class *(page 51);* Language Arts *(page 58);* Learning from Mistakes *(page 267);* Math *(page 72);* Note Taking *(page 79);* Parent-Child Conflict *(page 393);* Planning *(page 176);* Performance Standards *(page 91);* Recording Assignments *(page 107);* Resistance to Help *(page 282);* School Anxiety *(page 406);* Self-control *(page 287);* Spelling *(page 112);* Teacher-Child Conflict *(page 293);* Teacher-Designed Tests *(page 132);* Test Anxiety *(page 420);* Underachievement *(page 143);* Visual Discrimination *(page 343);* Visual Memory *(page 360);* Working Independently *(page 302).*

Phonics

▲

Refers to a codified system that governs the pronunciation of letters, syllables, and words.

▲

The debate over whether to teach children to read phonetically or with the "sight method" appears to have been won by the proponents of phonics, at least for the time being. Currently, most American schools are committed to the phonics approach. Elementary-school teachers using this method systematically teach children to "attack" words by breaking them down into constituent sounds, blending the sounds into groupings of sounds (typically syllables), and melding the sound groupings so that words can be deciphered and accurately pronounced.

The phonetic instructional methodology is predicated on children being able to recognize and articulate precisely a range of basic sounds or phonemes. These phonemes are the building blocks of all words that conform to phonetic conventions.

Proponents of the phonics method contend that children who can identify, differentiate, and pronounce the sounds produced by consonants, vowels, blends, and syllables possess an invaluable resource that will enable them to decode and spell most English words. They also argue that teaching students how to connect visual symbols with their spoken equivalents and apply rules that govern how letters and combinations of letters are pronounced is the most efficient way to help children attain reading fluency and confidence. Three requisites are necessary to making a phonics-based system work effectively:

- a well-trained and enthusiastic teacher
- methodical instruction
- ample opportunities for students to practice attacking words and blending sounds together

The advocates of the sight method have a very different perspective on how to teach reading. They point out that many words in the English language do not conform to consistent phonetic rules and that children are better served if they are taught to identify and pronounce entire words without having to attack and sound them out laboriously. These sight-method proponents argue that phonics is unwieldy, inconsistent, and perplexing and that the painstaking process impedes reading fluency. If teachers carefully control the difficulty level of newly introduced *sight words* and provide adequate opportunities for practice, students can quickly learn to recognize most English words and can expeditiously achieve reading fluency.

Whatever instructional methodology is employed, some students are destined to have great difficulty learning to read. These difficulties are invariably attributable to specific perceptual-processing deficits. In the case of the sight method, the deficits may involve visual discrimination, visual memory, and/or auditory memory. These deficiencies can interfere with the child's capacity to recall written words and their pronunciation.*

Perceptual-processing deficits can also cause students to struggle when they are being taught to read phonetically. Children may have difficulty recognizing phonemes, recalling the sounds associated with letters, sequencing the sounds accurately, and differentiating letters and sounds. This notwithstanding, research has unequivocally documented that a phonics-based program is the more effective instructional program when students are struggling with reading problems. Highly specialized phonics-based remedial programs such as the Lindamood Phonemic Sequencing (LiPS) program and Fast Forward have been developed to enhance phonemic awareness, word attack, and blending skills. These programs methodically train students to identify, pronounce, and recall basic sounds and letter groupings.

High-tech brain scans using functional magnetic resonance

---

*Chronic reading inaccuracies involving letter, word, and number reversals, letter and word omissions, and transpositions are primary symptoms of dyslexia.

imaging (fMRI) have recently revealed the cerebral physiology involved in reading. These scans indicate that reading deficiencies are directly linked to faults in the way the brain is hard-wired to decode written symbols. Specific areas in the back of the brain that are normally involved in deciphering words are underactive, while other areas in the front of the brain that are normally involved in speech production are overactive. Because of this neurological anomaly, the sounding-out process is inefficient, and children with reading problems must work considerably harder to analyze the sound patterns produced by written symbols. Intensive and methodical phonics instruction specifically addresses this problem and helps students compensate successfully for their inefficient decoding skills.

Children who are able to process sensory data efficiently can learn to read using either a phonics or sight method. Only challenging multisyllable and/or nonphonetic words require multiple exposures and extensive practice. As adults, these "natural" readers will probably never even remember how they were taught to read.

Poor readers, on the other hand, will probably never forget their struggle to learn how to read. By the middle of first grade, many have already been placed in the lowest reading groups. By third grade, those who have been officially diagnosed as learning disabled are probably receiving remedial assistance in the school resource program. For a great many of these children, reading aloud is a nightmare. Because of their painful associations with deciphering words, these students are at risk for becoming resistant to reading and, in some cases, reading-phobic.

As oral and silent reading play such central roles in academic achievement, children who struggle to read with fluency are at risk for concluding that they are "dumb" despite the fact that they may actually be as, or even more, intelligent than many of their classmates who read effortlessly. Lowering their expectations and aspirations accordingly, these struggling readers often choose the path of least resistance and shut down in school. The embarrassment and humiliation they are forced to endure every day can cause permanent emotional scarring and trigger a profound aversion to reading that could persist throughout life.

In response to a nationwide epidemic of poor performance on standardized reading tests, textbook publishers periodically introduce new and innovative programs that are designed to teach reading more effectively. Whole Language is an example of a methodology that was eagerly embraced by many school districts. Rather than provide formal, systematic reading or phonics instruction, the program integrates reading into the science, math, history, and language curriculum. Research indicates, however, that learning-disabled students generally make far more reading progress when taught the traditional and methodical phonics method.

Although phonics has proved to be the most effective instructional program for children with reading problems, there are still many words that do not conform to the rules of phonics. These include words of foreign origin, such as *buoyant, sergeant, lieutenant,* and *colonel,* and words whose pronunciation has evolved but whose spelling has not. Examples include *two, could, through, thought, rough, bought, bough, though, although, count, loud, caught, laugh,* etc. In Middle English, these words were pronounced precisely the way they were spelled. All of the "ough" words, for example, had the same guttural pronunciation. These foreign and nonphonetic words must obviously be learned by sight even in a phonics-based system.

In addition to the systematic remedial program previously described, other highly effective remedial methodologies have been developed to help children with reading problems. Most of these methods, which include Orton-Gillingham, Slingerland, neurological impress, and neurolinguistic programming, incorporate multisensory instruction. Resource specialists and private educational therapists may choose to use either a "packaged" program or a more eclectic and individualized approach that incorporates components of several different remedial methodologies.

SYMPTOMS OF PHONICS PROBLEMS

- difficulty with auditory discrimination (hearing the difference between sounds)
- difficulty with auditory memory (remembering what is heard)
- difficulty with auditory sequencing (remembering the proper order of verbally communicated information)
- difficulty identifying phonemes and linking them with the sounds that specific letters produce (phonological processing delays that impede efficient word attack)
- difficulty with phonemic sequencing (deciphering sounds in the proper sequence)
- difficulty articulating and blending sounds accurately (melding phonemes and forming syllables and words)
- difficulty with visual discrimination (seeing the difference between letters)
- difficulty with visual memory (remembering what is seen)
- difficulty with visual sequencing (remembering the proper visual order)
- difficulty with visual tracking (seeing letters and words accurately and perceiving letters and syllables in the proper sequence)

SEE: Articulation *(page 429)*; Auditory Memory *(page 322)*; Brain Dysfunction *(page 326)*; Decoding *(page 332)*; Dyslexia *(page 335)*; Grades *(page 25)*; I'm Dumb Syndrome *(page 388)*; Incomplete Assignments *(page 256)*; Keeping Up with the Class *(page 51)*; Language Arts *(page 58)*; Learning from Mistakes *(page 267)*; Mastery of Academic Content *(page 67)*; Performance Standards *(page 91)*; Phonics *(page 346)*; Psychological Overlay and Psychological Problems *(page 399)*; Reading Comprehension *(page 100)*; Reading Fluency *(page 351)*; Resistance to Help *(page 282)*; School Anxiety *(page 406)*; Self-concept *(page 410)*; Spelling *(page 112)*; Standardized Tests *(page 116)*; Teacher-Designed Tests *(page 132)*; Test Anxiety *(page 420)*; Underachievement *(page 143)*; Visual Memory *(page 360)*; Vocabulary *(page 150)*.

Reading Fluency

▲

Refers to the ability to decipher and pronounce words accurately and smoothly when reading orally.

▲

Children in elementary school are continually required to read aloud in class. Those who struggle to decode words accurately, fluently, and with proper intonation are at a significant disadvantage and often feel embarrassed, inadequate, frustrated, and self-conscious. These youngsters are acutely aware of their reading deficits, and their negative experiences with oral reading can undermine their self-confidence and cause significant emotional scarring. To read with fluency in a phonics-based reading program, children must be able to "attack" words, blend sounds, and track letters and words efficiently as the eyes scan the material being read. They must also be able to read nonphonetic (or "sight") words, such as *straight*, and words that are spelled the same but pronounced differently, such as *caught* and *laugh* and *cough, rough, through,* and *thought.* In addition, they must be able to read words of foreign origin that have become part of the English language, such as *sergeant, colonel,* and *lieutenant.*

Two methodologies are typically used to teach reading. Phonics is now by far the most common instructional program.* In this method, children are taught how to "attack" phonetic words that conform to consistent rules of spelling and pronunciation. Students use these sound-letter correspondence rules to identify and pro-

---

*The instructional pendulum periodically swings. Whereas phonics is currently the program of choice in most schools, it is conceivable that this traditional method may once again fall into disfavor in five years. Programs such as Whole Language and Read to Write have also enjoyed popularity in some school districts. Many innovative reading methods, however, are trendy and then disappear because the publishers' claims and the educators' and administrators' expectations are not validated by achievement test scores. Publishers argue that the new programs are designed to enhance reading skills and compensate for less-than-adequate teaching. Another obvious motive for creating new methods and materials is to make existing programs obsolete and sell millions of new textbooks.

nounce the individual phonemes (sounds and syllables) and then
blend the sounds together to form words.

In schools committed to a phonics-based reading program, the
instructional methodology requires specific decoding skills that include:

- phonological awareness and auditory discrimination (recognizing
  and being able to pronounce the different sounds that letters and
  combinations of letters make)
- auditory memory (recalling the sounds that letters and letter combinations make)
- word attack (breaking words down into phonetic units)
- blending (putting phonetic units together)
- tracking (seeing letters and words accurately and in proper sequence)
- visual discrimination (being able to identify and differentiate letters
  accurately)
- visual memory (being able to recall and read common sight or nonphonetic words)

To acquire the decoding skills that are requisites to reading fluency in a phonics-based program, children must be able to process
sensory data efficiently. Those who have perceptually based learning
disabilities and who struggle to process sensory data are clearly at a
major disadvantage. Some of these children have dyslexia and reverse letters and numbers or flip a word such as *saw* and see the word
as *was*. Some may have ocular-motor inefficiency and may have difficulty tracking (seeing letters, syllables, and words in the proper sequence). They may lose their place when reading, insert nonexistent
letters and syllables into the words they are attempting to decode,
omit syllables or words, or transpose words or phrases from one
place in the sentence to another. Other children have auditory-
and/or visual-discrimination and memory deficits and struggle to
identify, distinguish, associate, and recall the sounds that letters and
combinations of letters make. The repercussions from these perceptual-processing deficits include labored reading, frustration, demor-

alization, reading phobias, self-concept damage, and possible academic shutdown.

The second teaching methodology encourages children to learn words "by sight." Utilizing visual-memory skills, students are exposed to new words that they then add to their warehouse of recognizable words. This word-recognition approach requires repeated exposure to core words and extensive practice, especially in the case of difficult multisyllable words. Some children have no difficulty learning to read using this method and retain newly introduced words easily. Other children, especially those with perceptually based learning disabilities, can have monumental difficulty recognizing and visually imprinting new words. If these children do not have a good foundation in phonics, they will lack the requisite skills to "attack" and sound out not only unfamiliar words but also words that they have been exposed to but do not recall how to read. This will trigger frustration and demoralization that could cause learning-disabled students to become even more reading-phobic. Phonics-based programs have proved the most effective method of teaching struggling readers, and most specialists in the field strongly recommend this approach over the sight-word methodology.

Currently, the sight method of teaching reading is out of favor in most schools. In view of the generally dismal reading performances of children on standardized reading tests in many areas of the United States, the prevailing pedagogical attitude is "Let's return to the basics," and the basics translate into teaching phonics.

Because of the numerous phonetic exceptions and anomalies in the English language, most teachers incorporate both phonics and sight-recognition techniques in their instructional strategy. Children are taught to sound out words that conform to standard phonics rules and to memorize those that do not.

Irrespective of the teaching method, poor visual efficiency (seeing and tracking letters, words, and syllables accurately) can make oral reading a nightmare for children. To read efficiently, both eyes must be able to converge *(focus in tandem on a point)* and scan letters and words smoothly from left to right *(ocular pursuit)*. If the child's convergence and/or visual tracking are inefficient, the child may transpose or omit letters, syllables, words, or even phrases when reading.

Static tracking problems usually manifest as letter and/or number reversals ("b" perceived as *d* or *q* perceived as "g"). The child may also have up/down reversals (6 perceived as 9 or *n* perceived as *u*). *Kinetic tracking problems* usually manifest as flipped words. *(Was* perceived as *saw,* and *bad* perceived as *dab.)* If the brain is unable to decode the letters because of an anomaly in the brain's structure or wiring, the child will be at a significant disadvantage in the classroom. This condition is generally referred to as dyslexia.

Children with oral-reading deficits may also have difficulty hearing the difference between sounds. (e.g., *e* may be perceived as "i".) This condition is described as an auditory-discrimination problem and can usually be remediated with intensive phonetic-discrimination training. Methodical programs such as Fast Forward and LiPS have been specifically designed to provide this intensive training.

Children who are embarrassed by their reading difficulties may attempt to compensate by doing everything possible to avoid reading aloud. Because of their painful associations, these children could develop a profound aversion to reading, and the phobia can produce disastrous emotional, academic, and vocational repercussions. Since reading is a common gauge by which children assess their abilities and intelligence in the lower grades, those who are struggling with a reading disability are at risk for suffering severe self-concept damage.

Many children, especially those receiving learning assistance, attempt to compensate for their oral-reading deficiencies by reading more slowly and meticulously. On the surface, this compensatory behavior would appear laudable, but there is a downside to such diligence. The laborious sounding out of each difficult word usually causes the oral reading of these children to be choppy and monotonous. Struggling readers are caught on the horns of a dilemma. If they read fast, they will make mistakes. If they read slowly and carefully, they will put their classmates' "toes to sleep."

Stress can also interfere with oral-reading fluency. Self-conscious children with poor oral reading skills have usually acquired deeply imprinted, painful associations with reading and may become quite anxious whenever they are asked to read aloud. Their insecurity, anxiety, and fear of making mistakes and embarrassing themselves in front of their classmates may cause them to make even more errors. The antidote is to help these children acquire the skills they need to read efficiently. This necessitates providing intensive, effective, and highly focused remedial assistance. By carefully orchestrating successes and effusively affirming progress, empathetic teachers, resource specialists, and tutors can reduce the fears of these children and incrementally build their self-confidence. Acknowledgment and praise for even small gains will stimulate effort, motivation, and pride. The objective is to convince struggling readers that they can, in fact, learn how to read with fluency. Creative, focused, and effective instruction, patience, and effusive praise for progress are the most potent means for improving children's reading fluency and enhancing their reading confidence.

STRATEGY FOR IMPROVING STUDENTS' ORAL-READING SKILLS

- Let struggling readers know in advance what sections they will be asked to read aloud.
- Have students prepare assigned sections with their parents or the teacher before class. (During practice sessions, parents could read a sentence aloud and have the child reread the same sentence. This procedure should be repeated until the child has mastered the section and feels self-confident.)
- Treat struggling readers with extra sensitivity and provide effusive praise, encouragement, and affirmation for progress.
- Identify specific reading deficits and provide appropriate and effective specialized remedial intervention in school and/or after school.
- Teach struggling readers anxiety-reducing relaxation techniques (closing eyes, visualizing oneself reading fluently and confidently, taking three deep breaths before beginning to read).

> • Encourage the parents of a struggling reader to read aloud with their child at home and provide reassurance and effusive praise for improvement.

▼

SEE: Attention Deficit/Attention Deficit Hyperactivity Disorder *(page 214)*; Attention to Details *(page 223)*; Auditory Discrimination *(page 317)*; Auditory Memory *(page 322)*; Avoiding Responsibility *(page 227)*; Brain Dysfunction *(page 326)*; Conduct and Attitude *(page 235)*; Decoding *(page 332)*; Defense Mechanisms *(page 373)*; Dyslexia *(page 335)*; Grades *(page 25)*; I'm Dumb Syndrome *(page 388)*; Incomplete Assignments *(page 256)*; Keeping Up with the Class *(page 51)*; Mastery of Academic Content *(page 67)*; Passive Learning *(page 84)*; Performance Standards *(page 91)*; Phonics *(page 346)*; Psychological Overlay and Psychological Problems *(page 399)*; Reading Comprehension *(page 100)*; School Anxiety *(page 406)*; Self-concept *(page 410)*; Test Anxiety *(page 420)*; Underachievement *(page 143)*; Visual Memory *(page 360)*.

Verbal Directions

▲

Refers to the ability to understand, follow, and recall orally communicated instructions.

▲

Students are exposed to a continual barrage of verbal instructions during the course of a typical school day. Teachers tell them where to put the remainder in long-division problems, how to convert fractions into decimals, how to format a book report, how to fill in an answer sheet on a standardized test, and where to place the footnotes in their term papers.

Whenever possible, good teachers try to reinforce verbal instructions with written ones. For example, they might discuss an assignment in class and also write key information on the chalkboard or distribute a handout that contains the information. This multimodality instruction, however, is not always practical, and teachers might announce to the class: "Turn to page ninety-two and answer the questions about the first unit. Do the odd-numbered questions in class and the even-numbered questions for homework. Use complete sentences and skip a line between each answer." Children who struggle to follow verbal directions are likely to be overwhelmed by these explicit instructions. In desperation, they will probably look around the classroom and desperately try to figure out what their classmates are doing.

The capacity to assimilate verbally communicated directions efficiently is an essential academic survival skill. Children who become chronically confused and anxious whenever their teachers are explaining something are at a significant disadvantage. Those who cannot understand the instructions or retain the information are likely to submit work that does not conform to their teachers' directions. This will result in lowered grades, diminished expectations, and reduced self-confidence.

Some students struggle to make sense out of even the most basic directions. These youngsters are often in a constant state of bewilderment, and their chronic confusion, anxiety, and frustration usually lead to discouragement, demoralization, and resignation to marginal performance.

Children who have difficulty following oral instructions often try to compensate by:

- repeatedly asking the teacher for clarification
- attempting to figure out what their classmates are doing
- doing assignments without having understood the directions
- accepting their "limitations" and going into cerebral shutdown whenever their teacher gives verbal directions

Confused students who ask for repeated clarification can upset the rhythm and pacing of the lesson and exasperate their teachers, who may communicate their frustration with statements such as: "If you would only listen, you would understand what I am saying." To avoid embarrassment, befuddled students may ask a child seated nearby for help and in the process get into trouble for talking in class. As their feelings of inadequacy increase, their behavior and attitude will deteriorate. Those who are repeatedly reprimanded for not paying attention may conclude that their situation is hopeless and react by turning off and shutting down whenever information is verbally communicated. From the vantage point of the child who cannot follow oral directions, there can be only one explanation for his ineptitude: "I must be dumb."

On the surface, chronically poor listeners may appear unmotivated and apathetic. Typically on the receiving end of a great deal of negative feedback, their seeming indifference is usually a coping mechanism. While they struggle to make sense out of what their teachers are saying, they can see that their classmates are effortlessly following the instructions and assimilating the information. Negative comments, poor grades, embarrassment, and frustration will confirm their feelings of inadequacy and exact a major toll on their self-confidence.

If poor listeners are to improve their ability to follow verbal directions, they must be taught compensatory techniques that will allow them to process, understand, recall, and respond to auditory input more effectively. They must be taught how to reinforce the auditory modality by automatically forming visual pictures in their mind that *paint a picture* of what they are hearing. By learning to use the visual modality to compensate for their auditory-processing deficiencies, these students can significantly enhance their listening comprehension and retention. As their teacher gives instructions, they must mentally see themselves, for example, writing their name on the right-hand side of the top line of their paper. They must visualize placing the numbers next to the red line on the left side of the paper, skipping a line between each answer, writing in complete sentences, beginning each answer with a capital, and ending each sentence with a period.

Before children can realistically be expected to compensate

successfully for their listening deficits, their teacher, resource specialist, or parents must provide them with effective compensatory tools. They must:

- teach them how to form mental pictures of verbally communicated directions
- provide them with opportunities to practice visualization techniques in verbally loaded instructional situations
- praise them for their progress

Poor listeners who master visualization techniques can level the playing field. The method will become an invaluable resource that will allow them to break the cycle of poor auditory comprehension, poor recall, confusion, frustration, demoralization, catastrophic expectations, and deteriorating self-confidence.

SOURCES OF DIFFICULTY FOLLOWING VERBAL DIRECTIONS

- sensory impairment (a hearing loss)
- auditory memory deficits (recalling verbal information)
- auditory sequencing deficits (recalling information in the proper order)
- concentration problems (ADD/ADHD)
- difficulty with receptive language (understanding what words mean)

INDICATIONS OF DIFFICULTY FOLLOWING VERBAL DIRECTIONS

- work that doesn't conform to the teacher's instructions
- poor retention of orally communicated information
- continual confusion when directions are given
- difficulty working independently
- incomplete assignments
- lack of self-confidence in verbally loaded situations
- continual requests that the teacher repeat or explain verbally communicated information

- difficulty sequencing tasks as explicitly directed
- stress and anxiety whenever verbal instructions are given
- diminished academic self-confidence

SEE: Aptitude *(page 15)*; Attention Deficit/Attention Deficit Hyperactivity Disorder *(page 214)*; Attention to Details *(page 223)*; Auditory Memory *(page 322)*; Brain Dysfunction *(page 326)*; Decoding *(page 332)*; Grades *(page 25)*; I'm Dumb Syndrome *(page 388)*; Incomplete Assignments *(page 256)*; Keeping Up with the Class *(page 51)*; Mastery of Academic Content *(page 67)*; Math *(page 72)*; Parent-Child Conflict *(page 393)*; Psychological Overlay and Psychological Problems *(page 399)*; Recording Assignments *(page 107)*; School Anxiety *(page 406)*; Self-control *(page 287)*; Standardized Tests *(page 116)*; Study Skills *(page 127)*; Teacher-Child Conflict *(page 293)*; Teacher-Designed Tests *(page 132)*; Test Anxiety *(page 420)*; Underachievement *(page 143)*; Working Independently *(page 302)*.

Visual Memory

▲

Refers to the ability to recall accurately what is seen or read.

▲

The American educational system has traditionally been "visually loaded." The requirement that children be able to recall what they read begins in first grade. As students progress into the upper grades, the demands on their visual memory expand exponentially. Students are expected to remember symbols, facts, formulas, rules, procedures, vocabulary definitions, historical dates, and irregular Spanish or French conjugations. Those with good visual retention clearly have a distinct advantage in classes in which their teachers emphasize the retention of facts and details.

Visual-memory skills are especially invaluable resource when children spell. Students who can "see" words in their minds invariably make fewer spelling errors than those who laboriously attempt to sound out words or who try to apply spelling and phonics rules. This capacity to imprint and access mental pictures of words can be especially useful when spelling words that are commonly mispronounced *(e.g., prerogative),* nonphonetic *(e.g., allegiance, through,* and *bought)* or foreign *(e.g., sergeant, lieutenant,* and *potpourri).* When proofreading, good spellers are likely to say: "This word doesn't look right." They may not always know how to spell the word, but they know that they need to look up the word in a dictionary or run it through spell-check.

People with exceptional visual recall are often described as having a "photographic memory." This analogy is accurate. Their eyes function as a camera lens; their brain, as a roll of film onto which they instantaneously imprint visual information.

The value of having good visual-memory skills is certainly not limited to spelling. In every academic subject area, children are required to recall written information. Those who can "see" imprinted on their minds the date when the Declaration of Independence was signed, the chemical formula for nitric acid, the conjugation of the irregular Spanish verb *entender,* or the formula for determining the circumference of a circle are likely to get better grades than students who cannot visually imprint and access this information.

Not all children, of course, learn in the same way. Some are auditory learners. Some are visual learners. Others are tactile or kinesthetic learners. Children who intuitively identify their preferred learning modality and figure out how to capitalize on their natural learning strengths are able to understand and recall information with greater facility than those who beat their heads against a wall trying to recall information in their nonpreferred modality.

Children often unconsciously signal their preferred learning modality with their choice of vocabulary. Auditory learners are likely to say, "I hear you." Visual learners are likely to say, "I see what you mean." Tactile or kinesthetic learners are likely to say, "That feels right."

Auditory learners have a very different learning modus operandi. Instead of attempting to imprint visual information on a roll of film, they record the information on a mental *audiotape*. They read something, identify the important information, and repeat the facts orally, subvocally, or mentally until the information is impressed. (e.g., "The moon is 254,000 miles from the earth . . . the moon is 254,000 miles from the earth. . . .") This natural ability to record information auditorially can be especially useful when teachers lecture. Auditory learners tend to listen intently to the lecture and digest the content as it is being presented, while visual learners attempt to record as much of the information as they possibly can in their notes so that they can digest the information later.

As a general rule, visual imprinting is a more effective tool when memorizing large quantities of factual data written in textbooks, in notes, and on the chalkboard. Children who can form mental pictures of what they are reading and learning usually find memorization chores less onerous than those who record mental audiotapes. Students who are blessed with both a visual and auditory facility are likely to utilize both modalities when studying. This is the equivalent of a one-two punch.

Possessing first-rate visual-memory skills does not necessarily guarantee good reading comprehension. A student may be able to retain and regurgitate a plethora of facts but may not understand them or be able to apply the information. Nonetheless, visual-memory abilities generally serve students well when they take multiple-choice, true/false, and short-answer tests that emphasize details.

Teachers who stress the rote memorization and the warehousing of facts without requiring critical thinking and thoughtful application discourage active learning. Answering the question "When was the telephone invented and who invented it?" demands considerably less cognition and insight than writing an essay in response to an item on a test that instructs students to "Discuss the effects that the civil-rights movement has had on American culture and cite specific ways in which it has altered our society."

Students tend to forget quickly information that is poorly understood, not reinforced by discussion and application, and/or perceived as irrelevant. Children who are required to memorize the names of the bones in the hand will usually forget this information soon after taking a test. Their long-term retention usually increases if they are provided with an opportunity to assemble a model of the hand (kinesthetic/tactile learning), draw diagrams (visual learning), discuss and describe the information verbally (auditory learning), and interact with other students in a cooperative learning context. When active multisensory learning is reinforced by encouraging students to create mental visual pictures, recall is further enhanced.

Students who think strategically capitalize whenever possible on their natural and preferred learning styles and learning strengths. At the same time, these students are pragmatic. If they are required to memorize a great many facts, dates, names, or formulas and if they conclude that visual imprinting is the most effective way to assimilate and retain the information, they are likely to shift into the visual modality. Visual imprinting may not be their natural or preferred learning style, but they may conclude it is the most effective method of getting the job done. This tactical, pragmatic thinking differentiates achieving students from their less successful classmates.

With effective instruction and adequate opportunities to practice, all children can learn to imprint mental visual pictures and in the process improve their visual memory.* These visualization skills will provide them with an invaluable asset that they will use throughout life.

---

*A systematic and highly effective program called Visualizing/Verbalizing, developed by Nanci Bell, has been specifically designed to help students learn how to form and imprint visual images when reading.

SEE: Aptitude *(page 15)*; Attention Deficit/Attention Deficit Hyperactivity Disorder *(page 214)*; Attention to Details *(page 223)*; Auditory Discrimination *(page 317)*; Auditory Memory *(page 322)*; Brain Dysfunction *(page 326)*; Decoding *(page 332)*; Dyslexia *(page 335)*; Grades *(page 25)*; I'm Dumb Syndrome *(page 388)*; Intelligence *(page 45)*; Keeping Up with the Class *(page 51)*; Mastery of Academic Content *(page 67)*; Math *(page 72)*; Note Taking *(page 79)*; Passive Learning *(page 84)*; Phonics *(page 346)*; Reading Comprehension *(page 100)*; Reading Fluency *(page 351)*; Recording Assignments *(page 107)*; School Anxiety *(page 406)*; Self-concept *(page 410)*; Spelling *(page 112)*; Standardized Tests *(page 116)*; Study Skills *(page 127)*; Teacher-Designed Tests *(page 132)*; Test Anxiety *(page 420)*; Underachievement *(page 143)*; Visual Discrimination *(page 343)*; Vocabulary *(page 150)*.

Written Directions

▲

Refers to the ability to follow, understand, and retain instructions that are communicated in writing.

▲

Students are expected to be able to assimilate instructions written on the chalkboard, in textbooks, on handouts, on tests, and in workbooks. Those who struggle to understand and follow these written directions face monumental academic challenges that will increase exponentially as they progress into the upper grades.

Some children are negligent about following written directions because of focusing deficits. Their carelessness may be attributable to ADD/ADHD and specifically to difficulty staying on task, filtering out distractions, attending to details, and controlling impulsivity.

Perceptual-processing deficits, such as dyslexia, can also make it difficult for children to decipher, understand, recall, and apply written information. Children who misread the explicit directions on a test are likely to answer the questions incorrectly. If they cannot accurately decipher the data written on their homework-assignment sheet (i.e., they might read page 96 and perceive it as page 69), they are going to end up doing the wrong assignment. They might become confused when reading a handout that tells them how to format a term paper. They might misinterpret, or not be able to recall, instructions in their science textbook, and as a consequence, they may do an experiment improperly. These miscues will not only lower their grades; they will also damage their academic self-confidence. In cases in which difficulty following written directions is clearly attributable to a perceptual-processing dysfunction and poor reading skills, remedial intervention is vital.

Children who see their classmates effortlessly following written directions and working efficiently while they are in a continual state of confusion are likely to become frustrated and discouraged. They are also likely to feel hopelessly incompetent. Convinced in advance that they will not be able to understand what's expected of them, they may panic whenever they encounter written instructions. To protect themselves from feeling inadequate, these children often acquire a range of coping behaviors. They may repeatedly ask for clarification and explanations from their teachers or parents, or they may attempt to mimic what their classmates are doing without understanding the directions or the objectives. In extreme cases, they may simply shut down when confronted with written directions. Whatever compensatory behavior they select, children who cannot follow written instructions are clearly at a significant academic disadvantage, and their deficiencies will become increasingly problematic as they progress into middle school and high school.

Children can be taught practical and productive (versus counterproductive) compensatory mechanisms for dealing with their difficulty following written directions. One of the most effective compensations is for them to break complex instructions into small chunks that can be more easily understood and assimilated. This methodical "divide and conquer" procedure permits children to identify, isolate, and sequence the specific bits of information contained in a series of directions. (i.e., "Let's look at these directions one step at a time, and let's not panic because they seem complicated.") The method provides students who might otherwise be overwhelmed with a practical and easy-to-apply tool for handling instructions. Once they master the procedure and get into the habit of using it consistently, written instructions will seem less intimidating and confusing, and their anxiety and stress will be significantly reduced.

Another method of compensating productively involves forming visual mental pictures that imprint the step-by-step details of the instructions. The child whose preferred learning modality is visual might methodically create a graphic mental "map" that guides him through each of the steps described in the instructions.

Auditory learners might prefer to create a soundtrack that imprints the step-by-step details contained in the instructions. The child might silently recite: "The directions say to fold the *paper* in half vertically. Okay, I know what vertical means. I need to hold the paper lengthwise and then fold it so that I have two equal columns...."

The key to helping children improve their capacity to follow written directions is to encourage them to develop an alternative representational system that capitalizes on their learning strengths and preferences. Once children acquire a functional, practical, and productive compensatory system, their ability to understand written instructions and their self-confidence should improve significantly.

FACTORS THAT CAN CAUSE DIFFICULTY FOLLOWING WRITTEN DIRECTIONS

- visual impairment (acuity deficiencies)
- visual-decoding deficits (such as dyslexia)
- reading-comprehension deficits
- distractibility and impulsivity (ADD/ADHD)
- visual-memory deficits
- visual-sequencing deficits (recalling information in the proper order)
- anxiety (panic when required to follow directions)

INDICATIONS OF DIFFICULTY FOLLOWING WRITTEN DIRECTIONS

- confusion
- intimidation when confronted with directions
- incomplete assignments
- late assignments
- inaccuracies and lack of precision when following explicit instructions
- difficulty working independently
- need to have directions repeatedly explained
- difficulty accurately decoding words
- poor reading comprehension
- panic and anxiety when confronted with written directions
- expectations of disaster
- feelings of incompetence and inadequacy
- diminished academic self-confidence
- frustration and demoralization

SEE: Attention Deficit/Attention Deficit Hyperactivity Disorder *(page 214)*; Attention to Details *(page 223)*; Brain Dysfunction *(page 326)*; Decoding *(page 332)*; Disorganization *(page 251)*; Dyslexia *(page 335)*; Grades *(page 25)*; Identifying Important Information *(page 41)*; I'm Dumb Syndrome *(page 388)*; Incomplete Assignments *(page 256)*; Keeping Up with the Class *(page 51)*; Parent-Child Conflict *(page 393)*; Passive Learning *(page 84)*; Planning *(page 176)*; Priorities *(page 180)*; Psychological Overlay and Psychological Problems *(page 399)*; Reading Comprehension *(page 100)*; Reading Fluency *(page 351)*; Recording Assignments *(page 107)*; School Anxiety *(page 406)*; Standardized Tests *(page 116)*; Study Skills *(page 127)*; Teacher-Child Conflict *(page 293)*; Teacher-Designed Tests *(page 132)*; Test Anxiety *(page 420)*; Time Management *(page 138)*; Underachievement *(page 143)*; Visual Memory *(page 360)*; Working Independently *(page 302)*.

PSYCHOLOGICAL FACTORS

Learning problems and psychological distress are often directly linked. Children who look around the classroom and see that their classmates are "getting it" while they are confused and unable to do the assigned work usually conclude, on either a conscious or unconscious level, that they are incompetent. That they must struggle while other students learn effortlessly confirms their feelings of inadequacy.

Having a child who is convinced she's "dumb" can be one of parenting's most heart-wrenching experiences. The anguish is all the more acute when parents see the day-by-day deterioration of their child's self-concept and feel powerless to prevent the damage.

A steady diet of failure, frustration, and discouragement can chip away at the emotional resources of even the most "together" child. A basic survival instinct impels children who feel vulnerable to protect themselves. Unfortunately, the defense mechanisms to which these academically defeated children typically resort—blaming, denial, laziness, procrastination, irresponsibility, acting out, and resistance—offer no protection. The self-defeating behaviors only exacerbate their learning problems.

On the surface, a child's counterproductive attitudes and behavior may appear quite willful. Most children, however, do not consciously plan how they're going to compensate for their feelings of inadequacy. They do not say to themselves: "I'm doing poorly in school, and I feel frustrated and demoralized. I think I'll misbehave and slug this kid sitting next to me or talk back to my teacher so that I can let everyone know how unhappy I am." The behaviors are unconsciously driven, and most children are not even aware of the predictable scripts they have created to handle their emotional vulnerability. One child may shut down and refuse to study or complete his assignments. Another may become hostile, disrespectful, resistant, and/or rebellious. Another may escape into a fantasy world. And another may compensate by avoiding academic responsibilities and by focusing exclusively on athletics or developing video-game skills.

Pushed to despair by the struggling child's maladaptive behavior, teachers and parents may conclude that the child is acting out to *get attention* when the child is actually resorting to these behaviors in a desperate attempt to *deflect attention* from his or her inadequacies and hide feelings of inferiority. If the child's unconscious could give voice to the underlying feelings that are driving the behavior, it would probably say: "I feel so stupid! If I act this way, you won't see how dumb I really am and how much I dislike myself. If I act this way, I won't have to deal with my pain."

A struggling child's frustration, anger, fear, insecurity, and feelings of incompetence may implode and manifest as depression or explode and manifest as hostility, aggression, rebellion, antisocial behavior, and/or behavioral disorders. Between these two extremes are countless possibilities for a child to express pain, resentment, demoralization, sadness, and anger.

The signs of emotional distress are sometimes blatant and sometimes subtle and difficult to detect. The evidence, in fact, may be so inconspicuous that critically important danger signals may be overlooked by teachers, parents, and even mental-health professionals. The effects of this oversight can be calamitous. Internal conflict that might have been quickly resolved in first or second grade is often far more challenging to treat by the time a child enters eighth or ninth grade.

Many factors can influence a struggling child's unconscious selection of psychological defense and coping mechanisms. Primary determinants include the:

- quality of a child's rapport with the classroom teacher
- effectiveness of the school learning-assistance program, special day class, or after-school remedial program

- quality of parental support (i.e., encouragement, guidance, supervision, affirmation, and empathy)

Academically deficient children who can see that they are making substantive progress are less likely to resort to and/or hang on to counterproductive behavior. Conversely, those who become convinced that their situation is hopeless and that effort is futile are likely to become increasingly frustrated, demoralized, and defended.

In the following section, school-related factors that can affect your child emotionally are examined, and the red-flag symptoms that indicate psychological distress are described. This information is intended to help you identify and address issues that could negatively affect your child's mental health.

Defense Mechanisms

▲

Refers to behaviors designed to offer protection from feelings of inadequacy and deflect responsibility for dealing with problems.

▲

The struggle to survive in school can wear down the emotional resiliency of learning-disabled children and cause them to become resistant to help, unmotivated, irresponsible, and psychologically defended. To cope with their frustrations and feelings of incompetence and to avoid accountability, many of these children acquire behaviors and attitudes that they believe will hide their inadequacies, insulate them from humiliation, and deflect attention from, and responsibility for, their learning difficulties.

Struggling children can be masterful at rationalizing their counterproductive modus operandi. Classic excuses include:

1. "The teacher is unfair."
2. "School is boring."

3. "The work is dumb."
4. "What's the use of studying for the test? I'll do poorly, anyway."
5. "I forgot."
6. "The test didn't cover what the teacher said it would cover."
7. "The teacher never told us it was due today."
8. "The teacher didn't explain the assignment."
9. "I did check over my work."
10. "Don't worry. I can go out with my friends and finish studying when I get home."
11. "I did all my homework in school."
12. "The teacher didn't assign any homework today."

These justifications, rationalizations, and fabrications are usually transparent to most parents and teachers. The conundrum is figuring out how to respond effectively to the counterproductive behavior. Children's defense mechanisms can make everyone's life miserable. Constantly having to prod children to do their homework and study can wear down the resolve of even the most dedicated parents, and the continual battle of wills can take an emotional toll on everyone in the family.

By denying responsibility, blaming, and making excuses, academically defeated children try to convince themselves and others that they are okay. The illusion inevitably shatters when report cards are sent home.

Unfortunately, parents and teachers are often so preoccupied with reacting to the defended child's maladaptive behavior that they may lose sight of the fact that the exasperating behavior is actually a red flag signaling the child's discouragement, demoralization, and feelings of futility. Reprimanding and punishing children and taking away their privileges rarely prove effective because they do not address the source of the counterproductive behavior: poor skills and a sense of hopelessness and despair. Behavior modification based exclusively on negative reinforcement seldom works. To avoid the punishment, children usually become more devious and manipulative.

Emotionally defended children can avail themselves of a range of ingenious methods to disguise their deficiencies, insecurities, and vulnerabilities. Some may refuse to study, complete their homework, submit their assignments on time, or check over their work for spelling and computational errors. Some may misbehave, become disruptive in class, or assume the role of class clown. Others may retreat into daydreams. The common denominator is the conviction that effort is futile, and the primary concern is somehow to make it through the day without suffering too many bruises.

When the bell finally sounds at the end of the school day, the ordeal is not over. Struggling children must now face the prospect of returning home and confronting concerned, demanding parents who typically want them to sit down immediately and begin their homework.

Many discouraged students choose the path of least resistance and do everything in their power to avoid studying. Those who become passive or resistant learners unconsciously delude themselves into thinking that if they don't really try, then they can't really fail. Their lack of effort only accentuates their deficits, but defended children are usually so enmeshed in their evasive system that they do not recognize this paradox.

Ironically, children with the greatest need to study diligently are frequently the ones who are the most resistant to studying. Fearful of exposing their deficiencies and vulnerabilities, they desperately try to distance themselves from their problems, believing that by running away, they can escape the pressure of having to confront and deal with seemingly insurmountable problems. To them, the outcome is inevitable: If they continue trying, they will fail again.

The accurate identification and effective remediation of children's learning deficiencies is the most potent antidote for eliminating defense mechanisms. With focused learning assistance, emotional support, clearly defined and consistently applied rules and performance guidelines, and affirmation for progress, struggling children will usually begin to relinquish their defense mechanisms. As their skills improve, they will start to experience success. Their achievements will produce self-confidence, emotional resiliency, and self-reliance. They will begin to feel good about themselves and proud of their accomplishments, and the compelling need to defend themselves will usually dissipate.

Defensive, counterproductive behavior tends to become increasingly entrenched over time. For emotionally vulnerable children with significant learning problems and poor self-esteem, defense mechanisms function as a fortress. The fortress is, of course, also a prison, but psychologically defended children prefer not to confront this contradiction. As maladaptive coping behaviors can become deeply entrenched, older children who have struggled unsuccessfully for years with learning problems and who are addicted to their defense mechanisms may require counseling in addition to effective educational intervention.

COMMON DEFENSE MECHANISMS

- rationalizing ("School is dumb.")
- assuaging ("Don't worry, I'll get my homework done.")
- minimizing the implications ("Who cares about getting good grades?")
- deflecting ("Why do you always complain about me and never about my sister?")
- denying ("Stop bugging me. I'm doing fine.")
- blaming ("The teacher never told us to study that.")
- running away ("Who cares about doing well in math? I want to be a professional skateboarder.")
- hiding ("My stomach hurts. I want to stay in bed.")
- evading ("I don't think the teacher assigned science homework.")
- lying ("I didn't sign your name to the report card!")

COMMON COPING BEHAVIOR

- cavalier attitude about school and academic obligations
- passivity
- resistance
- manipulation
- helplessness and dependency
- laziness
- rebelliousness
- procrastination
- self-pity
- irresponsibility
- poor motivation
- disorganization
- inattentiveness to details
- disregard of deadlines
- incomplete and late assignments

SEE: Anger *(page 201)*; Apathy *(page 208)*; Attention to Details *(page 223)*; Bouncing Back from Setbacks *(page 232)*; Conduct and Attitude *(page 235)*; Critical Thinking *(page 161)*; Dealing with Consequences *(page 241)*; Depression *(page 378)*; Disorganization *(page 251)*; Fear of Failure, Success, and/or Competition *(page 383)*; Goal Setting *(page 165)*; Grades *(page 25)*; I'm Dumb Syndrome *(page 388)*; Incomplete Assignments *(page 256)*; Judgment *(page 260)*; Keeping Up with the Class *(page 51)*; Learning from Mistakes *(page 267)*; Logic *(page 171)*; Mastery of Academic Content *(page 67)*; Parent-Child Conflict *(page 393)*; Passive Learning *(page 84)*; Peer Pressure *(page 272)*; Performance Standards *(page 91)*; Planning *(page 176)*; Priorities *(page 180)*; Problem Solving *(page 185)*; Procrastination *(page 278)*; Psychological Overlay and Psychological Problems *(page 399)*; Recording Assignments *(page 107)*; Resistance to Help *(page 282)*; School Anxiety *(page 406)*; Self-concept *(page*

410); Self-control *(page 287);* Strategic Thinking *(page 189);* Study Interruptions *(page 122);* Study Skills *(page 127);* Teacher-Child Conflict *(page 293);* Teacher-Designed Tests *(page 132);* Test Anxiety *(page 420);* Time Management *(page 138);* Underachievement *(page 143);* Working Independently *(page 302).*

Depression

▲

Refers to the despondency triggered by frustration, futility, guilt, anger, and feelings of hopelessness.

▲

Children who are struggling with learning problems, particularly those who are not making progress in school, are especially vulnerable to becoming depressed. The origins of their despondency can usually be directly linked to the frustration, discouragement, and sense of futility they are experiencing.

Being asked to read aloud can be a nightmare for children who have perceptual-processing deficits, such as dyslexia. Being required to complete homework and in-class assignments designed for children with better skills can be equally traumatizing. For these struggling children, school and learning become synonymous with pain, humiliation, and hopelessness.

Frustration invariably takes a cumulative psychological toll on students who learn differently. The daily embarrassment they experience can undermine their already fragile self-esteem and trigger despair.

Some frustrated children express their unhappiness and feelings of inadequacy by acting out. Their hostility is pervasive, and they express their anger aggressively. When triggered by a setback, a negative comment, or a real or imagined slight, the anger explodes and envelops those in proximity. These children may be defiant, disrespectful, resistant, antagonistic, hostile, oppositional, and/or rebellious. They may get into fights during recess, disrupt the class, or become bullies who terrorize weaker or younger children. As teenagers, they may join gangs and become nihilistic and, in extreme cases, sociopathic. Unless there is effective intervention, many of these children are destined to end up mired in the criminal-justice system.

Other children handle their frustration and despair very differently and are unconsciously driven to hide their negative feelings. Sensitive to parental and societal disapproval of venting unpleasant or "unacceptable" emotions, they disguise their anger and express their frustration and sadness through *passive-aggressive behavior.* They may resort to sarcasm, teasing and taunting, or lies and manipulation. They may say something hurtful and then immediately add the caveat "Just kidding." They may derive pleasure from getting other children or their siblings into trouble and from spreading malicious rumors. Because their hostility is convoluted and their means of expressing their feelings is distorted, most of these children do not consciously realize that they are enraged.

Other children who cannot handle the disappointments, embarrassment, and feelings of inadequacy caused by their learning problems warehouse their sadness and feelings of futility. Their frustration and anger *implode,* and this implosion triggers depression.

Depressed children may isolate themselves socially and escape into a fantasy world of daydreams and books. They may become fixated on video games or the occult. They may become chronically shy or excessively narcissistic. Their depression and their inability to relate successfully to others usually cause them to become increasingly alienated from their family and peers. These children are signaling that their coping mechanism cannot handle their problems, but despite the sometimes subtle and sometimes obvious warning signs, their parents and teachers may be either oblivious to, or in denial of, their plight. The consequences can be disastrous, as attested to by the alarming increase in acts of senseless juvenile mayhem in American schools. These acts reflect the detonation of intense, unstable, repressed hostility that finally breaks down the walls of the emotional warehouse where it was contained.

Depression, of course, can be triggered by many factors other than learning problems. Family disharmony, trauma, loss of a parent or sibling, and psychological, physical, or sexual abuse can cause children to conclude that their situation is hopeless and that they are helpless. These feelings will produce despair, which in turn will cause depression.

Children who are overwhelmed by life and by a sense of gloom must be evaluated by a mental-health professional. Because the cloud of depression may temporarily lift of its own accord, parents may conclude that the problem has disappeared and that intervention is unnecessary. Chronic mood swings and repeated episodes of depression are red flags that should not be disregarded. The underlying issues must be examined and sorted out so that children realize that there are viable alternatives to repressing their feelings, warehousing their frustration and anger, and becoming depressed. In some instances, mood-altering medication may be an important component in the treatment protocol.

Depression attributable to school frustration often dissipates when a child's learning problems are effectively remediated. This type of depression, which is a symptom of scholastic difficulty, is described as *psychological overlay* and can be differentiated from depression attributable to a *psychological problem* caused by family dysfunction, trauma, or abuse.

In many cases, depression can be linked to several overlapping factors. A child may, for example, be despondent because she is struggling in school and also because of seemingly intractable family problems. Such a child will require learning assistance to deal with the school-related issues and psychotherapy or family therapy to deal with the psychological issues.

SYMPTOMS OF DEPRESSION

- shyness, withdrawal, fear of social situations
- excessive fears, phobias, and/or anxieties
- difficulty creating friendships
- chronic bed-wetting
- inappropriate social behavior
- chronic sleep disturbances
- chronic eating disorders
- chronic dissatisfaction and complaining
- isolation
- chronic manipulative behavior
- memory loss
- disorganized thinking*
- sudden change in friendships or peer group
- lack of interest in play or social interaction
- excessive sensitivity to real or imagined criticism
- unwillingness to accept constructive criticism, help, or advice
- mistrust of authority figures
- extreme critical attitudes (about self or others)
- chronic physical problems (vomiting, headaches)†
- overeating or no appetite
- unwillingness to accept consequences of behavior (denial, lying, or blaming others to avoid the truth)
- sudden change in personality or behavior
- disregard, or discounting, of one's own abilities
- no interest in personal achievement
- delinquent behaviors (stealing, truancy, running away, using drugs or alcohol, sexual promiscuity)
- verbalization of suicidal thoughts ("There is no reason to live." "I wish I could die.")**

---

*This may indicate mental illness, and a psychiatric consultation is vital.

†This may indicate serious physical illness, and a physician should be consulted.

**Threats of suicide must be taken very seriously, and a qualified mental-health professional should be contacted immediately.

- excessive inappropriate behaviors (need for constant attention, shyness, inability to make sense when communicating*)
- chronic nightmares
- excessive tiredness
- rigid, judgmental, inflexible attitudes
- chronic self-esteem deficiencies
- feelings of profound inadequacy and incompetence
- excessive passivity

▼

SEE: Anger *(page 201);* Apathy *(page 208);* Attention Deficit/Attention Deficit Hyperactivity Disorder *(page 214);* Attention to Details *(page 223);* Avoiding Responsibility *(page 227);* Bouncing Back from Setbacks *(page 232);* Conduct and Attitude *(page 235);* Critical Thinking *(page 161);* Dealing with Consequences *(page 241);* Defense Mechanisms *(page 373);* Disorganization *(page 251);* Fear of Failure, Success, and/or Competition *(page 383);* Goal Setting *(page 165);* Grades *(page 25);* I'm Dumb Syndrome *(page 388);* Incomplete Assignments *(page 256);* Judgment *(page 260);* Keeping Up with the Class *(page 51);* Learning from Mistakes *(page 267);* Mastery of Academic Content *(page 67);* Parent-Child Conflict *(page 393);* Passive Learning *(page 84);* Peer Pressure *(page 272);* Performance Standards *(page 91);* Planning *(page 176);* Priorities *(page 180);* Problem Solving *(page 185);* Procrastination *(page 278);* Psychological Overlay and Psychological Problems *(page 399);* Resistance to Help *(page 282);* School Anxiety *(page 406);* Self-concept *(page 410);* Self-control *(page 287);* Strategic Thinking *(page 189);* Study Interruptions *(page 122);* Teacher-Child Conflict *(page 293);* Teacher-Designed Tests *(page 132);* Test Anxiety *(page 420);* Time Management *(page 138);* Underachievement *(page 143);* Working Independently *(page 302).*

---

*Chronic communication difficulty may also reflect a language disorder such as dysphasia. An evaluation by a speech and language clinician is advisable.

Fear of Failure, Success, and/or Competition

▲

Refers to a conscious or unconscious apprehension that causes children to feel anxiety about the consequences of making a goal-directed effort. This apprehension can cause children to sabotage themselves.

▲

A powerful instinct compels children to protect themselves from harm. When confronted with real or imagined danger, the child's brain triggers an involuntary neurological, hormonal, psychological, and behavioral chain reaction. Adrenaline surges through the body, and reflexes automatically respond to the perceived threat. The child may run, fight, assume a defensive posture, or attempt to neutralize the peril.

When the protective instinct is functioning properly, fear serves as a warning signal that alerts children when the risks are excessive. Ideally, this instinct will inhibit them from diving headfirst into water of unknown depth, getting into a stranger's car, stealing from a store, using cocaine, or entering a gang-infested part of town.

Fear, however, is not always an ally. When it is irrational, inappropriate, or disproportionate, it can distort judgment and perceptions and cause children to become emotionally and mentally dysfunctional.

Academically demoralized children are particularly vulnerable to fear. The continual struggle to survive in school can exact a heavy psychological toll, especially when the situation appears hopeless. Faced with the prospect of seemingly unavoidable failure, defeated learners often become school-phobic. As their self-confidence and emotional resilience deteriorate, the temptation to run away from situations that might potentially cause additional pain or frustration becomes compelling.

Once children are convinced that effort is futile and that failure is preordained, their primary concern is to protect themselves at all costs from feeling worthless. Typical self-protecting behaviors include laziness, procrastination, resistance to help, irresponsibility, manipulation, denial, blaming, cheating, lying, and/or codependency. These behaviors, of course, offer no real protection; in fact, they call attention to the very learning deficiencies psychologically defended children are attempting to cope with and camouflage. Insecure children, however, are usually so entangled in their defense mechanisms that they cannot perceive this contradiction.

Some children react to their frustration and demoralization by acting out. Others shut down, retreat into a shell, and refuse to venture outside the perimeter of their psychological fortress. Fearful of doing anything that might disrupt the dynamics of their protective zone, they reduce their expectations, eliminate their aspirations, and eschew effort. Lacking self-confidence and unwilling to take risks—at least in the academic arena—they repress their natural desire to compete and succeed and instead become consumed by their need to avoid additional failure. Their counterproductive behavior preordains failure, but emotionally defended children are usually too invested in protecting themselves to recognize this cause-and-effect link. Exceedingly sensitive to criticism and the real or imagined derision of their classmates, they run from challenges and give up as soon as they encounter difficulty.

Often traumatized by their negative school experiences, learning-disabled children may perceive any new challenge as a potential defeat, and they may react to every setback as a further confirmation of their inferiority. To avoid the possibility of another failure, they may capitulate *in advance* and then unconsciously rationalize that they haven't really failed because they haven't really tried.

Struggling children may become so habituated to doing poorly in school that they may actually find the prospect of success threatening. Their marginal performance may provide them with a sense of identity and a type of distorted security. To children who are resigned to being incompetent and unintelligent, achievement could be an upsetting disruption in the accustomed status quo. Having unconsciously concluded that they *cannot succeed* and do not *de-*

serve to succeed, these youngsters will do everything in their power not to succeed.

Ensconced in a comfort zone where relatively little is expected of them, many defeated learners actively or passively resist all efforts by their parents and teachers to dislodge them from their haven. Driven by their fears and insecurities, they may feel compelled to run away from any situation that places them in competition with other children who they believe are more capable.

For defeated learners, competing and winning can be as anxiety producing as competing and losing. Were they to begin to achieve in school, they would need to revise their assessment of their own abilities and potential. This reevaluation could be profoundly unsettling, and the prospect of altering their accustomed modus operandi could be traumatizing. Their relationships with their parents and teachers would need to change. D's or C's would no longer be accepted. Their parents and teachers would probably begin to expect them to get B's or even A's in school, and they would be less willing to accept excuses for poor grades or offer help. Meeting the new expectations and performance standards would require additional effort, and they might be rejected by their nonachieving friends without any guarantee that they would be accepted by achieving students.

The fear of failure, competition, and/or success is not readily overcome, and the associated defensive habits and behaviors are not easily changed. The antidote is to reorient children so that they begin to derive pride and pleasure from their accomplishments. This reorientation requires patience, insight, careful planning, empathy, acknowledgment of progress, affirmation for achievement, and appropriate learning assistance.

Before fearful children will relinquish their defense mechanisms, their self-concept must undergo a gradual transformation. To stimulate this shift in self-perception, parents and teachers must effusively praise even small successes, and they must encourage struggling learners to establish specific attainable short-term goals such as a C+ on the next book report. As children begin to achieve, their fears are likely to slowly dissipate. Ideally they will begin to set specific performance objectives for themselves, and they will be more willing to take reasonable risks to achieve these objectives. When children conclude that success is attainable, their motivation, effort, and desire for additional success usually improve commensurately.

Altering the dynamics of a child's fears can be a slow, challenging, and arduous process. Emotional associations with failure, success, or competition can become indelibly imprinted, and assistance from a trained mental-health professional may be necessary when children are unresponsive to their parents' efforts to help them overcome their fears. This intervention is especially vital when the fears are debilitating and are causing children to remain academically and emotionally dysfunctional.

Effective learning assistance is clearly a critical component of the reorientation process. Once struggling children master the basic decoding and encoding skills they need to read their textbooks, retain information, and express their ideas in writing, they must be taught the advanced reasoning, critical thinking, strategic thinking, and study skills that are required for success in upper-level courses. The goal is to guide academically phobic youngsters toward the realization that with the improved skills and sufficient effort, they *can* achieve and that the payoffs for success far exceed any that are derived from being fearful and defensive.

NEUTRALIZING THE FEAR OF FAILURE, SUCCESS, AND COMPETITION

- Identify the specific nature of your child's fears. (e.g., Is he afraid of succeeding because he would then be expected to work more independently? Is he afraid of failing because he is very sensitive to your disapproval? Is he afraid of competing because his sibling is a good student or is a top-notch athlete?)
- Determine if your child perceives himself as unworthy of succeeding. (e.g., Does your child repeatedly say "I'm so dumb!" or

"I hate myself!" If so, an assessment by a mental-health professional is vital.)

- Identify your child's emotional and academic strengths and deficiencies.
- Make certain your child's learning deficits have been accurately identified and are being effectively remediated.
- Encourage your child to develop her natural talents and aptitude.
- Observe how your child responds to setbacks. (e.g., Does your child get defensive and depressed? Does your child give up easily?)
- Identify your child's negative and positive payoffs. (e.g., Does he act like a clown to get attention? Does he act helpless to elicit assistance? Does he intentionally try to elicit sympathy and concern? Is he willing to work for tangible, extrinsic rewards?)
- Identify what triggers your child's anxiety and stress (e.g., having to work independently, write legibly, or study for a spelling test).
- Identify the possible underlying sources of your child's fears (e.g., being ridiculed, unrealistic expectations from parents and teachers, having to transition from a nonachieving peer group to an achieving peer group).
- Plan with the teacher how to help your child improve his academic skills and self-confidence and how to orchestrate successful school experiences (e.g., providing tutorial or educational therapy assistance, requesting extra time with the resource specialist, enrolling your child in a study-skills program).
- Urge the teacher to make reasonable accommodations until your child improves his skills (e.g., reducing the number of spelling words that he's required to learn).
- Effusively praise your child for each success and express confidence in her ability to prevail over her learning difficulties.
- Request that the teacher acknowledge and praise your child whenever possible.
- Encourage your child to discuss and examine situations that frighten her and recommend possible solutions to these problems.

I'm Dumb Syndrome

▲

Refers to profound feelings of inadequacy triggered by chronically poor school performance.

▲

Chronic academic deficiencies invariably produce emotional repercussions. The fallout typically includes diminished self-confidence, elaborate defense mechanisms, and feelings of inadequacy and worthlessness.

That children who struggle academically are likely to feel incompetent should come as no surprise. Poor grades, negative feedback, embarrassment, and frustration are bound to take an emotional toll. Some children who feel they are a disappointment to their parents may react by feeling guilt and shame. Some may become resentful about the pressure their parents and teachers are exerting on them and may act out. Others may become hostile, rebellious, or alienated. Still others may become cavalier about their schoolwork and seek alternative venues in which to excel.

Children who wrestle with specific learning disabilities are particularly at risk for experiencing self-concept damage. As they watch their classmates reading with fluency, comprehending the content of their textbooks, understanding the teacher's instructions, and completing class assignments and homework assignments with little apparent difficulty, their own inadequacies become all the more glaring. For these children school is a never-ending battle to decipher words, understand and remember information, follow directions, do math problems, spell accurately, and express their ideas in writing. Frustrated and demoralized, many of these children are at risk for concluding that their scholastic situation is hopeless and that effort is futile. Once they do, they are likely to shut down in school. Learning becomes secondary. Their primary concern is to make it somehow through the day with the minimum amount of anguish.

From the perspective of a despairing child, there can be only one plausible explanation for his poor academic performance: "I'm dumb." The psychological repercussions of this conclusion are likely to affect the child throughout his entire life. His diminished self-esteem and self-confidence will cause him to accept marginal performance and to lower his expectations and aspirations accordingly.

Unless there is effective remediation and substantive scholastic progress, children who have become convinced in elementary school that they are incompetent are likely to carry this negative self-assessment into middle school, high school, and beyond. Each real or imagined defeat, perceived embarrassment, and poor grade will confirm and solidify their feelings of inferiority. Once they conclude that their situation is futile, these demoralized youngsters will accommodate to their insufficiencies and settle into a comfort zone where they feel safe and protected. Expecting little of themselves and wanting others to do likewise, they will actively or passively resist the efforts of their parents and teachers to help them prevail over their problems.

Children who are convinced they are dumb often acquire an elaborate system of defense and coping behaviors. They may continually make excuses or blame others for their problems. They may resist doing their homework and rationalize that there is no need to work diligently because they are going to fail, anyway. They may hand in assignments late or simply refuse to do them. They may neglect to proofread their essays or check over their math homework for computational mistakes. They may become dependent on their parents or tutors to help them do their assignments, even those that they are actually capable of completing on their own. They may resist help, continually complain, and blame others for their predicaments, or they may become passive and apathetic and retreat into daydreams or a fantasy world of toys or video games. Some will seek surrogates that provide them with a sense of accomplishment. Others will continually sabotage themselves with flawed choices, poor judgment, and compulsive escapism.

Defeated learners who are convinced they are dumb expect disaster, and their negative attitudes and maladaptive behavior guarantee that their expectations will become self-fulfilling. A recycling loop of marginal performance, reduced effort, and diminished self-confidence precludes self-actualization.

Achievement is the single most potent remedy for reorienting the negative attitudes and catastrophic expectations of children who are convinced they are dumb. Parents and teachers, special educators, and school psychologists must make every effort to identify the specific learning deficits, provide effective remedial assistance, and orchestrate repeated opportunities for struggling students to experience success. Telling demoralized students that they are intelligent and capable is an exercise in futility. Before they will believe this, they must have substantive proof. As demoralized children begin to experience success at increasingly difficult tasks, a transformation in their self-image will usually occur. At first, this transformation may be almost imperceptible, but the changes in self-concept will accelerate as children become increasingly convinced that they are actually capable of succeeding in school. With careful engineering by parents and teachers, the "I'm dumb" mind-set will begin to shift to "Maybe I'm not so dumb, after all." The ultimate goal, of course, is for children to conclude: "Hey, I'm a lot smarter than I thought!"

Unfortunately, orchestrating successes for struggling learners is not always a magic bullet. Children with significantly damaged self-esteem may be highly resistant to altering their negative self-assessment. These children will require professional counseling.

ATTITUDES AND BEHAVIORS LINKED TO THE "I'M DUMB SYNDROME"

- poor academic self-confidence
- fear of failure
- fear of competition
- fear of success
- emotional fragility
- dependency on others
- jealousy
- negative expectations
- difficulty bouncing back from setbacks
- depression
- confusion
- elaborate system of defense and coping mechanisms
- resistance to establishing short- and long-term goals
- diminished effort and motivation
- lack of emotional resiliency
- complaining
- blaming
- procrastination
- irresponsibility
- diminished aspirations
- resistance to accepting help

Parent-Child Conflict

▲

Refers to negative feelings triggered by poor communication and a child's unwillingness or inability to meet parents' expectations and performance guidelines.

▲

The likelihood of friction developing between parents and children with learning problems increases significantly when struggling children resort to counterproductive behavior in a misguided attempt to insulate themselves from feeling academically inadequate. Common defense mechanisms include chronic irresponsibility, laziness, procrastination, incomplete assignments, and careless errors, and these behaviors invariably trigger recurring arguments and confrontations whose dynamics are scripted and whose consequences are predictable. Children get upset at their parents for nagging, reprimanding, and punishing them, and parents get upset with their children for generating constant stress and anxiety in everyone in the family.

Parents may recognize the origins of their child's maladaptive behavior and realize that their child is using the behaviors to cope with scholastic problems that appear insoluble. They may also recognize that their child's defense mechanisms are erecting major barriers to successful remediation. These insights, however, do not necessarily equip parents to handle a youngster who should be devoting his energy to improving his academic skills and who is instead preoccupied with evading his obligations and denying responsibility for his actions.

Defended children typically blame their teachers for their difficulties, make excuses for their deficient effort, and use manipulative behavior to avoid doing their work. Common justifications, rationalizations, and deceptions include:

- "The teacher didn't assign any homework tonight."
- "I did my homework in school."

- "Don't worry, I'll get it done after this TV program is finished."
- "I already studied for the test."
- "It was an unfair test."
- "The teacher never gave us that assignment."
- "The teacher never told us when the book report was due."
- "The test covered stuff we were never told to study."
- "Someone took my homework."
- "The other kids cheated."

Acutely aware that these excuses and attitudes are compounding their child's learning problems, concerned parents often resort to an arsenal of traditional "weapons": lectures, admonitions, sermons, nagging, and punishment. Most parents discover, however, that these interventions are ineffectual. Struggling children who are convinced that their coping behavior is essential to their survival will desperately hold on to the behavior until they become convinced that there are better alternatives. These children either do not realize or refuse to acknowledge that their resistance to studying, incomplete assignments, disorganized binders and book bags, disordered study areas, shoddy work, unwillingness to record assignments, and failure to bring home vital study materials offer no real protection. The defense mechanisms simply guarantee continued poor performance and call attention to their deficiencies. Enmeshed in a web of resistance and denial, these children continue to sabotage themselves and in the process drive their concerned parents to despair. Their behavior, however, does provide them with a convenient rationalization for their lack of success: "If I'm not really trying, then I'm not really failing."

Coaxing struggling children to relinquish self-defeating defense mechanisms requires consummate patience, planning, and fortitude on the part of parents. The behaviors provide a haven for children who perceive themselves as deficient, vulnerable, and incompetent. By refusing, resisting, complaining, blaming, rationalizing, and manipulating, children can delude themselves into thinking that they are exercising control over their lives. They can retaliate against life's injustices by pressing their parents' hot buttons and eliciting a predictable negative response.

Before parents can reasonably expect defeated learners to accept more demanding performance and behavior standards, work diligently, and risk failing, they must intentionally create a context at home and in school that allows children to alter their self-perception. Children must become convinced that they are capable of confronting and handling academic challenges. They must begin to see that they are making progress. They must start to derive satisfaction and pride from their accomplishments. They must be effusively affirmed for their improvement and rewarded for their achievements.* Only then will they be willing to relinquish their maladaptive coping mechanisms.

To effect this transformation in a child's self-concept, parents must first make certain that their child's learning problems have been accurately identified and are being effectively remediated by means of formal learning assistance in a resource program, private tutoring, educational therapy, and/or peer tutoring. Parents must also make certain that fair and reasonable accommodations are made in the classroom until their child is able to keep up with the class. These accommodations may include untimed tests, modified assignments in the classroom, and modified homework assignments.†

Parents must also establish fair, reasonable, and consistently applied rules, standards, and performance guidelines at home. They must be supportive, empathetic, and affirming without encouraging helplessness and dependency. If they suspect that significant psychological overlay or psychological problems are contributing to their child's self-sabotaging behavior, they must be prepared to seek counseling for their child.

The alternative is to do nothing, endure continued conflicts and confrontations, and *hope* that somehow "everything will work out." This is both risky and naive. Serious learning problems do not go away of their own accord, nor do chronic family conflicts that are

---

*Rewards can be extrinsic or intrinsic. The goal is for a child to make the transition from working for extrinsic rewards (a prize or money) to working for intrinsic rewards (pride and satisfaction).

†See accommodations listed below and Appendix II for a more comprehensive list of accommodation.

generated by a child's recurring self-sabotaging behaviors. These conflicts will not only trigger resentment and upset; they could also profoundly damage the relationship between parents and their children. A constant diet of conflict at home and poor performance in school cannot help but warp a child's perceptions about his abilities and prospects in life. Unless parents commit themselves to developing an effective strategy to identify the underlying problems and provide learning assistance and, if appropriate, psychological assistance, the disharmony will persist, with potentially disastrous repercussions.

STEPS FOR REDUCING PARENT-CHILD CONFLICT

- Make certain that academic deficits and specific processing deficits have been accurately identified.
- Make certain that the child is receiving effective learning assistance that addresses his or her specific academic deficiencies.
- Make certain that reasonable accommodations are being made in school.
- Establish fair and reasonable performance standards and guidelines at home.
- Identify the specific issues that trigger conflict and confrontations at home.
- Involve the child in the process of identifying underlying issues and brainstorming solutions.
- Encourage the child to establish reasonable short-term and long-term goals.
- Help the child create a study schedule.
- Provide reasonable help while discouraging dependency.
- Give praise and rewards to the child for progress and effort.
- Express confidence in the child's ability to prevail over problems and challenges.
- Provide tutoring or educational therapy if appropriate.
- Provide psychological counseling if appropriate.

IN-CLASS ACCOMMODATIONS THAT CAN REDUCE
AT-HOME CONFLICTS

Adjustments in Classroom Instruction

- Provide study guides.
- Provide a written model for how assignments are to be completed.
- Back up oral directions with written directions.
- Check for understanding of newly introduced material.
- Hand out printed homework assignments for the week.
- Send home simple daily and/or weekly progress reports.
- Verify that instructions and directions are understood.

Classroom Management

- Provide consistent structure and clear performance guidelines.
- Provide a clear explanation of the consequences for failure to meet guidelines.
- Seat student near positive role model.
- Keep rules simple and clear.
- Provide affirmation for progress.

Concentration Deficits

- Clearly define behavioral limits.
- Minimize distractions.
- Provide additional structure to reduce inattentiveness.
- Use nonverbal signals to help student stay on task.

Homework

- Break assignments into smaller projects.
- Urge student to keep track of performance on tests and homework.
- Making certain student accurately records and understands homework assignments.

Motivation

- Emphasize affirmation for achievement rather than negative consequences.
- Make a performance and behavior contract with student.

Organization and Self-management

- Urge student to define realistic short- and long-term goals.
- Show student how to plan and execute long-range projects.
- Show student how to budget time and create a schedule.

Performance

- Provide peer tutoring.
- Assign volunteer homework buddy.
- Utilize study groups in which good students help struggling students.
- Pair students to check each other's work for errors.

Study Skills

- Teach student how to study, get organized, take notes, identify key information, budget time, and prepare for and take tests.
- Teach memorization techniques (e.g., methods of creating visual pictures of information being learned).

SEE: Anger *(page 201)*; Apathy *(page 208)*; Attention Deficit/Attention Deficit Hyperactivity Disorder *(page 214)*; Attention to Details *(page 223)*; Avoiding Responsibility *(page 227)*; Bouncing Back from Setbacks *(page 232)*; Conduct and Attitude *(page 235)*; Critical Thinking *(page 161)*; Dealing with Consequences *(page 241)*; Defense Mechanisms *(page 373)*; Depression *(page 378)*; Developmental Immaturity *(page 246)*; Disorganization *(page 251)*; Fear of Failure, Success, and/or Competition *(page 383)*; Goal Setting *(page 165)*; Grades *(page 25)*; I'm Dumb Syndrome *(page 388)*; Incomplete Assignments *(page 256)*; Judgment *(page 260)*; Keeping Up with the Class *(page 51)*; Learning from Mistakes *(page 267)*; Logic *(page 171)*; Mastery of Academic Content *(page 67)*; Passive Learning *(page 84)*; Peer Pressure *(page 272)*; Performance Standards *(page 91)*; Planning *(page 176)*; Priorities *(page 180)*; Problem Solving *(page 185)*; Procrastination *(page 278)*; Psychological Overlay and Psychological Problems *(page 399)*; Recording Assignments *(page 107)*; Resistance to Help *(page 282)*;

Self-concept *(page 410)*; Self-control *(page 287)*; Strategic Thinking *(page 189)*; Study Interruptions *(page 122)*; Study Skills *(page 127)*; Teacher-Child Conflict *(page 293)*; Time Management *(page 138)*; Underachievement *(page 143)*; Verbal Directions *(page 356)*; Working Independently *(page 302)*; Written Directions *(page 364)*.

Psychological Overlay and Psychological Problems

▲

Refers to a pattern of counterproductive, maladaptive, and often self-sabotaging behavior and attitudes that can be attributed to either an emotional reaction to learning difficulties or to emotional trauma, temperamental predisposition, and/or family dysfunction.

▲

Children with learning problems can be profoundly affected by their negative school experiences. They may be agonizingly embarrassed when they are asked to read aloud. They may cringe in fear and be overwhelmed by catastrophic expectations whenever they take a test. They may crumble when they receive a poor grade and feel humiliated when they cannot answer a question in class or do a math problem at the chalkboard. As they see their classmates effortlessly doing the assigned work while they battle to decipher words, follow directions, and understand the content of their textbooks, these children cannot help but feel frustrated, discouraged, and defective.

For many struggling students, school is a recurring torment. Each day, they face a series of monumental challenges, seemingly insoluble problems, and demoralizing failures. Dreading situations that might expose their inadequacies and subject them to real or imagined ridicule, these children often feel compelled to defend themselves. Their selected defenses are invariably maladaptive and offer no real protection, but insecure children cannot see this obvious paradox. Consumed by an unconscious need to deflect attention from their deficiencies, they may retreat into daydreams, act out, or become the class clown. They may refuse to study and do their homework. They may submit incomplete assignments and miss deadlines. The work they do hand in may be illegible and replete with careless mistakes.

Defeated learners are at risk for becoming school-phobic. Many experience paralyzing performance anxiety whenever they are asked to read, do math problems, or write an essay. Their stress may cause them to complain of stomachaches, sore throats, and headaches on school mornings, and in school they may tell the school nurse that they are sick and need to go home.

When unpleasant school experiences trigger negative psychological reactions, these reactions are described as *psychological overlay*. The emotional symptoms often include avoidance, demoralization, depression, denial, blaming, withdrawal, irresponsibility, diminished self-confidence, and profound feelings of incompetence.

Children with learning problems who become convinced that effort is futile are clearly at emotional risk. These children are prime candidates for acquiring psychological overlay. If they do not qualify for formal learning assistance in school or are unresponsive to the help that is provided, the likelihood of their latching onto a range of counterproductive behaviors increases significantly. Acutely aware that they are making little or no progress, they are likely to become increasingly defended. Once they conclude that pain and humiliation are inescapable no matter how hard they try, they will simply shut down. They may passively go through the motions of being educated, or they may rebel, act out, and develop chronic conduct problems.

Having to return home at the end of a miserable school day and spend additional agonizing hours doing homework compounds the agony of struggling learners. These children know what awaits them: concerned and often nagging parents who insist that they spend hours studying from textbooks they can't understand, drilling number facts they can't retain, composing essays they can't write, and doing math problems they can't solve.

Some discouraged children will retreat behind the walls of a psychological fortress, pull up the drawbridge, and become resistant and uncooperative. Some will ensconce themselves in a comfort zone in which they can avoid responsibility and clearly demarcate what they are willing and unwilling to do. Some may become helpless and dependent on their parents, teachers, and tutors. Others may become depressed, angry, rebellious, alienated, and/or antisocial.

SYMPTOMS OF PSYCHOLOGICAL OVERLAY

- apathy
- anxiety
- manipulative behavior
- self-sabotaging behavior
- passive learning
- aggression (active or passive)
- hostility
- depression
- helplessness
- irresponsibility
- lying
- immaturity
- procrastination
- daydreaming
- acting out
- clowning
- blaming
- complaining
- reduced motivation
- denial
- feelings of being oppressed

- lowered expectations and aspirations
- resistance to studying
- fear of failure, success, and/or competition
- resistance to help
- resistance to authority
- identification with a nonachieving, alienated, rebellious, and/or antisocial peer group

The symptoms of psychological overlay are often identical to the symptoms of a psychological problem, and this overlap can lead to misdiagnosis and inappropriate intervention. Unlike psychological overlay triggered by negative school experiences, psychological problems are usually triggered by emotional trauma, family dysfunction, or genetic predisposition. A child who has witnessed a horrifying incident or who is enmeshed in a volatile, hostile, and dysfunctional family system that elicits fear, anger, shame, and/or guilt is clearly at risk psychologically. So too is the child who has been physically or emotionally abused or molested or the child who has experienced the loss of a parent or sibling. Children may also have an inherited genetic predisposition to psychological problems, such as bipolar disorder or schizophrenia. Whatever the causal factors, psychological problems can induce and/or magnify learning difficulties and generate anger, depression, phobias, insecurity, anxiety, resistance, irresponsibility, and diminished self-confidence.

Determining whether a child is wrestling with psychological overlay triggered by learning problems or with a psychological problem that is causing or exacerbating his learning problems can be extremely challenging. Is a child depressed and rebellious because he is doing poorly in school, or is he doing poorly in school because he is depressed and rebellious? Making this judgment call can be difficult for even a highly competent school psychologist. Do you address the learning problem first and hope that the emotional symptoms will disappear as the child resolves her academic difficulties? Or do you

have the child evaluated by a mental-health professional and hope
that the learning deficiencies will disappear as the child begins to
sort out and resolve her underlying emotional distress?

In many instances, the symptoms of psychological overlay will
disappear as children begin to make academic progress and experience success. This is not always the case, however. Older children
who have been struggling with learning problems for many years
and who have been profoundly scarred by their negative school experiences may not readily relinquish their counterproductive behavior and attitudes. Deeply embedded psychological overlay may have
become an integral component of their persona, and it may have
metamorphosed into a full-blown psychological problem. At this
juncture, psychotherapy may be the only recourse for repairing the
self-concept damage.

Some children wrestle concurrently with both psychological
overlay and psychological problems. A child may be emotionally defended, insecure, and anxious because she is dyslexic. At the same
time, her distress may be compounded because her parents are going
through a bitter divorce. Such a child usually requires both learning
assistance and counseling.

Teachers and parents who are perplexed and frustrated by a
child's behavior may conclude that the self-sabotaging behavior is
the source of their child's learning difficulties. "If only she would be
more diligent (responsible, motivated, attentive to details, etc.), her
grades would improve!" Certainly, maladaptive behaviors can magnify a child's scholastic problems, but in most instances these behaviors are *symptomatic* of an underlying condition, in much the same
way that a fever and muscle aches are symptoms of a viral or bacte-
rial infection. The fever and discomfort are a reaction to the illness
and not its cause.

Accurate diagnosis of the underlying causal factors and effective treatment are the two most effective antidotes for children's
counterproductive behavior and attitudes. The efficacy of these antidotes hinges on early intervention. The sooner a child's learning
problems and/or emotional problems are accurately diagnosed

and addressed, the less need the child has to hang on to self-sabotaging behaviors and attitudes and the lower the risk of lasting psychological damage.

RED-FLAG SYMPTOMS OF A POSSIBLE PSYCHOLOGICAL PROBLEM

Disorganized Thinking

- lack of orientation (awareness of time, place, and people)
- delusions (grandeur or persecution: "My teacher hates me!")
- sensory distortions (auditory and/or visual hallucinations)

Maladaptive Behaviors

- social withdrawal (seclusion, detachment, inability to form friendships)
- excessive sensitivity
- unwillingness to communicate
- tantrums
- superstitious activity (rituals that must be performed before doing a task)
- extreme mood changes
- excessive fantasizing
- phobic reactions (fear of people or germs)
- fixations (excessive and exclusive interest in something)
- suicidal tendencies or threats
- chronic explosive anger or hostility
- depression
- excessive fearfulness
- excessive anxiety
- chronic manipulative behavior
- chronic bullying
- chronic lying
- chronic stealing
- chronic need to control others

Physical Dysfunctions

- bed-wetting (in older children)
- incontinence (in older children)
- repeated stomachaches or headaches (also may be symptomatic of a physical problem)
- chronic sleep disturbances

SEE: Anger *(page 201)*; Apathy *(page 208)*; Attention Deficit/Attention Deficit Hyperactivity Disorder *(page 214)*; Attention to Details *(page 223)*; Avoiding Responsibility *(page 227)*; Bouncing Back from Setbacks *(page 232)*; Conduct and Attitude *(page 235)*; Critical Thinking *(page 161)*; Dealing with Consequences *(page 241)*; Defense Mechanisms *(page 373)*; Depression *(page 378)*; Developmental Immaturity *(page 246)*; Disorganization *(page 251)*; Fear of Failure, Success, and/or Competition *(page 383)*; Goal Setting *(page 165)*; Grades *(page 25)*; I'm Dumb Syndrome *(page 388)*; Incomplete Assignments *(page 256)*; Judgment *(page 260)*; Keeping Up with the Class *(page 51)*; Learning from Mistakes *(page 267)*; Logic *(page 171)*; Mastery of Academic Content *(page 67)*; Parent-Child Conflict *(page 393)*; Passive Learning *(page 84)*; Peer Pressure *(page 272)*; Performance Standards *(page 91)*; Planning *(page 176)*; Priorities *(page 180)*; Problem Solving *(page 185)*; Procrastination *(page 278)*; School Anxiety *(page 406)*; Self-control *(page 287)*; Standardized Tests *(page 116)*; Study Interruptions *(page 122)*; Study Skills *(page 127)*; Teacher-Child Conflict *(page 293)*; Teacher-Designed Tests *(page 132)*; Test Anxiety *(page 420)*; Time Management *(page 138)*; Underachievement *(page 143)*; Working Independently *(page 302)*.

School Anxiety

▲

Stress and apprehension attributable to concerns and self-doubt about being able to meet academic challenges.

▲

Children with learning problems are especially vulnerable to school anxiety. A pattern of negative experiences—or even just one particularly powerful negative experience—can cause them to imprint painful associations that could significantly affect their motivation, resiliency, self-confidence, expectations, and aspirations.

Some children experience generalized anxiety and apprehension every school morning. Others experience anxiety that is triggered by specific stimuli. For example, a dyslexic child may become highly fearful whenever she is asked to read aloud in class. As she waits her turn, her feelings are those of a condemned prisoner awaiting execution. By the time the teacher calls her name, her apprehensions may have reached crescendo proportions. Fear of making mistakes and appearing foolish in front of her classmates and teacher consumes her. Beset by panic, she stumbles over simple words that she would normally be able to decipher. Each error is a further confirmation of her inadequacies, and if she could, she would run from the classroom. What began as anxiety has escalated into a panic attack.

For an insecure child with deficient skills and a fragile self-concept, having to perform in front of the class can be traumatizing. The embarrassment of stumbling, appearing incompetent, and looking foolish can leave an indelible mark the emotional impact of which could persist throughout life.

Chronic anxiety can make a child's expectation of disaster self-fulfilling. The child who has imprinted profoundly negative associations with math may struggle because he has difficulty grasping concepts or performing specific operations, such as dividing fractions. If he concludes that it is impossible for him to understand the material, he may experience dread whenever he is asked to do a problem at the chalkboard. As he stares at the problem, anxiety may cause his mind to shut down. Unable to do the problem, he returns to his seat, crushed by the experience of having once again embarrassed himself in front of his classmates. To the mortified child, the debacle confirms that he is "dumb," and the public humiliation further undermines his already tenuous self-concept.

Insecurity, apprehension, and self-doubt attributable to emotional and/or family problems can also trigger school anxiety. Children who are in conflict with themselves and who feel undeserving are likely to be fearful of any context in which they are expected to perform or compete. These children may manifest their inner turmoil by becoming depressed, chronically shy and tentative, and afraid of situations they cannot control. To a child who feels unworthy, not only can failure be disastrous; so, too, can success. Because achievement conflicts with the child's self-concept, it can produce debilitating emotional dissonance.

A child affected by family disharmony, a divorce, a bitter custody battle, or the death of a parent or sibling is also clearly at psychological risk, and the pain is likely to spill over into the classroom. Lacking emotional resiliency, the child may panic whenever she encounters a challenge in school. Anxiety-producing situations may include reading aloud in class, answering probing questions, solving problems at the chalkboard, or taking tests.

Identifying the source of a child's angst is the most logical antidote for chronic school anxiety. Children with suspected learning problems must be evaluated and provided with learning assistance. To reduce their stress, reasonable teaching, testing, and homework accommodations must be made. These accommodations, which are mandated by federal law (Section 504 of the Rehabilitation Act of 1973), might include untimed tests, less demanding homework assignments, modified curricula, peer tutoring, and multimodality instruction.*

---

*See Appendix I for a description of federal-law provisions that apply to learning disabilities.

If traditional teaching methods have proved unsuccessful, innovative, individually tailored strategies must be devised that capitalize on the child's learning strengths. For example, the child who is convinced he will never be able to do problems involving fractions must be guided to a different conclusion. Creative instructional techniques must be used that will help him master the concepts and do the mathematical operations. These methods might involve the use of manipulatives (cardboard or plastic strips of different dimensions that can help the child grasp in concrete, rather than abstract, terms the part/whole relationships that are central to the concept of fractions).

If children are to overcome their school anxiety, they must acquire the skills to do the work required of them. They must also be "set up" to succeed. The goal is to convince them—by means of a series of carefully engineered positive experiences—that they can, in fact, do what is expected. As their self-confidence improves, their anxiety will diminish.

If the child's chronic anxiety is attributable to family or psychological factors, intervention by a skilled mental-health professional is vital. As the child examines and sorts out his underlying feelings with the help of the therapist, the emotional conflicts that are controlling him will loosen their grip, and his anxiety will diminish.

SOURCES OF SCHOOL ANXIETY

- history of pervasive learning difficulties
- skills deficiencies in a specific subject
- family problems
- emotional problems
- performance apprehension
- deficient self-esteem
- fear of success, failure, and/or competition
- temperamental predisposition to being fearful
- traumatic associations with particular academic material
- intellectual limitations
- teacher-child conflict

SYMPTOMS OF SCHOOL ANXIETY

- resistance to going to school
- chronic complaining or blaming
- fear of having to perform
- frustration
- anger
- demoralization
- feelings of inadequacy
- sense of hopelessness
- depression
- dependency
- anticipation of disaster
- panic
- sense of being overwhelmed
- resignation
- feelings of futility
- diminished expectations
- diminished aspirations

SEE: Anger *(page 201)*; Aptitude *(page 15)*; Avoiding Responsibility *(page 227)*; Bouncing Back from Setbacks *(page 232)*; Conduct and Attitude *(page 235)*; Critical Thinking *(page 161)*; Decoding *(page 332)*; Defense Mechanisms *(page 373)*; Depression *(page 378)*; Disorganization *(page 251)*; Dyslexia *(page 335)*; Fear of Failure, Success, and/or Competition *(page 383)*; Goal Setting *(page 165)*; Grades *(page 25)*; Identifying Important Information *(page 41)*; I'm Dumb Syndrome *(page 388)*; Incomplete Assignments *(page 256)*; Intelligence *(page 45)*; Judgment *(page 260)*; Keeping Up with the Class *(page 51)*; Language Arts *(page 58)*; Learning from Mistakes *(page 267)*; Logic *(page 171)*; Mastery of Academic Content *(page 67)*; Note Taking *(page 79)*; Parent-Child Conflict *(page 393)*; Passive Learning *(page 84)*; Performance Standards *(page 91)*; Planning *(page 176)*; Priorities *(page 180)*; Problem Solving *(page 185)*; Psychological Overlay and Psychological Problems *(page 399)*;

Self-concept

▲

Refers to a child's underlying feelings about his or her abilities and intrinsic worth.

▲

Self-esteem is the engine that drives most human behavior. A child's conscious and unconscious feelings about his or her intrinsic value as a person cannot help but influence the child's choices, goals, aspirations, expectations, motivation, judgment, reactions to challenges, problems, and setbacks, capacity to love, ability to create and experience happiness, and zest for life.

Children who have a positive self-concept, appreciate and respect themselves, and feel worthy and deserving think and act in ways that reflect and preserve their positive feelings. This *acting-in-conformity-to-underlying-emotions principle* also affects children who have a poor self-concept, do not appreciate or respect themselves, and feel undeserving. Because the innermost feelings of these children are negative, the external manifestations are equally negative. Their conscious and unconscious assessment of their intrinsic self-worth will color their perceptions and create an agenda that dictates their attitudes, controls their behavior, and determines the denouement of their life.

Children spend fifteen hundred hours each year in school. It is the arena where they are expected to develop talents, acquire skills, perform, compete, and achieve. Those who prevail in this arena are far more likely to feel good about themselves and their abilities than those who continually struggle and perform poorly.

Learning disabilities can obviously erect significant obstacles to the development of a positive self-concept. Children who have difficulty decoding words, comprehending what they read, following instructions, recalling spoken and written information, and expressing their ideas orally or in writing are at a severe disadvantage. The constant battle to master skills and keep up with the class and the continual need for help can cause these children to feel incompetent and become emotionally defended. Perceiving their deficient skills and poor grades as a confirmation of their inadequacies, learning-disabled children may attempt to deal with their distress by latching onto surrogates for academic achievement, retreating into daydreams, becoming withdrawn, acting out, becoming resigned, or becoming depressed. Some may attempt to cope with their feelings of inadequacy by denying that they have problems. Some may become helpless and attempt to manipulate their parents and teachers into continually rescuing them. Some may attempt to deflect responsibility by blaming others. Others may simply shut down.

Children with poor self-esteem may express their frustration and anger by misbehaving. They may become *actively aggressive* (e.g., bullying or fighting) or *passively aggressive* (e.g., teasing, testing the limits, acting irresponsibly, lying, and/or being resistant). Older children may intentionally cultivate an appearance that clearly signals their disaffection. They may pierce and tattoo their bodies and/or affect a demeanor that unequivocally conveys alienation, rebelliousness, arrogance, hostility, or antisocial attitudes.

Feeling unworthy, children with poor self-esteem typically project their negative feelings about themselves onto others and are often convinced that other people cannot possibly appreciate, respect, or love them. They may express their lack of self-appreciation by refusing to establish personal goals and by running away from problems and challenges. Lowering their expectations and aspirations, these children will then perform congruently with their diminished ambitions. Some may seal their fate as nonachievers by consciously or unconsciously sabotaging themselves with chronically flawed choices and ineffectual effort.

In contrast, children who possess a positive self-concept are convinced that they deserve to succeed. Because they appreciate and respect themselves, they cannot imagine others feeling differently about them. They expect to achieve and prevail over problems and challenges. They also realize that success in school and in life is governed by basic cause-and-effect principles, and this insight guides their attitudes, behavior, and decisions.

CHARACTERISTICS OF CHILDREN WITH A POSITIVE SELF-CONCEPT

- are goal oriented
- are achievement oriented
- establish new goals after attaining those previously coveted
- seek opportunities to test themselves
- are convinced they deserve to prevail
- compete with intensity
- work diligently
- are capable of thinking and working independently
- take pleasure in developing their skills and natural talents
- revel in their accomplishments
- take pride in their work
- learn from mistakes
- bounce back from setbacks
- handle frustration
- take responsibility for their actions
- are aware of the potential consequences of their choices and actions
- accept established rules
- strive for excellence
- select like-minded friends who share their values, interests, goals, and motivation

CAUSE-AND-EFFECT PRINCIPLES RECOGNIZED BY CHILDREN WITH A POSITIVE SELF-CONCEPT

- Effort produces achievement.
- Good judgment improves the likelihood of success and reduces the likelihood of disaster.
- Challenges offer opportunities for developing and improving abilities.
- Goals stimulate effort and motivation.
- Practice enhances skills.
- Success generates pride.
- Winning produces joy.
- Achievement enhances self-confidence.

Parents cannot give their child self-esteem, nor can they guarantee its development by continually trying to make their child happy and by protecting him from all unpleasantness. In fact, these efforts work at cross-purposes with the development of self-esteem. By attempting to shield their child from difficulties, disappointments, setbacks, rejections, and frustration, parents unwittingly deny him the opportunity to overcome adversity and develop character and grit.

Chronic failure and demoralization must be distinguished from occasional setbacks and discouragement. No one can escape sporadic defeats in life, and learning how to handle these conundrums is a requisite to becoming a fully functional adult. Parents who try to protect children from all frustration are preventing them from developing their emotional and problem-solving resources. Self-esteem grows as a function of being able to handle life's positive and negative experiences with increasing efficacy and independence.

Parents may not be able to bestow self-esteem on children, but they can certainly play a vital role in nurturing the development of self-esteem by creating a safe, supportive, and loving family context, by urging children to develop their talents, and by helping them figure out who they are, what they are good at, and what they want in life. Appreciation, praise, and affirmation for progress and accomplishments encourage children to respect themselves and value their abilities. These children will become convinced that they are entitled to the best that life has to offer.

Self-esteem must be differentiated from self-confidence. Although the two phenomena frequently overlap and are the cornerstones of a child's self-concept, there are fundamental differences. A child may be talented in sports and may feel supremely self-confident on the basketball court. Off the court, he may feel insecure and inadequate. He may project self-assurance and bravado when dribbling or shooting the ball, but he may feel intellectually inadequate, socially inept, and insecure in any situation not involving sports.

Although self-confidence may not be the equivalent of self-esteem, it can be an important resource for children who are struggling academically. When children with learning problems possess other talents and excel in sports, drama, music, or chess, they have a refuge from the storm and a means of assuaging the impact of their scholastic trials and tribulations. The pain of failing a test can be partially mitigated by going out and shooting baskets or hitting a tennis ball.

The ideal is to help children develop *both* self-confidence and self-esteem. Initially, promoting the acquisition of self-confidence may be all that is realistically possible until the underlying academic, psychological, and/or family issues that are preventing the growth of self-esteem are identified, addressed, and resolved.

COMMON MISCONCEPTIONS ABOUT SELF-ESTEEM

- Parents can give their children self-esteem.
- Parents can guarantee self-esteem by lavishing attention, economic advantages, or educational advantages on their children.
- Parents can enhance self-esteem by shielding their children from life's trials, setbacks, uncertainties, frustrations, and unhappiness.
- Self-confidence is the equivalent of self-esteem.

Parents can play an instrumental role in helping children acquire self-confidence by encouraging them to develop their abilities, establish personal-performance goals, and apply themselves assiduously. At the same time, they will need to affirm progress effusively, praise effort, and applaud achievement.

Entrenched negative attitudes, behavior, and expectations are not easily discarded. Children with poor self-esteem often settle into a comfort zone. Resigned to marginal performance, nominal effort, and minimal payoffs, these children often unconsciously sabotage themselves so that they can maintain the status quo. Within the confines of the comfort zone, everything is predictable, and this predictability provides a sense of security and control. To children with a poor self-esteem, retreating into a safe haven can be appealing and addictive.

Carefully orchestrating opportunities for achievement is the critical first step in improving a child's self-concept. When parents realize that the lament "I can't" has become "I can," they will know that their child has begun to make the critically important transition from feeling ineffectual and inadequate to feeling capable and proficient.

Significant self-esteem deficits will not disappear of their own accord, especially if feelings of guilt, shame, and unworthiness are deeply imbedded. These emotions are psychologically corrosive and can have disastrous repercussions. Unless there is intervention by a well-trained mental-health professional, the feelings are likely to affect children negatively throughout life.

GAUGING SELF-CONCEPT

	Yes	No
My child:		
• has a realistic sense of her strengths and weaknesses	___	___
• has personal short- and long-term goals	___	___

	Yes	No
• develops realistic strategies for attaining goals	___	___
• perseveres despite obstacles	___	___
• is able to handle setbacks and glitches	___	___
• is willing to accept challenges	___	___
• delights in challenges	___	___
• believes he can prevail and deserves to prevail	___	___
• is self-reliant	___	___
• thinks independently	___	___
• is able to establish and maintain social relationships	___	___
• selects friends who share positive values and goals	___	___
• feels connected with family	___	___
• is able to analyze and solve problems	___	___
• is able to handle setbacks	___	___
• has success-oriented attitudes and behavior	___	___
• has a zest for life	___	___
• can express positive feelings	___	___
• feels secure	___	___
• is self-confident	___	___
• is optimistic	___	___
• assesses situations realistically and rationally	___	___
• focuses on the positive rather than the negative	___	___
• feels loved and deserving of being loved	___	___
• is capable of accepting and expressing love	___	___

A pattern of *yes* responses generally indicates a positive self-concept. A pattern of *no* responses indicates the opposite.

GUIDELINES FOR ENHANCING CHILDREN'S SELF-CONCEPT

- Express love, acceptance, respect, and pride.
- Provide security, stability, safety, and constancy.
- Define family values.
- Establish reasonable and consistently applied rules, limits, performance guidelines, and expectations.
- Insist that your child assume reasonable, age-appropriate responsibilities.
- Express appreciation for your child's talents.
- Express positive expectations.
- Communicate honestly.
- Be sensitive and empathetic to feelings and fears.
- Practice and model ethics.
- Intentionally orchestrate opportunities for success.
- Encourage independence and self-sufficiency.
- Permit your child to experience a reasonable amount of frustration.
- Teach and model how to analyze and solve problems.
- Help your child identify and develop his talents.
- Encourage self-expression.
- Validate your child's feelings and ideas if they are reasonable—even if you are not in complete agreement.
- Listen and communicate nonjudgmentally.
- Encourage your child to establish personal short- and long-term goals.
- Encourage your child to establish priorities.
- Help your child develop a practical strategy for attaining her goals.
- Encourage your child to challenge himself and improve his skills.
- Help your child realize that she is responsible for her own happiness and accomplishments in life.
- Provide academic and/or psychological support if underlying learning or emotional issues are preventing your child from developing self-esteem.
- Carefully orchestrate successes.
- Affirm progress.

- Praise accomplishments.
- Express faith in your child's ability to handle problems and challenges.
- Encourage self-appreciation and self-acceptance.

CHARACTERISTICS OF A POSITIVE SELF-CONCEPT

- sense of worthiness
- self-acceptance
- desire to achieve
- recognition of personal talents
- desire to establish short- and long-term goals
- willingness to work diligently to attain goals
- motivation to seek challenges
- desire to test skills and abilities
- awareness of cause-and-effect principles that affect success and failure
- faith in ability to prevail over problems and challenges
- capacity to handle frustration
- willingness to suspend immediate gratification
- ability to develop a well-conceived plan for getting from point A to B
- capacity to analyze and learn from mistakes
- focused, goal-directed effort
- capacity to rebound from glitches and setbacks
- ability to weigh the pros and cons and make wise decisions
- realization of responsibility in determining the outcome of endeavors
- determination
- perseverance
- pride in accomplishments
- self-reliance

SEE: Anger *(page 201)*; Apathy *(page 208)*; Aptitude *(page 15)*; Auditory Memory *(page 322)*; Avoiding Responsibility *(page 227)*; Bouncing Back from Setbacks *(page 232)*; Conduct and Attitude *(page 235)*; Critical Thinking *(page 161)*; Dealing with Consequences *(page 241)*; Defense Mechanisms *(page 373)*; Depression *(page 378)*; Developmental Immaturity *(page 246)*; Disorganization *(page 251)*; Dyslexia *(page 335)*; Fear of Failure, Success, and/or Competition *(page 383)*; Goal Setting *(page 165)*; Grades *(page 25)*; I'm Dumb Syndrome *(page 388)*; Incomplete Assignments *(page 256)*; Intelligence *(page 45)*; Judgment *(page 260)*; Keeping Up with the Class *(page 51)*; Language Disorders *(page 433)*; Learning from Mistakes *(page 267)*; Logic *(page 171)*; Mastery of Academic Content *(page 67)*; Parent-Child Conflict *(page 393)*; Passive Learning *(page 84)*; Peer Pressure *(page 272)*; Performance Standards *(page 91)*; Planning *(page 176)*; Priorities *(page 180)*; Problem Solving *(page 185)*; Procrastination *(page 278)*; Psychological Overlay and Psychological Problems *(page 399)*; Resistance to Help *(page 282)*; School Anxiety *(page 406)*; Self-control *(page 287)*; Strategic Thinking *(page 189)*; Study Skills *(page 127)*; Teacher-Child Conflict *(page 293)*; Teacher-Designed Tests *(page 132)*; Test Anxiety *(page 420)*; Time Management *(page 138)*; Underachievement *(page 143)*; Verbal Directions *(page 356)*; Working Independently *(page 302)*; Written Directions *(page 364)*.

Test Anxiety

▲

Refers to apprehension and dread of taking exams that is motivated by fear of doing poorly.

▲

Having to take a test is an anxiety-producing experience for most students. As they wait for the test to be handed out, children often feel misgivings and uneasiness similar to the butterflies actors experience before the curtain goes up. In most cases, the anxiety and apprehension dissipate once they become involved in answering the test questions and discover that they know the answers.

Chronic and incapacitating test anxiety is far more deleterious. Convinced that they are going to do poorly, some students become paralyzed by fear and stress, and their expectations of disaster can undermine their ability to think effectively and recall the information they have learned. In extreme cases, the anticipatory dread can cause sleeplessness the night before the exam, panic attacks, and depression. By the time these chronically apprehensive children are finally handed the test, they may be mentally and emotionally dysfunctional. As they scan the questions covering material that they diligently reviewed, they panic and immediately conclude that the questions have nothing to do with what they studied. Their mind shuts down, and their fear of failing becomes self-fulfilling. The subsequent poor grade only serves to confirm their feelings of inadequacy and reaffirm their feelings of futility.

Profound test anxiety can usually be traced to several sources. The most common is a learning disability. Children with learning problems often do poorly on tests, and their imprinted negative associations with test taking and their expectations of disaster can be paralyzing. Knowing that they have to take a science test on Friday and realizing that they have never done well on previous science tests can throw them into an emotional, mind-numbing tailspin.

Some learning-disabled youngsters simply resign themselves to failure. They may go through the motions of studying and preparing for tests, but their studying is passive and ineffectual. These children may become so inured to frustration, discouragement, and demoralization that they may present as unconcerned or even flippant about their poor test performance. Their affected flippancy, however, is actually a smokescreen designed to camouflage their pain, feelings of incompetence, and tenuous self-esteem.

Learning-disabled children who are resigned to doing poorly on tests may also defend themselves psychologically by refusing to study. They typically justify their behavior by rationalizing: "Why try? I'm going to fail, anyway."

The negative-expectations/negative-outcome loop can be represented graphically:

NEGATIVE-EXPECTATIONS/NEGATIVE-OUTCOME TESTING LOOP

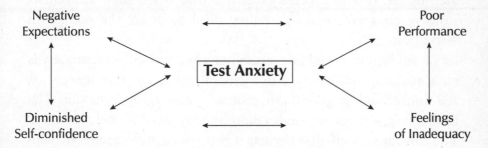

The arrows in the preceding diagram point in both directions to underscore that each component in the loop can reciprocally affect the other components.

Once the test anxiety cycle becomes firmly entrenched, it can have disastrous academic and psychological consequences and can cause potentially capable children to become academically dysfunctional. Without effective intervention, children enmeshed in a negative-expectations/negative-outcome loop will usually lower their expectations and aspirations. Potential abilities may never be developed, and doors to higher education and rewarding careers may never open.

The most obvious antidote to chronic test anxiety is to teach test phobic children practical relaxation techniques that can calm their fears. Apprehension-reducing techniques typically incorporate:

- deep breathing to soothe nerves (not too many breaths, as this can cause children to hyperventilate)
- positive visualization (forming a mental image and actually seeing themselves taking the test, knowing the answers, doing well, and feeling proud and confident)
- a "mantra" of positive statements recited silently and repeated several times while the child studies for the test and later as the child waits for the test to be handed out ("I will do well on this test. I know the information. I have prepared conscientiously.")

Children pass through a critical-anxiety threshold during the highly stressful moments when they are waiting for a test to be distributed. It is at precisely this juncture when their apprehensions reach a crescendo that they need to apply the relaxation techniques.

Counseling should be considered when a child's test anxiety is incapacitating and is linked to a general pattern of fear, insecurity, self-doubt, and/or maladaptive or self-sabotaging behavior. The underlying sources of the foreboding may need to be examined. The child who feels that she can never please her parents or who has experienced a great deal of overt or implied criticism is far more likely to be excessively anxious about having to validate herself by doing well on a test. If the child feels undeserving of success, she may consciously or unconsciously sabotage herself. Having a panic attack, forgetting what has been studied, and doing poorly on an exam could be the means of enacting this unconscious self-defeating agenda.

Parents who suspect that underlying psychological factors are triggering their child's excessive test anxiety are advised to seek professional help. The sooner this intervention occurs, the lower the risk of severe and lasting damage to their child's self-concept.

SOURCES OF TEST ANXIETY

- the conviction, real or imagined, that one is not adequately pre-pared for a test
- a track record of poor test performance
- a history of learning difficulties that have undermined academic self-confidence
- difficulty mastering the content of a particular subject, such as math or chemistry
- a fear of failure linked to fragile self-esteem
- a fear of success linked to fragile self-esteem (e.g., "If I do well on this test, everyone will expect me to do well on the next test, too.")
- feelings of unworthiness
- a conscious or unconscious self-sabotaging agenda linked to poor self-esteem
- generalized anxiety and self-doubt exacerbated by the need to perform

SYMPTOMS OF TEST ANXIETY

- expectation of disaster
- escalating dread and apprehension
- sleeplessness
- obsessive fixation on the upcoming test
- trembling
- difficulty breathing
- sweaty palms
- paralyzing fear
- inability to recall what has been studied
- panic that interferes with intellectual reasoning
- generalized dysfunctionality that undermines performance

SPEECH AND LANGUAGE

The quality of a child's verbal communication hinges on two over-lapping capabilities: speech and expressive language skills. Children who have a speech disorder have difficulty pronouncing letters and words properly. They may omit sounds, saying "at" instead of "cat," or substitute one sound for another, saying "pag" for "bag"); distort sounds, such as the *r* and the *l,* or distort words, saying "furog" for "frog."

Other forms of speech disorders include lisping, stuttering, and stammering. These disturbances in speech rhythm may be caused or exacerbated by physiological, genetic, or emotional factors. In extreme cases, the child's speech difficulties may be so significant that the child's communication is incomprehensible.

Speech disorders can be a serious source of embarrassment. Children who struggle to communicate intelligibly are often self-conscious, apprehensive, and insecure. Their articulation difficulties may cause other children to tease them, and this derision can undermine their self-confidence and warp their perceptions about themselves and their abilities. To protect themselves from feeling inadequate and defective, children with speech disorders may acquire a range of psychological defense mechanisms and become chronically shy, withdrawn, and uncommunicative.

Children with less severe speech problems sometimes slip through the diagnostic screen and are never provided with speech therapy. These children may have difficulty articulating only one or two sounds (e.g., the *l* sound), and their parents and teacher may assume that the mispronunciations will correct themselves naturally. Some parents may even find the articulation problem to be "cute."

Others may choose to disregard age-inappropriate "baby talk" and hope that their child will ultimately outgrow the problem.

Articulation problems become less "cute" as children mature and can be a source of profound embarrassment. Chronic mispronunciations can undermine self-confidence and limit vocational choices and career advancement. The adult who cannot pronounce the letter *l* and who says, "I'm rearning," when he wants to say, "I'm learning," is not likely to be promoted to an upper-level career position.

Language disorders can also be psychologically, academically, and vocationally debilitating. Children with a language disorder have difficulty finding the words to express *(encode)* their ideas, emotions, insights, knowledge, and perceptions. For example, a teacher may ask a student to read a math word problem aloud in class and explain how to solve the problem. If the child can decipher the written words and symbols, understands the math concepts, and can do the required calculations but cannot intelligibly describe the problem-solving procedure, her difficulty is probably attributable to an *expressive-language disorder.*

Children with serious and chronic expressive-language problems are described as *dysphasic* or *aphasic.* Whereas dysphasic children are able to communicate but have difficulty finding the proper words to express their ideas, aphasic children have virtually no communication skills.* Both conditions require intensive language therapy, and children with these conditions are usually placed in specialized language-disorder programs.

Language disorders can erect formidable educational and emotional barriers. Children who cannot find the words to express their needs, ideas, insights, and feelings are at risk for feeling frustrated, demoralized, isolated, and depressed. Early intervention and specialized language therapy are vital.

---

*The terms *aphasia* and *dysphasia* are generally used interchangeably, even by professionals. This usage is technically inaccurate, as it fails to indicate that aphasia is a far more profound language disorder.

Chronic communication deficits should be interpreted as red flags signaling a potential language disorder. The most obvious indication is delayed language acquisition. If the normal developmental progression from cooing to babbling to speaking isolated words does not occur or if this progression is interrupted, the child's pediatrician should be consulted. Other warning signs include the inability of a six-year-old to verbalize the names of colors, identify basic shapes, recite the days of the week or the months of the year, count out loud, or sing the words to the songs taught in class.

In the following section, you will find a more complete description of the symptoms, causes, and implications of speech and language disorders.

Articulation

▲

Refers to the actual physical production of sounds in speech. An articulation problem manifests as difficulty pronouncing certain sounds and words properly. The problem may reflect a speech disorder if the mispronunciations are chronic and persist past kindergarten, first grade, and beyond.

▲

Speech is produced when air passes from the lungs through the larynx or voice box. The vocal cords vibrate, and the sound is altered by the palate, tongue, lips, and teeth. Difficulty with articulation is often attributable to the incorrect placement or movement of the articulation muscles in the lips, tongue, velum, and pharynx.

Articulation skills are acquired sequentially. At specific developmental stages, it is relatively common for children to have difficulty pronouncing certain letters and words. These difficulties should not necessarily trigger concern, especially if the child responds to gentle feedback and is able to correct the mispronunciation. A three-year-old who says "wawa" instead of "water" may not have yet developed the ability to pronounce the *t* and *r* sounds.

As children mature, their articulation skills should improve. Significant mispronunciations by children in kindergarten may indicate a possible *speech disorder*. Children with chronic mispronunciations require monitoring. By three to four and a half years of age, children should be able to make most of their verbal communication understood, and their words should be at the minimum 70–80 percent intelligible.

Developmental Milestones in Articulation

Age	*Developed Sounds*
3 years and 5 months	b, p, m, w
4 years and 5 months	t, d, g, k, ng, y
5 years and 5 months	f, u, s,* z
6 years and 5 months	sh, l, th, r

A four-year-old's difficulty pronouncing *l* should not necessarily trigger concern, but it could be a red flag if the problem persists in first grade or if the child makes multiple articulation errors. There is justification for concern, however, when a six-year-old struggles to pronounce *b* or *t* correctly. If articulation problems persist, parents should consult a pediatrician, who will advise them if a speech evaluation is advisable.

Parents of school-age children may request an evaluation by a speech-and-language pathologist at their child's school, or they may elect to have their child assessed privately. Preschool children ages three to five are also entitled to a public-school speech evaluation if they are struggling to articulate sounds they should developmentally be able to produce. It should be noted, however, that many

_____

*Difficult sounds such as *s, l, r, sh, ch, y, v, z, dg*, and *th* may not be completely acquired until age seven or eight.

minor articulation problems disappear of their own accord by age eight or nine.

Subtle articulation difficulties may involve relatively common pronunciation difficulties. A child may omit sounds and say "at" instead of "cat" or substitute one sound for another and say "pad" for "bad," distort specific sounds such as *r* and *l* and say "cally" instead of "carry," or distort words by inserting dipthongs and say "furog" for "frog." Articulation problems may also present a lisping (distorting the *s* sound and difficulty differentiating the *s*, *sh*, and *th* sounds). In cases of severe articulation difficulty, a child's communication may be incomprehensible.

Although *stuttering* (repetition of sounds, prolongations, or blockages) and *stammering* (stumbling and hesitating) affect speech, these conditions are considered to be *disturbances in speech rhythm*. The difficulties may be caused or exacerbated by physiological or genetic factors and are considered to be *organic* (a physiological abnormality).

Other physiologically and/or neurologically based conditions that can affect speech include:

- dysarthia: weakening of the sound-producing muscles of the face due to disease of the central nervous system
- oral ataxia*: an inability to coordinate voluntary muscular movements of the mouth attributable to a nervous-system disorder
- apraxia*: loss or impairment of the ability to execute movements that is not attributable to paralysis

Emotional factors, such as anxiety or fear, can also contribute to speech-rhythm disturbances. There also appears to be a higher incidence of speech disorders and language disorders in children born prematurely and/or of multiple births. Although most children with

---

*The terms *ataxia/dystaxia* and *apraxia/dyspraxia* are often used synonymously. Technically, this is inaccurate. The prefix "a" means total (e.g., ataxia: the *total* inability to coordinate voluntary muscle movements). The prefix "dys" indicates a less severe condition. This is usually the more precise description.

articulation difficulties are physiologically normal (i.e., the problems are of *nonorganic* or *nonmetabolic* origin), some children (approximately 15 percent) struggle to speak clearly because of specific organic and neurological abnormalities.

SYMPTOMS OF ARTICULATION DIFFICULTIES

- omitted sounds when speaking or reading
- substituted sounds
- distorted sounds
- distorted words
- self-consciousness or embarrassment when talking
- auditory-discrimination deficits
- reluctance to communicate, especially if teased
- diminished self-confidence
- defensive behavior
- motor-coordination deficits (in face or body)

DIAGNOSTIC TOOLS

Formal Assessment

- Goldman-Fristoe Test of Articulation: uses picture stimuli to assess the ability to produce consonants and consonant blends in words and guided narrative (i.e., retelling a story). This is a commonly used testing instrument. Age range: 6 to 16+.
- Khan-Lewis Phonological Analysis: used with Goldman-Fristoe Test to analyze articulation errors.

Informal Assessment

- Arizona Articulation Proficiency Scale (AAPS): uses picture stimuli to measure articulation errors in single words. Determines percentage of correct sound productions and provides an intelligibility rating.

▲

TREATMENT PROTOCOLS

Most speech-therapy programs are eclectic and nonformularized. The speech-and-language clinician typically uses a range of specialized methods to correct identified deficits. Usually, the therapist will work initially on sounds that are easiest for the child and progress to more difficult sounds that are critical to more intelligible speech. The therapist will model the sound and then help the child reproduce it. Repetitive practice is an integral part of the intervention process. "Let's Articulate" is an example of a systematic program that some clinicians may incorporate into the speech-therapy procedure.

▼

See: Auditory Discrimination *(page 317)*; Auditory Memory *(page 322)*; Brain Dysfunction *(page 326)*; Decoding *(page 332)*; I'm Dumb Syndrome *(page 388)*; Language Disorders *(page 433)*; Phonics *(page 346)*; Psychological Overlay and Psychological Problems *(page 399)*; Reading Fluency *(page 351)*; School Anxiety *(page 406)*; Self-concept *(page 410)*; Spelling *(page 112)*.

Language Disorders

▲

Refers to the inability to communicate ideas and feelings effectively using spoken language.

▲

Speech is a genetically programmed and biologically hard-wired ability that is linked to chronological phases of child development. Babies progress from cooing to babbling. By the time they become toddlers, they can use single words to describe what they see, hear, and touch. They can say "wawa," "mamma," "blanky," "dadda," "cookie," and "doggie," and by exerting some effort, their parents can usually understand what they are trying to communicate. Soon after, they begin to put two words together to form phrases and sentence fragments.

Most children progress smoothly through this language-acquisition sequence and effortlessly develop the ability to communicate in spoken language. By the age of two, they can link words with concrete objects. They soon begin to add adjectives and action verbs to their ever-expanding vocabulary and incorporate these words into simple sentences. As their language skills expand, they are able to respond to environmental stimuli and express their basic needs and feelings. As they decipher (decode) sensory data received through their five senses, they can select words to express (encode) their perceptions, feelings, and thoughts.

Children's choice of words and the quality of their expressive language are affected by eight interrelated factors that include:

- age
- intelligence
- sensory stimulation
- experiential opportunities
- language aptitude
- home environment
- social interaction
- educational instruction

If these interactive components are conducive to language development and if a child's family promotes verbal expression, most children will learn to communicate effectively. When the natural sequence of language development is impeded and children fail to develop effective verbal skills, the causal factors need to be identified and addressed.

Expressive-language difficulties range from subtle to severe. Profound communication disorders are usually associated with a condition of neurological origin called *dysphasia,* or in extreme cases, *aphasia* (total inability to use language).* Because children afflicted with these language disorders can obviously become frustrated, discouraged, demoralized, and isolated, a professional assessment and intervention in the form of intensive language therapy is essential.

Children afflicted with aphrasia often present as emotionally distant, noncommunicative, and nonemotive or inappropriately emotive. Children with more subtle expressive-language deficits do not necessarily manifest these characteristics.

In some cases, a severe expressive-language disability may be linked to autism, a puzzling and poorly understood disorder that appears to be of neurobiological, neurochemical, and/or genetic origin. Autistic children struggle to communicate, but their condition is anatomically distinct from dysphasia or aphasia.

Difficulty with receptive language can also trigger an expressive-language disorder. Children who do not understand what is being said to them have difficulty responding to even the most basic verbal cues, such as "Open the door." Their confusion and difficulty processing language (a decoding dysfunction) will affect their capacity to communicate appropriate verbal responses (an encoding dysfunction).

With systematic instruction, patient support, and sensitive, empathetic feedback from their parents and teachers, many mildly inarticulate children can significantly improve their verbal skills. Providing these children with repeated, nonstressful opportunities to practice using language is vital. Feedback should be selective, constructive, and communicated with sensitivity, and children should be repeatedly acknowledged and affirmed for progress. ("I like the way you described the game!") Correcting every mistake

---

*Through common usage, the term *aphasia* is used by both professionals and non-professionals to describe a language disorder irrespective of its severity. This is technically incorrect. Most children with significant communication problems still have some language ability and are actually *dysphasic* and not *aphasic.*

can be an agonizing experience for a child who is already insecure and verbally tentative. Continual criticism will invariably cause the child to become even more anxious, inhibited, language-phobic, and noncommunicative.

Children with even relatively minor communication problems can be extremely sensitive about their language deficiencies, and their struggle to express themselves can trigger profound feelings of inadequacy, anxiety, and vulnerability. Every effort must be made to protect them from being ridiculed or teased by other children in school and at home. Teachers must be particularly vigilant in the classroom and on the playground.

The more significant children's communication deficits, the more defended and language-phobic they are likely to become. To protect themselves, they may resist discussing their feelings, thoughts, and observations. They may respond grudgingly to direct questions, answer in monosyllables, and recoil from any situation in which they might be required to speak in public.

Unless the specific language deficits (i.e., vocabulary deficiencies, grammar and syntax errors, or disorganized thinking) of children with language disorders are identified and treated, these children are likely to become increasingly isolated and alienated from other children and perhaps even from their family. An evaluation by a speech-and-language pathologist is essential. This assessment will indicate if language therapy and/or psychological counseling are required.

Some insecure and chronically shy children may present as having a language disorder. These children may actually be quite verbal and articulate in private conversation with those they know, trust, and feel at ease with, but they may be traumatized by the prospect of talking to strangers or speaking in public. To overcome their fears and anxiety about speaking in public, these exceedingly self-conscious children must be gently coaxed to communicate, repeatedly affirmed, and effusively praised for progress. Their parents and teachers must also make a special effort to convince them that they're not being critically judged when they speak. Allaying their fears and building their self-confidence will require time, patience, emotional support, planning, affirmation, and carefully orchestrated and deliberately acknowledged successes.

Parents and teachers should intentionally create opportunities for children with poor communication skills to express their ideas and feelings. Even the most rudimentary comments and statements should be positively acknowledged. When children make unclear statements, parents and teachers must use their discretion. In many instances, it may not be appropriate to correct the errors, especially if the child might be embarrassed in front of others. In other instances, providing sensitive, supportive, and constructive feedback can play an instrumental role in helping children improve their communication skills.

Parents and teachers must also be sensitive to the fact that oral communication is more difficult when children attempt to respond to complex stimuli, such as their reaction to feeling embarrassed or when they attempt to describe complex issues, such as the plot of a book. Children with communication deficiencies who try to describe an event, an idea, or a feeling are taking a major risk, and they require extra patience, encouragement, and empathy.

Verbally tentative and insecure children should be intentionally drawn into family discussions. As they become more self-confident and competent, they should be gently encouraged to participate in class discussions, make short oral presentations, express their reactions to current events, and summarize verbally what they've read in their textbooks. Although initially these experiences will trigger anxiety in children who are phobic about public speaking, the anxiety can usually be overcome with affirmation and praise for progress.

Excessively fearful children obviously require extra coaching, rehearsals, encouragement, acknowledgment, praise, and instruction in basic relaxation and visualization techniques. A series of carefully engineered successes can be a powerful elixir in building their self-confidence and a powerful antidote for their stage fright.

Children who can communicate effectively possess an invaluable resource that they'll be able to use throughout their lives. Logic prescribes that teaching effective verbal skills should be one of our highest educational priorities. Unless our educational system recognizes this priority, American high schools will continue to "crank out" graduates with a working vocabulary of one thousand words. Struggling to express their most basic feelings and thoughts comprehensibly, these youngsters will characteristically preface each incoherent statement they utter with the words "you know." Unfortunately, these inarticulate teenagers are destined to discover that their deficient expressive-language skills will exclude them from many of the most coveted careers and vocations.

Children suspected of having a language disorder should be evaluated by a speech-and-language pathologist as soon as possible. The sooner a language disorder is identified and treated, the lower the risk of psychological damage.

SYMPTOMS OF A LANGUAGE DISORDER

Auditory Processing Deficits

- difficulty paying attention to auditory stimuli
- difficulty discriminating sound versus no sound
- difficulty locating where sound is coming from
- difficulty discriminating different sounds
- difficulty distinguishing primary sounds from background sounds
- difficulty associating sounds with source of sounds
- difficulty filtering out extraneous sounds
- difficulty sequencing ideas
- oral reversals (e.g., "emeny" instead of "enemy")
- circumlocutions (imprecise, roundabout communication—e.g., "that place down there where they sell the thingamajig")

Linguistic Processing Deficits

- poor grammar
- wrong verb tenses
- use of only broad meanings of words

- lack of understanding of subtle meanings or differences between words
- difficulty understanding spatial prepositions (e.g., "beside" or "beneath")
- difficulty understanding comparatives, opposites, and superlatives (e.g., bigger/biggest, far/near, rough/smooth, fast/slow)

Cognitive Processing Deficits

- difficulty following oral directions
- difficulty expressing thoughts and information
- difficulty classifying
- difficulty putting events in sequence or order
- difficulty making comparisons
- difficulty understanding or expressing the moral of a story
- difficulty predicting the outcome of a story or event
- difficulty differentiating between fact and fiction
- difficulty remembering and expressing facts

Evaluation Deficits

- difficulty drawing conclusions ("Why did she need her gloves?")
- difficulty relating to cause and effect ("What would happen if he forgot to put gas in the car?")

Aphasia/Dysphasia

- difficulty making facial motor movements to produce sound (This is called *dyspraxia*.)
- difficulty imitating sounds
- difficulty remembering words (but can repeat them)
- difficulty formulating sentences (but can use single words)
- difficulty naming common objects
- difficulty recalling a specific word
- difficulty recognizing common objects by touch

Sᴇᴇ: Aptitude *(page 15)*; Articulation *(page 429)*; Auditory Memory *(page 322)*; Brain Dysfunction *(page 326)*; Critical Thinking *(page 161)*; Decoding *(page 332)*; Defense Mechanisms *(page 373)*; Fear of Failure, Success, and/or Competition *(page 383)*; Grades *(page 25)*; Grammar and Syntax *(page 31)*; Identifying Important Information *(page 41)*; I'm Dumb Syndrome *(page 388)*; Intelligence *(page 45)*; Keeping Up with the Class *(page 51)*; Language Arts *(page 58)*; Logic *(page 171)*; Performance Standards *(page 91)*; Psychological Overlay and Psychological Problems *(page 399)*; Resistance to Help *(page 282)*; School Anxiety *(page 406)*; Self-concept *(page 410)*; Underachievement *(page 143)*; Visual Memory *(page 360)*; Vocabulary *(page 150)*.

Appendix I

Provisions of Federal Law

Individuals with Disabilities Education Act (IDEA)

The *Individuals with Disabilities Education Act* (IDEA-PL 105-17) prescribes specific procedures for providing assistance to children with learning disabilities and other handicaps and dysfunctions. Under this federal law, schools are required to:

1. Provide a free and appropriate public education to all handicapped children. This includes special education and related services to meet their unique educational needs.
2. Provide handicapped children with an education in the least restrictive environment on the basis of individual needs
3. Guarantee to each handicapped child an unbiased, valid assessment
4. Provide parents the opportunity to be involved in educational decisions concerning their child

Key Provisions of IDEA:

- Limits protection to those requiring and qualifying for special-education services
- Requires that children must meet certain diagnostic criteria to qualify for IDEA (thirteen categories of disability are specified).
- Requires a formal written IEP (Individual Educational Plan) that conforms to standard content and formatting criteria.
- Provides federal financial assistance to state and local school systems for support services and independent evaluations.

Section 504 of the Rehabilitation Act

This federal law also provides protection for children who are struggling in school and has proved especially useful for students with mild-to-moderate learning disabilities who might not otherwise qualify for special-education services. Section 504 states: "A not otherwise qualified individual with disabilities in the United States . . . shall not, solely by reason of his/her disability, be excluded from the participation in, be denied the benefits of, or be subjected to discrimination under any program or activity receiving federal financial assistance. . . ."

Key Provisions of Section 504:

- Provides protection to people with disabilities *throughout their lifetime.*
- School districts must provide a grievance procedure and have a Section 504 official to assure compliance with the regulations.
- Districts cannot pass on any associated costs to the student's family and cannot claim limited financial resources as a rationale for failure to provide accommodations.
- Districts can attempt to prove that accommodations would cause undue hardship for the entire district, although this contention rarely prevails, as most accommodations are relatively inexpensive to implement.
- Does not impose the restrictive stipulations of IDEA and applies whenever a functional impairment can be identified that "substantially limits a major life activity."
- Qualifies a learning dysfunction as an impairment.
- Requires that a *free and appropriate education* be provided to all children. This critically important provision is referred to as FAPE.
- Offers broader protections than IDEA and includes students who do not qualify for special education but who may need in-class accommodations to meet their distinctive learning needs.
- Does *not* require school districts to pay for independent evaluations but does require that school districts *consider* reimbursement for such evaluations when appropriate.

- Does not require a formal IEP but does require that an accommodation plan be created and implemented. This plan must address the struggling child's specific learning needs and must be formatted so that it is clear and understandable.
- Does not require an administrative hearing prior to seeking recourse from the Office of Civil Rights or from the courts.
- Individuals who believe their child has been damaged by discrimination can seek monetary compensation.

Americans with Disabilities Act (ADA)

This 1990 federal law specifically identifies the following as dysfunctions covered in both Section 504 and in the Americans with Disabilities Act:

- learning disabilities
- attention deficit disorder (ADD)
- attention deficit hyperactivity disorder (ADHD)

The Intent of Federal Law

Section 504 and ADA are essentially civil-rights laws intended to eliminate discrimination against people with disabilities in all programs and activities that receive federal financial assistance. The intent of these laws is to remove physical, organizational, and instructional/curriculum barriers that might prevent full participation in educational activities and opportunities. The laws stipulate that inflexible instructional procedures that prevent students from demonstrating their abilities be modified.*

---

*I am indebted to the *Learning Disabilities Association Newsbrief* (July/August 1995) for descriptions of the federal laws that protect the rights of learning-disabled children. See also Individuals with Disabilities Act (1997 Revised) and Regulations (1999).

Appendix II

Examples of Reasonable Accommodations As Stipulated under Section 504

Classroom Instruction

- using different sensory modalities when teaching (auditory, visual, tactile, and kinesthetic)
- using specialized, less difficult curriculum
- taping lectures for students with auditory-processing deficits
- using manipulatives (hands-on materials) to reinforce learning
- providing a written model for how assignments are to be completed
- reinforcing oral directions with written directions and reinforcing written directions with oral directions
- breaking instructions down into smaller units
- modifying reading level of in-class and homework assignments
- identifying and capitalizing on student's preferred learning style
- using visual aids to explain content of lectures and textbooks
- reading directions on worksheets and in textbooks to student
- reducing emphasis on spelling accuracy
- checking for understanding of newly introduced material
- blocking off, masking, or highlighting assignments to facilitate focus and mastery
- handing out printed homework assignments for the week
- sending home simple daily and/or weekly progress reports
- verifying that instructions and directions are understood
- providing a written outline of textbook or lecture content
- asking student to repeat instructions
- having student summarize information orally
- providing before- and after-school tutoring

- reducing length of instructional segments
- using computers to assist in learning, reinforcement, and skill mastery
- allowing extra time to complete tasks
- reducing the number of worksheets handed out at one time

Classroom Management

- seating struggling student near teacher or positive role model
- standing closer to student when presenting lesson or giving instructions
- providing consistent and reasonable consequences for misbehavior
- keeping rules simple and clear

Concentration Deficits

- allowing students short breaks between tasks
- clearly defining behavioral limits
- minimizing distractions
- allowing time out of seat
- providing additional structure to reduce inattentiveness
- increasing space between desks
- using nonverbal signals to help student stay on task
- using nonembarrassing time-out procedures

Grading

- deemphasizing handwriting as a grading criterion
- allowing extra credit for student-initiated projects and for in-class participation
- reducing the number of correct answers required to achieve a decent grade

Homework

- reducing the number of problems assigned
- breaking down large assignments into smaller projects

- making certain student accurately records and fully understands the assignment
- modifying homework so that the student with deficient skills can complete assignments

Learning Strategies

- helping students identify their preferred learning style (how they learn most effectively and efficiently)
- encouraging students to experiment with different ways of learning assigned material

Motivation

- emphasizing rewards for achievement rather than negative consequences for mistakes and poor judgment
- providing more immediate rewards for accomplishments
- making performance and behavior contracts with students

Organization and Time Management

- urging students to define realistic short- and long-term goals
- showing students how to plan and execute long-range projects

Parent Instruction

- providing workshops that teach parents effective at-home instructional methods (tutoring, review, drilling)
- modeling how parents can provide effective emotional support and guidance
- examining appropriate versus inappropriate intervention techniques
- teaching parents how to motivate children to learn

Peer Assistance

- encouraging peer help with planning, organization, and time management
- providing peer note taking

- providing peer tutoring
- assigning volunteer homework buddy
- forming study groups in which superior students help struggling class-mates
- pairing students to check each other's work for errors

Psychological Support

- encouraging self-monitoring of behavior and performance
- providing group and individual counseling
- helping children acquire better socialization skills
- encouraging students to be sensitive, understanding, and supportive of classmates with special needs

Study Skills

- providing methodical instruction in how to study, take notes, and iden-tify important information
- helping students develop personalized learning strategies congruent with individual learning style
- teaching students how to prepare for and take tests
- teaching memorization techniques

Teacher Training

- providing in-service training for teachers to help them better understand learning deficits and manage associated behavior problems
- creating a team of master teachers and resource specialists to provide classroom teachers with guidance on how to help struggling children learn more effectively

Testing

- allowing students to answer test questions on tape
- highlighting key information and test-taking instructions

- making certain that students understand exam directions
- marking students' correct answers as opposed to mistakes
- using frequent short quizzes as opposed to long exams
- permitting open-book and take-home tests
- reading test items to student
- using multiple-choice and short-answer questions rather than essays to assess mastery

Bibliography

Armstrong, Thomas. *In Their Own Way.* Los Angeles: Jeremy P. Tarcher, 1987.

Bell, Nanci. *Seeing Stars.* San Luis Obispo, Calif.: Gander Educational Publishing, 1997.

———. *Visualizing/Verbalizing.* San Luis Obispo, Calif.: Gander Educational Publishing, 1986.

Bell, Nanci, and Kimberly Tuley. *On Cloud Nine.* San Luis Obispo, Calif.: Gander Educational Publishing, 1997.

Coles, Gerald. *The Learning Mystique.* New York: Pantheon, 1987.

Cronin, Eileen M. *Helping Your Dyslexic Child.* Rocklin, Calif.: Prima Publishing, 1994.

Dias, Peggy. *Diamonds in the Rough.* E. Aurora, Colo.: Slosson Educational Publishing, 1989.

Doub, George T., and Virginia Morgan Scott. *Family Wellness Workbook.* Santa Cruz, Calif.: Family Wellness Publishing, 1987.

Gardener, Howard. *Frames of Mind.* New York: Basic Books, 1983.

Greene, Lawrence J. *Finding Help When Your Child Is Struggling in School.* New York: St. Martin's Press.

———. *Kids Who Underachieve.* New York: Simon & Schuster, 1986.

———. *Learning Disabilities and Your Child.* New York: Fawcett, 1987.

———. *1001 Ways to Improve Your Child's Schoolwork.* New York: Dell, 1991.

———. *Think Smart—Study Smart.* Englewood Cliffs, N.J.: Center for Applied Research in Education/Prentice Hall, 1994.

———. *The Life-Smart Kid.* Rocklin, Calif.: Prima Publishing, 1995.

———. *Getting Smarter.* New York: Simon & Schuster, 1984.

Greenspan, Stanley I., and Serena Wieder. *The Child with Special Needs.* Reading, Pa.: Perseus Books, 1998.

Harwell, Joan M. *Complete Learning Disabilities Handbook.* Englewood Cliffs, N.J.: Center for Applied Research in Education/ Prentice Hall, 1989.

Jensen, Eric. *Student Success Secrets.* Hauppauge, N.Y.: Barrons, 1989.

———. *You Can Succeed.* Hauppauge, N.Y.: Barrons, 1989.

Lindamood, Patricia, and Phyllis Lindamood. *LiPS.** Austin, Tex.: Pro Ed Publishing, 1997.

Macroff, Gene L. *The School Smart Parent.* New York: Times Books, 1989.

McCarney, Stephen B. *The Parent's Guide to Attention Deficit Disorders.* 2nd Ed. Columbia, S.C.: Hawthorne Educational Services, 1995.

Rief, Sandra F. *How to Reach and Teach ADD/ADHD Children.* Englewood Cliffs, N.J.: Center for Applied Research in Education/Prentice Hall, 1993.

Siegal, Lawrence M. *The Complete IEP Guide.* Berkeley, Calif.: Nolo, 2001.

Taylor, John. *Helping Your Hyperactive/Attention Deficit Child.* 3rd Ed. revised. Rocklin, Calif.: Prima Publishing, 2001.

---

*Lindamood Phonemic Sequencing.

Index

Attention Deficit/Attention Deficit Hyperactivity Disorder (*cont.*)
classroom environment and, 218;
dependency issues and, 305; failure to
record assignments, 108; genetic link, 220;
handwriting problems and, 37, 38; helpful
suggestions for productive functioning,
218; intelligence and, 216; interventions
and treatment, 222; IQ testing and, 49;
judgment and, 264; learning disabilities
accompanying, 215, 216, *216*; math difficulty and, 74; medications prescribed for,
220–21; mistaken as misconduct, 215;
percent of American children with, 217;
planning problems and, 177–78; puberty
and diminishing of, 221; punctuation and,
97; reading comprehension and, 102, 104;
Ritalin, 38, 220; self-control, poor and,
288, 289–90, 291; selective capacity for
focusing, 217–18; stimulation, limiting,
218; stress in classroom and, 219; symptoms, 221–22; teacher-child conflict and,
297; terminology and types, 215, 317,
317n.; thoughtless and impulsive behaviors, 243; time management problems,
139; underachievement and, 216, 219;
written directions, difficulty with, 364
Attention to details, 223–26; ADD/ADHD
and, 224–25; behavior that indicates
inattentiveness to detail, 225–26; cognitive behavior modification to train for,
225, 225n.; learning disabilities and lack
of, 224; psychological factors impeding,
224; punctuation and, 97; resistance to
correction, 224, 225; visual-acuity and
visual-efficiency deficits and, 225
Attitude. *See* Behavior
Auditory discrimination deficits, 317–21;
diagnostic tools, 319–20; learning problems with, 13; neurologically based dysfunction, 318; phonics-based reading
programs and, 318, 352; spelling problems, 112; symptoms of auditory
discrimination problem, 319; symptoms
of auditory processing deficits, 438;
treatment protocols, 318–19, 320–21;
word attack and, 318
Auditory learner, 105, 361–62, 366
Auditory memory, 322–26; ADD/ADHD
and, 324; compensating for deficit,
324–25; deficit, 13; decoding deficits
often occurring with, 322–23; failure to

record assignments and, 108; lecturing
as teaching style and, 324; phonics-based
reading programs and, 352; physiology
and neurochemistry of brain and, 323;
symptoms, 323, 325
Auditory-sequencing difficulty, 108, 322
Avoiding responsibility, 227–31; behaviors
signaling addiction to a comfort zone,
230–31; comfort zone and, 227–28, 385,
415; interventions, 230; manipulating
environment and dependency, 228–29;
negative behaviors and, 227;
temperament and, 228

Behavior, 86–87, 199–201; acting out, 372,
384; ADD/ADHD, common behaviors
with, 217; ADD/ADHD, counterproductive behaviors and, 219; aggression, 411;
anger and, 201–7; associated with resistance to help, 286; brain dysfunction
symptoms, 330; common coping behavior, 377; conduct and attitude problems,
235–40; counseling interventions for
irresponsibility, 258; counterproductive,
110–11, 236, 245; defensive, 13–14,
108–9, 186, 236, 269, 282, 285, 373, 337;
dependency and, 227–40, 302–8;
discouraging misconduct, steps to take,
200–201; homework resistance and
avoidance, 130; "I'm dumb" syndrome,
attitudes and behaviors linked to, 391;
imprinting mental reflex before acting,
243; indications of difficulty following
verbal directions, 359–60; indications of
difficulty following written directions,
367; indications of difficulty handling
setbacks, 234–35; indications of
difficulty learning from mistakes, 270;
indications of difficulty mastering content, 70–71; indications of
inattentiveness to detail, 225–26; indications of language-arts demoralization,
64–65; indications of passive learning,
86, 89–90; indications of poor judgment,
265–66; indications of problem-solving
deficiencies, 187–88; indications of
strategic thinking deficiencies, 194–95;
maladaptive, understanding causes, 200;
maladaptive and red-flag of psychological problem, 404; mindless, 244, 245,
268; oppositional behavior, 109; parenting, rules, and guidelines for, 243;

LAWRENCE J. GREENE, a graduate of the Stanford University Graduate School of Education, is an educational diagnostician and therapist with over thirty years' experience in special education. He is author of thirteen books, and his study skills and strategic thinking programs have been used in thousands of schools in the United States and Canada.